CHRISTIAN HIGHER EDUCATION
THE CONTEMPORARY CHALLENGE

"Wetenskaplike Bydraes van die PU vir CHO"

SERIES F

INSTITUTE FOR THE ADVANCEMENT
OF CALVINISM

F3. Collections no. 6

CHRISTIAN HIGHER EDUCATION
THE CONTEMPORARY CHALLENGE

IN U LIG

CHRISTIAN HIGHER EDUCATION

THE
CONTEMPORARY
CHALLENGE

Proceedings of the First International

Conference of Reformed Institutions

for Christian Scholarship

Potchefstroom,

9 — 13 September 1975.

Potchefstroom

Institute for the Advancement of Calvinism

1976

ISBN 0 86990 320 9

378
P48c
114692
July 1980

Distributed in Canada and the U.S.A. by Wedge Publishing Foundation, 229 College Street, Toronto, Ontario, Canada.

Printed by the Potchefstroom Herald (Pty) Ltd., P.O. Box 156, Potchefstroom 2520, Transvaal, Republic of South Africa.

Preface

A year has passed since the International Conference on Reformed Institutions for Higher Education was held at Potchefstroom during September last year. And with the passing of time clearer perspectives and greater maturity of thought have come to the fore in more ways than one.

Having as point of departure the carefully prepared papers collected in this publication, we were treated to penetrating discussions, and as the thoughts matured we now truly proclaim that this laudable enterprise has clearly been a first assault on the problematics of Christian Higher Education.

This reconnaissance programme has revealed amongst other things

>*that there are yet greater depths in this area to be explored in order to come to clearer understanding;*

>*that it will probably result in the identification of important differences of opinion on Christian Higher Education;*

>*that we will have to view one another with great tolerance in order to avoid elevating conclusions to principles capable of separating bone and marrow;*

>*that there are regional conformities in which similar patterns of thought occur;*

>*that there are encouraging signs of a will to find one another in our common pursuit of an honest appraisal of the Christian principle in higher education;*

>*that those who have come a long way with Christian education, have accepted as their own the problems experienced by those who are yet at the beginning of this struggle and in so doing have made manifest a helpful brotherhood in Christ.*

It is my sincere conviction that this first and pioneering publication will reveal many facets of our problem in such a way that it will become a valuable asset for those yet to join in this attempt at ecumenicity within the context of Christian Higher Education.

It is our hope and prayer that this publication may serve as forerunner in anticipation of a worthy enterprise in a world sorely lacking in Christian faith.

Prof. dr. H. J. J. Bingle
(Rector, Potchefstroom University for Christian Higher Education)

Contents

PROGRAMME

INTERNATIONAL CONFERENCE OF

REFORMED INSTITUTIONS FOR HIGHER EDUCATION

Potchefstroom 9—13 September 1975

Reformed Institutions for Higher Education as a bulwark for

the Kingdom of God; present and future

Monday, 8th September: 14h00—17h30 Registration at Kasteel.

FIRST DAY: Tuesday, 9th September

08h00—09h00 Registration: Concert Hall, Conservatoire of Music.
09h00—10h00 Official Opening.

Chairman: Prof. Dr. H. J. J. Bingle (South Africa).

(a) *Scripture reading and Prayer.*
Prof. Dr. Tjaart van der Walt (South Africa).
(b) *Words of welcome.*
Prof. Dr. Hennie J. J. Bingle, Vice-Chancellor and Rector,
P.U. for C.H.E.
(c) *Formal matters.*

THE CHRISTIAN INSTITUTION

Questions relating to the rest of the twentieth century

1. A RADICAL NEW ORDER?

Chairman: Prof. Dr. J. D. Dengerink (The Netherlands).

10h00—10h40 First Paper:
Prof. Dr. Hennie J. J. Bingle — Rector, P.U. for C.H.E., South
Africa.
10h40—11h00 Tea.
11h00—11h30 Second Paper:
Prof. Dr. Hendrik van Riessen — President, Vereniging voor
Calvinistische Wijsbegeerte, Professor in the Centrale Inter-
faculteit, Vrije Universiteit, The Netherlands.
11h30—12h30 Discussion.

2. THREATS TO THE CHRISTIAN CHARACTER OF THE CHRIS-
TIAN INSTITUTION

Chairman: Prof. G. N. M. Collins (Scotland).

14h30—15h10 First Paper:
Prof. Dr. Pierre Courthial — President, Faculté Libre de Théo-
logie Réformée, Aix-en-Provence, France.
15h10—15h30 Second Paper:
Prof. Dr. John H. Kromminga — President, Calvin Theological
Seminary, Grand Rapids, U.S.A.
15h30—16h20 Discussion.

3. THE SERVICE MOTIVE AS A FUNCTION OF THE MODERN

CHRISTIAN UNIVERSITY

Chairman: Prof. Dr. M. D. Barnes (U.S.A.).

16h30—17h10 First Paper:
Prof. Dr. Hendrik Hart — Senior member in Philosophy, Institute for Christian Studies, Toronto, Canada.
17h10—17h30 Second Paper:
Prof. Dr. Henry J. S. Stone — Vice-President, Vereniging vir Christelike Hoër Onderwys, Professor of Education, University of South Africa, South Africa.
20h00—21h00 Discussion (after dinner).

4. THE NATIONAL AND INTERNATIONAL STRUCTURE AND TASK OF THE CHRISTIAN INSTITUTION FOR HIGHER EDUCATION

Chairman: Prof. A. Barkley (Australia).

21h00—21h30 Paper:
Dr. Zacharias Rittersma — Principal, Gereformeerd Paedagogische Academie, The Netherlands.
21h30—21h40 Propositions for Discussion:
Prof. Dr. P. G. W. du Plessis, Professor of Philosophy, Randse Afrikaanse Universiteit, South Africa
and
Dr. B. J. van der Walt, Director, Institute for the Advancement of Calvinism, P.U. for C.H.E., South Africa.
21h40—22h30 Discussion.

Prayer: Rev. F. D. Sakala (Zambia).

SECOND DAY: Wednesday, 10th September

09h00—09h20 *Scripture reading and Prayer.*
Rev. A. R. Kayayan (France).

CHRISTIAN LEARNING/SCHOLARSHIP/SCIENCE
Fundamental and existential problems

1. CHRISTIAN LEARNING/SCHOLARSHIP/SCIENCE AND/OR CHRISTIAN SCHOLARS?

Chairman: Prof. Dr. E. Schuurman (The Netherlands).

09h20—10h00 First Paper:
Prof. Dr. Nicholas Wolterstorff — Professor of Philosophy,

Calvin College, Grand Rapids, U.S.A.

10h00—10h20 Second Paper:
   Prof. Dr. Hendrik G. Stoker — Formerly professor of Philosophy,
   P.U. for C.H.E., South Africa.

10h20—10h40 Third Paper:
   Prof. Dr. J. Chris Coetzee (Sr.) — Formerly professor of Education and rector, P.U. for C.H.E., South Africa.

10h40—11h00 Tea.

11h00—12h30 Discussion.

2. PROBLEMS AFFECTING THE DEVELOPMENT OF CHRISTIAN
   LEARNING/SCHOLARSHIP/SCIENCE IN THE MODERN WORLD

A. In non-Christian countries.

   Chairman: Prof. Dr. Kun Sam Lee (Korea).

14h30—15h10 First Paper:
   Prof. Ryuzo Hashimoto — Acting President, Kobe Reformed
   Theological Seminary, Japan.

15h10—15h30 Second Paper:
   Prof. Anthony H. Nichols — Facultas Theologia, Universitas
   Kristen "Satya Wacama", Indonesia.

15h30—16h30 Discussion.

16h30 Group photo.

3. PROBLEMS AFFECTING THE DEVELOPMENT OF CHRISTIAN
   LEARNING/SCHOLARSHIP/SCIENCE IN THE MODERN
   WORLD

B. In dechristianizing (dechristianized) countries.

   Chairman: Rev. I. Achineko (Nigeria).

20h00—20h40 First Paper:
   Prof. Dr. Sidney H. Rooy — Facultad Evangelica de Theologia,
   Buenos Aires, Argentina.

20h40—21h00 Second Paper:
   Prof. Dr. George van Groningen, Reformed Theological Seminary,
   Jackson, Mississippi, U.S.A.

21h00—22h30 Discussion.

   Prayer: Rev. J. G. M. Maseko (Malawi).

Thursday, 11th September

07h30 Depart on excursions.
20h00 Official dinner.

Hosted by Prof. Dr. H. J. J. Bingle, Rector, P.U. for C.H.E.
Address by the guest of honour.
The State President, Dr. N. Diederichs.
Venue: "Voorhuis" Residence, Dining Hall.

THIRD DAY: Friday, 12th September

09h00—09h20 *Scripture reading and Prayer.*
  Prof. E. S. Nchephe (South Africa).

THE CHRISTIAN SCHOLAR
Problems concerning relationships

1. THE POSITION OF THE CHRISTIAN LECTURER, TEACHER
   AND STUDENT AT THE CHRISTIAN INSTITUTION, WITH
   SPECIAL REFERENCE TO THE EDUCATIONAL TASK

   Chairman: Prof. Dr. H. N. Ridderbos (The Netherlands).

09h20—10h00 First Paper:
  Prof. Dr. Johan A. Heyns, Faculty of Theology, Nederduits
  Gereformeerde Kerk, University of Pretoria, South Africa.
10h00—10h30 Second Paper:
  Prof. Dr. Takeshiro Kodera — Professor of Economics, Former
  President, Kwansei Gakuin University of Kobe, Japan.
10h30—10h50 Tea.
10h50—11h30 Discussion.

2. THE POSITION OF THE CHRISTIAN LECTURER, TEACHER
   AND STUDENT AT THE SECULAR INSTITUTION, AND OF
   THE NON-CHRISTIAN STUDENT AT THE CHRISTIAN INSTI-
   TUTION

   Chairman: Dr. D. Roper (New Zealand).

11h30—12h10 First Paper:
  Prof. Dr. W. Stanford Reid — Professor of History, University
  of Guelph, Ontario, Canada.
12h10—12h30 Second Paper:
  Dr. David R. Hanson — International Secretary, IARFA, Lecturer
  in Ear, Nose and Throat Surgery, University of Leeds, England.
14h30—14h50 Third Paper:
  Prof. Dr. Jong Sung Rhee — President, Presbyterian Theological
  Seminary of Korea, Seoul, Korea.
14h50—15h30 Discussion.

3. AUTHORITY AND DISCIPLINE AT CHRISTIAN HIGHER EDUCATIONAL INSTITUTIONS

Chairman: Rev. E. C. Esterhuize (Rhodesia).

15h30—16h10 First Paper:
Prof. Dr. Schalk C. W. Duvenage — Dean of the Faculty of Theology, P.U. for C.H.E., South Africa.

16h10—16h40 Second Paper:
Dr. Paul G. Schrotenboer, General Secretary, Reformed Ecumenical Synod, Grand Rapids, U.S.A.

16h40—17h30 Discussion.

4. ACADEMIC FREEDOM IN CHRISTIAN PERSPECTIVE

Chairman: Drs. K. Veling (The Netherlands).

20h00—20h40 First Paper:
Prof. Dr. W. van 't Spijker — Theologische Hoge School, Christelijke Gereformeerde Kerken, Apeldoorn, The Netherlands.

20h40—21h10 Second Paper:
Prof. Dr. F. J. M. Potgieter — Teologiese Kweekskool, Nederduits Gereformeerde Kerk, and Faculty of Theology, University of Stellenbosch, President, Vereniging vir Christelike Hoër Onderwys, South Africa.

21h10—22h30 Discussion.

Prayer: Rev. D. D. Sceats (England).

FOURTH DAY: Saturday, 13th September

09h00—09h20 *Scripture reading and Prayer.*
Dr. Susumu Uda (Japan).

CO-ORDINATION BETWEEN CHRISTIAN INSTITUTIONS

1. REVIEWING THE STATUS QUO OF REFORMED CHRISTIAN STUDY FACILITIES AROUND THE WORLD. POSSIBILITIES AND METHODS FOR IMPROVEMENT OF THE SITUATION IN VARIOUS PARTS OF THE WORLD

Chairman: Prof. Dr. N. Shepherd (U.S.A.).

09h20—09h40 *The British Isles:* Mr. Richard A. Russel — The Christian Studies Unit, England.

09h40—10h00 *The America's:* Prof. John van der Stelt — Associate Professor of Theology and Philosophy, Dordt College, U.S.A.

A radical new order ?

Prof. Dr. H. J. J. Bingle

1. *Introduction*

This international conference begins with a theme formulated as
a question, not without good reason and intent. Questions are being
raised about the university as such — the neutral as well as the
Christian university — sometimes to the extent of general reference
being made to "crises". This almost automatically results in thoughts
about new orders, not always and everywhere against the same
background or with the same motive. There is an entire spectrum
of phenomena and motives, from the most revolutionary to the
mildest reformative approach. Irrespective of the diverse manifestations of these phenomena, there is one certainty: the university
finds itself in the midst of numerous accelerations demanding the
urgent attention of all concerned.

Let us first of all turn our attention to those crises so often
heard about today.

2. *Crises in the university world*

It can generally be accepted that there is not just one but a number
of crises at the university. One may go so far as to say that the
entire university finds itself in a state of crisis. There is hardly any
facet, from the most physical to the most fundamental, which
does not labour under one or other threat. And even where there
is no visible threat, there is the reformative stance constantly
attempting to align theory and practice with the demands of contemporary life, without resulting in disruption of one kind or another.

Modern technological society with its incessant demand for
trained and even semi-trained manpower requires leaders for this
host of workers which the institute for higher education is unable to
train in terms of the traditional basis of professional standards and
stringent selectivity. The large number of unselected students entering the university, necessarily affects the very nature of the university.

In addition, these numbers place an enormous financial burden
on the university in respect of grounds, buildings, equipment and
staff, resulting in contributions to the university by the private
sector being minimized by this colossus of large financing. The

15

state has to provide assistance to such an extent that according to some opinions university autonomy is at stake.

And this student has entered the university with the express purpose of bringing about a change in this structure. He states his demands in virtually every section of the university, and this, in more than one way, has resulted in various crises.

Let us consider this situation in greater detail.

In the context of contemporary society — the disappearing "establishment" which has been rejuvenated — the view of man, the aims, the curricula and syllabuses, the methodology, organization, standards, and discipline of the university have acquired new meanings and/or nuances so that in many cases the university has been unrecognizably transformed.

Man is being stripped by the student and the university of all the norms and values accepted up to now, originating in a time during which a set of human values was built up with the greatest scientific care, although it was not necessarily rooted in the Christian faith. The student is co-assessor of the ultimate goal of university training as well as co-determiner of where he wishes to find himself upon completion of his studies. Questions concerning the relevancy and priorities of the curriculum are determined by the student's assessment of the demands of the times. Thus a far higher premium is placed on the applied as opposed to the basic sciences and the student, with his university, slips away from the essential scientific structure without which no applied knowledge is viable. And the more the university accedes to the demands of the students, the greater becomes the influx of students and the more the problems of the university escalate.

The new generation demands justice and peace, with the connotations it attaches to these concepts, instead of the social order and status with the meanings given to these by its adult environment. And while his parents are occupied by the pursuit of their own careers and he is free to work out his own priorities within a self-created culture and his own society, the generation gap widens. The disenchantment of these young people entering the university has reached such proportions due to what they have found there, that the university has been unable to meet all the social demands of its students; and the university has been equally powerless to maintain its so-called neutrality which has been used by the students as a means of breaking down the social order. To this is added an even more fundamental factor for the neutral university, namely the new scepticism denying the possibility of objective, rational thought so vaunted by the modern university. The simplistic faith

16

that rational man will increasingly understand his environment to the evolutionary advantage of mankind, is a concept which has been progressively devalued with each passing year. In its stead there has arisen a mysticism and a belief that somewhere in the dark recesses of the mind, in the senses and sensations, in emotion rather than in thinking, truth is more likely to be found than in an objective study of the world around us.

Even university methodology has not escaped the onslaughts of the modern philosophy of life. The heavy demands made upon the selected, the intelligentsia, being trained as scientists and then as professional people, could no longer be maintained in an institution which had become a national school for the people. The scientific method has gradually come under pressure from the limited capabilities of the majority of modern students as well as from the claim of the modern student himself that there is no longer any relevance in being scientific, or in constructing his own methods in confronting life, all of this gradually being replaced by a set of mental recipes which fit the requirements of the community to be served.

This inevitably resulted in the breaking down of standards. If everything up to this point, where the result has to be determined, has landslided towards an impoverishment, then nothing more can be expected of the standards. Deterioration of scientific standards can reach the point where one can hardly use the term university any longer.

In the final instance so many changes have been wrought in the character of the university in the modern context that the institution has become unrecognizable. All the essential features of the university have become involved, sometimes making it difficult to recognize these institutions as places of learning where science in all its implications is practised, where according to accepted standards individuals are shaped as human beings and as scientists, where professional people are provided for all branches of the national economy, where service is rendered to state, church, society, culture, art, economy — in short, an institution that stands as a tower of light in a world sorely in need of it.

3. *Interpretation of the crises*

Upon closer inspection of the above types of disaffection with the university, it becomes clear that they contain aspects of a purely organizational-administrative nature, as for instance the size of the university, its financing, the buildings etc. It matters little whether a university has 5 000 or 20 000 students, whether it is wholly or partially subsidized by the state or only for 80 per cent or 50 per cent, whether the buildings have been grouped or constructed in a specific pattern — problems at this level do not result in more than discomfort, although there are those who contend that the essence of the university is affected when student enrolment exceeds a certain number (although no-one has indicated the exact danger-point); or that university autonomy is linked to the amount of state subsidy received (again without the dividing line being indicated); or that science as such is influenced by the specific confluence of buildings although this is valid only for the degree to which it functions more effectively. These are problems that can be overcome by ingenious organization and administration.

In the second place, however, there are also assaults mentioned above which are directly aimed at the university as a practitioner of science. These crises are of a more serious nature for they affect the essence of the institution. Therefore they require closer analysis.

When it is accepted that the university no longer caters for the select few, for the intellectually highly gifted, but that the masses irrespective of ability may enter, converting the university into a national school for the people, it becomes inevitable that the nature of the institution will change. It will no longer be the practitioner of science, nor the unfettered moulder of scientists and professional people. This will have such an incisive effect on the university that the entire human way of life, our modern science, art, culture and technology will be denuded and impoverished, becoming in the end a bloodless mass of moribund tissue.

This result will inevitably bring about a revolutionary new order in all facets of human existence.

But the university is also affected in its function as educator aiming at the development and shaping of individuals according to their inherent talents and in accordance with convictions about the nature of man. Where it is demanded that the immature should be self-determiner of his being, of his educational aim — usually so limited that it cannot avoid being naive yet no less serious in its effect on the nature of the university — of the means to be employed along that road, the manner of their employment, of the result being aimed at; and where all of these lead towards the denigration of values and norms carefully and diligently evolved through the centuries, tested, verified — that is, scientifically validated as exhaustively as possible — there the university, in the face of this assault, finds itself on the edge of an abyss from which it will no longer be able to escape as an institution known to us as a university. There can still be an institution but stripped of its present character, an institution radically different from its predecessors.

Fourthly, the assaults mentioned above affect the university as the practitioner of science and as a social community in that one of its elements has forcibly become the focal point to the extent that the university is no longer free but a slave of the student and particularly of the immature student. Anyone who disrupts the harmony between the constituent elements of the university as a social community must accept impairing this social institution to the point of doing so much harm that it must produce a fundamentally different substance. But it is the express purpose of this assault to revolutionize the university in line with the undoing of contemporary society aimed at the acquisition of a radical new order. The result — a radical new order at the university. And to our alarm it must be added that even some of our Christian institutions justify acceptance of the forcibly advanced role played by students in the control of the university as being not all that serious and say that it can even be accepted as advantageous!

Finally we must come to the crisis which rests in the creed of the university. Mere acceptance of the fact that a university has a creed has been thrown overboard by the majority of modern universities. They cannot accept that a specific view of life is valid for scientific knowledge as it cannot lead to pure scientific practice, it cannot educate correctly for it must end up as indoctrination, it restricts the freedom of the university and the individual in all respects to the extent that both are impoverished and forced into a straight-jacket resulting in such confinement that the university is dismantled. What is so disturbing here is again some of our institutions that would like to remain conservative, while adopting the point of view that this restricts the freedom of the university, that it gives offence to those who think differently, that it is completely irrelevant in the field of science where it would involve the aim of objectivity and the scientists themselves through dogmatic pre-suppositions.

From this classification and interpretation of the crises it must be clear that our concern here is about the most serious affairs of the contemporary university, both Christian and neutral. These are progressive processes, usually maturing slowly due to the university being such a complex institution, so that it sometimes takes generations for the university to be completely overturned. But the signs are evident that there is consistent progress in this direction, and possibly taking place more rapidly than ever before because we live in an era where the universities themselves are producing the methods for their rapid and total restructuring. And if modern man overturns and dismantles virtually every facet of life, and if the entire contemporary order, the establishment, is engaged in destruction, this process can be accelerated to the point where it becomes a hurricane sweeping everything along and leaving destruction in its wake. This is not impossible, particularly if we have a closer look at the crisis makers.

4. *The crisis makers*

From the reasoning expounded so far it can be deduced that there is a variety of crisis makers in the university world.

It is surely not far-fetched to contend that the modern university is the most serious crisis maker of all, due to a process it has maintained for generations and which is now coming to fruition. The persistent subscription to the humanist point of view in respect of virtually every aspect of the university, the elevation of man to an omnipotent god, the idolization of the idea of progress, necessarily had to result in a generation destroying everything in a culture evolved over a period of centuries; the university has received what it wanted — its own Frankenstein that would mutilate it beyond being recognizable by its own people.

The student of the second half of the twentieth century and those who during this period have been taken up in the teaching community, have come to the fore with their creed of revolutionary thought and dangerous living as the inevitable product of a cumulative process. They are the revolutionary crisis makers.

It is not really so difficult to grasp the motivation behind these crisis makers. Modern enlightened paganism is guided by the principle which destroys those existential norms transcendentally received by mankind and which have refused to bow before the idols of this world. It cannot lead to anything but destruction, not necessarily now, but beyond any doubt somewhere in the future.

Opposed to these crisis makers are the serious reformers. This contrastive group is also guided by a principle of life, a principle that stands as the opposite of the former. They do not disparage the establishment, or the godgiven norms. They are restlessly engaged in combating the imperfect, the sinful in the existing order, reaching out towards serving God more purely. They do not labour under the false premise that leads the university from one bondage into the other, or lands itself from one colonialism into another.

This search for reform mentioned above finds its total and exclusive justification in the Calvinist creed which implies, also for the university, liberty in the freedom we receive through Christ, until the perfect is found in eternity.

20

Our age cries out for a polarization of the crisis makers so that each one can be clearly identified.

The Calvinists of the Christian university are also, and must of necessity be, crisis makers, in order to advance with the university on the path towards sanctification. We are not in search of a new, unknown, radically different order in higher education, but we are aiming at the perfection of that which has been developed by generations and which may sometimes appear to the uninitiated as a radically new design. We accept the established constitution of the university with all its fundamental characteristics and we submit it all to the light of God's Word for us to see the light.

5. *The Christian university of the last quarter of the twentieth century*

The intention in this final part, which concomitantly concludes this discussion, is to arrive once again at a creed of the Christian university. During the course of time, not just due to the influence exerted by the absence of a firm foundation at the neutral university, but also under the influence of the peculiar ideas held at such universities by Calvinists who from there attack the Calvinistic institution, there has arisen uncertainty and confusion about principles which we had assumed to be firmly established. From this angle misplaced sympathy has been generated, even by Calvinists at Calvinistic institutions. Without taking these deviations as criteria in determining the order of the following discussion they will nevertheless be consistently reviewed. Neither will we be able to examine critically each facet of the Calvinistic university, simply due to a lack of time.

Just a few theses, acutely relevant to the very nature of the university, are to be proposed here.

Thesis 1: *It is in keeping with its character for the university to have a creed*

This thesis has been phrased deliberately in such a way that there is no choice about having a creed or not. There are universities that allege they have no creed, others that their members have creeds but that the university as such cannot follow suit. The so-called neutrality that this attitude displays, is just as much a creed as that of the Christian university, even though those universities allege that for scientific reasons they have no creed. How strange that even fellow Calvinists at neutral universities allege that they are more at home there than they would be at a Christian university

21

because there nobody is supposedly forced into a mould to the possible detriment of his personal creed. There are even some of these Calvinists who maintain that no university can have a creed just as they maintain that there can be no Christian school. Without trying to be facetious one cannot arrive at any other conclusion than that these erudite persons probably see the university as a collection of buildings and not of people, for in no other way can they come to such a conclusion.

This places the Christian university before a formidable enemy from its own ranks and here in South Africa we know many of these. It is difficult enough to battle agains disbelief, but to be opposed by one's own people, Bible in hand, is a double burden and who has any counsel here?

We do not hesitate in acknowledging that we have a creed. On the contrary, we consider it such a tremendous honour and privilege to confess that our creed qualifies every facet of our university that we proclaim it at every available opportunity. All the scientific work, the teaching being done, the professional training, the services rendered to the community, state, church, indeed all thrive under this life-giving creed.

The Christian university states and proclaims that the entire institution finds itself in the midst of God's Kingdom on earth.

The university is by virtue of its nature a product of human culture and finds the justification for its existence in the cultural injunction proclaimed in Genesis 2 : 15 to "work" and "preserve". And this leads the Christian university assiduously onwards to attempt tirelessly and without pause to bring about congruency between the boundaries of created reality and the boundaries of God's Kingdom on earth. It proclaims the sovereignty of Jesus Christ over every facet of the university according to Rom. 11 : 36, and in all its scientific practice, in its education, in its government it seeks the guidance of God and wishes to take no step except under this sterling guidance with which it has been graced.

Whoever subscribes to this point of view, must expect to be accused of preconceptions within the field of science as if those with all their pretence at being unaligned are not similarly bound, with the difference that they labour under the yoke of the obverse side of the highest good.

He will have to carry the burden of abuse for not being free, for being an injudicious person incapable of separating on the one hand the world of science and knowledge from that of faith on the other hand, this abuse being levelled also by fellow-believers worshipping in the same church and serving on the same church council. These schizophrenics with their dual personalities have become the norm also for the community of believers and this normative attitude is revealed, like the Christian creed, in every facet of the university.

He will constantly be accused of indoctrination due to his demand that a new field of knowledge, namely that of religion, be taken into account at every level of the university in order to attain full understanding of all phenomena.

These accusations can be multiplied to the point of writing off all the work of the Christian university. To us, however, it makes no difference, we are not impressed by it, for we know that a slanted foundation can produce only a slanted building. For this conference it means nothing more than once again experiencing the responsibility and unutterable privilege of freedom in Jesus Christ. Here lies the basis for the amalgamation of the Christian universities throughout the world in their common service to God.

Thesis 2: *The nature of the Christian university requires it to practise a Christian science*

The university is the practitioner of science. It is one of its essential functions. The Christian university practises a Christian science. And with this — as with the creed — we find ourselves confronted by one of the essential features of the Christian university.

This is not the opportunity for an explanation of Christian science; it will be done later during this conference. Let it suffice to state that for the Christian university, science is not complete without its Christian perspective, for this is the only road to full comprehension. To all the methods being applied, from the most spiritual to the most mechanistic-technical, there has to come in the final instance a meaningful breakthrough, with the assistance of these additional elements, in order to uncover the full nature of the phenomenon.

This is controversial ground. Unbelief rejects a Christian science as unscientific, subjective, a confusion of faith and reason. This does not disturb us. That there are, however, fellow Christians, even reformed brethren, to whom a Christian science is unacceptable because at the scientific level one operates with the intellect where faith is irrelevant, is a matter for grave concern. They succeed in removing an important field of human endeavour from the sovereignty of Jesus Christ without affecting their creed, for they still insist on being called Christian scientists. It is apparently impossible for them to rid themselves of this schizophrenia.

That we still lack complete unanimity as to what Christian

science encompasses and that the ramifications of this question hove not yet been fully explored, does not detract from the need and compulsion of doing so; nor from the sense of achievement in the field of scientific practice.

In respect of a Christian science this conference has the task of participating in the world-wide construction of the edifice of science, erected in the light of God's Word.

Thesis 3: *The Christian university is essentially an educational institution*

A few decades ago it was generally accepted that the term "education" in its wider connotation was not applicable to the university in its concern with adults whose upbringing had been completed. There was a time in the history of the university when this was the case. The modern university, however, has undergone at least two major changes in this respect: students have in general become so much younger that they can no longer be considered adults, and secondly the years of youth have been extended to the point where most students pass through university without having attained adulthood.

Although we call the university a corporation of scholars, of lecturers and students, exploring science at an advanced level and in all its seriousness and profundity, we are still concerned with mature and immature individuals engaged in a calculated process of the moulding of people, and where this process is executed, a host of questions about matters of principle are raised which can only be answered in terms of a philosophy of life.

Once again this is not the place to expound the pedagogical act in all its ramifications at the university level. Let it suffice to state that it is a fundamental task of the Christian university to explore this facet of its being to the very foundation of this phenomenon as a whole, just as scientifically as the rest of its work, in which there is the full unfolding of the basis of the pedagogical act or of man, the final objective, the way between these two that has to be filled by the content and method, organization and administration of the pedagogical act.

And here this conference is faced with a third equally important task, and that is to proclaim the Christian university as an institution where people are formed to occupy their full place in the Kingdom of God on earth. This institution cannot produce any split personalities, for it contains within itself the harmony of the unity of science, of the unity which underpins all creation.

24

Thesis 4: *It is a secondary task of the Christian university to train professional people*

It is a fundamental task of the Christian university to train scientists in the process of practising science and the moulding of people. To satisfy the requirements of the world in which it functions, the university has to accept as a secondary task the third necessity of arriving, through the moulding of people and the training of scientists, at the training of professional people who have to occupy their place in life as exemplifiers of basic principles and especially as method innovators in the field in which they operate.

It is an essential characteristic of training at the tertiary level of education that general education and scientific training can be applied to all spheres of life. We could consider this to be a strange phenomenon because its existence is at present merely recognized without being fully understood. Here lies a vast unexplored field with tremendous demands on the Christian university.

This conference must be concerned about coming to the full richness of shaping Christian professional people for each branch of national life where it is relevant, to be able to meet the demands made on the people of God's Kingdom on earth.

Thesis 5: *The modern Christian university is in the midst of the world without being of the world*

The rendering of service by the university is fully discussed at a later stage.

Here it is sufficient to state that it is a necessary demand levelled at the Christian university for it at all times to pass along to life in all its variety, everything which it has explored for the advancement of church, state, society, art, culture, the economy and what you will. It is the vocation of the Christian university to provide well-considered direction at an advanced level in such a sober manner that it will become the leader on the road to reformation, preventing life from degenerating to the condition discussed at the beginning of this discourse. It will not be going too far to maintain that the Christian university cannot lead towards chaos, being prevented by its creed. This would only be possible if the Christian university were to be separated from its foundation.

This conference has to demand for itself that its institutions for tertiary education should come to the fore in providing the leadership so sorely lacking in the world.

Thesis 6: *The control of the university is determined by the nature of the university as a unique social community*

The people concerned with the university are the teaching staff, the students, all those in society with a need for tertiary education and who publicly demonstrate this in support for the institution, and the state. In the interests of the university they are bound together in a new social institution, an institution in which each individual irrespective of his point of origin, functions with the rest in a new capacity. Here there is no one more important than the other and the one may not be dominated by the other. Should this happen, the university becomes the slave of the one who predominates.

Should we accept this view of control of the university, harmony would naturally result and numerous contemporary crises mentioned at the beginning of this discourse would disappear. Should the state, the society concerned, or the teaching staff, or the students, acquire dominance over the university, it must be expected that this institution will become warped.

In this unique design each one of the interested factions is indeed responsible for the entire university because corporate control is exercised by all of them. And yet on the other hand, also as part of the character of the university, it is just as true that each one of them is more involved in a specific facet of the university than in the other. If there is any deviation here, the result almost without exception is disharmony that could end in chaos.

Without going into details I would like to refer to the evils which have resulted when the state exceeds its powers in wanting to determine the character of the university, or the parents wish to usurp judicial powers, or the teaching staff when they wish to take over the management, or the students when they wish to take over control — or just as bad — wish to determine academic standards.

This conference declares that the Christian university in terms of control of the institution, can only flourish on the basis of justice towards all concerned.

Thesis 7: *The Christian university places a premium on the student*

By virtue of the nature of the university the student is an integral part of the university, and this has to be taken into account at all times.

This is more true for the Christian university because its view of man demands that it must place a premium on the bearer of the image of God. There is no question, therefore, of disregarding the student, just as he may not be elevated to the point of becoming the deciding factor at the university. Due to his immaturity during part or the whole of his training period, it is self-evident that at most of these levels, it is only the mature student — alumnus or member of the convocation — who will join in this responsibility. Should it develop differently, the natural consequences are multiple disasters for the university as displayed throughout the world during the last two decades.

There is, however, a specific field of activity for the student, irrespective of age. For this he cannot be too young to accept the responsibility because without it he can never fully develop.

This field is contained in the essential contribution made by the student to the university, namely being co-worker with the lecturer in the pursuit of knowledge, science, education, training. The student is being shaped in each one of these fields, but conclusive results cannot be achieved if he is not prepared to participate purposefully in his own development. He is educated towards the acquisition of all those virtues we have already mentioned, but he is at university during that stage in his life where he has to participate in his self-training and self-education.

He is also called upon to create his own niche in the extra-curricular activities of the student community in the lobbies and the forum, in the residences, in cultural activities, on the sports fields — in all the richness of student life.

Thus the student is faced with a full programme leaving no time for anything else. Without neglect here he will not be able to act elsewhere without damage to himself. Those who diligently apply themselves to this vocation, can be assured of a full richness being experienced in their lives.

This conference proclaims that the Christian university considers its supreme vocation to be the moulding of the student, lawfully and in justice, towards a fully conscious bearer of the image of God. In this there is for the student no question of indoctrination, only the fulfilling of a vocation which must result for him in the autonomous choice of the freedom with which Christ has set us free.

6. Conclusion

We posed the question whether we should strive for a radical new order at the university level. I think I have shown that this is not a prerequisite for the Christian university to flourish. That which during the passing of the centuries has crystallized about the form and content of the university and which has been the result

27

of the work of the faithful and unfaithful at this level, offers all that is necessary to bring the Christian university to full deployment.

The modern neutral university maims the university in more than one respect and it cannot be ruled out that the ultimate result in these hands could be such radical changes that the institution may lose its character.

The Christian university does not need it, but it is clear that there will have to come a polarization between it and the secular university, even if in practice it means that each one will have an institution with an essentially different character.

However, this is not of great importance to the Christian university. What is imperative though, is that the two principles of life guiding the various universities should be clearly stated as opposites, for this is of the greatest importance to the Kingdom of God on earth. And the Christian university may not shrink from doing this.

I believe this conference has to lead towards the consolidation of Christian institutions for higher education, their propagation and the concomitant rejection of the neutral university in its present form or in whatever form it may present itself. And for this no new order of the university is required.

With this, this conference succeeds, without it, it fails.

The university as it is and as it ought to be

Prof. Dr. Hendrik van Riessen

It seems to me that the decisive background of this conference and at any rate of my lecture could be summarized as follows:

The Law of God, or the Word of God, for all creation is the command to exist of God, through God and unto God. Uniquely concerning man, the content of this command is that he has to choose to serve God in order to exist fully and truly.

While man failed in this calling, Jesus Christ, both the Son of God and the second Adam, fulfilled the Law of God. Thus He reconciled creation with God and delivered it to its destination.

Through faith in Jesus Christ the christian is given new life, that is life in Him, and as such the christian is motivated towards a meaningful existence, to the service of God in every respect.

Confining myself to the university as a field of man's activities, our problem is to discover what is the service of God in this case and in our time.

I consider it as my task to deal with some fundamental aspects of this subject from a philosophical point of view.

In the first place we have to know what we are talking about, what the university is.

The investigation will lead us in the second place to a very special problem with which christians are confronted concerning the university. I have in mind the possibility and actuality of a specific kind of apostasy in the case of the university.

Furthermore, we have to look into the complications of this problem. One could summarise it in this way: The apostasy does not succeed; as a falling away from God it is but an appearance. On the one hand this appearance has an effect on man, in practice and in history; on the other hand all things remain integrated within creation, which exists to the honour and in the service of God.

After this introduction we will contemplate the contemporary university, its situation and motivations.

Finally we will consider the christian approach to the university of the future.

1. *The university*

Some are inclined to deny the existence of "the university" as the common denominator of the phenomena which we call universities. There is no lasting structure, they say, because this phenomenon too is determined by the course of history. I am not bothered by this idea. Our intuition knows that it is better to choose one word for a kind of institution which has been in existence in our civilization for at least 900 years. The difficulty is of course to bring this intuition to expression.

What we are looking for is a normative principle, actualized by mankind, dependent on the historical situation. The actual university will therefore be a thing in development, but exhibiting confused issues, mostly with a tendency to one or to the other extreme.

But how can these facts lead us to the sought-after principle? Here we touch upon a very general difficulty for human knowledge. It can never be avoided. We can analyse the confusing ambiguity, we can state the tendency towards an extreme idea, by means of general normative principles, but in the end we will have to transcend the given facts in order to envisage the conjecture of a normative principle for the university which satisfies us at least for the present, concerning both the inner unity of meaning of the university and its meaning-coherence with society.

Let us test some ideas. Is the university the place where the elite of society is formed? Such was the opinion of Schelling and Fichte, also of Jaspers. With Newman it was the place where the gentleman was educated, or as Ortega Y. Gasset puts it, the cultural man. Although in another sense, namely essentially critical with respect to society, Marcuse also nurses this idea of a general education of the elite.

One can admit that the loss of a general education at our universities not only degrades the university as such, but also (while turning out all kinds of narrowminded specialists) deprives society of men at university level who are trained to be aware of the problems which really trouble our world in distress.

None the less, the idea of the education of an elite is not typical enough and in fact wrong. It presupposes, moreover, both too much and too little. Too much, because the tools of the university, science and even philosophy, are too onesided for such a goal. Too little, because no justice is done to the fact, which has been present from the start of the university: particular training for professions.

Let us now look into the idea that the university offers the highest training for professions. It certainly meets an essential external goal of the university, but the idea does not provide us

30

with an inner unity of the university. It results in a multi-university as Kerr saw it. We observed already that such a university lacks the general education which society at present needs more than anything else.

Moreover, in this case too, the idea does not penetrate to the university in its particularity.

In my opinion we are on the track of this particularity when we pay attention to science being at home at the university. I include in science the humanities, as well as philosophy.

It is, however, not my intention to look at the university as an institution for research. We would then forget the student, who in relation to science is the heart of the matter. But not all of it. One could study at home. We have to add that the study of science is placed in a community of learning, a community of "learning" students and of teachers "learned" for that purpose.

Could we describe the relation of student and science as a relation of education? It is a good description, especially as it surpasses the idea of gathering scientific knowledge. But it is not good enough. I prefer the description training in science. The education is preparatory. In the end guidance of the teacher has to make room for the student as his partner in the student's attempt to prove, independently, mastery in his field. He has to prove it in original work at the frontline of science. It shows the necessity of research at the university. There are other types of research at the university. I mention the research of the teacher as a basis for his teaching task. He will, moreover, investigate fields which are more remotely connected with his teaching task at hand. Many times the aim will be the publication of the results. The same is valid for research performed by teams about more general problems. In my opinion the criterion of such general problems too must be that the research in some way and at some time can be used for the teaching and training of students.

To illustrate my point that the essence of the university is the training in science I observe that lectures too are preparatory. They prepare the student for independent study, the results of which he has to prove and defend in the community of learning.

Nowhere else than at the university can the study of science reach this level. When the university fails to provide the student with this opportunity to prove himself a scholar, it will be no more than a pretension of what a university has to be.

Summarizing I propose the following normative principle for the university. It is the institution of communities of learning for the training of students in science.

The reason for a number of communities existing in one university is firstly that the sciences are directed towards different fields of investigation which are irreducible to each other, secondly that a scholarly community has to be limited in the number of its members.

The difficulty, especially at present, is of course, that the communities have to be integrated into the whole of the university. I will confine myself to two observations. This integration is not merely a problem of organization. It has to be a human whole. One source of the present difficulties is that the student experiences himself as part of an impersonal mass, ruled by an autonomous organization. Limitation of the number of students, at whatever cost, is imperative.

The second remark concerns the coherence of the sciences. Groups to promote these coherences ought also to be formed. The role of philosophy becomes especially apparent here.

I have now developed the normative principle for the university. It makes, however, no mention of the education for professions. In my opinion we have to distinguish the principle of the university itself according to its own nature, and the meaning-coherence of the university with society outside. The inner principle is conducive to the outer goals of the university, has to be worked out for the service of the professions. But we must avoid the pragmatistic mistake of replacing the inner principle by the external goals.

There is yet something else that needs to be said about the normative principle I tried to formulate. To know a norm implies that we judge reality by means of it and also that we know the direction of what we have to do and what we have to reject, whether the norm is expressed or not. That is the way, the only way, everyone of us acts.

It is not always necessary to express the norm. Mostly we know intuitively what is good and what is bad. And when we need the expression, as in our case, we can never make it complete. In our case we are of course in need to know what is meant with study, community, science, etc. And even this knowledge would not be enough. It is not proper to consider for instance study and science isolated from man's true life, the service of God. Neglect of this feature would be sin in the essential sense of the word, anomia and missing the goal.

I need this remark because, while the restricted expression of the norm will be useful later on, we can not truly understand this use if we had not considered firstly the religious question concerning the university and science, viz. the questions of the service of God and of sin in its essential features.

2. *Science and the university in apostasy*

There is no thought or deed of man, nor the projection of it in reality, which does not show the tendency of every one of us to fall away from the service of God, be it in part or totally.

Science and its home, the university, have added, however, a new feature to this falling away from God: a systematic apostasy. For 2 600 years already, science and philosophy have cherished the pretension of knowledge and mastery of the world in human independence. I don't know of any weapon of Satan against the Kingdom of God which is more powerful than this one. The idea cherished by mankind is not only that with regard to the knowledge of science and philosophy, man is independent and autonomous, but also that this knowledge gives man mastery over the world. The belief that the university has to educate the elite has its origin here. It is not only an elite in the field of truth, but also with regard to human activity. Mostly hidden, but openly confessed by Socrates and elaborated by Plato, the jump from the truth to the good is made. The person who knows more is the better person. The philosopher, therefore, is the best person there is.

Why was this tool suitable for a systematic apostasy so that it could become a lasting and extremely powerful institution of man? The possibility for it lies in the method of science, including philosophy. It is the method of analysis and abstraction. Due to that method, science can provide us with trustworthy universal knowledge, which of course makes us very powerful. As universal knowledge it is trustworthy, inasmuch as the abstraction frees it from man's feelings, interest, preferences and beliefs. It is therefore called objective knowledge. That is why science could become a tool and a lasting institution, to a certain extent independent of man.

Let us then consider that science is taken to be the thing that makes man independent from God. It follows that science then has to exist in that same way with regard to man himself, because it has to be independent from man's faith and religion.

The irony of the systematic apostasy by means of science is, therefore, that the tool man created in order to be independent from God thus also has to be considered as independent from man. That is not only a repetition of the idea of autonomy, disproving the autonomy of man himself. Throughout history the development of science has shown that in its autonomy it became a prison for man and is at the bottom of the crisis of western civilization.

Apostasy of man to become entirely free from God does not lead to freedom but, on the contrary, to slavery in the service of an idol, science in this case.

It is, however, a slavery made by man himself and an appearance at that. The idea of the independence of science from man is as much a fiction as its premise, the independence of man from God.

But what is the scientific origin of the wrong turn man took from the start in science? In my opinion it is the abstraction being considered as absolute. Abstraction as such is lawful and of great value for human thought and action. But here, for the purpose of man's independence, it is taken as the entire dissociation of scientific thought from belief. Consequently it results in the dissociation of science from man. That is the idea of an absolute objectivity.

In fact abstraction, not misused as is the case here, is a very complicated subject. It is something in between mere distinction and isolation. But where about? In other words and for example, what in science is rightfully abstracted from man, from his beliefs especially, and what is not? A very important question and a fine subject for a thesis. I am unfortunately 30 years late.

It is clear that absolute abstraction and objectivity cannot be proved. Philosophy never proved it. That did not astonish or worry the philosophers and the scientists with regard to their conviction that man in science is independent from God and therefore from faith. Their conviction is of course a belief which is not even bound to science. If it proves useless for its original purpose, it is thrown away as such, as is the case in our time. Christian belief, therefore, is not confronted with science and its arguments, but with the belief of apostate man.

The belief in the autonomy of science has in 2 600 years gathered the strength of tradition. The power of tradition gave the idea of the autonomy of science, and the belief that science has nothing to do with christian faith, the halo of selfevidence.

Most christians accepted it. One could be a christian and at the same time be dedicated to science as an activity for which God did not exist. They did not understand that behind the separation lay an antithesis of beliefs, a struggle in western history in which christian faith in our civilization has been defeated and science is now celebrating its Pyrrhic victory.

There is, however, another reason why many christians think it justified to stay at what is to me the wrong side of the barricade.

3. *The complication of the apostasy*

An example of what I mean has already been discussed. The idea

34

of an absolute abstraction does not wipe out the abstraction as such. Because the idea does not start in The Truth it does not lead to The Truth, but that does not imply that it leads into the opposite direction. Such a science will also result in valuable knowledge, be it of a mixed character.

We touch here, of course, upon a universal feature of sin as the falling away from God. Sin does not walk upon an independent road. It is attached to reality, which keeps on existing to the honour of God. It has no other possibilities than those given in the Law of God. It even appears in the disguise of that Law.

The mixed character of scientific truths varies from science to science for various reasons. Both this mixture and the variety in it are conducive to the supposition that the relation of science and faith can be neglected or does not even exist. We find it in the natural sciences, but also in the other ones in so far as they preserve a neutral, so called theoretical, field.

Such suppositions stand in the way of true science, because they show the tendency towards autonomy which will always mix untruth in its results. On the other hand, it seems sensible not to speak of christian science in general.

Our intentions will become more clear when we dedicate ourselves to the christian approach to science. It means an obedient openness to what God in His revelation is telling man about reality. In my opinion such an openness is the condition for scientific freedom, while the idea of neutrality stands in the way of scientific openness.

But even when we are aware of this condition it is far from easy to apply it. Science never starts with a faith content. It starts with problems about certain facts of reality, encountered in wonderment about these facts. It carries on with the investigation of such problems and with reasoning about them. This is also the case in philosophy, where Dooyeweerd called the correct method the transcendental method, rejecting the transcendent method which he called dogmatic. But where then and how does the faith content enter the reasoning? Another fine subject for a thesis.

In all my lectures and publications I have struggled with this problem. This time I have begun with the expression of my belief. Was that wrong? I am not sure. But it is perhaps not good enough. I tried to save my lecture from the fate of many publications of christians, positive with regard to our problem, but who never stepped outside of the area beyond which they kept their faith. But I am sure there is a more genuine way to do it.

4. *The university of today*

We have to look at the situation of the contemporary university and its dominant motivations. These two are interdependent. The situation induces motivations and motivations shape the new situation. The problem is very complicated, but we have to try to understand it.

As to the situation, we observe a very swift development of the sciences on a road towards even more specialization. Decomposing as a whole, the unity of science is at stake.

Furthermore, the number of students has grown extraordinarily. They study at a mass-university which, generally speaking, has lost the human outlook and its communality of learning.

Finally, science has systematically turned to the application of its results to society, in a way which is entirely new in history. These three are, of course, interdependent. But in my opinion the latter is dominant. The new possibilities of science in practical life are a magnet for the young people, while the high standard of living, resulting from the new powers, has made their study possible. The rapid development of the sciences is of course due to the tendency to cover the whole of society and due to the requirements of a society rapidly on the move in history.

It means an impressive change in the character of the university. Its aim is no longer knowledge and the shaping of an intellectual elite, but it aims at mastery in society and shaping rulers. Not wonderment to know as such, but the problems of society (and all of them) have become the problems of science, and this decides the practical issues. The tools for the new dominion of society are, next to science, modern technology and organization, both on a scientific basis.

Motivated to master society, the university experiences in return the mastery of society over it, urging the university to teach professions and nothing more. Viewed in the light of the principle of the university, that is a serious loss, not only with regard to training in science, but remarkably, also with regard to the scientific contributions which society really needs in our time.

However that may be, I have to draw your attention to a still more important feature of our new situation, dominated by the university. In our century the leadership of western civilization has shifted from the church to the university with its tool, science. One could interpret this shift as the result of man's striving for independence from God and mastery over the world. It is in the spirit of our time, this definite shift from dependence on God to independent, powerful man in a closed world.

At the front of this movement we experience a departure from the church on a tremendous scale, an adaptation of the official church in words and deeds to the secularized world, but also the rise of a more radical christianity, on a small scale but very promising.

Let us return to the university. The victory over christian faith did not result in a resolute leadership over society and its future. It is, on the contrary, caught in a crisis of motivation.

In the light of the nearly explosive development of the universities all kinds of confusions, also about the general direction, could be expected. But that is not the heart of the matter. The university shares with our entire civilization the crisis of meaning which such men as Nietzsche and Camus understood to be inevitable in a closed world.

At the university the crisis was focussed on science. From the beginning its adepts expected that science would be able to solve the problems and to have all the answers. But now being ready for it, conqueror of christian faith and master of the field, it appeared that science was entirely blind to the decisive question of the meaning of life and the world. Science therefore was degraded by an irrationalistic movement. As a basis for man's autonomy it was, moreover, undermined by the results of science itself. Freud, and others, considered autonomy of human thought and reason to be a fiction.

Although the autonomy of science is maintained tacitly by most, the idea of autonomy has switched to man's mastery over practical life, as could have been expected from the turn towards applied science.

But here too, the promise of man's final independence and mastery turned out to be a disappointment. We already touched upon this subject as a repetition of the idea of autonomy. What man and the university are doing is in fact following the course of the independent powers in their automatic development. This independence, as we saw, is an appearance. But due to the belief of most men in it and their lack of motivation by the true meaning of life the appearance projected in society has become effective.

A protest against this situation of diminished freedom was to be expected. It arose at the university among the students. They advanced the idea of a new, critical university. Its motivation was not only the critique of the adjustment-university but more in general a critique of the present society in its one-dimensional development.

One has to admit that the students had serious reasons for protest. It even belongs to science that the university has a critical approach. Yet we need a closer look at what the students mean and do.

They accepted the leadership of what is called neo-marxism. It is a return to the younger Marx. With him they were moved by the bondage of mankind. While many neo-marxists understood that the theory of Marx was essentially not corroborated by history, they took from him his dialectical method and practice.

It needs a short explanation. Dialectic implies here an actual and radical conflict between two poles which are irreconcilable but presuppose each other.

The dialectic can take various shapes. In our case it is the dialectic between the adjustment university and the critical university, the former being negated by the latter in an actual struggle.

Well then, to understand our situation it is important to observe that the battle is not fought within the dialectic actually existing in our civilization, but within another one. The actual dialectic is the one between human freedom and the human powers. It is implied in the idea of autonomy and it has become more extreme in proportion to the closing of our world. The dialectical battle fought by the neo-marxists and the students is the one against authority and for democracy.

While the real dialectic is hopeless due to the loss of meaning, the dialectic between authority and democracy is a shadowshow. I will briefly try to explain it.

In case the battle against the people in authority is won and authority is overthrown, nothing has been achieved for the cause of freedom. Other people will be at the helm of the same autonomous powers which deprive man of his freedom.

But why don't the neo-marxists attack the autonomy of these powers? Because they are convinced that the powers in their rationality are inevitably as they are, autonomous.

The battle for democracy is just as vain. The rejection of authority as such is understandable, because in a closed world there is no one left to give authority to some. All people are equal and together they decide all issues. In practice this extreme raises, however, the other extreme: the tyranny of an elite and the loss of the common man's freedom.

The lesson to be learned, from this revolt too, is that true authority is the precondition for freedom and actual responsibility of all the people for the common cause.

The adjustment-university and the critical university battle vainly against each other and for the deliverance of society from its evils in search of a promising future because they have lost the guidance of the Law of God giving human existence its meaning in the Kingdom of God.

5. *Some remarks about a christian university*

Bearing in mind that all the speakers will have their point of gravity in this subject and will certainly within their field talk competently about it, I can confine myself and in view of my ability have to confine myself to some conclusions about a christian university, which could be drawn from what I said about the principle of the university, in relation with what I said about the present situation and its origin.

They will concern: the basis of such a university; science and its study at the university; the university and the outside world; the university as an institution and a community.

If the decay, distress and near collapse of western civilization is understood and if it is also understood the measure in which science and the university have been its causes, it will also be understood that christian education and a christian university are of the utmost importance. Because we need at such a christian or reformed university a joint impetus and a mutual correction it ought to have a basis to which one could appeal. This basis has to imply the motivation and the direction in teaching and research, corresponding to what ought to live in our heart, even though always poorly expressed. But that is not the point. One should love it and start from it, not undermine it in order to be able to escape from its obligation. The seduction to do so is always at hand because our attempts are not very convincing, here especially.

The important thing, however, as in every field of christian activity in the service of God, is the recognition that the blessing of the Lord is more important than the activity of man. It should be expressed in the basis and it should be practised in the community in the manner of listening and speaking to Him.

Our second topic concerns science and its study.

The Christian concept of science is the critical question because it is the fundamental question and the most difficult one. On the one hand christians in science belong to the entire community of science, learning from it and contributing to it; on the other hand they have their own approach to science. The temptation is not in the tendency to stand apart but in the tendency to conform, due to the overpowering influence of established science.

The struggle for a good balance, while holding the community together, is very difficult. It needs loyalty to the basis, a strong belief, perseverance and alertness. Every scientific result has to be reviewed not in order to reject it but in order to look through it in the direction of the facts and how they were chosen and interpreted; also to track down the presuppositions. The collaboration of the sciences and philosophy is always needed here. With regard to the existence of presuppositions, theology too needs the aid of philosophy but on the other hand philosophy needs the aid of theology with regard to their content. A better understanding and collaboration between these two than is generally the case would be a cause of great joy.

In the christian approach one always has to be aware of these two features of science: its limitation and its relativity or dependence on presuppositions. The limitation not only means that scientific knowledge can never exhaust reality, but also that science cannot replace (let alone surpass) other types of knowledge such as practical knowledge. This consideration is of supreme importance with regard to applied science. We have to reject the idea that science could master the world and its problems. It can in fact strive for this mastery, but in doing so it makes a mess of society. We have already some experience.

The recognition of the relativity of science is of course the rejection of its autonomy. Especially here philosophy has a task. I will only make one remark. In my opinion a new approach to thought and belief instead of the idea of their duality could free us from the old and strong tradition that this duality is nearly or even wholly a separation. The unity of the human mind and its transcending acts has to be put first and foremost. In it thinking, imagining, believing, etc. are always and integrally present. We can distinguish them by means of the qualification of the act. But thinking is never without believing, etc. It is especially belief which makes the transcending character of human acts possible.

The problem is therefore not as it has always seemed to be: how to bridge the separation. But it is: how can distinction be made in what is at bottom, one.

As to the study of and the training of the students in science, we generally reject the situation of the present university, even if it is at the price of the christian university being rejected by society. We have something in mind which would in the end serve society better than it is being served by the universities at present: true study up to the highest level, namely scientific independence with respect to society, scientific maturity. This has to take place in real communities of study at a university small enough to entertain overall human relations and to cultivate a community spirit of the whole staff. In other words, a university where human relations can be prevalent over organizational relations.

It would ask a lot of sacrifices, but in my opinion it would not be impossible to make them. One has, moreover, to take into consideration with regard to the tremendous number of applications at present that most of the students will prefer to study at the various higher schools for professions which have to be distinguished from the universities.

I grant that the prevailing trend is to wipe out difference, whereby the university is the loser. It is perhaps not possible to turn this trend, but that does not mean that a dedicated attempt of christians to establish a university as proposed here, or to change an existing one gradually into it, could not succeed.

I proceed to the relation of the university with the world outside. The other universities are there. To the ones which pretend to have no basis the christian university will have a mixed relation of opposition and collaboration.

Society at large is there too. It needs and requires students trained for various professions. The christian university has to prepare the students for this goal but it has to do this in its own way. Not as society usually thinks of needing them, but as society actually and normatively needs them.

The relation could best be understood if we bear in mind that the university takes the detour of science, justified by its method of abstraction, in order to free itself from the ties of society for the purpose of scientific knowledge as such. At the detour the university does not forget about the need of professional men and the desirability of the application of science in society, but it is not ruled by them. It is motivated by science and the training of students in it.

I will conclude with an observation about the university as an institution and a community. Actually it is my intention to finish with the outline of some unsolved problems in this respect and in the style that suits philosophy so well. This philosophical mood, that there are more problems unsolved than solved, will perhaps take away a wrong impression from the other parts of this lecture, that there would be no problems left.

In a short time some remarkable changes have taken place at the university. I have already mentioned some of them: the tremendous growth of the sciences; the university as a mass institution; the dominant turn to the application of science.

We have to add some more. The sovereign professor of old is past. Perhaps not yet here in South Africa. But wait and see.

The student has lost considerable freedom in his study. His curriculum is extensively regulated and he studies under stricter supervision. All this at a lower level of learning.

The fate of the professor is not only due to the protest of the students and the fate of the student not only to the number of students. There is a tendency at the university to control and master it centrally by means of planning and organization, while there is a general tendency in government to control the universities in the same way. This collectivistic trend produces, as we saw, an automatic control by autonomous powers and a considerable loss of freedom.

We observe therefore opposing trends. On the one hand the staff, other than the professors, and the students have gained a lot of influence, meaning more freedom in responsibility. On the other hand the university is gradually becoming a victim too of organocracy. That is the same dialectic I spoke about. It shuttles between the extremes of chaos and tyranny.

At the university I outlined, due to another motivation and another situation, amongst others a reduced size, these problems need not arise. But there remain some serious problems which I will put before you.

Such a university recognizes and respects authority. God has revealed to us that He ordains and sustains authority. The university will also try to realize the norm of a good balance between authority and the freedom of the people to responsibility, also with respect to the common cause.

Well then, at each side of this balance a problem arises.

Authority at the university covers two quite different fields: The authority in teaching and over research, and the authority over the institutions as such. I leave the question of a hierarchy in both aside.

Could these fields be separated, there would be no problem. But that is not the case. They are intertwined, e.g. at the board of a faculty.

The professor is supposed to be qualified for authority in teaching, examinations and in research. But he is certainly not qualified to preside over assemblies, to plan, organize, manage and control the university and its parts. Mostly to the contrary. Formerly there were nearly no such problems. The professor did as he liked and was in fact in charge of his own "university". But now some people have to be in charge of these aspects of the university. If other people are appointed for this authority there will not only be a divided authority dealing with e.g. matters of the faculty, the teaching curriculum and the integration of research, but also the qualified responsibility of the professors for teaching and research, the centre of the university, will be challenged and easily overruled by people who are not qualified in these fields.

This problem has to be solved and I don't know how.

The second problem concerns the responsibility of all the participants for the common cause. It also complicates the first problem.

Of course I don't have in mind democracy in a literal sense. On the other hand responsibility in the sense of advice and committees for it would not be a problem nor the good custom of consultation with the students about all kinds of matters.

The problem arises when decisionmaking committees are aimed at after the example of the representation of the people in the state.

It is of course not necessary to do so but in my opinion it would not only be useful but also a consequence of the idea of the responsibility of the participants. The relations between authority and the committees could of course be fixed in the laws of the university.

The difficulty is, however, that the responsibility has to be tuned to the ability of the person in question. In matters of teaching, examinations, research, nominations, etc. the differences in ability between students, assistants, fellows, professors, technical and administrative employees are so great that it seems impossible to resolve them for the decisionmaking committees in terms of their composition and the extent and content of their task.

Threats to the Christian character of the Christian institution

Prof. Dr. Pierre Corthial

1. *Introduction: History in review*

The question is asked, and must be asked: how could christian institutions established by sacrifices of every kind and by faithful, confessing Christians, how could and can they slip and degenerate, more or less rapidly, and come to minimize, dispute, contest if not actually to corrupt or repudiate and reject the basic principles on which they had been founded?

How could Harvard, established in 1636 with a well defined christian character, the first institution for higher education in America, how could it, within 65 years, deviate to such an extent that Yale is founded in 1701, only to enter from 1805 onwards, one century later, the dark fog of unitarianism.

How did Yale in its turn lose its way?

And how did Princeton, this fearless and wise bastion of the reformed faith, established in 1811 and coming to clear expression in the work of Archibald Alexander, the Hodges, Benjamin B. Warfield, W. H. Green, R. Robert Dick Wilson, J. Gresham Machen and so many others, how did it come to abandon its basic principles and its faithful tradition to justify in the end the establishment, in 1921, of *Westminster Theological Seminary* of Philadelphia?

How could the Free University of Amsterdam, inaugurated less than a century ago, on 20 October, 1880, gift of God, result of the faith, prayers, struggles, love, offerings, the hope of a whole reformed people of the Netherlands, carried along by the genius of Abraham Kuyper, how could it arrive at the alarming stage where we find it today?

And how, in France, could a brilliant reformed Academy like the one at Saumur, how could it from before the middle of the seventeenth century, and little after the ecumenical reformed Synod of Dordrecht, let itself be invaded by a more or less camouflaged armenianism which would, alas, spread itself almost everywhere in my country?

I have only mentioned examples of universities, academical

institutions; but I could also mention the unfortunate examples of missionary societies, medical or professional institutions, Sunday school societies, magazines and papers, churches or church associations etc., which after a time of faithfulness and ardour of their first love, did not know how to "keep" what they had "received", and then had to see the golden chandelier which was their light and their glory taken away from them.

But, in talking to you, to you who listen to me now, I must surely speak about our own struggles of today. My speech shall not consist of a retrospective analysis of histories, some of which I have just recalled. Even if historical situations can be the same, they are never identical. Of course, we can occasionally retain lessons learned from historical similarity, but because of the difference, the non-identity, we must rather search in the unique Word of God for the warnings, the promises and the orders which are really valuable for us now and which we need. "When I want to know the latest news", said Léon Bloy, "I read St. Paul !"

2. Invisible powers, affliction and perseverance

It is with this warning of St. Paul that I am going to start. Ephesians 6 : 12: "For we wrestle not against flesh and blood, but against principalities, against powers, against the rulers of the darkness of this world, against spiritual wickedness in high places".

We must know how to receive this revelation. It means that our environment, from the time of Pentecost till the coming in glory of Jesus Christ, contains in its depth this terrible invisible reality against which the New Testament warns us and puts us on our guard. Our vision of threats to the christian character of christian institutions would lack reality, would deceive us, would delude us and would dull our vigilance, if it only took into consideration the "visible". In fact, we are surrounded by an atmosphere saturated by "invisible" powers animated and directed by the prince of darkness. These powers model, remodel and use the "Directive Ideas" that prevail at a certain time. These Directive Ideas present themselves in the beginning with so much subtlety that we inhale them, that we breathe them unconsciously. Afterwards they can progressively oppress with such a weight that they end up by crushing us to death.

Every christian institution as a whole, and every one of its members, has to cope with constantly renewed temptations, with formidable snares, skilfully set by the Adversary who "walks about as a preying lion, seeking whom he may devour" (1 Pet. 5 : 8). With and behind the men, the organizations and the states which oppose themselves, openly or surreptitiously, to God and to the Faith handed over to the Saints, with and behind the pseudo-christians, the false brothers, those who teach the lie, who are in the churches and the christian institutions without being of Christ and of the Church, behind and with these, are the demons and their Prince who maintain their watch, acting in different ways, and do not fail to find accomplices in what remains of sin even in the most faithful Christians. We must know this and never forget it.

But something which is even more important not to forget and which is even more important to know, is that the temptations never come up without the will of our Father in Heaven, who allows them, and who presents them by His own hand to His children as afflictions through which, by the strength He gives, He calls them to triumph. These two opposites: the demonic temptation and the divine affliction (which are often indicated by one word, *peirasmos*, in New Testament Greek) coincide antinomically in the purpose of the victorious decision of the faith, in our spatio-temporal reality. In this coincidence the vicious intention of the Adversary is to tempt us to sin, to seduce us, to make us fall and perish; whilst the good intention of God over and against the Adversary is to afflict His children only to make their faith more firm and pure, and to let His Name be thus glorified.

Also, instead of becoming discouraged or to despair, the threats to the christian character of the christian institutions of whom we are the responsible managers must push us towards vigilance, towards spiritual progress and ardour in our struggles.

By the faith in and the sovereign grace of God, who in Jesus Christ, predestines those who belong to Him for glory, we know that every saint who is elected will persevere till the end and that nothing "shall be able to separate us from the love of God which is in Jesus Christ our Lord" (Rom. 8 : 39). And we know that the holy elected church will persevere till the end and that "the gates of hell shall not prevail against it" (Math. 16 : 18). We can put it in another way: we believe in "the perseverance of the saints" and "the perseverance of the Holy Church".

But on the one hand, it is exactly this perseverance-hymn of praise to the merciful faithfulness and almightiness of God which calls for and includes at the same time the humble recognition of our weakness and the necessity of a constant appeal to the "arms (weapons) of God"; and on the other hand, the indestructible promises of God as far as the fundamental indefectability of the elect is concerned and the Church-as-Bride, do not concern this or that particular church or even more so this or that given christian institution. We are not allowed to have any personal negligence or any blind confidence in such an institution.

3. *The first threat is in ourselves*

The first threat, the first danger, is always inside ourselves. The frontline in which we must fight, hold on, and conquer, passes through our own lives. In the first place we must constantly be on the watch for ourselves. Our pride, our self-love will only disappear with our present life on earth and the first way to battle against pride is to recognize it and to confess it. "Wherefore, let him that thinks he stands take heed, lest he fall", said the apostle Paul in 1 Cor. 10 : 12, showing thus that one must never here below "think that he stands" as if one could in fact stand all alone.

Our weakness consists exactly in this foolish belief that we could be strong in ourselves. Our inclination always to come back to a will of independence, of autonomy. A will which is the mark itself of self-love, of pride.

The dominical exhortation "Watch and pray!" asks us in the first place to discern the complicity that the enemy still finds and, alas! always finds in us, in everyone of us personally.

"And take heed to yourselves" said Jesus to His disciples (Luk. 21 : 34). "Pray lest you enter into temptation" (Luk. 22 : 46). "But every man is tempted when he is drawn away of his own lust, and enticed", said James (chapter 1 : 14). "Take heed unto yourself" wrote St. Paul to Timothy (1 Tim. 4 : 16).

So must every one of us, together with the psalmist, cry to God "Search me, O God, and know my heart, try me, and know my thoughts; And see if there be any wicked way in me and lead me in the way everlasting" (Psalm 139 : 23—24). And also "who can understand his errors? cleanse me from secret faults" (Psalm 19 : 12).

As humiliating as it may be for every one of us, we must recognize and confess that *the most immediate threat* against the christian character of the christian institution *is in us,* is composed of our weakness, of our self-love, of our pride. It is to us, the responsible managers of some or other christian institution, to every one of us personally, that the call is addressed to recognize and confess this.

4. *The christian institution must form one body*

It is proper to say a word here, no more about the vigilance that everyone must have toward himself, but about the vigilance that the responsible managers of the christian institution must exercise as a whole on the body which consists of them.

"It is not good that man is alone". Jesus often sent his disciples two by two. The apostles formed 'the twelve'. The New Testamental churches were led by 'the Elders'. Even he who presides over a christian institution must preside 'in council', that is to say, not alone but in communion with others.

A very serious threat against the christian character of the christian institution becomes evident, grows and becomes quickly mortal when the council, the team which directs it, is no more homogeneous and when its members don't pull together. The devil is the divider. "If a house is divided against itself, that house cannot stand" (Mark. 3 : 25). Thus, every member of a council of a christian institution must watch himself, and the whole of the council of a christian institution must also watch itself, so that this council forms and persists to form a "body"; a body which is "one", with the diversity of talent and of services allowed to everyone; a body in which every member knows, and finds, that he needs the others; a body where jealousy does not reign but where when "one member is honoured, all the members rejoice with it" and when "one member suffers all the others suffer with it" (1 Cor. 12 : 4—31).

That is why doctrinal accord is not enough for a council to be really one body. There must be also a *psychological accord* established and maintained by a common and reciprocal love which "envies not, vaunts not itself, is not easily provoked, thinks no evil but rejoices in the truth" (1 Cor. 13 : 1—31).

In such a body where everybody is attentive to the others and where all are attentive to everybody and where the common well-being excels, humility, kindness, mutual support, *nouthesía* can develop, defining at the same time the christian character of the institution; thus truth is professed in love and "the whole body fitly joined together compacted by that which every joint supplies according to effectual working in the measure of every part, makes an increase of the body unto the edifying of itself in love ..." (Eph. 4 : 16). And if there is occasionally a movement of anger, the day does not end without confession, fraternal correction and reciprocal pardon. (See Eph. 4 : 26, Math. 5 : 21, Luk. 17 : 3—4, etc.).

5. *"Hypomonè" or endurance*

Every christian institution, from the moment when its qualification as "christian" is more or less authentic, becomes the target of threats and offences of the Enemy. The situation, even if it appears peaceful, is never a situation of neutrality. The demonic strategy is never short of tactics, and every method is good enough: cold war or warm war; open actions or camouflaged actions, from outside or from inside. We must, therefore, never let ourselves be distracted or rocked asleep; but we must always be on the watch-out, on the rampart, ready to act, in a state of attentive watch: "Watch... pray... watch... pray..." is the constant password of Jesus and of the apostles which we must practise.

In the New Testament a unique virtue named *hypomonè* appears which makes perfect faith, love, and hope.

Confronted by the threats and by the offences of the demonic strategy we must exercise *hypomonè*.

The Greek word is variously translated in our versions by endurance, patience, perseverance, etc.

Its etymology is enlightening: *Hypo* meaning "under" and the verb *menô* meaning "to hold". To exercise *hypomonè* is to "hold under", in other words to "support".

But what do we have to support? We must support at the same time the trials by which God wishes to try our faith in the way one tempers steel by fire, (1 Pet. 1 : 6) and the duration of time, necessary for the accomplishment of the divine mystery (1 Thess. 5 : 1 ff., 2 Thess. 2 : 1 ff.). As far as the trials are concerned *hypomonè* is essentially *endurance;* as far as the duration of time is concerned, the *hypomonè* is essentially *patience;* and, on the whole, endurance and patience constitute *perseverance.*

To "hold under", to "support", to exercise endurance, patience, perseverance, one must be *strong.* But now, as we have said, in ourselves we are weak. Therefore we cannot be strong if it is not by the power which is given to us and renewed from Above (Deut. 8 : 18, Isaiah 14 : 29—31); if it is not by the power which comes from the Holy Spirit and which unites us with Jesus Christ, in Jesus Christ (Eph. 3 : 16—20). This power is given and renewed for the faithful who ask for it, who implore about it (Math. 7 : 7—11); it is the only way which makes it possible to endure the trial and its duration and to be victorious in the end (1 Cor. 10 : 13).

6. *The "hypomonè" must qualify and make perfect our faith*

A christian institution is, by vocation, confessing. Whether it has adopted an already existing ecclesiastical confession of faith, or whether it has established a particular declaration of faith according to its specific objectives, it shows and makes public in this way its basic principles in the conviction that these conform to the Word of God and are demanded by faithfulness to his Word. Being or becoming a responsible member of such an institution, is to accept *cordially and without any reservation in mind,* to respect and practise the basic principles confirmed in this way.

Surely, it is more difficult to respect and practise the principles than to enunciate them. But we must force ourselves to go on in this respect and with this practice, being managers of this institution. And we must give mutual help in doing so.

But history, even the most recent, shows that, alas, even in the christian institutions the most elementary loyalty is not in fashion or is no longer in fashion for many.

We have seen and we see people who do not cordially subscribe to the basic principles of a christian institution, demanding nevertheless to be part of this institution and who are willing to sign the promise of faithfulness to these principles when asked to do so.

We have seen and we see people who want to stay in a christian institution, sometimes people who have important posts, whilst they do not anymore consider some or other of its basic principles true.

Some seem hardly to realize the hypocrisy of such situations, whilst others willingly mask their own convictions and objectives. But whether it is to obtain or to maintain a place by different interests or whether it is for subversive purposes, we have seen and we see men who sink so low that they only subscribe superficially to the clear and well defined basic principles to which they are at best indifferent, or even worse, which they intend to combat or to reverse.

There are in all this, threatening realities for the christian character of the christian institution, whether it is for some a "force of inertia" (which does not mean neutrality) which is going to weigh down the institution or to paralyse it, or whether it is, for others, a real "fifth column" operating in the institution to pervert it.

Faced by these hostile threats, which have become internal to the institution and therefore much more formidable, only *hypomonè,* perseverance and faith can be victorious by practising on the one hand an ardent and continual return of the faithful to the teaching of Scriptures and to prayer, and on the other hand by the correct practice of discipline.

In fearless loyalty towards the basic principles of the institution, united to the Lord and Saviour Jesus Christ, the responsible, faithful members must ask to be sanctified by the *Word of God* which is the Truth (John 17 : 17); they must "continue grounded and settled in the faith" (Col. 1 : 23); they must "resist steadfast in the faith" (1 Pet. 5 : 9). They must "hold the beginning of confidence steadfast unto the end" (Hebr. 3 : 14) and at the same time, they must reject the teachings of the 'false teachers' (2 Pet. 2 : 1 ff), who "distort the meaning of the Scriptures" (2 Pet. 3 : 17), who are "with us without being of us" (1 John 2 : 19); who are "ungodly men turning the grace of our Lord into lasciviousness" (Jude 4).

But if the spiritual combat of *hypomonè*, of perseverance, of faith, with the weapons of the Word of God and prayer, aims to strengthen the faithful, it implores us to have the courage to practise discipline, so necessary in the heart of institutions like those for which we are responsible. Neither friendship, nor the consideration of certain qualifications and academic diplomas, nor, even more so (we will come back to it) questions of prestige or money, must prevent us from warning, for a first and second time, firstly man to man and then in council, and then to exclusion if there is no repentance and reparation, one who shows himself notoriously unfaithful to the basic principles of the institution of which we are the responsible managers. (Compare Math. 18 : 14—20).

The cowardice, the slackness of one group of people towards the practice of discipline is also culpable, if it is not more culpable, than the despising or the rejection of the principles by the others. The letters to the churches of Pergamon and Thyatira in Revelations (2 : 14—16; 20—22) show clearly that God asks us to repent of certain intolerable tolerances and not to let the field open to the seducers of the saints.

Let us be on our guard against false invocations of love, peace and liberty when we start talking of discipline.

I say 'false invocations of *love*' for it is neither loving God, nor loving one's brothers to give over by slackness a christian institution to subversive activities and to the power of the Enemy, to leave the christian institution to transform itself to its opposite. On the other hand, it is for the love of God and one's brothers that one must know how to practise fair discipline at the right time.

I say "false invocations of *peace*" because there can be no real peace where one yields to the Enemy by all sorts of compromises and concessions, where one lets the truth of the Scriptures be disputed and rejected, where a clearly stated divine proposition is given over to reduction or to negation in the name of conjectures of philosophy and the human sciences. It is exactly in order that the real peace, troubled for a time, can be re-established that one must exercise the indispensible discipline.

I say: "false invocation of *liberty*", because it is important to know on which side is legitimate liberty: on the side of those who disloyally despise the basic principles of the christian institution, of its faithful and living tradition, of the sacrifices made by its founders, friends and members, undermine or attack from within the specific confessed or declared faith of this institution, or on the side of those who respect the basic principles of the institution for which they are responsible, in faithfulness to its tradition and at the price of new sacrifices, only practise discipline to keep the institution in the direction traced out by its vocation?

7. The "hypomonè" must qualify and make perfect our love

In the centre of the Holy Scripture is the commandment concerning love. In the same way as we must persevere in enduring the trials and duration of time in faith, we must also persevere in love.

But if it is true that real faith has as a result that the beginning of real love of God and our neighbour, springs up and grows in us, it is also true on the other hand that threatening idols invite us continually to prefer them: the idols of Number, of Money, of Science, of Power, etc....

"Little children, beware of idols" exhorts and pleads St. John, at the end of his second letter which is specifically 'on love'.

"The world" (in the sense of St. John) loves Number, Money, Science, Power, rather than God. All these idols fascinate the world, seduce it and drag it along. St. John also writes: "Love not the world neither the things that are in the world. If any man love the world the love of the Father is not in him, for all that is in the world, the lust of the flesh, and the lust of the eyes, and the pride of life is not of the Father, but is of the world, and the world passes away and the lust thereof: but he that does the will of God abides for ever" (1 John, Chapter 2 : 15—17).

We can never say enough to what extent the christian character of christian institutions was damaged, corrupted and finally destroyed because the love of one or more idols (Number, Money, Science, Power, etc.) prevailed over the love of God.

Spiritual adultery starts from the moment that one looks at an idol to desire it; and "the light of the body is the eye!" (Math. 6 : 22).

Well, shall we say, must we therefore not wish for a christian institution to grow in numbers? Surely! But wait! We must know that with this wish the threats of the idol Number can define or manifest itself. It is a good thing to desire and to ask for the normal development of a christian institution and to rejoice when one sees it; but one very quickly runs the risk also of looking for increasing numbers only *for itself,* at the price of all sorts of concessions: in the domain of publicity, for example, which becomes untrue; or in the domain of the qualifications of the members of the institution, which, soon, are no longer examined closely enough.

The first growth that we must ask for and search for is the

growth "in grace and truth". It is a fact, and a sad one, that where the numerical growth of christian institutions was pushed, this growth was often accompanied by progressive reductions of the christian character; the reason being that the people there rejoiced more in numbers than in truth.

It is, moreover, to be anticipated that in an institution with too large numbers, social relations (for example in an establishment for education, between professors and student, between students and professors) will be dehumanised and therefore dechristianised, and the administrative system will have a weight which will become less and less supportable.

When an institution becomes too large it is certainly better to create a second parallel institution. The christian character of an institution, in fact, demands a fraternal communion of prayer, thought, and sharing of enterprise, to which numbers are inevitably a threat.

Well, it will also be said, must one not desire that the christian institution should have something of which to live? Doesn't the christian institution need buildings, libraries, money to pay its managers? Certainly! But one must also be on the watchout for the threats of the idol Money. We cannot love and serve, at the same time, God and Mammon (Luk. 16 : 13). It is not for nothing that the New Testament talks to us of "unjust" (Luk. 16 : 11) or "rotten" (James 5 : 2) riches and that Jesus curses those who find their *paraklesis,* their consolation, their assurance, in their riches (Luk. 6 : 24); instead of finding it in the paraklete: Jesus Christ; and in the other paraklete: the Holy Spirit (John 14 : 16).

Poverty is not something to be desired: we must have what is necessary. And God knows what we need. But the love for Money is always frightening: because of money christian institutions have lost their christian character because of compromises, because of the egoism and the envy which it had provoked.

Let us remember: it is in fear of being short of something that the people of Israel, in the desert, grumbled against God (Exod. 16 : 4, 19, 20; Numbers 11). Jesus ordered His people not to take thought for tomorrow (Math. 6 : 19—34), but to "seek first the Kingdom and the justice of God". It may happen in certain circumstances that God orders us to take precautions (Gen. 6 : 21; Gen. 41; Luk. 22 : 39), but our normal duty (which to our fallen nature is extraordinary) is, according to the title of a work by Isabelle Rivière, "the duty of want of foresight", because we are in Jesus Christ the adopted children of a Sovereign God, who in His wisdom, in His goodness, and in His allmightiness, knows, predestines and foresees what we need. Good "economy" is to use what God gives to His glory and according to His promises and His commandments, day after day, month after month, year after year; being rich sometimes, but without loving richness; being poor sometimes, but without recriminating nor envying; and always in the love of God and in works of grace.

Solomon already said: "He that trusts in his riches, shall fall" (Proverbs 11 : 28). But He who is "more than Solomon" said to His disciples: "my children, how hard is it for *them that trust in riches to enter into the Kingdom of God. It is easier for a camel to go through the eye of a needle than for a rich man to enter into the Kingdom of God!"* (Luk. 11 : 31; Mark. 10 : 24—25).

It is chiefly by the generosity, by the love for God of a whole reformed peasant people of the Netherlands, that Abraham Kuyper more than a century ago, got the necessary money for the foundation of the Free University of Amsterdam; and for the love of God, that the first professors of this institution were willing to receive smaller salaries than elsewhere (2 Cor. 9 : 7—13).

Well, it will also be said, is it not desirable for the christian institution to have competent people in its highest posts? In an establishment for christian education, for example, must the professors not also be as learned as possible? Certainly! But the threats of the idol Science must not take us unawares. God wants to be recognized as Lord and Saviour in every domain, also the domain of science. The love for Science which wrongly has been made absolute must not make us turn away from the love of God.

In fact, scientific fetishism, instead of increasing and improving our knowledge, as it pretends to do, reduces it and brings it down; even worse, it deforms and degrades it, and that all the more when it disposes of more and more efficient instruments and means. Also remarkable techniques in service (alas!) of the idol Science, instead of serving the living God, end up in an abominable depersonalisation of man created to "the image of God". Certain biological, psycho-analytical, political or hermeneutical "experiences" of today are precisely demonic experiences.

And, nevertheless, we see responsible members of christian institutions giving place to this degrading fetishism without even wanting to become conscious of it (whether it is in the wish for apologetics (bad apologetics!) or whether it is in the wish to see themselves admitted in the circle of the recognized learned); we see these people ready to recognize, in this or that scientific domain, dogmas which are taboo, contrary to Scriptural Revelation.

Well, it will finally be said, must one not wish a christian institution to have an impact, to gain in influence, on the church and the world? Certainly! But the threat of the idol Power comes up immediately.

We live in a time in which efficiency is preached everywhere. Under the pretext of being efficient, states and parties become more and more totalitarian. Handed over to propaganda and publicity of all kinds, everywhere pouring out their sounds and images, man allows himself more and more to be accommodated by them. Under the pretext of recycling, many are manipulated by techniques said to be "group" techniques; many are also enslaved by drugs (chemical or intellectual).

The *hypomonè*, the perseverance of love, must expel from a christian institution which is being threatened, all these abusive forms of power and every respect for them; and *that* in the name of the power of the Lord and for His honour; He who never treats human beings like puppets but who reigns sovereignly and mysteriously over them in the consideration of their responsibility as creatures created in His image, responsibilities which he had given them and which He maintains for them in His grace as in His judgement.

There are also proceedings, methods, ways of being and of doing, which christian institutions and their members must repudiate if they do not want to lose their christian character.

Witness? Yes. But only by moulding the spirits? No.

Education? Yes. But brainwashing? No.

Firmness? Yes. But shutting off? No.

It is in taking up the risk of responsibility, and therefore of liberty and of human dignity — in the faith in Him who reigns over every risk — that the christian institution avoids surrendering to the threat of the idol Power.

8. *The "hypomonè" must qualify and make perfect our hope*

There must be and there is, if it could be possible, even a closer relationship between *hypomonè* and hope than between *hypomonè* and faith, or between *hypomonè* and love; so close that *hypomonè* and hope end up by identifying one another. That is why several times in the New Testament the trilogy "faith, love, hope" is replaced by the trilogy "faith, love, *hypomonè*" (2 Thess. 1 : 3—4; 1 Tim. 6 : 1; 2 Tim. 3 : 10; Titus 2 : 2 and Rev. 2 : 19).

How could one endure without the *hope* of the certain victory of divine love over the enemy forces, a hope which gives and nourishes the real faith? (Hebr. 11 : 1).

The faithful keep on, endure, persevere, because they know that by grace, by faith, their hope shall not be deceived, that their patient expectation will sooner or later be fulfilled beyond all measure.

Faith, perseverance, hope. These form a whole for the faithful; thus they endure also the trial and its duration (2 Cor. 6 : 4—10).

The threats against the christian character of a christian institution can never make those responsible for this institution lose heart when they exercise, and hulp one another to exercise, the *hypomonè* of faith, love and of hope.

When these threats become only greater from the *outside,* they can in certain cases end up in the interdiction, the suppression of some or other christian institution. We have seen this in France after the revocation of the Edict of Nantes (1685). We have seen this and we can still see this in the 20th century in totalitarian countries. But the *exterior* threats could never efface the *christian character* of the christian institution.

The only real threats against the christian character of a christian institution are those which are born *inside,* those which are *interior,* those which involve the responsibility of the members themselves, of this institution.

While there is still time, that is to say whilst the institution has not yet arrived at the point where it rejects openly its basic principles, while it has not already lost the whole christian character, its *faithful members* must counter-attack, strengthening themselves on the rock of the Word of God, by prayer and by demanding that just discipline should be used against the unfaithful members.

And if, in some or other institution, it is the wicked, the apostate, which were to carry it away, the faithful members would owe it to God to leave, with grief, but without despair, knowing that the Lord, He who is always faithful to His redeeming alliance, would set up soon, elsewhere, a new institution to again take up the torch.

In every case the practice of *hypomonè* must be and shall be followed up: "Be of good courage and He shall strengthen your heart, all you that hope in the LORD" (Psalm 31 : 25).

The threats to the Christian character

of the Christian institution

Prof. Dr. J. H. Kromminga

Preface

It is of course an honour to be invited to present a paper for such a conference as this. It is furthermore a delight when the organizing committee assigns a definite topic and goes on to specify what the general outlines of the treatment might be. The writer has been asked to give attention to the main factors leading to the undermining of the Christian character, to the possible ways in which it may be purposefully undermined, and to the measures to be taken to ensure as far as possible the maintenance of the original character of the Christian institution.

With such a well-defined mandate it might be supposed that all one would have to do would be to fill in the blank spaces. But it has appeared preferable to take some liberties with the assigned subject, while attempting to remain true to its basic thrust. It will be in order to state in a few introductory paragraphs the nature of those modifications.

What follows will not be a global pulse-taking or temperature-reading. No attempt will be made to state what actions have been taken by a government in one country or an academic community in another to threaten the Christian character of the Christian institution. If this is what is desired, an hour's round-table discussion at such a conference as this would produce more data than a year's study by an isolated researcher. Perhaps such a discussion will take place at some time during this conference. If so, we would all benefit. But this paper will not attempt to supply such information.

From another point of view, this paper will range somewhat more widely than the precise field indicated in the title. It is difficult to make a hard and fast distinction between a "threat", narrowly defined, and such problems, crises, and difficulties as may be addressed by other speakers at the conference. There will probably be some overlapping, accordingly, between this paper and others to be presented. The focus, however, will remain on the threats, and perhaps the discussion can proceed accordingly.

The difficulty in isolating this subject from the others applies chiefly to the distinction between external threats and internal weaknesses. The dimensions of a threat which comes from without are determined largely by the internal weaknesses to which it appeals. These will be separated as far as possible in this paper, but both will have to be discussed.

Accordingly, and without further apology, we will describe not many threats, but basically only one; and will add to that the description of a difficulty, a weakness, and several dilemmas. While this may not seem to answer precisely to the assignment given, it does fit the nature of the problem as this writer sees it.

The perspective from which this paper is presented is largely that of the United States of America. The underlying assumption is that this perspective is not basically parochial, but worldwide. To the extent that the conditions described below vary from area to area, the discussion will have to serve for correction and a truly global perspective.

One final introductory comment: when one is asked to deal with threats to the Christian institution, the discussion must of necessity be somewhat negative. But it is not the writer's desire or intention to present a pessimistic recital of difficulties, permeated by an atmosphere of gloom and doom. The Christian educational enterprise is not destined for early collapse. But a realistic address to its task requires a clear recognition of the difficulties to be met and mastered.

1. *The basic threat: A shrinking God-concept*

Our concentration will be on a single massive threat which has many ramifications and comes in many guises. It is the shrinking concept of God and His relevance to the world, which is so prevalent in modern thinking. This, it is contended, is the one all-pervasive threat to the Christian character of the Christian educational enterprise.

This attitude, which is not so much argued as presupposed, poses a threat not to Christian instruction alone, but also to the vitality and very existence of the Christian religion itself. It threatens, in fact, not only the Christian religion, but any religion which purports to be a world and life view. This threat is really not new, but it has gained new prevalence, new acceptance, and new power in our day. The removal of God from a position of authority, of influence, of importance in learning has had a long history. Such secularism today sits confidently in the saddle. It pervades the thinking and actions of various parties which influence higher education. At worst, it invades the very citadel of Christian higher education and threatens a fatal weakness from within.

The massive presupposition of secularism is that God — whoever he may be, and if he exists at all — is irrelevant to the interests of mankind. For purposes of illustration we will look at the influence of this assumption for national interests, popular interests, and the interests of education. This presupposition may well lead to overt hostility to the Christian cause. But even if this is not the case, the threat is real and dangerous.

God and His revelation, it is assumed, are not relevant to governmental interests. Obedience to God is not necessary for the good government of the people. A national government making this common assumption may under certain circumstances actively seek to subvert the Christian character of Christian institutions. This has happened here and there in the past, and it is happening here and there today. Governments are by definition interested in national unity. Christian education may be opposed as introducing a divisive note into national unity. It may be opposed as being a waste of energy inasmuch as it is not directed to the recognized national interests. Particularly when it is most true to its calling it may be given the ultimatum to conform or be suppressed.

In many parts of the world, however, such open opposition has not yet made its appearance. But this does not mean that the threat is non-existent. The attitude of many governments is more characterized by the absence of the positive than by the presence of overtly negative positions. Christian institutions and their contribution to the national interest are damned with faint praise. The government expresses general appreciation and some measure of support for the "private" institutions, whatever their religious orientation, if any. But there is little or no conception of a positive evaluation of what is really the heart of a Christian educational enterprise. This is fundamentally unsatisfactory to the Christian institutions, which cannot be content with tolerations as manifestations of a healthy diversity or of free enterprise. Surrendering to such a relegation to a side-eddy is to be untrue to the Christian calling.

The situation is quite similar with respect to the populace in general. God and His revelation are not relevant to the popular interests. The citizenry of a nation are likely to approve of and support higher education if it is understood somehow to serve their interests. But what is really distinctive about a Christian institution is usually seen to be quite isolated from the interests of the people. Increasingly the needs of the people are seen to be needs involving social justice, economic advantage, or material betterment. Both the haves and the have-nots share this attitude; but the danger of hostility increases as the voice of the have-nots is more insistently heard.

Christian higher education is challenged to show that it is at least as relevant to the crying needs of the world as is secular education. Such demonstration is difficult at best because this is a game to be played on someone else's field and according to foreign rules. But to make matters worse, the Christian enterprise has not bent itself to this task as it should have done. In a hungry world, a world filled with injustice, this lack of ability or will to demonstrate relevance, threatens a growing likelihood of open hostility.

If the masses should rise, and revolution should come in any guise, the Christian institutions may either be abolished or so transformed as to lose their identity. The philosophical spearhead of such opposition is the Marxist theory; but this theory gains its greatest support where there is a Christian vacuum, a situation altogether too prevalent in the world today.

Educational leaders have their own version of this negative presupposition. God and His revelation are not relevant to the interests of education. Educational leaders and spokesmen who fancy themselves as the master-planners of national and international programs sometimes consider Christian institutions an intolerable obstacle to true progress. Thus far this mailed fist has usually been clothed in a velvet glove. But conditions need only ripen slightly before such opposition emerges openly, purporting to be the educated voice of the will of the people and the expert advice to the people's government. And, whether or not the opposition becomes overt, this pervasive assumption of the educational irrelevance of the Christian vision creates a most difficult climate for Christian institutions.

Open interference in Christian education, as suggested above, is a reality for some and only a vague threat for others. There is, however, a sense in which it is a real and present danger for all Christian higher education. This is due to the fact that there are weaknesses within the Christian educational enterprise making it vulnerable to this threat. We will not deal with this aspect of the problem at the moment, but will return to it below. For the moment we must give passing attention to a new difficulty which encumbers the Christian task.

2. *A growing difficulty: The problem of a unified worldview*

Attention must be given to one aspect of modern life which poses a vast new challenge to Christian education. Since the days of the early Christian apologists the distinctive effort of Christian learning has been to establish and maintain a comprehensive view of the world and history in the light of God's revelation. Since God is one, and since He is the sovereign creator, His dealings with mankind must have an inner unity and wholeness. Of Him, through Him, and unto Him are all things. Christian education accepts the challenge of recognizing this fact, tracing its outlines, and bringing it to organized expression.

In medieval times this task was relatively easy, although one should not denigrate the gigantic labours of medieval scholars or overlook the real differences which existed among them. With the coming of the modern period, the task became more difficult, not least of all because the driving will to do this has weakened. But the proliferation of data available to scholarship has presented an unprecedented challenge to those, whether Christian or otherwise, who wish to understand truth as a unity.

There have been many attempts to cope with this problem. Christian philosophy has worked at the task. Other scholars, not specifically Christian, have sought to revive medieval systems and apply them to modern times. Other efforts have been primarily economic, nationalistic, or otherwise in their orientation. All of these attempts resemble efforts to push back the tide. Even the most confident of the sciences find the onrush of statistics, discoveries, and theories threatening to engulf them. Today's frantic attempt to organize all of knowledge becomes obsolete tomorrow. In the absence of any comprehensive view which meets with general acceptance, even the continuing attempts to provide such a view are presented very tentatively. There is a growing tendency toward a sort of resigned materialism. This view wins the day more by default than by choice. It seems no longer possible to do more than live by the day, adjust endlessly to new situations, and see what tomorrow says about this open universe.

Without a clearcut understanding of the origin and destiny of mankind, various views find themselves competing on the basis of showing how they are useful to man here and now. For any attempt to impose wholeness on a mass of data this is difficult, if not unfair, competition. But for the Christian viewpoint it threatens to become a disaster. Other philosophies, however important they consider such unified understanding to be, may find it finally non-essential. But the Christian enterprise cannot consider this task non-essential. It is of its essence to interpret the world and history — not just side eddies and passing moments — in the light of God's revelation. For the Christian scholar, every discipline and every discovery within that discipline is part of a whole. While that whole need not at every moment have a proper niche for every one of its parts, the effort to make things fit must go on without end.

The question facing Christian scholarship is not whether this pursuit is valid. That is more a matter of faith; we know by faith that the unity exists. But finding it is infinitely more difficult than it used to be. No one has deliberately created this problem in an effort to unseat a Christian position. It is a challenge created by modern techniques; but it is a gigantic challenge which calls for intellectual capacities which are rare, if, indeed, they exist at all.

3. *Internal weaknesses*

The threats posed to Christian institutions would not be half so severe were it not for internal weaknesses which undermine resistance to them. These have been referred to from time to time; the time has now come to examine some of them. The subject of weaknesses probably does not fall properly within the purview of this paper, but its importance to this discussion is so great that some attention must be given to it here.

As we have noted one basic threat to the Christian character of the Christian institution, so it might be said that there is one basic weakness. The weakness consists in the fact that the assumption of Christian irrelevance tends to seep into the Christian camp itself. It is not impossible to detect an air of defeatism in the Christian scholarly world. This absorption of the assumption of irrelevance is a subtle influence, which is much more insidious, and therefore more dangerous, than a threat posed from without by some enemy or other. When students, parents, teachers, or administrators unconsciously resign themselves to the position that the Christian interpretation of reality is of less than paramount importance, the termites have made their way into the Christian structure.

There are many factors which contribute to this situation. They are of various sorts and of varying importance. The catalogue of contributing forces given below is not complete. It is a sampling, although hopefully a representative one, of factors which weaken Christian resistance to the threat which it faces.

3.1. Disunity and diversity in Christian higher education

To compete in today's scholarly world, the Christian scholar, like any other, must specialize. The more narrow his area of specialization, the more likely he is to produce some new insight, make some contribution to the sum of knowledge, establish a name for himself. The diversity of offerings demanded of Christian institutions by their constituencies (students and parents) contributes to that need for specialization.

But at the same time, this scholar-specialist must integrate his learning into the unified whole of knowledge. He need not necessarily do this alone; in fact, the presumption is that he does this in co-operation with other Christian scholars. But specialization makes this very difficult. It is not uncommon on a Christian campus to hear a scientist say, "Here are my data; I'll leave their harmonization with a Christian view to the theologians". Meanwhile, the theologian feels himself totally incapable of dealing with data which are quite outside his sphere of understanding. What is true within one faculty is even more true between two Christian campuses. When one considers the problem on an international basis it is even more hopeless.

This may be viewed as a problem of communication, and it is that in part. It is further complicated by human frailties when departments within one school or the faculties of two different schools are at odds with each other and argue with each other to gain advantage. But even when communication is open and rivalries subdued the problem remains. The sheer size of the task of bringing many refined specialties together is staggering. The temptation is always present to say, "Since I cannot fit my data into a comprehensive scheme, I will simply submit them to the public and leave them uninterpreted". "Since I feel ill at ease with my interpretation, I will find a narrower specialization and make that my contribution". But when one fails to make the extra effort to interpret one's findings, one has not only surrendered; one has joined the enemy.

3.2. Confessional inadequacies

Another item in the weakness of the Christian position is the inadequacy of its confessional base. Institutions of Christian higher education base their positions variously on the historic Christian confessions. This provides the framework in which Christian scholars do their work and Christian faculties maintain their unity, internally and with their supporting constituencies.

The historic confessions on which many schools base their work are three to four hundred years old. Sound though they are at the core, they do not address today's situation at many crucial points. They contain little recognition of the minority role of the Christian community in a secularized world. They are much more likely at any point to address differences in theological interpretation than to consider the responsibility of Christ's people to the world. The Christian scholar could look to them for much more support if they would indicate more clearly, for instance, how the Holy Spirit operates in the world at large or what kind of eschatological expectation the Christian ought to have.

Perhaps the confession called for should not be a new church confession, but some kind of creed for the academic community. Perhaps the production of agreed confessional answers to the burning questions of the day is an impossible task. But what a temptation it is to the Christian scholar to say, "These statements do not help me where I need help. Perhaps the Christian faith as confessed in the church *is* outmoded". But to say, or even think, such things is to go far toward accommodation to a modernity which confesses nothing because it has no faith to confess.

3.3. The hermeneutical problem

A third element in the internal weakness of the Christian position is provided by the problem of Scriptural interpretation. Mutually agreeing to reflect the teaching of the Bible, institutions differ among themselves and within their respective faculties as to the manner in which the Bible is to be interpreted. Not only the differences of some experts, but the uncertainties of the many who are not expert in this area hamper the vigorous effort to apply the Scriptures to the various disciplines. The problem is accentuated by the necessary willingness of Christian scholars to take seriously the new findings of science which call into question long-held assumptions. Christian teachers acting in good conscience make adjustments to changes when the changes cannot be denied. But they lack a firm base on which to apply the witness of the Scriptures to these developments.

Without doubt some of the developments with respect to Biblical hermeneutics are well-based and sound. But a host of problems arises. Not all of the hermeneutical theories are consistent with the Christian faith; what is the criterion of judgment? An older, less sophisticated hermeneutic provided simpler answers to what were probably at the same time simpler questions. Difficulties multiply when at one and the same time the questions become more profuse, while the techniques for handling them become more and more the property of a narrow coterie of experts.

The temptation, once again, is toward resignation and surrender. If there is no hermeneutical standard which is at once clearly recognized, commonly accepted, and applicable by a wide variety of scholars, the response may be either of two possibilities. The scholar may abandon the task of interpretation and harmonization entirely — in effect making his speciality his Bible. Or, seeking to be faithful to the task of harmonizing his findings with the Bible, he may opt among the various theories for one which conflicts least with what his specialized research brings forth. The effect in either case is to lose the vital contact between written revelation and research. Such a hermeneutic is in effect no hermeneutic at all. The Christian character of Christian scholarship is lost. Biblical irrelevance has ceased to be a threat from the outside, and has become a fatal weakness within the body.

3.4. Financial pressures

For the final illustration of weakness from within over against the threat of secularism, we turn in a very different direction. An ivory tower theoretician might sneer at the mention of financial pressures in this connection, but those engaged in the practical work of Christian education will hardly find it necessary to do so. Unacademic and mundane as this consideration is, it remains one of the elements which make Christian higher education susceptible to threats from without.

To carry on a distinctive Christian witness to the various aspects of higher education is a costly task. The Christian college is threatened by declining enrolments as students and parents find education much cheaper in secular institutions. The Christian seminary is caught in the price spiral, and many smaller schools cannot meet the demands of efficiency.

Complicating this problem are the trends toward specialization among students and professors and the diversification of programs. Christian liberal arts education is under pressure to add constantly greater vocational dimensions to its offerings. Otherwise the competition for students becomes even more hopeless. But this in turn adds a potentially limitless list of courses and programs which strain budgets to the breaking point. Theological schools also find it necessary to proliferate programs and to tailor their offerings to individual and small-group needs. Schools of small size find the competition ruinous. In the American theological arena "clustering" has been proposed as a solution. This means the pooling of faculties from schools of various kinds, with only a narrow range of subjects taught under direct denominational supervision. This presents difficulties for those who wish to maintain a pervasively consistent interpretation.

Relief from the financial squeeze is not easy to find. Assistance from government funds may be out of the question in some countries. Even where it is available it raises the problem that "he who pays the piper calls the tune".

All of this may seem very remote from the philosophical threat to the Christian character of the Christian institution, but it is not. The problems of finance tempt the institution to compromise, to cut corners, to sell its soul for the wherewithal to exist. Together with the other difficulties which have been mentioned — and others could be added — this contributes to the internal weakness which makes Christian higher education vulnerable to pressures and temptations from without.

4. *Dilemmas facing Christian higher education*

Having fundamentally covered the subject in the pages above, we propose briefly to traverse the same territory once again by way of listing certain dilemmas which confront Christian higher education. The listing, once again, is partial. No claims are made for its completeness. It will be satisfactory if some of the central concerns are treated. The four dilemmas described below do not present new issues. The presentation meets its purpose if it provides an alternative way of seizing upon the issues already dealt with.

4.1. The dilemma of isolation versus absorption

Involved in this dilemma is the question as to what "Christian" means when we speak of a Christian educational institution. In minimal terms, the appellation "Christian" cannot apply if the institution is indistinguishable from any other institution of higher education. But the point which raises the dilemma is that an institution completely isolated from other institutions and their concerns is not fully Christian either.

Christian educational institutions are part of a Christian community, to which they owe responsibility. But they are also part of an educational community, and to it also they bear a responsibility. The education offered in a truly Christian institution must take into account a wide variety of viewpoints, including those indifferent to and those hostile to the Christian approach. The contact with divergent views may be in some sort of an adversary relationship; it may not be friendly at all under some circumstances. But it must be a vital contact. Some might think that this is a threat rather to the educational than to the Christian character of the institution. But this is a false antithesis. The Christian must be concerned with

66

the truth as it is reflected in God's world.

Perhaps this is more accurately described as a balancing act than as a dilemma. How does one gain a hearing in the academic community? How does one establish one's authenticity as a scholar? How is meaningful conversation to be established when even techniques are governed by presuppositions alien to the Christian mind? There are many ways of approaching this problem, all of them fraught with difficulties and even dangers to Christian integrity. But the responsibility remains.

4.2. The dilemma of fundamentalism versus liberalism

This dilemma is perhaps experienced most acutely in the North American scene, where fundamentalism and liberalism have often been seen as the sole alternatives for Christian education. The problem, however, undoubtedly exists in some form or other elsewhere in the world. In an oversimplified, but widely held categorization, fundamentalism has presented itself as the champion of Christian faithfulness and purity, while liberalism has claimed to stand for educational integrity. This tension can frequently be observed within a single Christian faculty. It is not hard to find in the relationship of one Christian college with another, or for that matter in the relationships of two theological seminaries.

The premise on which Christian higher education is built is that it is possible and necessary to bridge this gap. The dilemma, in theory, is false. But the fact remains that the tension exists. That it exists so plainly and can be found so readily is a sign that there is work still to be done on developing the answer of Christian education to its challenge. Perhaps that task is even further from a satisfactory solution today than it was in an age now past. The most painful manifestation of this difficulty arises when individuals or schools united in one basic task see themselves as divided because of real or suspected defections toward one side or the other. Here improved communication and developing trust are clearly called for. The task is too great to allow for the luxury of petty animosities and unjustified suspicions.

4.3. The dilemma of academic freedom versus confessional fidelity

What is at stake here is not so much the final outcome of the educational effort as what goes on during the process. The agreed confessional positions represent the mind and heart of the Christian community, and the Christian scholar must be true to that community. But he may, and often does, have a conception of the true interests of the community which differs from the uncritical assumptions made by the community at large. He needs the freedom — not easily obtained — to hypothesize, experiment, engage in trial and error, not for the sake of breaking down, but for the sake of building up the total understanding of truth. He needs the right to be wrong on occasion, so that the right may emerge in the end. But he needs also the grace to admit when he has been wrong, so that the gift of trust given him by his supporting community may not be abused and, in the end, forfeited.

This suggests what might be isolated as a separate dilemma, that between traditionalism and innovation. Several considerations sharpen this dilemma. The prevalent fear induced by the shaking of foundations makes the Christian community apprehensive and defensive. At the same time, the very challenge of modern unbelief makes the developmental task more important, while financial considerations make a unified, confident effort more necessary.

4.4. The dilemma of Christian versus secular graduate education

One more aspect of the Christian scholar's relationship with the wider academic community concerns his graduate training. Is it possible, is it necessary, and is it wise to have Christian scholars trained entirely in Christian graduate schools? On the one hand, if he is given his final training, if his skills are honed and tuned, in a secular institution, will his work at its most crucial point be Christian? And on the other hand, if he has no such contact, will his work speak to a world which he does not know?

With respect to these and other difficulties confronting the Christian scholar, it is of first importance to develop contact between Christians involved in higher education. Efforts of various sorts have been made in this direction. The present conference is a major effort to promote such contact. The threats, difficulties, weaknesses, and dilemmas noted above will not be banished with a mere wave of the hand. Nor will we soon be rid of them with the best unified effort we are able to put forth. But the best progress is sometimes made in small steps. The further development of a community of Christian scholars, with frequent meetings, definite programs, mutual support, and a responsible journal would certainly assist Christian higher education in moving forward on a broad front.

The idea of Christian scholarship

Outline and notes for an exploratory discussion*

Prof. Dr. Hendrik Hart

PART I: GENERAL COMMENTS

0. *Terms*

0.1. Idea

The word "idea" in the title of this paper can best be interpreted to refer to the attempted formulation (via theoretical reflection) of the intuitively known meaning of a norm which is to give positive guidance (led by the Christian faith) to the shaping of an academic enterprise in the contemporary situation. The idea, therefore, functions as a conditional hypothesis (not a hypothetical condition), meaning that *if* it has true meaning, it *should* lead to certain consequential responses; or, *if* we are to have Christian scholarship, the actual shape of it *should* be characterized by that idea. As idea, it is an open-ended response to and a dynamic departure from a fixed point of orientation. The idea of Christian scholarship is known and becomes known only as the meaning of the norm is unfolded in our continued response to its calling. Distinct knowledge of the norm's particular identity is known only intuitively and sure knowledge of its guidance is known only confessionally. Within the limits of this intuitive certainty the idea is to show us the path along which we are to proceed in the fulfilling of our task in truth.

0.2. Christian

The word "Christian" as it qualifies the word scholarship is not to be taken as an adjectival accident, as a gratuitous addition to

---

* NB 1: This paper is a revised and greatly expanded version of an address presented to a Christian Reformed Ministers' Conference in Grand Rapids, Michigan, U.S.A., in 1968, subsequently published in a slightly revised edition in the U.S. and South Africa in 1972. The original title was: *The Idea of a Christian University.*

NB 2: The address at the Potchefstroom conference was taken largely from Part II of this text, which is new almost in its entirety.

an otherwise unrelated entity. It neither signifies one qualifier among many others, nor does it stand for the most important qualification. The two words point to a relationship that cannot be conceived either in terms of being kept separate or of being added. "Christian scholarship" is intended to be understood as we understand expressions like visible sign, legible script, straight ruler, just law, white snow, funny joke. The adjective expresses what the totality of meaning involved in the noun is meant to be. For that reason, "Christian" can never derive its true meaning from the observed behaviour of Christians, but must rather be discovered from our being oriented to the directives of the Word of Truth, our being driven by the Spirit of Truth and therefore from our truly developing the character of the task at hand. For that reason also, the word "scholarship" must in principle mean just what it is meant to be, neither more (e.g. "source of truth") nor less (e.g. theological analysis).

0.3. Biblical foundations

The idea of Christian scholarship is an idea of scholarship that is in and of Christ, that signifies a new creature, a new creation; scholarship that is an incarnate symbol of redemption and reconciliation, a visible enterprise in the redemptive service of the Gospel of God's Kingdom (Cf. Eph. 4 : 24, Col. 1 : 20). Many scholars, even some Christians, object to the idea of Christian learning. Their antagonism is based, I believe, on other ideas such as the objectivity or neutrality of science, the autonomy of the university, the freedom of the academy, the a-religious character of theoretical methods, the secular nature of science, the ecclesiastical nature of religion, etc. Since this paper is addressed primarily to Christians, I would suggest to those who have objections to the idea of Christian scholarship that, at this introductory stage of the paper, the idea as proposed so far may be worth entertaining on the basis of Romans 8 (esp. 19—22), Ephesians 1 : 9, 10 or Colossians 1 : 15—20, where the Scriptures indicate that no creature, nor any part, piece, dimension, aspect, process, act, event, thing or relation in creaturely existence falls outside the scope of redemption in Christ. This does not, of course, in and by itself constitute a full and final answer to all objections. But the Biblical witness to the idea that such obviously creaturely phenomena as operational methods or scientific theories do not lie beyond the pale of salvation should at least make the idea of a radically Christian engagement in academic matters a worthwhile idea for Christians.

1. *The idea of a free university*

In the context of the contemporary upheaval in university circles around the globe, it strikes me as particularly meaningful to investigate the idea of Christian scholarship in the context of a free university.[1] The perspective for this investigation is Galatians 5 : 1, the command to stand firm in the freedom of Christ and not to submit again to a yoke of slavery. Any standpoint will be a yoke if it does not accept the standpoint of Christ in full submission to the will of our Father. The slavery meant by Paul is the pagan life as well as the tying down of God's Word by his own people to whatever they obediently understood of it within a particular historic setting: not only the heathen are slaves, but also the Jews who fossilated the Spirit of the Word in the Letter of the Law. From that the new creature is set free in Christ and he is commanded to stand fast in that freedom, i.e. from now on only to submit in obedience to the Word in the Spirit, according to the Scriptures.

1.0. Meaning of Freedom

This freedom has, I believe, at least two basic features related to our present concern. One is that, in Christ, man is slave to no creature, but lordly servant of all creation. This is the fulfilment of Psalm 8 of which Hebrews 2 tells us. The other is that man's deliverance in Christ enables him to live again in obedience to the law which our Redeemer fulfilled and in subjection to which creation truly unfolds itself. These are, of course, two sides of the same coin. Man freely occupies his lordly position in the creation only in subjection to the Creator's will. The beginning of the Sermon on the Mount as well as the end (cf. Matth. 5 : 17—20, 7 : 21—27; also 22 : 34—40 and Jn. 2 : 7) testifies to our calling to a new obedience. Freedom in Christ means to be an obedient servant, rather than a disobedient slave; in the sense that obedience means service, disobedience means slavery; in the sense that freedom means fruits of obedience to God's Word, his Law. Christ frees man from the curse of the law, in order that the law may bring life again. (Cf. Ps. 19 : 7—19, 119, Eccl. 12 : 13.)

1.1. Two Tasks

A Christian academic community standing firm in this freedom has two basic tasks. The first[2] is that of being a faithful servant of Christ in casting out the demons of the academy in his name. (Cf. Matth. 10; Mk. 6 : 7—13; Lk. 9 : 1—6; 10 : 1—37.) This is the task of liberating the university from the spells and charms that enslave the academic world. To serve the Lord in this field is the specific task of those members of the body of Christ who are engaged in the world of scholarship. The evils which they will meet in the academic world are many. There are, of course, the external powers that are being exposed today as dominant controls foreign to the true character of the academy. All over the world the usurpation and exploitation of the university by combined interests of capital and politics have been called into question.[3] The expulsion of internal evils is, however, becoming our concern as well. There has been a beginning of the challenge of the myths of objectivity and neutrality by the Marxists.

Many of the destructive powers, however, still occupy our lecture halls. They present themselves in the claim that theory is the perfection of knowledge, that physico-mathematical methods are models for all other sciences, that science is autonomous or that truth is an operational plurality of approaches. They also surface in the various kinds of isms, such as evolutionism, behaviourism, historicism, sociologism, specialism, scientism and many others. In these positions, as human convictions attach themselves to them in faith, lies the origin of motives that provide the spiritual direction for communities of scientists. The greater the conviction and the more its origin and function are hidden, the greater the power of its influence. It is the evil consequences of these convictions that caused much of the unrest in the university around the beginning of our decade. But the tragedy is that the generation of students and young scholars who denounced the evils is often motivated by the same ultimate conviction that is at the very root of these evils. Idolatrous notions of freedom, autonomy and individuality have driven the university into its present disarray, but lack of a radically critical self-analysis has hidden these false principles from detection. Thus they continue to motivate the new generation in its struggle to overcome the destructive consequences of faithful adherence to these very principles. Love and redemptive concern compel the Christian scholar to contend with these powers in the name of Christ.[4]

Such love and concern imply a second task. True liberation can only be achieved when it is understood that displacement of destructive powers is at best preparatory for unleashing the powers of redemption and reconciliation. The former is necessary to provide room for the latter. But it is precisely in this area that all the problems come to the surface. Not only will there be strong resistance on the scientific scene itself to the exposure of its idols, but the idolatrous position of science in our civilization at large will tend to enlist all who have faith in theory to come to its defence, driven by the fear that its erosion will undermine our very existence. Consequently, attempts at demonstrating the redemptive power of Word and Spirit will be experienced as suicidal attacks on the most cherished foundations of our culture. And besides that, the Christian knows that whatever signs of shalom he is given to erect will always be earthen vessels, destined not to last and pointing only to something that is to come and that is not of this present earth. Thus, the Christian's task is complicated by the fact that in his redemptive service he exhibits features that are themselves unredeemed.

1.2. Provisional Conclusion

Although not much has emerged from our discussion so far by way of a well defined and substantially detailed outline, I believe that a more or less tangible perspective is showing itself, which allows us to conclude provisionally that the idea of Christian scholarship in the context of a free university is closely related to the ideas of freeing and rebuilding, of liberation and reformation. Abraham Kuyper called "his" academy in Amsterdam a free reformed university *(universitas libera reformata)* and I believe that we could do worse than stick to that characterization, so long as we understand "free and reformed" to refer to a norm for our call to service and not to an accomplished *status quo.*[5]

But indeed, the idea is yet too vague. Many difficult problems are still to be encountered. What makes Christian learning Christian in terms of a noticeable difference? Is there a real difference? Does it make sense to speak of a Christian approach to physics? If the eye does not perceive a difference, is there none?[6] With respect to the problematics of these questions it is interesting to notice that the mighty works that Moses and Aaron performed before Pharaoh as men of God could apparently be duplicated, at least some of them, by the unbelieving magicians. (Cf. Ex. 7 and 8.) On the other hand, we have an account in the same book of the Bible about the work of Bezalel and Oholiab and we are told that their technical craft was impossible except the Spirit of God inspire them. (Cf. Ex. 35 : 31). And yet another question is: supposing that the above problems could be solved and we knew what Christian scholarship was all about, would we also need to actually have a Christian university? Some of these problems, and others, need to be discussed now, in order to work out our idea of Christian learning somewhat more. This requires that we deal with the structure and direction of the academic enterprise within our present historical context. What is an academy? What is academic freedom? What is academic responsibility? What is the scholar's right and what is his duty? Within the context of these issues the idea of a Christian university as a liberating and reforming institution in the academic world can take on more concrete shape.

2. *Is there a difference?*

Let us begin our approach to these problems by asking what an academic enterprise is. We should look for an answer that is not merely descriptive in the sense that the picture is recognizable, but also prescriptive in the sense that a norm is indicated which points to minimal conditions of anything that is to be an academy. In other words, the answer is to be found in a process of inquiry which is more properly called discovery than invention, whereas the search for a contemporary shape of the university would be more inventive. Now, if we look for a characterization of the scholarly community in terms of its task, in terms of a normed function, I would think that a university embraces a community of scholars whose pursuit is to gain scientific insight into reality and to make their theoretic finds serviceable to society. To that end it engages in research, educates researchers and educates those who will translate the insights of the academy in terms of social functions for leaders in our culture. The accent in this characterization lies on theory, scholarship.[7]

2.0. Theory

At this stage it is helpful for just a moment to sketch in a few words the meaning of the theoretical nature of this task.

Theory can be identified as the abstract and systematic structure-analysis of functional fields or of functional wholes in their functional interrelationships, with a view to discovering the conditional framework which constantly underlies the experienced patterns of regularity and of general trends in reality. This has two important implications. One is that theory thus brings the scholar into contact with the universally valid constitution of experience and that therefore no man can escape that conditional expanse of real patterns holding for all men, even when he does not always recognize or acknowledge it. Secondly, one does not get at these constant conditions unless one deliberately breaks up one's experience and pulls parts of it out of context.[8] For that reason theory is always a broken and distant kind of knowledge. It deals with "bits" of reality that do not exist in that way and are not normally experienced in the way that theory deals with them. Its facts are such "bits" of information. The chemical formula H_2O refers to water and symbolizes a valid physical approach to a dimension of what we know as water. Water is, as a matter of fact, H_2O, i.e. chemically speaking. But what men know to be water is never exhausted in the fact. However, knowledge of necessity always tends in the direction of fulness, wholeness, contextuality and integrality.[9] In order to really "know" what goes on in the theoretic context, therefore, its findings must be experienced in a fulness of reality which can, for the theoretician, only be found if his endeavour finds its place in the full context of the communal affairs of man. Further, the affairs of man cannot be truly called communal unless they arise from a common commitment which moulds them into a spiritually integrated body and in terms of which they understand the radical unity of all of reality.

2.1. A Difference?

Against the background just presented it may be possible to put the problem of the distinctive character of Christian theorizing in a meaningful way. To introduce the problem let us face it in the form of the retort so often put forth by sceptics confronted by the idea of Biblically oriented scholarship: "Is there a Christian way of adding two and two?" In earlier days of reflection about this problem, this simplistic rhetorical device of the sceptic tended to produce an (equally simplistic) answer in faith: "Yes!" However, a barrier was hidden in the question, which allowed hard work at answering it, in a more concretely worked out demonstration, only within its own limits, Consequently, much frustration was encountered. People hung on in faithfulness to the idea, but beyond *a priori* arguments nothing convincing was produced to demonstrate the truth of the simple answer. Finally it seemed that the question had driven the faithful into the arms of the sceptics, had driven those who sought to answer it to a fitting response: "No, there is no different way of adding numbers!" Therefore, the idea of Christian learning in terms of distinctly different scholarship has steadily lost ground: adding numbers is adding numbers. But is it?

2.1.0. Logical reduction

In a sense, a logical sense, adding numbers is adding numbers. According to the simple rule known as the law of identity, adding numbers is, analytically speaking, adding numbers. Such a tautological statement is indeed known as an analytic judgment: $A = A$. But is any A what it is analytically? Or, if it is recognized that there may be "more to it" than that, is any A "essentially" what it is analytically? Let us see. As an example we will take an uninformed visitor to a camp where the cook customarily calls the people to dinner by blowing a trumpet. Question from the visitor: "What's the man who is blowing the trumpet doing?" Answer in the style of our previous paragraphs: "He's blowing the trumpet". But our visitor is not all that uninformed. He knew that and yet now he still does not know a thing. The answer should have been: "That is the way he calls people to dinner". To say in *this* case "he is blowing the trumpet" is only correct as an abstraction. And in the way of abstraction a great many more answers could have been given, like "He is forcing air through a delicately formed copper tube for producing sounds". Such abstract answers are reductionistic. In the same way to speak about mathematics in terms of "adding numbers" is reductionistic. *Is* "adding numbers" anything? Is it anything concretely speaking? Can it be observed? As such? Just "adding numbers"? Is it anything that goes on? Something that people do? Suppose the latter, is it conceivable apart from people?

When we get ourselves to think about these questions, it will soon become apparent that what we call "adding numbers" is a verbally concretized abstraction, which in fact can only be encountered as a phase or an aspect of a very complex process in which humans engage. We can abstract that aspect and give it a substantivizing, noun-like name, capturing it in a thing-like sounding word. But that does not make the process any more independent or substantial. In short, persons wanting to see the "difference" demonstrated in terms of "ways of adding two and two" are presupposing the correctness of their reduction of the whole complex thing called "science" to this kind of simplistic abstraction. Indeed, the "difference" in this case should begin right then and there, when the question is put. A helpful response could come in the way of questions that seek to extract from the questioner what he *means!*

2.1.1. Abstraction and meaning

With the question of meaning, the problem of "a difference" acquires another setting altogether. For if anything *is* what it *means,* if it is experienced, understood, known to be what it means, then both a person asking a question and a person answering that question understand what they are talking about within a meaning context. Thus, before entertaining the question whether or not the *position* of the Christian is to make a difference with respect to any X, the prior question of what is *meant* by X should be considered first. Consideration of this prior question, however, carries with it a peculiar difficulty in the case of theory. For the latter is concerned with conditional contexts of a universal character, properly investigated in a context of abstraction and reduction. This could suggest that perhaps the problem of a different position, since it depends on context for a solution, cannot be solved and is a pseudo-problem in the case of theory. The suggestion does not hold up, however, for at least two reasons. One is that abstraction and reduction are complicated processes, which are determinative for the results obtained by them. They are, so to speak, not themselves abstractions. The other is that the validity of the result is also determined by the original context within which the theoretic process began. Insofar as both the history of theoretic endeavour and the totality of the experienced world (neither of which are abstractions) are involved in the theoretic endeavour, we could say that theoretic abstraction and reduction are not to be understood as abstraction and reduction *from* meaning, but *of* meaning.

3. *Freedom and responsibility*[10]

We can probably enter into the problem just a little more deeply if we consider for a moment the questions of academic responsibility and academic freedom.

3.0. Responsibility

Very specifically linked up with the responsibility of the scholar is his operational distance from the concrete situation. Since his responsibility is the obedient fulfilment of his task, the nature of theory directly characterizes his responsibility. The agricultural scholar is not normally concerned with any particular crop failures. His concern is to find out why under such and such conditions a failure of such and such a kind occurs in crops. And he is concerned why these conditions are there. His attention is directed to a regularity in occurring relationships of a structural, predictable and leading-to-control character. When he is finally done with his research, his theories and hypotheses no longer deal with *any one* situation in particular, precisely because they deal with *all possible* situations under certain conditions. Since he deals with structural relations in their constancy, his statements deal abidingly with all situations and as such his work is unlimited, in its appeal to a universal validity. But since he deals with no situation in particular and since his theories always only approach reality and are not to be identified with it, his work is also limited. Keeping these limitations in mind belongs to the very responsibility of the scholar. Responsible scholarship can only be preserved when it is consciously embedded in a fully contextual reality and with a view to having scholarly work take a place of service in that context. The truth of the scholar's work depends on its function in this context.

3.1. Freedom

This brings us to the correlative of academic responsibility, viz. academic freedom. The latter is essentially the scope one has in which to carry out one's task responsibly. And this implies in the case at hand to take distance and to be *in*different. However, the all-important question is: what is the proper distance and what the proper indifference; proper in the sense of belonging to specifically academic freedom and responsibility? And the answer has to be, at least in part, that theoreticians can never be indifferent to universally valid conditions, since it is those with which they must deal. Their freedom is conditional upon being bound to these structures. And these structures are by no means exclusively thought-structures or even logical structures. Organisms, e.g., do not behave logically but organically. Concepts relating to the organic world are, therefore, not just logical but biological concepts. It is theoretically unrealistic to consider as contingent in reality whatever is not logically necessary. Thus, a concept of biological necessity must deal with organic necessity. Academic freedom is not the licence to investigate whatever seems theoretically possible. The room one has in which to be a responsible scholar is not bound*less*. It has the same conditional framework which outlines those responsibilities. Theory is *free from* conditions and controls foreign to its proper character (such as state or corporate-industrial interference), just because it must be *free to* submit itself to those conditions that provide the framework for meaningful work.

3.2. Some bonds

Part of the universally valid expanse of conditional frameworks binding the scholar is his own humanity.[11] He can take distance from and be indifferent to his own personal likes and dislikes. But he cannot escape what is human. This includes the fact that one is fully bound by one's religious commitment. It is not so that one *should* bind oneself to it, but one *is* so bound. Failure to recognize this or attempts to mask it lead to destructive bondage. Any attempted escape from that bond will immediately result in unfreedom. Scholarship is always carried on fully within the framework of commitment, confession, world-and-life view, philosophy and special theory.

78

Science can in some instances help in bringing about some changes in these frameworks, but never can it change the fact of being so bound, nor can it rise beyond the level of theory to that of ultimate commitment.[12] It then ceases to be science.

Finally, the idea of Christian scholarship can never be entertained except in radical openness to the Word of God. This always involves a bond. God's Word and Spirit bind his people together into a body, a community. They are one. The openness of Christian scholarship is, therefore, related to a corporate responsibility. The freedom of that body should then also be exercised within a corporate framework.[13] This implies a common philosophic outlook. For philosophy is the academic tool meant to bring unity and coherence into the diversity of special scientific points of view. The desire to escape from this can in principle only yield a dictatorial unfreedom.

4. *The present situation*

Before we move on the second part of this paper, in which suggestions will be made concerning special problems requiring a specific contour for Christian scholarship in our age, this first part needs to touch on one more general issue, viz. do we always need specifically implemented and institutionalized forms of Christian scholarship? It seems to me that this is the case only when certain conditions prevail.

4.0. *One* is that the redemptive need of the situation must be obvious. In the situation in which the question of need arises, the historic power of sin must have taken on alarming proportions. An organized concentration by the Christian community must always have redemptive significance. And since our forces are both small and weak, they need to be concentrated on issues of priority. It is no accident that we have seen examples of this precisely in the fields of education, labour and politics; three key areas of modern culture and three areas also in which the power of idolatry had progressed far. According to this criterion we can safely say that there is definitely a need for Christian scholarship today.

4.1. A *second* criterion I would like to consider is that existing channels must make it practically inadvisable to work effectively within them. If the Christian community can have historically effective, redemptive influence through existing channels, because they provide sufficient elbow room, then it would seem to be unwise to establish a Christian university. In the light of this I would say that some institutionalized effort is in place in our world even though it need not take the form of a traditional university.

4.2. The *third* criterion which now suggests itself is that when the Christian community is forced by the above considerations to start thinking about Christian scholarship it must not begin till it knows what it ought to be doing. A Christian university, e.g., is not just any university with a no-smoking sign on its entrance hall. It is a university and not a moralistic hothouse; not for conservative morality and not for new-morality either. Thus, e.g., it is not a place for the humanization of man either, nor a seedbed for political revolutions.[14] And this means that it is no use beginning such an institution until one has at least the conviction that one has to be academically Biblical.

With these considerations in mind we can now take a brief look at the shape that might make Christian scholarship especially meaningful in our times. That shape, I believe, would be the shape of service.

PART II: SPECIAL CONSIDERATIONS: THE FORM OF A SERVANT

— A biblical key to our responsible presence in today's academic world

0. *Biblical introduction*

Why would one choose service as a theme that is peculiarly suited to characterize the norm for Christian academic endeavour today?[15] Are there not themes that can be Biblically anchored and that are at the same time more in keeping with acknowledged aims in the secular academic world? We could choose love, relevance, respect, the liberation of humanity and several others which, rightly so, stand in the centre of attention today. The reason for the choice of service is in my opinion a matter of perspective. The perspectival context within which the secular academic community views these important concerns of our world is largely one of rights, of individual autonomy. The Scriptures have a different emphasis. They often centralise many of today's legitimate concerns around the theme of service as the individual's place in a community of obedience.

0.1. Old and New Testament themes

Perhaps I will be allowed a few moments to present a Biblical basis for this opinion, before I go on to work out this theme for our present topic. Between chapters 42 and 53 in the book of Isaiah we find many of the concerns that occupy us today described as the very mission of Christ. He will bring justice, open blind eyes, bring out prisoners, deliver those in darkness and set his people free. But notice that the mission he is on is one of service and obedience. He comes to bring justice, suffering injustice. He gave life to all in the death of himself. And for that very reason he is glorified. Indeed, the four songs pointing to Christ on this mission (42 : 1—9, 49 : 1—6, 50 : 4—11, 52 : 13—53 : 12) are known as the *Songs of the Suffering Servant.* It is this very theme which Paul recommends to us when he encourages the Philippians to have the same outlook which Christ also had. (Phil. 2 : 5—13.) Paul says that Christ, who is God, took on the image of man: the reverse of the creation story. Then Paul says: that being the case, he did what is typical for man in God's world: he humbled himself and became obedient.[16] Being in the likeness of man, he became a servant even to the point that it brought him to his own death. And as was already said in Isaiah, this was the very reason why he became exalted above all. By becoming an obedient man he again became the image of God.[17] Against this background the themes that have received so much priority in our world can also become our themes. We, too, must serve the cause of liberation. Not only did Christ come to set us free, but he came to set us free for freedom. (Gal. 5 : 1.) So we are free and our freedom is to serve and our service is to liberate, to serve in the cause of the coming of full freedom in Christ. Our freedom is that through love we serve one another. (Gal. 5 : 13.)

0.2. The Free Servant of Liberation

All of this is made plain by Jesus himself, not in an involved doctrine, but in a simple exercise of hygiene and social courtesy. The point of the washing of the disciples' feet is not so much to show how much Jesus loved his followers.[18] Rather, it comes in a simple and dignified demonstration of the true nature of the Son of Man. There is only one Master, God. All of us are his servants. The disciples were still at the stage that they could experience their dignity only in terms of being served in such a menial task. We today are more at the stage that we think no one ought to have his dignity undermined by being made to serve others. But Christ is free to be Himself, the Son of Man, truly man. He calls no man his master. And he is ready to serve all men. The old spirit in our world, the one from which our world seeks liberation, is to seek one's exaltation in being served, in being master. That is a left-over of the desire to be as God. And it is right that we should seek to be liberated from that. Yet our world seeks that liberation in the wrong direction. It now wants to make masters of all men, that is how it wants to achieve the goal of having no man call another master. But Christ shows us that our true liberation is in our all becoming servants. And so he acts as a liberated person when he washes the feet of his disciples. He is free to do that, it does not offend his dignity, but accents it. The humility and obedience of the servant attitude is not punishment for man's sin, but the restoration of man to his glory.

1. *Clarification of the title*

1.0. Man as servant

Having thus indicated what I hope to be a Biblical ground for the choice of this theme, allow me also to make a few preliminary remarks about the intended meaning of the title and subtitle of this part. First of all about man in the form of a servant. Not all service in creation is human. There is Biblical evidence to warrant a characterization of all creatures as servants, as creatures who find their being in obeying God's Word. (Cf. e.g. Psalms 147 and 148.) If this is so then we must conclude that the peculiar service of man is that he represents God among the other creatures. His service is to bear God's image, to administer God's Will, to be a minister of the Word. In representing the Master, the servant who does this becomes a delegate of the author of creation and bears authority. This bearing of authority, this peculiarly human service, is to be exercised in complete obedience to the author. Thus man is the lordly servant of which Psalm 8 and Hebrews 2 speak. As all creatures are, so man too is a servant. But as the image of God-bearing creature he is a lordly servant, an authority-bearing creature. And for us this peculiar service must become concrete in terms of the academic context. The ministry of the Word to which the academic is called is one of scholarly service and thus of scholarly authority and we must try to explore the meaning of this from the perspective just indicated and with reference to our peculiar situation.[19]

1.1. Normativity of Scripture

Our responsible presence as academics in an academic world that is itself embedded not only in human society but in the entire creation, must be understood in the light of a Biblical norm. In our times it is not sufficient to appeal to traditions within historic Christianity, whether past or present. Our times are marked by a renewed openness toward the fallible nature of our traditions, so that not one of them has sufficient historic authority to survive an appeal without serious challenge. At the same time, we do not want to cut ourselves loose from tradition, nor do we want to stand outside of our own contexts in this world. We want to identify with our world without losing our identity in it. We do not want to regard any of our traditions, even the most hallowed, as having the eternal dependability of God's Word, lest we be tempted to think that the new earth is our culture or our tradition. But at the same time we want to remember that the coming of God's Kingdom has its implications for our very present cultural situation. We must receive our norms by letting the Spirit of the Word open the Scriptures and by letting them indicate to us the meaning of our situation.[20]

1.2. Contextual limits

Our situation itself, of course, also presents us with a norm. It is not normative, but it requires that we recognize it as the only context for our service. Today's academic world is the only field of service about which we in the context of this paper can meaningfully be concerned. Its needs must be met, its misery relieved, its talents explored, its tasks taken up. At the same time it indicates the limits of our service. Our task is not political, our calling as academicians is not to break down or to undergird political systems. Neither are we expected to preach sermons or to pastor. Changing or maintaining economic policy is not our calling. However, we are more than academicians as people and as people we have more callings, just as it is true that the world in which and to which we must minister expects us to serve it exactly in those areas in which we ourselves are not competent to serve. Our service is limited, though not isolated.[21]

2. *The academic servant in a service-conscious academy: forces of liberation*

In accordance with the perspectival sketch and the clarification of terms just presented we should be looking for the peculiar ways in which scholarly authority can serve the cause of liberation in our global twentieth century culture. Therefore, only those dimensions of the academic task will come to the surface that will allow us to get a close-up view of the particular theme under investigation. There will, of course, be related issues that will either be seen as out of focus or will not be in view at all. But if the emphatic view of some important details does not actually produce disturbing distortions, we can suffer the incompleteness for the sake of greater clarity.

2.0. The limits of possible freedom

One of the characteristic processes going on in the university is that of definition. The scholar centres his activity around the problems connected with defining what something is. The something that needs to be defined may be a thing, a relation, a function of something, an event of some kind, a kind, or whatever else. Just what defining is, is itself a matter of concern to some scholars. Some say a definition is descriptive, some say explanatory, and others claim that it is prescriptive. Again, people differ about what it is that defines a thing. Some believe that essences do, while others may feel more at home with behavings or operations. And there is no agreement either about the relation of the definition to what it defines. Some may say that it causes the thing. Others may be more convinced that it only states our agreement about the thing by convention. And yet others say that it indicates the true identity of what is defined.

My own provisional conclusion about the matter, which cannot now be analysed or defended, is as follows. Stating definitions is what defines scholarship. Something is defined when we can state the limits within which it maintains its continued identity during the time in which it essentially remains what it is. A definition is an essential identity statement. Defining is making statements about what delimits something, what determines it. The definition is not itself that which limits, nor is it the scholar who determined. Confessionally speaking, the limits of things are ordained by God (Psalms 147, 148), who sets the bounds of things. The limits discovered and stated by the scholar are in Scripture proclaimed to be God's ordinances; provided, of course, that the scholarship is carried on in truth. Thus true scholarship is disclosure of the limits of existence from a structural point of view. The definition as statement of limits describes the general structure of what things must be. The statement is descriptive of what itself is prescriptive. The structural limit does not cause anything to be, but determines what they must necessarily be. And what they must necessarily be is not all that they can be. All things are free to be what they want to be, within the limits that are the necessary conditions for what they must be.

Thus my conclusion is that essentially the scholar is the person whose task it is to disclose the general limits of possibility, within which all things are free to be themselves. Thus, if for some context an adequate definition of distance is stated to be a function of time and velocity, neither the time nor the velocity are thereby stated to be determined. They are left free to be any time and any speed. The definition simply states the limits of all possible distances in this context, not of any particular distance. It only indicates that any distance, if there is to be a case of distance in this context, is necessarily a function of time and velocity. Even where the distance is given, the time and the speed are still free to be any instance of many possible combinations. But all possible combinations are now determined to be of one kind necessarily, viz. such as will together yield the given distance. In short, the scholar helps us to discover what, in the case of any X, we must necessarily expect to be the case.

2.0.0. Limits of possibility give scope

One of the freedoms we gain from this service is that of scope, of broadness of vision. True scholarship helps us to get away from the possibly confining restrictions of the here and now. Prejudice and harmful side effects of otherwise beneficial relations can benefit from scholarship. Experience of some kind may have taught some people that poverty is caused by laziness and that wealth is to be defined as the blessed reward for hard work. A scholarly investigation of the relationship between these states and attitudes will come to the conclusion that, although these experiences may be justified and the conclusions valid, they are not justified and valid for all possible cases of poverty and wealth and that we cannot by way of a valid definition conclude that all the rich are necessarily blessed and all the poor necessarily lazy. The investigation may even come to the conclusion that in other cases the wealth was a curse and the laziness caused by poverty. And in that way the scholar structurally opens up ways of acting that otherwise would perhaps never have become known.

2.0.1. Liberation from conservatism

Scholarship that truly opens our horizons is, therefore, an important resource for the battle against conservatism in our world. Conservatism seen within our present context is the attitude which mistakenly identifies the status quo as the definition or prematurely concludes that the status quo is the best possible case of all possible cases. Conservatism is found wherever, e.g., a church claims that every deviation from its structure is a deviation from the definition of the church. It is also found wherever a church claims that it is the best of all possible churches, though not the only possible. Reformed ecclesiology is, by and large, conservative for these reasons. It can be served by the liberating forces of dedicated New

Testament scholarship. Another example would be the destructive conservatism which claims that science is the best possible kind of knowledge. It can be served by a patient investigation of the structures of research. In most cases the best method for preventing liberalism of all kinds is to attack the conservatism that usually causes it.

2.0.2. The freedom of foreseeing the possible

The disclosure of limits of possibility also helps us to predict what may happen or even what must happen or will definitely happen. A diabetic who is travelling in a car on a road which has a speed limit of 60 mph, who needs some food before the next hour is over and who is 80 miles away from the nearest place where food is found will almost certainly be in trouble if he does not know the necessary relations between distance, time and velocity. But if what scholars long ago disclosed about this is known to him, he is free to act before the trouble arrives. He can decide to transgress the speed limit, he can decide to risk being 20 minutes late, or he can stop and try to find edible plants that will help him. Prediction is possible only when structures of possibility have been disclosed.

2.0.3. The freedom of limits

When freedom has limits, when it is play room within certain limits and when definitions state what determines the room we do have, scholarship can also free us from both the fear of the boundless and the pride of the unlimited. Lack of limits or of knowledge of determining structures can make us very uncertain and even afraid. When will inflation stop? Does it have limits? Can they be discovered? Without scholarship these questions are almost beyond answer. But lack of awareness of limits can also foster pride. We can then act in our economic policy as though economic growth has no limits. Scholarship has not been free enough to warn us about those limits. If it had been, we could earlier have been delivered of our selfish yearning for possessions. As it is, the limits themselves are showing their teeth, without our really having insight into their structure.

2.0.4. Critical analysis

It is unfortunate that in our day not the church but Marxism gave the vital impetus to the exercise of the critical function of scholarship. Much Marxist scholarship has once again laid bare the distinction between the present situation and the expectations we are allowed to have on the basis of known structural configurations. This scholarship has confronted us once again with the fact that, e.g., the determining limits that allow us to define justice are not only to be identified with any particular instance of justice, but are also the basis for necessary criticism of many instances. Thus Marxism has demonstrated that even though every instance of X is necessarily some sort of X, it is not necessarily a good X or a good sample of X. And that in turn means that conservatist-empiricist approaches which define things by means of describing present samples of them, are not able to muster a critical definition. However, when the community of scholars is aware of its task, it will understand that part of its service is that of criticizing the present. Because of its disclosure of limits of necessity and possibility, the nature of scholarship is by definition critical. For that reason it is not only dangerous for the academy to be controlled by ecclesiastical, industrial or political powers, but it is even risky for the community of scholars not to be able to criticise these institutions or to be afraid of embarrassing them. Because the academy is then not in a position to serve society with liberating exposures of limit transgression or of poor concretization of structures.[22] The academy must remain free to warn society of disastrous consequences of certain courses of action, simply because the academy is in a position to foresee such consequences. A critical community of students and teachers which exercises its critical function responsibly is not a danger but a service to society.

2.1. The limits of academic service

Most of the service functions that I have mentioned so far have been known by scholars and have been exercised by them to a greater or lesser degree, in more or less awareness of the real nature of these functions. Sometimes vigorous exercise of them has been accompanied by lack of awareness of the proper limits of this task. However, if the liberating effect of scholarship is truly to be a service to mankind, it must be free to observe its own limits. This requires the insight that the power and the authority to define, the freedom and responsibility to disclose limits is itself limited to just those tasks that will result in providing society with an awareness of the limits it needs. And that means that defining the limits of all possible instances of X is a completely different task from that of deciding responsibly in a given situation how X is best given concrete shape within those limits. This implies that the scholar, in order to be of real service, should keep the following in mind when going about the particular kind of liberating task that is proper to the academy.

2.1.0. Advice, not decision

The scholar is competent to advise. He is, *qua* scholar,[23] quite incompetent to make decisions about the affairs in which he must advise. He has no experience in assessing the concrete factors that shape the concrete instance within the limits he has found. Furthermore, as a specialist he is likely to be aware only of the structural limits of a certain dimension of the matter at hand. Thus, governments that tend to listen too closely to economic theorists often wonder why these theorists cannot help them overcome certain bad results of a particular economic policy; especially if the ministry of economic affairs closely followed the suggestions of the economists. Both the governments and the economists forget, however, that governments, in distinction from economic theorists, do not abstractly deal with economic generalities. Rather, they deal with flesh and blood citizens whose economic decisions are affected by many more factors than those behaviours that can be measured in terms of economic models only.

2.1.1. The subjectivity of disclosure

In addition, the scholar cannot be too careful to remember that even though the limits and conditions he discloses are so-called objective states of affairs, his disclosure of them is itself a subjective process. And certainly in the case of the human sciences, the disclosure activity itself follows a kind of Heisenberg uncertainty relation, i.e. the disclosure affects the objectivity of the investigation.[24] The service of liberation provided by the scholar is therefore truly honest only when the relativity of the validity of his advice is clearly passed on to those who receive the advice.

2.1.2. Dangers of activism

Both the lack of practical experience and the lack of certainty in principle, which always accompany the discoveries of the scholar, should warn the theoretician, as theoretician, not to regard himself as an expert in the practice of the field which he has studied. If he sees that the practice he observes deviates from the model he has disclosed, he should remember that the model is not a model of the actual practice in a specific situation, but a structural and general representation of the conditions and limits, subject to which all possible practice of that kind must proceed. An actual, practical situation is never a mere copy of a theoretical model. In theory masses can be treated as moving along a path of motion without friction. But no actual mass behaves that way. Calculations based on such theories deal with abstracted dimensions and generalized behaviours, never with concrete situations. For physics that is not so hard to realize. But the same general truth holds for sociology and its present futuristic ambitions. If some sociologists would truly understand the nature of their insights they would be more careful in the service they render on behalf of planning departments of governments.

3. *In-house service a first requirement*

In connection with the observations just made it must be said that a problem which, though beginning to be recognized, does need much more attention, is that of the need for the scholar to gain a more scholarly appreciation for and insight into his own work. There is mounting evidence today that the service of liberation rendered by sincere scholars is rendered with closed eyes and tied hands. There is evidence that the scholarly community, which has been so convinced of its freedom, its impartiality, its objectivity and its unfettered service to mankind, is actually little aware of its own prejudices and is therefore servile to unknown forces. Science and scholarship have been so idolized and spoiled in Western cultures, that they have not been open enough to the dangers of an objectivism that did not acknowledge the environment, of an empiricism that did not criticise the *status quo* or of academic freedom bought for a price from government and industry. But the service of liberation rendered by the scholar is of value only in so far as he is free himself and aware of his service and its own limits and conditions. The following suggestions are meant to help us, as scholars, to be more aware of ourselves.

3.0. The science of scholarship

There is a long tradition in the history of Western thinking which occupies itself with thinking about thinking. But only in the last two decades or so has tradition been seriously, significantly and with increasing support fleshed out into a full fledged investigation of the actual procedures that are followed in scholarship. The science of research, the disciplined investigation of actual procedures of inquiry, the analysis of concrete scientific procedure is becoming an adult art today. The close study of scholarship will help to separate facts about the actualities of theorising from the fancies that have for so many centuries been held by theorists. Today the church can no longer function as the scapegoat for the scientist's guilt feelings about Galileo. The Christian scholar especially should earn his marks of distinction by being in the forefront of informing colleagues about the true structure of theoretic endeavours.[25]

3.1. The scholar's self-awareness

There exists the strange phenomenon in our academies that most scholars are trained only for half of their job. They are taught the ins and outs of the field of research they are going to be investigating. But they get little or no training in the procedures of analysis. Neither are most confronted with the structure and history of theorising. Against this background it is no wonder that many scientists fall easy prey to false dogmas about the nature of science and that many others are incapable of being critical scholars. They may be able to critique the goings on in the field they are investigating. But the procedures of investigation themselves, in their field, are not open to critical scrutiny for lack of training in the proper manner.

3.2. Fundamental issues

Neither do many scientists profess to be sufficiently aware of the presence of differences of opinion on foundational problems in the area of their interest. The nature of scholarly authority, the character of scientific certainty and truth, the ontic basis for definitions, the meaning of order, the origin of laws and generalisations and many other issues lie far outside the scope of the average practitioner of theoretic analysis.

3.3. Foreign influences

Even further away from the horizon of awareness of the average scientists is the question of influences that originate from beyond the borders of science itself. Questions of cultural inheritance, religious conviction and present priorities in our environment are normally thought to be irrelevant to theory and to have no appreciable influence on its procedures. But contemporary research is becoming aware of the fallacy of this assumption and the danger of this ignorance.

3.4. The return of coherence

A helpful way of insuring that as many problems as possible, from as many angles as practicable, begin to function in the actual practice of scholarship, is to proceed in a more interdisciplinary way. By that I do not mean that courses are provided at universities in interdisciplinary procedures. No special courses can take the place of what should be normal routine procedure. Already in grade and high schools we learn the lesson that learning is best promoted by doing and that because the universe does not proceed in sliced processes of forty minutes each our curricula are too artificial. But in the arena of scholarship and theory that lesson must yet be learned almost completely. I would propose that one of the Christian influences toward more meaningful service of the academic community could come from a renewed emphasis on the unity of experience, the unity of existence and the interrelatedness of every process ever encountered in reality to all the rest of what exists.[26]

4. *Related and relative as aspects of service*

Integrated scholarship in which the experience of coherence and unity is part and parcel of every day procedure will also have less problems with the humility that must accompany every form of service that is truly liberating. For it will not only experience that in isolation there is no truth but only the despotic claims of absolutisms, but also that its own service is meaningful only so long as it is placed alongside of and in the context of other contributions in the ever ongoing development of human history.

Aware as we should be that the Kingdom of God, which is here and has come, is also still coming, we must be aware as well that the service of Christian scholarship can be meaningful only if in self denying consciousness of the centrality of God's redemption in Jesus Christ we demonstrate our seriousness by acting as sign posts of the shalom of the new earth. The redemption of the scholar's task must become visible now; not because it is indispensible and not because this earth is our focal point either. Rather, it must be seen that nothing on this earth is beyond redemption; even though the fulness of renewal lies beyond the horizons of our present experience.[27]

Consequently, every stand we take should not merely verbally confess its own inadequacy, temporary nature and incompleteness; but should concretely demonstrate in its own procedures that the future is not here. At the same time, that should not prevent us from taking recognizable stands and from working them out so far as and in so far as we are able. But always flexible, showing that our subjective appreciation of the truth is not eternal. Always historically relevant and self-critical, knowing that true truth enters into and takes on historical form. Always trying to demonstrate our own unity in Christ without taking on the dreadful garb of uniformity.

A free community of Christian scholars would, in the interest of service, not do all the jobs done by a secular institution. It would concentrate on central problems in which the sin-corrupted nature of scholarship would cry loudest for redemption. And it would at the same time concentrate on problems that confront us more easily than others with the evidence of such corruption. Such problems lie in border areas between the sciences, between them and philosophy and between theory and every-day life. We must become free to pursue the problems that have intrigued the Christian scholar for many generations and for which practically no one has had real time and freedom to analyze them. Our work must be foundational, encyclopaedic work.[28]

It should be understood that such scholarship must have the courage to be a failure time and again. Christian scholars must not become nervous if after a few generations they have not found the answers they had once hoped to find. Perhaps all they will find after some generations is that the questions were wrong. But in Christ a Christian tradition is free from the curse of the law and in that freedom it can continue to seek to be obedient. We will simply have to be patient and to trust that it will take time to learn to be redemptive.

In no case should failure lead to abandonment of the idea. The idea of Christian scholarship can neither be verified nor falsified! It is literally the confession of a principle. The point of departure of such an endeavour is Col. 1 : 15—20. It is a point of departure to which we shall constantly have to return after having found out that we went in the wrong direction.

The central criterion is that of the coming of the Kingdom of God and of our having to be of service in it. This will almost certainly mean that many jobs will have to be left undone, that available resources should be exploited to their maximum and that none should be wasted. Much that is done on a secular campus cannot be done in a Christian context. Party because the resources are not available, partly because to do them at this critical time in history would be inopportune, and partly because the need for redemption is not — if it can be said this way — equally great all over.

5. *Conclusion*

The idea of Christian scholarship to me is filled with intrigue and challenge, with hardship and trouble, with joy and reward, with sin and misery, with salvation and redemption and above all with need. There are those who sneer at the idea and there are others who believe with perhaps some romantic nostalgia that the idea has had its time. Well, it is an idea with plenty of frustration attached to it and we should beware of standing above those who have succumbed to it. Maybe it should teach us that the suction of modern scholarship away from redemption is greater than we had thought it to be. In that case let us have the humility to see the need for implementing the idea of Christian scholarship.

John Dewey said of science: "It is the supreme means of the valid determination of all valuations in all aspects of human and social life". The Scriptures say: "See to it that no one makes a prey of you by philosophy and empty deceit, according to human tradition, according to the elemental spirits of the universe, and not according to Christ. For in him the whole fulness of deity dwells bodily, and you have come to fulness of life in him, who is the head of all rule and authority". The clash between these two statements is what is involved in the idea of Christian scholarship in the service of liberation.

PART III: SELECTED BIBLIOGRAPHY[29]

Apel, K. O.: *Analytic Philosophy of Language and the "Geisteswissenschaften"*. Dordrecht, Reidel, 1967.
Austin, J. L.: *Sense and Sensibilia*. Oxford, 1970.
Buytendijk, F. J. J.: *Prolegomena of an Anthropological Physiology*. Duquesne U.P., 1974.
Coulson, C. A.: *Science and Christian Belief*. Fontana Books, 1967.
Dewey, John: *Logic, the Theory of Inquiry*. New York, 1938.
Dooyeweerd, H.: *A New Critique of Theoretical Thought*. Philadelphia, 1953—1957, 4 vol.
Feguson, Thomas: "The Political Economy of Knowledge and the Changing Politics of Philosophy of Science". In: *Telos*, 1973, 124—137.
Habermas, J.: *Knowledge and Human Interest*. Boston, Beacon, 1970.
Hanson, N. R.: *Patterns of Discovery*. Cambridge, U.P., 1958.
Hart, H.: *The Challenge of our Age*, Ch. I—III, Toronto, Wedge, 1974.
Hempel, C.: *Aspects of Scientific Explanation and other Essays in the Philosophy of Science*. New York, Free Press, 1965.
Jeeves, Malcolm A.: *The Scientific Enterprise and Christian Faith*. IV Press, 1971.
Kalsbeek, L.: *Contours of a Christian Philosophy*. Toronto, Wedge, 1975.
Kerkut, G. A.: *Implications of Evolution*. Pergamon, 1960.
Köhler, W.: *Gestalt Psychology*. New York, Mentor Book, 1947.
Kolakowski, L.: *The Alienation of Reason*. New York, Doubleday, 1968.
Kuhn, T. S.: *The Structure of Scientific Revolutions*. Chicago, U.P., 1962.
Lakatos, I. and Musgrave, A. (eds.): *Criticism and the Growth of Knowledge*. Cambridge, U.P., 1970.
Laszlo, E.: *Introduction to Systems Philosophy*, New York, Gordon and Breach, 1971.
Lorenz, K. and Leyhausen, P.: *Motivation of Human and Animal Behavior*. New York, 1973.

MacKay, Donald M.: *The Clockwork Image,* IV Press, 1974.
Maslow, A. H.: *The Psychology of Science.* Chicago, Gateway, 1969.
Piaget, J.: *The Psychology of Intelligence.* Totowa, Littlefield, Adams & Co., 1973.
Polanyi, M.: *Personal Knowledge,* London, Routledge and Kegan, 1958.
Popper, K.: *The Logic of Scientific Discovery.* New York, Basic Books, 1959.
Popper, K.: *The Poverty of Historicism.* Boston, Beacon Press, 1957.
Popper, K.: *Conjectures and Refutations.* New York, Basic Books, 1963.
Radnitzky, Gerard: *Contemporary Schools of Metascience.* Chicago, Henry Regnery, 1973.
Runner, H. Evan: *The Relation of the Bible to Learning.* Toronto, Wedge, 1967.
Suppe, F.: *The Structure of Scientific Theories.* Chicago, U. Illinois, 1974.
Toulmin, S.: *The Uses of Argument.* Cambridge, 1974.
Wagner, F.: *Die Wissenschaft und die Gefährdete Welt.* München, Beck, 1969.

---

1 I have in mind here the Free University of Amsterdam, which was conceived to be *free from* the foreign controls of church and state and *free to* be religiously open to the Biblical faith. I also have in mind the contemporary free universities, viz. the groups clustering around an establishment university, conceived to be free from sterile objectivity and free to engage in relevant inquiry.

2 The order is not necessarily like this. What is mentioned first here may be accomplished by what is mentioned second. I am primarily concerned to bring out the two sides of the process.

3 No university is, of course, a-political; nor can any academy survive without money. In addition, there are the "internal" external dangers: administration and organization interfere with the academic process, simply because of the size of the institution, which demands an over grown machine, which must in turn protect itself from the university. Structures, rules and computers then kill spontaneous scientific creativity. Problems of *organization* can often (by definition) not be solved by more or better or different *organization.*

4 In some of the papers in this volume the contending is there, but the sympathetic tone of understanding too lacking.

5 Especially the two big and old establishments among us need to pay attention to this, viz. the V.U. (Free University) and P.U. (Potchefstroom). Both are around a century old and both have problems. The former, after the height of self confidence that marked the thirties, fell into an ideological vacuum which was (so it seems) recently filled by the left. It is consequently completely alienated from the latter, which is now in its period of over confidence and is consequently suffering from the over tight reigns of an established tradition.

6 The new literature on observation renders it questionable that observation is perspective-neutral.

7 Van Riessen stresses education more. I think he is wrong. His apparent differences with Bingle might not be so strong if agreement between them on this point were explored; especially the question of whether the university is in any sense (I think not) *in loco parentis.*

8 Wolterstorff misreads the nature of abstraction. Although it is true that abstraction requires focus, centred attention and selective concentration,

94

it is not true that wherever specificity of focus occurs, that there we also have abstraction. It is the deliberate rupture of natural context which makes an important difference here. Cf. his footnote no. 3.

9 Positivism has long prevented this insight from becoming common. Today it is breaking through. Cf. E. G. Polanyi, theological work on knowing (e.g. in Kittel's N.T. Dictionary), Maslow, Habermas, etc.

10 This section provides the link between and transition from PART I to PART II.

11 Scholarship is a *human* task, in spite of its abstraction from certain dimensions of humanity. If it does not want to run the risk of becoming inhuman (though even then it will be *humanly* inhuman, i.e. a form of transgression), it will have to strive to be noticeably humane, i.e. fulfil its duties to humanity.

12 Wolterstorff's paper would win in clarity, I think, if in the position he describes as foundationalism he would point out that theory and ultimate commitment are there fused into one.

13 Implicit here is the idea that the relation of the scholar to the rest of mankind is a corporate one, as well as his relation to other scholars. One could say that structurally mankind is the primary and total body, whereas the scholarly community is a secondary and functional body.

14 At the same time a campus should be politically aware and even fertile; cf. also note 11 (above).

15 Cf. the last two sentences of 3.0. in Part. I.

16 The sense of the word "is" here is not that of starting an observed fact, but of presenting a believed norm. Thus I use "for" rather than "of" man.

17 This is, of course, at best a one-sided statement. Yet it states a side that needs stating. In the area of theology we perhaps have learned too much to always state the whole truth at once and for all times. If so, then we could do more with stresses that are made primarily because they need emphasis at a certain time in history. Reformed theology has, in a needed reaction against Roman "works" theology and Arminian "free will" theology, stressed sovereign divine grace. I believe that today this reaction needs the balance of emphasis on the Bible's teaching about man's responsible role in salvation. Paul accepts the question: What must I *do*.

18 What I mean is: not a show of personal devotion. Rather, Jesus showed his love in a Johannine sense: vocation to serve the brothers.

19 The problem of authority in our circles is still suffering from an (illusory?) sense of being too well understood in its fundamentals. Wolterstorff echoed a fear of anarchy with too much influence from Schouls' analysis *(Insight, Power and Authority)* during the discussions. Though both Duvenage and Schrotenboer tried hard to show that ultimately authority is from God alone, their contributions still do not sufficiently come to terms, I believe, with the relationship of that insight to Christ's rebuke (no doubt *contextually* with reference to pharisaic abuse): Call no man your Master. But this contextual statement appeals to a context transcending principle. My own analysis has led me to conclude (cf. the section on the offices in the essay "Cultus and Covenant" ((*Will All the King's Men*)), which goes into a bit more detail) that "being in authority" is not a calling that some person can have to the exclusion of others. Thus I reject as wrong (though traditionally almost universally accepted) the

authoritarian position that comes through in Bingle's paper. At the same time, I do not see how this position can ultimately be avoided by Duvenage and Schrotenboer, for their position seems closer to Bingle than to Schouls.

20 A reduction of Word to Scriptures is Bibliolatry, a form of idolatry. Not acknowledging the Scriptures to be the Word of God is heresy. The Biblical position seems to be that of knowing the Word only *according to* the Scriptures.

21 In a healthy political climate, the political roles and responsibilities of non-political organizations will be very indirect and undramatic. But when serious problems arise or when the university is put under pressure, very dramatic roles can legitimately be expected. What I am indicating in the text of the paper is a norm, not an actual situation. If the independence (also independence to be sharply critical of a government) of a university is threatened, it may conceivably go to the barricades. It appears to me that in this respect the Potchefstroom University in its recent relation with the Free University is (acts?) almost irresponsibly naively, while the latter has almost identified itself as a mere political institution with sharply moralistic and "holier than thou" overtones.

22 One of the motives mentioned for Potchefstroom not allowing the Free University to include Naudé in its delegation was that this would probably embarrass the government. But surely, it is naive to believe that in such a relationship the university is really free to act as it should.

23 The person who is a scholar is, of course, never merely a scholar even when he is acting in the capacity of a scholar.

24 Gödel's theorems prove that a completely formal system can never be a complete or closed one. I believe this can be interpreted to mean that no theoretic system of any kind can in principle be self-contained. Only today is the significance of this understood in terms of the autonomy of reason, objectivity, neutrality, etc.

25 The bibliographical information at the end of the paper is designed to assist scholars in assessing the contemporary mind in this respect.

26 To achieve communal unity in scholarship *requires* relatively small institutions. Contrary to Bingle's notion that large numbers provide a mere organizational problem, I believe that big institutions are anti-normative in the contemporary context. His argument that no one can satisfactorily define the limits is arbitrary. The limit is felt wherever and whenever true community are no longer practically and routinely experienced in scholarly terms. In my experience those limits have already been exceeded at the P.U.

27 The Biblical tensions in the Christian life are many: God's Kingdom has come but is not yet there; we have eternal life and yet we sin; the Kingdom of Heaven is earthly but not of this earth; we must be in and not of this world; etc. But none of these are to be understood in terms of un-Biblical dualistic notions of heaven and earth, body and soul, nature and supernature, nature and grace, or church (institution) and world (of other social structures).

28 One of the greatest dangers threatening the Christian institution is that in trying to meet the requirements of being an academy according to modern demands, there is no time left to devote to finding out what it is to be a Christian academy. Work on the question of the special character is reserved for "when there is time left", meaning special conferences,

holidays, etc. When being a Christian institution is not a priority, but a hobby, a solid Christian *tradition* will never be established.

29 This bibliography consists of works that explicitly deal with or help understand the relation between the scholarly enterprise and the Christian faith. Those that do not do so explicitly contribute to our understanding of the problem by dealing with objectivity, neutrality, presuppositions, rational autonomy, scientism, verificationism, unity of experience, etc. For those who have limited time, the following books can be selected out of the list: Buytendijk, Hempel, Köhler, Kuhn, Laszlo, Maslow, Polanyi, Popper 1963, and Radnitzky. Some books mentioned are semi-popular lectures, e.g. Coulson, Hart, MacKay and Runner, yet they can be valuable as introductions to the problems. Kalsbeek is not a good introduction to Dooyeweerd for scholars or advanced students. It may be more helpful to the layman than its predecessor, Spier. But it does contain very valuable biographical material in English, French and German, about 40 pages of it. The book by Dooyeweerd is formidable, but for advanced reading in this area still a classic. Especially in the context of many of the other sources. If one book is to be chosen, I would recommend Polanyi. The first 115 pages of Wagner's book are the best that I know of by a Christian to interpret the history of theory from the Greeks through Descartes and Newton with respect to our particular problem. It is worth learning German for, and it is to be hoped that a translation of that section will become available.

Contextual possibilities for Christian
academic service

Prof. Dr. Henry Stone

I

Prof. Hart's excellent paper on *The Service Motive as a function of the Christian University* includes a very true statement about, as he calls it, "contextual limits" of service which reads as follows: "Today's academic world is the only field of service about which we in the context of this paper can be meaningfully concerned. Its needs must be met, its misery relieved, its talents explored, its tasks taken up" (Hart, 1975, 83). Hart then proceeds to describe the "academic servant in a service-conscious academy", explaining limitations and pointing out responsibilities. Both limitations and responsibilities, he says, are linked to the universal norms for scholarship, therefore to the nature of scientific activity; but they are also closely bound up with the so-called contextual limits in another sense, namely with the present day academic situation.

For the purpose of this (second) paper on "The Service Motive" I am going to rephrase Hart's expression, "contextual limits", to *contextual possibilities for academic service* in order to embark on a slight elaboration of the context of our Christian scholarly service within the university.

The context, as Hart (also Dengerink and others) has pointed out so clearly, is first of all the scope presented by science itself and by the nature of the university. But the context, secondly, also represents the stage in the history of civilization that we presently experience. The present day academic situation is closely interwoven with the present day world. The possibilities and limitations of present day scholarship are to some extent linked with new developments, new perspectives in the academic field; new horizons have also been opened for further and deeper research. Service to the academic realm and through scholarship to society and civilization has been given new scope and dimension. In a sense it is correct to speak of other times, other universities.

II

Speaking about the context of scientific service and its relatedness to the present stage of civilization, it is first of all necessary to point out several lines of development.

Characteristic of the second half of the 20th century (especially) is a tendency to orientate or relate scientific research to the problems of today. In Britain for instance Brian Holmes has become internationally well-known for his so-called "problem approach" in Pedagogics. There is a growing concern to bridge the gulf between education as a science and educational practice, and this has been reflected in publications and conferences, especially during the past two decades. And this phenomenon of a growing mutual involvement of scholarship and life, of science and practical decisions, coincides with an exodus of science from its previous ivory tower existence. For centuries the university was the only place for scientific endeavours, and science was exercised for the sake of science.

The change then that occurred in this situation reveals three lines of development:

Firstly scholars developed an interest in the significance that science has for, or the bearing it has on, everyday life, especially with a view to decisions that have to be taken, with a view to planning, and formulation of policy. Life is directing a very strong appeal to scientists.

Probably as a result of a more direct need of scientific knowledge for the solution of pressing societal problems, research is gradually also being undertaken outside the university. The result is that research is even more directly related to the problems of practice. In the realm of Education, for instance, research bureaux and national and international institutes and organizations have mushroomed.

In a twofold sense, therefore, science has stepped out of the ivory tower: in becoming related to societal problems, and by being undertaken also outside universities.

Secondly, from this involvement of science in life a fresh concern for the relation between science and presuppositions has also developed, the latter being an important part of the pre-scientific views of reality in society (Van Riessen, 1973, 115).

Thirdly the above-mentioned two lines of development should be viewed in the context of, on the one hand, the dynamic dimension twentieth century society has acquired, and, on the other hand, the progressive shrinkage of the globe caused by developing communication techniques. One should perhaps say that the former two lines of development are framed by the third.

This is, I think, the contextual framework which limits the possibilities for Christian scholarly service at the university — old and new possibilities. The question to be considered now is: In what way does this context offer possibilities for service to a service-conscious academic community founded upon faith in Christ?

III

It is necessary to have clarity on the limitations presented by the nature of science and the structure of the university before one should embark on an effort to answer this question. Much has been said on these limitations, by Prof. Hart too. Very concisely formulated, I believe that one should be guided by two principles. Firstly by the principle of the sovereignty of spheres, i.e. that each social structure has its own competency according to its own nature. Secondly by the principle of the universality of spheres, i.e. of an intrinsic interwovenness and interrelatedness of the different spheres of society. These two principles are directives for avoiding two errors. On the one hand one is safeguarded against identification of science and faith, or practice, or propaganda — also against identification of the university's competencies with those of other social structures, such as the school or the church or political bodies. On the other hand one is safeguarded against the error of an ivory tower conception and practice of scholarship. These two principles lead to the realization that isolation of the university and of science from society, or disregarding of the true nature of scholarship and of the university confuses the issue of the true context of academic service. At the same time, keeping these two principles in mind, the implication of a twofold rôle of the university is clear: namely a service to scholarship, and also a service through scholarship to society and civilization.

With this in mind one can now proceed more safely to answer the question: In what way does the context, outlined in the three lines of development of scholarship (above), offer possibilities for service to a service-conscious academic community?

We have highlighted two sides of the exodus of scholarship from the ivory tower: science has become more related to practical life, and scholars have become more interested in the relation between science and faith. Reaction has set in against the emphasis on the so-called autonomy of science and of the university to such an extent that these are isolated from or have become unrelated to society. Reaction has also been noticed against the notion that objectivity and neutrality of scientific method, i.e. of analysis and abstraction, can be pursued to such an extent that science is separated from man's (ultimate religious) convictions. (Indeed, such a notion is yet another unsuspended conviction underlying science.) It is felt, and truly so, that a scholar's deepest beliefs and insights cannot be sidestepped.

Notwithstanding this fact it must be conceded that science *is* different from either practice or faith. Abstraction and logical analysis indicate that science is not directly linked to faith and to practical life, but indirectly. Through analysis and abstraction knowledge of a general nature is achieved, knowledge that shows a systematic coherence, knowledge representing an effort to formulate the truth in respect of an aspect or structure of reality.

IV

The responsibility of serving the Kingdom as a *scholar* should therefore be seen within the boundaries of science. It lies within the possibilities and limitations presented by scholarship according to its nature. According to this three major possibilities for service can be identified. If you prefer: three major responsibilities of the university.

Firstly there is the responsibility of finding new possibilities for revealing the riches of reality. This applies not only to the natural sciences but just as much to the so-called humanities. Unfolding the riches of reality is a service to society and civilization and is a deed of renewal or reformation of life. This should be done through honest and dedicated scientific research. The Christian scholar should never let his sound pre-suppositions make him careless in respect of methodology or let him overestimate his effort just because his motivation and point of departure is Christian. Scientific service should be delivered through prima scholarship.

The fact remains, however, that science can never be isolated from a scholar's deepest convictions, or from his often unconscious pre-suppositions, hypotheses or insights, or from his so-called "obviousnesses" and "self-evidencies".

Therefore a *second* responsibility rests upon the scholar, namely to exercise, in a scholarly way, transcendental critique on his own scholarship as well as that of others. The transcendental-empirical method is well-known in this respect (Hommes, 1973, p. 118).

The discovery and scholarly exposure (not witch-hunt) of pre-

101

suppositions underlying science and university teaching is a service of reformation of science, provided that this is accompanied by a positive substitution with and application of Christian pre-suppositions. Through the application of science pre-suppositions take effect in society. A study of this should be included in the scholarly service of discovering and substituting underlying pre-scientific conceptions. *In this way* not only science but also society could be perpetually reformed by the university.

Interwoven with the foregoing *scholarly* context of service, is the context of a very dynamic society on a shrinking globe, together with all the problems, all the challenges and all the appeals that it presents. Scholarship should *thirdly* therefore be related to the present society and prevalent civilization if it wishes to deliver to it a service of renewal. The university together with its sciences, in research as well as in teaching, is intrinsically interrelated in a thousand ways to society. Like the state, church, school and other social structures the university also has to answer the call to build, keep and dominate the earth. It should answer in its *own* way the questions put forward by society; it should contribute to the renewal of civilization; it should create insight into and present knowledge about the problems of our day — problems emphasised by a shrinking globe, e.g. the lack of balance between unity and diversity; or questions (stressed by the dynamic dimension of modern society), i.e. problems concerning change and tradition.

New fields of specialization, new courses, re-arrangement of curricula to include or stress themes of special importance in our days should characterize our universities.

V

To these directives that I have given, I would like to add more general comment.

Fundamentally Christian scholarship through the university should be seen as a service of reconcilliation, therefore also as a service rendered with love and without fear. For if understood in its intrinsic relation to Christ as the Servant who has reconciled creation with God, the cultural mandate of man is essentially a service participating in this reconciliation. Reconciliation is a deed of love. And therefore the Christian university should render its academic service in obedience to the commandment of love and therefore also without fear in an often hostile world. The Christian scholar need not serve in a desperate way, for the Lord who uses him is victorious !

102

SELECTED BIBLIOGRAPHY

Coetzee, J. C.: Higher Education and Society. In Free University Quarterly, Vol. 6, 1959, pp. 262—276.

Dengerink, J. D.: Plaats en taak van de universiteit in de moderne samenleving. Lecture: twenty-fifth conference of V.C.H.O., 1975.

Hart, H.: The idea of Christian Scholarship. International Conference of Christian Scholars. Potchefstroom, 1975.

Kooistra, R. (1965): The university and its abolitions. Hamilton, Ontario, The Association for Reformed Scientific Studies.

Popma, K. J. (1969): De universiteit: idee en practijk. Amsterdam, Buijten en Schipperheijn.

Runner, H. E. (1970): The relation of the Bible to learning. Toronto, Wedge Publishing Foundation.

Runner, H. E. and others (1961): Christian Perspectives 1961. Hamilton, Ontario. Guardian Publishing Co.

Stellingwerf, J. (1971): Inleiding tot de universiteit. Amsterdam, Buijten en Schipperheijn.

Van Riessen, H.: Science between presuppositions and decisions. In: The Idea of Christian Philosophy. Essays in honour of D. H. Th. Vollenhoven (1973), p. 114—126.

Van Eikema Hommes, H. (1973): De Methode van de Encyclopedie, de Transcendentale kritiek van het wetenschappelijk denken en de hoofdlijnen van de geschiedenis der Rechts- en Staatsfilosofie. V.U. Boekhandel, Amsterdam.

The national and international structure and task of the Christian institution for higher education

Dr. Z. Rittersma

ONE cannot imagine the task of this institution without paying attention to the processes of change which occur on an international as well as a national level. For the practice of any science, however, it is not sufficient to note changes. In the midst of the battle of the spirits, we have to test the spirits, whether they be of God (1 John 4 : 1 and Rom. 2 : 18). The touchstone, God's infallible Word, has been given to us for that purpose. Whoever questions this touchstone, cannot make a correct evaluation of the processes of change and of the tasks which are related to these changes.

After trying to indicate some of the more marked changes, we will mention some of the ideals which play an important role in the processes of change. Then follows a look back into the history of higher education. Finally, we want to mention briefly our task as reformed scholars.

1. *Some marked changes*

1.1. A strong tendency to change that which exists

This tendency increasingly becomes an obsession. Changing of structures is not a more or less patient waiting for what is going to happen, but a turning around of structures and institutions; if necessary, or even preferably, by force. We see this kind of change in the differing or already different marriage concepts, in the levelling of authority relationships, in the internationalising of programs of education, etc.

In the area of pedagogy and education it is quite noticeable that people are continually busy with the formulation of new purposes. They prefer to depart from uncertain planning for the future, rather than from a clear definition of the point of departure. Institutions for higher education are therefore caught accelerating

104

in the rapids of a stream. Therefore they are often more directed to a new future than to acting for the preservation of what has appeared to be necessary in the past. The tendency is to be progressive and to ban conservatism. We are said to be "on our way", as it is called. But whoever asks the question "quo vadis?" certainly does not get a christian response.

1.2. Expansion of our horizon and of our reach

Because of exploration and exploitation the horizon of our knowledge has been enormously expanded. This cultural process of disclosure has been generated particularly by the specialization of scholarly work. This process of disclosure is related to man himself and to the structures of his society. Questions like: what holds the group together, what holds a nation together, or a people, or humanity, are not only put, but answered as well. But, however widely we expand the horizons, man remains central and so does his being together with others. The field of inter-personal relationships and interhuman ties is becoming as wide as the world itself. Whole areas of life are being internationalised. And this process is accompanied by tendencies toward levelling. There is strong protest against existing inequality. Today's equalisers put people and nations on a Procrustean bed of nails.

If the reach of a cannon used to be three miles, so that with its help the boundaries of territorial waters could be indicated, today the reach of a modern projectile is worldwide. Borderlines are honoured with much more difficulty and they can easily be transgressed. The results of certain sciences work in an analogous fashion. A publication, a small group of activities, can have far reaching results for all of humanity. It is simply clear that institutions for higher education can be the subject or object (with or without their permission) of this expansion of horizons, and with fear and trembling they see projectiles fall down in their national territory.

1.3. The relativising and mythologising of the Word of God

The above mentioned changes are nothing compared to what is happening in the area of Bible criticism. For, if the Bible is no longer trustworthy, the myth of science comes in its place. It is a power which catches many in its magic, because the power of error, of heresy, is hidden under the soft and warm robe of our calling to neighbourliness. The Christ of the Scriptures is being placed next to the gladiators of old.

When the sword of the Spirit is no longer wielded in the church of Christ, the deterioration in theology and also in other sciences will become manifest. Nobody should try to raise a reformed flag if he has hidden Bible-critical explosives in his baggage.

To be and to remain a confessor of the reformation means that in the exercise of scholarship we maintain the unity of pulpit and lectern. No longer keeping the truth, brings along the temptation of using false cries of unity and creating incorrect interecclesiastical ties. The church that is in the world is increasingly becoming the church of the world. The message of the pulpit is promoting the secularisation of life and of societal structures and promotes internationalisation in Babylonic style.

2. *These briefly noted changes have a world and life view as their background*

The following idols play a role in this respect:
1) The idol of freedom and liberation,
2) the idol of the choice between progressive and conservative,
3) the idol of supra-nationalising,
4) the idol of distancing our choice of church from our choice of field of scholarship.

2.1. Idols can only be discovered if the light of the Gospel enlightens our hearts

Well, true freedom teaches us, as for example in Joh. 8 : 36, that: "If the Son of man has made you free you shall be truly free".

The humanistic ideal of freedom does not truly liberate, whether the individual, or a people, or a nation. It certainly does not lead to the liberation of life by a free exercise of scholarship (however important this may be). For there is only one foundation, placed in this world, on which (both in our personal lives and in the life of a people or nation) life-saving work can be done: Jesus Christ. The pedagogy of freedom and liberation of Freud, Fromm and Marcuse, does confront us with the question of guilt, but indicates one or more wrong causes of sin, such as guilt feelings, frustrations, and above all, the Christian institutions.

2.2. The idol of choice between progressive and conservative seems simple, but isn't

The intention is that we choose for progress. In that case only you co-operate in the process of change and you don't share the bad name of conservatism. In characterising this choice the ethical concepts of good and bad are used illegitimately. Whoever allows himself to be led by these ideals, is no longer able to differentiate critically. Even the Christian may then be tempted to place parts of confessions and of the Bible on the altar of progress. Even the old idea of antithesis will be exchanged for a sympathetic going along with all who wish to break down things in a revolutionary mood and who think that only in this manner will all men have bread and happiness. Christians who co-operate in this way forget the travelling rules for God's Kingdom in this world and simply join an improvised parade without a real end.

The parade seems to be especially tiresome for those who work in the area of education.

2.3. Here too, an idol is destroying things, because existing and apparently useful structures and institutions are put aside

The concept "national" has been devalued. "National" increasingly becomes a synonym for being shortsighted, narrowminded, and parochial. National tasks are often in conflict with supra-national aspirations. All the structural changes that come along with this internationalisation, also confront us with the difficult phenomenon that everybody is going to make everybody else his business. Worldwide relationships are now given concrete shape in protest, boycott, strike and the placing of explosives.

The idea of the experience of unity, and thinking in worldwide categories is especially operative in the World Council of Churches. Church and world have joined hands here: (Revelation 17).

2.4. The idol of separating the choice of church relativises the confessions and promotes the secularisation of the sciences

In this manner the result is a two pronged approach. It works through not only in one's personal life, but also in the exercise of scholarship. In the past as well as the present, this can be demonstrated.

3. After having given some more insight into the state of affairs, we now want to say something about the history of the higher institutions and the universities

The exercise of scholarship in the Greek world, and long after that, proceeded from the Aristotelean idea that man was a free being, capable of developing in multiple dimensions.

In ancient times higher education was a matter of a free co-operation of teacher and student, i.e. a strictly private affair.

As society grew more hierarchical, and as large empires arose, higher authorities started to busy themselves with the erection and maintenance of these institutions. The emperor as well as the pope participated in this period. The name higher school is derived from the higher authority which started it or which maintained it. "High" therefore does not in the first instance indicate the character of scholarly education.

These ecclesiastical and political developments resulted in the growth of a certain discrepancy between the private and international character of this kind of education.

Because of the unity of language and the unity of religion, the higher schools, and later the universities, received an international character both with respect to the content of education and also with respect to their methods and structure. This character was strengthened because students from various countries registered at a certain university, which had famous men of science.

All colleges and universities had a hierarchical system of authority and a classical basis. There is, however, a clear difference in character between the religious universities and state institutions. Spiritual and secular authorities did not always harmonise.

The humanistic freedom principle of Aristotle had immense influence on the scholastics. The church had accepted the opposition of the areas of nature and grace, and this led to an exercise of scholarship which was more Aristotelean-humanistic than Biblical in its point of departure and in its purpose.

The reformation was of fundamental significance for the disclosure of life, also because it rejected humanistic ideals of science and pedagogy. It is useful in this connection to note the year 1559. This year was not only important because John Calvin's Institutes were completed, but also because in that year the national academy was opened.[1]

Calvin saw this academy as a national matter, which is understandable if one understands his church-state concept.

Calvin did not want a separation between ecclesiastical confession and the exercise of scholarship. He puts the full weight on the one office which man may occupy in the saving work of Jesus Christ.

Explicitly Calvin indicates that religion and science are not enemies. He appreciates the sciences as God's gifts. To his opponents, who libellously charge that science is not important for him, he gives the assurance that we ought to be no less serious about our business in this area than our enemies are in trying to destroy true obedience to God. Even though we let the Word of the Lord go first, we do not reject the sciences, which with justification take second place.[2]

Calvin wants to give lots of space to scholarship, even though he sees great dangers in its exercise. He sees this danger especially in separating scholarship and the Word of God. Outside of the Kingdom of God, he calls scholarship vain, a finite enterprise destined to disappear — and if it goes against the cause of Christ, even a dangerous pest.[3]

Calvin wanted to use his national academy to promote the well-being of the state and its citizens. We may never look at this national character of Calvin's work apart from his Scripturally faithful point of departure. The national task of scholarship is weighted down with the task of keeping the Word of God pure, of letting it work through into ordinary life and into the exercise of scholarship.

It is worth mentioning that Calvin and his friends viewed the academy as a battle community.

Calvin's model has had international significance.[4] Thus, we read in a decision of the Estates of Friesland in which they establish a university in Franeker: "since neither church nor political regime can be without learned persons".[5]

Calvin's model, which was born from the battle to save God's infallible Word from heresy, resulted in this, that when universities were started, the question of a link to the confessions was given a place. It is noteworthy and significant for today, that universities in the Netherlands were not afraid to bind professors to reformed confessions. Both in Groningen and Franeker these were signed. In Leiden the signing was prevented through the work of the Libertines.

After the sixteenth century the battle in and around the church puts a clear stamp on the manner of scholarship. The interests of the state and of private persons are continually in conflict. It seems difficult to arrive at the nationalising of the institutions for higher education. This is for example clearly visible in the United States. The original private college model of England was not a national model, yet it was taken over in the United States when Harvard University was started. The same was true for Yale. The development of many churches in the United States made the church-state problem even more acute.[6] Brubacher writes: "Perhaps most active in founding new colleges were the various denominations". The battle for the character of the university was fought in Dartmouth before the high courts. Dartmouth became the bulwark of academic freedom. This humanistic liberation is the continuation of the classic humanistic ideal of paedagogy on the basis of human freedom.

In the eighteenth century the problem arose in the United States of the beginning of the national university. Presidents such as

Adams and Jefferson thought it was advisable for the young republic to start a national university in order to expand knowledge for the sake of the state. This did not really succeed, because of the great protest from the North Eastern States. They did not want nationalization of the system of education and they were more given over to the idea of statism, rather than federalism. A few centuries later, somebody could still write that U.S. education is a true quilt.[7] When in the nineteenth century the influence of the state increased in the area of education (think of the various kinds of legislation), and when there came a separation between church and state, the national character of the different institutions received a new impulse. At the same time there were shared tendencies towards scholarly expansion in various countries. The national character at the same time had an international colour in so far as the structure of science was concerned. Increasing results of research and adoption of these results promoted the process of nationalization. They were also promoted by technical and political developments. In this connection one can think of the science of comparative religion and the science of comparative education. At the same time the secularization of our post-Christian era was increasing.

As a contemporary reformed confessor, it is educational to note a few matters from the year 1880. The founding of a reformed university had the sympathy of many people in the Netherlands.

In that year of the founding of the Free University (next to the non-free State Universities), Dr. A. Kuyper wrote a letter to the Christian Reformed Churches who had separated themselves from the Dutch Reformed Church since 1834. In that letter he asked for support. A large number of clergymen, among whom was the Rev. Lindeboom, reacted in an open letter to Dr. A. Kuyper, especially about the basis and the constitution.[8]

"In your circular letter for the Association for Reformed Higher Education", says this open letter, "nothing too much has been said when it was indicated that land and nation are being threatened by the State Universities". The letter continues: "The Christian people, especially reformed Christians, may not rest, until theology again glitters brightly and its light falls on *all* sciences and unity has in principle been restored between classically educated people in every area".[9]

But, in the open letter there is also some serious criticism: "How shall we be able to develop a reformed theology without a reformed church?" [10] And next: "You do admit, do you, that the doctrine of salvation and the scholarly investigation of it do not belong to private Christians, nor to some pastors, but to the church; that the

110

church needs to take care of its development, its expansion and its safekeeping? Therefore no theology without the church! Not an association for theology has given rise to the christian church, but the other way round: the christian church has given birth to theology and has nurtured and protected it. In the same manner, the reformed confessions and theology are the fruit of the reformed church. Now, since you are making plans without a reformed church, how shall you be able to safeguard the reformed basis? ... And if in this way there is no good feeding ground for reformed theology and the pastures for its grazing and the straight road for its development are lacking, does that not also mean that the christian character of the entire university is in danger? If theology does get a place in the cycle of sciences, but without guarantee of having sufficient and pure oil in its lamps, and if in this way its light would probably soon decrease and deteriorate, what certainty do we have that not soon, at a university which calls itself reformed, the classical moulding of lawyers and others will increasingly happen in the dark".[11]

"You too wanted to honour the reformed confessions and have them honoured by the people. But you cannot and may not and will not take articles 27 to 32 out of them, is it ... ?"

"How shall what is called the ecclesiastical question be solved or avoided, in the case of your important plan for the Free Reformed University which is so much desired both by you and by us? We would gladly help to erect a university, which in truth has at its basis the reformed confessions and therefore the Word of God. But then we also need to watch out together that no *vitium originis* cleaves to it — that its birth is not desecrated by not acknowledging main points of the confessions — then we need to watch out that if it is to be a true child of the reformed principles it be born from a sanctified marriage of the reformed church and science".[12]

From this short piece of history it appears that the national or international character of an institution for higher education, seen historically, was not primarily in question. National and international programs showed a lot of agreement and did not as such create a lot of problems. It is possible to have either the national or international character dominate the university, in which case the exercise of scholarship, which in the first place is the work of a small group of highly trained people, becomes unnecessarily difficult. It is more important that we arrive at a correct evaluation of the road that we have to go in the exercise of scholarship. Actually we see two roads.

The one road starts with Cain, the first sectarian. He followed the road of his own free choice over against God.

This freedom motive puts a stamp on the exercise of scholarship, and determines its character and purpose. The road for the free individual also becomes the road for a people, or a nation, or a race, or even a world population. Man looks for his fellow man in society on the same road. He forgets the God of creation and the Christ of salvation. Therefore he tends to get stuck in his exercise of scholarship, because liberation is actually a *fata morgana*. Nevertheless, much is accomplished. Man after the fall is still man. He still has gifts and he can still function. But not as God's image bearer, because he has left God's service.

The other road starts with Abel. In his case the road of faith has repaired what God required of us in His service. The exercise of scholarship on this road is based in our office which God has redeemed. The start of this is not our *humanum*, nor our *societas*, but the christian *Koinonia*. This was only possible by Christ's sacrifice. From out of this *Koinonia* it is possible for man again to see what is necessary for his fellow man, for people and for a nation. Again he can pay good attention to relationships and structures and institutions which God has created. In this way he can also fulfil a calling in the exercise of any science which can be a blessing to a nation or to people elsewhere.

These two roads do not coincide, even though all men of science work in God's one world. The decisive question remains whether one is willing to follow the Lamb, wherever it goes.

4. *The tasks for the Christian institution of higher education are many sided and dynamic in our days*

Much is in the process of changing and has yet to change. What remains is that we must accept our service before God the Creator and Christ the Redeemer and the Holy Spirit who sanctifies.

Whoever lives out of the truth also understands reality. The truth makes free.

Calvin said that a university was a battle community. In true ecumenical fashion he saw our one service from out of the pulpit and with it he connected the lectern.

Whoever talks about battles, thinks of fronts. The task of the christian institute of higher education is that of time and again placing itself in the right front. While doing that one has to remember that one can be attacked in the back by soldiers who stand right next to one. That is what the road of church history teaches us.

It is therefore necessary to support one another as well as keeping watch over one another. We have to support one another in learning to differentiate the spirits and in disclosing in a legitimate fashion God's created world.

Every one must see to it that he builds on the one foundation. The day of Christ's return will make it known whether our works will remain.

Our task is, however, a light burden! That is what our Saviour said. Anyone who loves him is from God and keeps his commandments.

---

1 *Vier redevoeringen over Calvijn*. D. Nauta, Smitscamp et al. Kok, Kampen, 1959, especially Nauta's essay "Calvijn en zijn academie in 1559".
2 Cf. id., p. 17.
3 Cf. id., p. 31.
4 Cf. "Calvijn's academie en de Nederlanden", id., p. 25.
5 Id., p. 29.
6 Cf. *A history of problems of education*, New York, 1947.
7 Cf. G. Linker: "Het Amerikaanse onderwijs een lappendeken", *Intermediar*, vol. 45, nos. 37—39.
8 Cf. *Open brief aan dr. Kuyper* by L. Lindeboom, Leiden, Donner, 1880.
9 Cf. id., appendix, p. I.
10 Cf. id., appendix, p. II.
11 Cf. id.
12 Cf. id., appendix, p. III.

The national and international structure and task of the Christian institution for higher education: Propositions for discussion

Prof. Dr. P. G. W. du Plessis

Dr. B. J. van der Walt

1. The Christian university is a servant in the kingdom of God. Services to be rendered in the Kingdom must be qualified by the typical functions of the university, i.e. *inter alia* teaching, research, application of knowledge, formative influence, cultural guidance. Consequently the institution for higher education must pay attention to various needs and opportunities in an academically responsible manner.

2. The Christian university selects a direction which differs from that of the neutral university as well as the utility university. Life is more than science or bread. The entire life of man is a vocation, an existence *coram Deo*.

3. As with man himself, the university finds itself in various relationships *(in casu* the national and international) but it is never absorbed by them.

4. The structure of the university is universal while the manner in which this structure is realized has a national character.

5. The Christian university will have to bear in mind that it will not be able to offer at a given moment everything that is interesting or important. At both the national and international level Christian universities ought to come together to work out programmes for amongst others the joining of forces, division and meaningful reduplication of work.

6. Contemporary practical application of science outside the university places a heavy responsibility on the university in respect of, for instance, consultation services and guidance in permanent education provided at various levels for individuals and instances.

7. The Christian university will have to assign the highest priority in

its teaching and research programme to the problem of the unity of science in order to avoid becoming merely a series of buildings connected to one another only by a service road, telephone or central heating system. The concern here is not about an additional course — because the Christian character of the university must be displayed in all its courses. Here it is a case of a new direction of thought in the selection of teaching material and teaching methods, for instance, an interdisciplinary approach. Both the what and the how of the teaching programme are important.

Commitment and theory

Prof. Dr. Nicholas Wolterstorff

I

How should a person who is both a Christian and a scholar relate his Christian commitment to his theorizing and his theorizing to his commitment? That is the topic I wish to discuss. Or better, one or two facets of this topic are what I shall discuss.

Originality is something my topic lacks to a striking degree. For as you all know the topic has been discussed by very many thinkers over the course of very many centuries. But though my topic is thoroughly traditional, in my treatment I shall depart from the tradition by not assuming the truth of that theory of theorizing known as *foundationalism*.

Foundationalists are of the conviction that the goal of scientific* endeavour is the formation of a body of theories from which all prejudice, bias and unjustified conjecture have been eliminated. They hold that to attain this goal the scientist must begin with a firm foundation of certitude; and on this foundation he must build the house of theory by methods of whose reliability he is equally certain. Austere and elegant, this theory has proved irresistibly attractive to Western man, shaping not only most discussions on "faith and reason" but our whole occidental image of the scientific enterprise.

It is worth stating the theory a bit more precisely. The basic question to which the foundationalist addresses himself is this: Under what circumstances are we warranted in accepting a theory? And the heart of his proposal is a rule for warranted theory acceptance. The rule can be stated thus: A person is warranted in accepting a theory at a certain time if and only if he is then warranted in believing that that theory belongs to genuine science *(scientia)*.

To understand this proposed rule we must understand what is meant by saying that a theory belongs to genuine science. On this the thought of the foundationalist goes along the following lines. A theory *belongs to genuine science* if and only if it is

---

* Throughout I shall mean by "science" what the Germans mean by *"Wissenschaft"*.

justified by some foundational proposition and some human being could know with certitude that it is thus justified. And in turn, a proposition is *foundational* if and only if it is true and some human being could know non-inferentially and with certitude that it is true.[1] Perhaps a diagram illustrating this view of the "logic" of genuine science would be helpful.

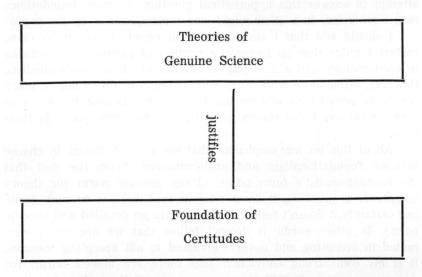

Foundationalism has been the reigning theory of theories in the Western world since the days of the high middle ages. Vast amounts of philosophical thought have been devoted to its elaboration and defence. It has been the dominant tradition among Christians as well as among non-Christians. Aquinas, Descartes, Leibniz, Berkeley, the logical positivists — all of them and very many more besides have been foundationalists. It is my own conviction, however, that the foundationalist's proposal is unacceptable. I do not believe it to be true that someone is warranted in accepting a theory at a certain time if and only if he is then warranted in believing that that theory could be known with certitude to be justified on the basis of propositions knowable non-inferentially and with certitude to be true. Consequently my discussion of the proper relation between a person's Christian commitment and his theorizing will not be set within the context of foundationalism.

My reasons for rejecting foundationalism are basically two-fold. No one has yet offered a satisfactory explanation of what it is for a theory to be *justified* by what the scientist takes as data, and I think it most unlikely that anyone ever will. And secondly, even if we did know what constitutes justification, the body of propositions

117

that we know non-inferentially and with certitude to be true constitutes far too slender a base for the justification of all acceptable theories.

Unfortunately, here I cannot even begin to develop these reasons for rejecting foundationalism.[2] So if you are not yourself convinced of its unacceptability you will have to regard my discussion as an attempt to answer this hypothetical question: *Suppose* foundationalism were false, how then might our topic question be answered?

I should add that I am not alone in rejecting foundationalism. In fact I judge that an increasing number of philosophers working in epistemology and philosophy of science are non-foundationalists. However, often those who reject foundationalism do so not so much for the reasons I have offered but because they believe there are no norms whatsoever for theory acceptance. "Anything goes" is their view.

About this let me emphasize that we are not forced to choose between foundationalism and antinomianism. From the fact that the foundationalist's formulation of the general norm for theory acceptance is mistaken it doesn't follow that there is no such norm, and certainly it doesn't follow that there are no detailed and specific norms. In other words, it doesn't follow that we are never warranted in accepting and never warranted in not accepting theories. It is my own strong conviction that there are indeed norms for theory acceptance. I shall assume so in what follows. My objections to foundationalism are not the objections of an antinomian.

I freely admit, though, that I am not in the position of being able to propose a formulation of the general norm to replace the foundationalist's proposal. But this gives me no qualms. For from the fact that someone does not have in hand a satisfactury formulation of the general norm for theory acceptance it does not follow that he cannot legitimately hold that people are warranted in accepting certain theories and unwarranted in accepting others.

Some theories specify what *ought to be done*. That is true, for example, of the foundationalist theory. But for our purposes we can set such normative theories off to the side and concentrate on descriptive theories — generalization to the effect that some or all members of a set of entities possess certain properties or stand in certain relations. Let us call the set of entities in question, the *scope* of the theory. For example, if I entertain the theory that all the chairs in my office originated in Amsterdam, then the set of chairs in my office belongs to the *scope* of that theory (and so do Amsterdam and my office). To propound a descriptive theory is to claim that the entities within its scope fit the generalization of

118

the theory.

Some theories, particularly those in the sciences, are predictive in character. But not all theories are predictive. Not all are even in any very natural sense of the word "explanatory". But all specify some pattern as present within the theory's scope.[3]

The scientist performs many different actions with respect to theories. For our purposes, though, we can concentrate on just one: The action of *weighing* a theory. That is, the action of deciding whether to accept or reject a theory. It is probably true, as several recent writers have suggested,[4] that those who work in the sciences spend relatively little of their time weighing theories. Rather, taking various theories for granted they spend most of their time making theories more precise, engaging in research suggested by theories, determining the data for theories with more precision, etc. Yet the weighing of theories is at the very heart of the scientific enterprise.

Let us consider some of the essential structure of theory weighing. In order to weigh a theory, with respect to whether there is in its scope the pattern claimed,[5] one must have beliefs concerning the entities within the scope. And at least some of these beliefs must be such that one takes them as *data*. That is to say, some must be such that one requires of the theory that at the very least it be consistent with these. This is minimal. If I have no beliefs about my office, the chairs in it, and Amsterdam, such that at least I require the Amsterdam-origination theory to be consistent with those beliefs if I am to accept it, then I cannot weigh the theory with respect to what it claims. Thus at the centre of all weighing of theory with respect to the presence or absence of the pattern claimed is a *decision* to take certain of one's beliefs about the entities within the theory's scope as data for one's weighing of the theory.

If foundationalism is indeed unacceptable for the reasons I have mentioned, this decision cannot be made by reference to a fund of foundational certitudes. For that would yield no data — or more cautiously, would yield far too little. If I am to weigh a theory's claim, there is no option to my taking as data that which I find myself believing to be true. Confronted as we are with the fact that we lack a foundation in certitude we each have no choice but "to one's own self be true".

Of course what repeatedly happens is that each of two competing theories is consistent with all that one takes as data. One's decision between them must then be made on other grounds. Yet it remains true: There can be no weighing of theory with respect to what is claimed without taking as data some of one's beliefs about entities in the theory's scope.

Now in one's weighing of a theory one always brings along the whole complex of one's beliefs. One does not strip away all but those beliefs functioning as data relative to the theory being weighed. On the contrary, one remains cloaked in belief — aware of some strands, unaware of most. I wish especially to single out two sorts of components from this cloak of belief.

There will always be, for one thing, a large set of beliefs such that one's holding them is a condition of one's accepting as data that which one does. Let us call these, *data-background beliefs*. If in weighing some theory I take as datum that this desk is brown, that may be because I believe that when I observed the desk my senses were in their proper state for discovering its colour by observation, etc. Those then are data-background beliefs.

It should be noticed that among the data-background beliefs for a given person's weighing of a given theory there will in turn be a great many theories. That which the scientist takes as data he does because of his acceptance of an enormously complicated web of theory. However, for the weighing of a given theory at a given time all such data-background theories are taken as unproblematic. They are themselves, on that occasion, not subjected to weighing.

For our purposes it is even more important to bring to attention another sort of component in one's cloak of beliefs. Everyone in the weighing of a theory has certain beliefs as to what constitutes an acceptable *sort* of theory on the matter under consideration. Everybody has certain *control beliefs,* as I shall call them: Beliefs about the requisite logical or aesthetic structure of a theory, beliefs about the entities to which a theory may correctly commit us, etc. Such beliefs function in two ways. Because we hold such beliefs we are led to *reject* certain sorts of theories. They are inconsistent with those beliefs, or if consistent with them they yet do not comport well with those beliefs. But equally because of such beliefs we are led to *devise* theories. We search for theories which are consistent with those beliefs. Or more stringently, we search for theories which comport as well as possible with those beliefs.[6]

For example, it was one of the control beliefs of the great physicist Ernst Mach that theories postulating non-sensory entities were unsatisfactory. Any theory falling outside the set of those satisfying this demand was rejected by him as not even a satisfactory candidate for acceptance. But in accord with this control belief he also set about reconstructing physics on a sensationalistic basis. In short, control beliefs function both negatively and positively in the propounding and weighing of theories.

This concept of control beliefs will be so central in what follows that it is worth citing one more example. Near the beginning of his *Beyond Freedom and Dignity* (pp. 14—15), B. F. Skinner forthrightly presents his requirements for acceptable sorts of psychological theories. He says:

> The task of a scientific analysis is to explain how the behavior of a person as a physical system is related to the conditions under which the human species evolved and the conditions under which the individual lives . . .
>
> We can follow the path taken by physics and biology by turning directly to the relation between bahovior and the environment and neglecting supposed mediating states of mind. Physics did not advance by looking more closely at the jubilance of a falling body, or biology by looking at the nature of vital spirits, and we do not need to try to discover what personalities, states of mind, feelings, traits of character, plans, purposes, intentions, or the other perquisites of autonomous man really are in order to get on with a scientific analysis of behavior.

Beginning with some person's weighing of a theory, I have made, within the fabric of his beliefs, the three-fold distinction between *data-beliefs, databackground beliefs,* and *control-beliefs.*[7] Two things about this distinction must especially be noticed. For one thing, it is a distinction as to how beliefs *function.* No belief is inherently a data belief. Secondly, it is a distinction as to how beliefs function relative to a *given* person's weighing of a *given* theory on a *given* occasion. What functions as a data-background belief or as a control belief in a given person's weighing of a given theory on a given occasion may on another occasion be the theory under consideration. On a given occasion Newton's laws of motion may be the theory which is being weighed, and certain beliefs about the optical features of telescopes may remain as background to the data. On another occasion — perhaps because of the occurrence of some anomaly within astronomy — the Newtonian theory may be moved into the background as unproblematic and various assumptions about the optics of the telescope may be moved into the foreground for weighing and testing. What also sometimes happens is that a belief which on a given occasion functions as a data belief against which a theory is weighed is on another occasion itself weighed by taking the theory as unproblematic.

It will be my contention in what follows that the religious beliefs of the Christian scholar ought to function as *control* beliefs within his devising and weighing of theories. This is not the only way they ought to function. They ought also to help shape his views as to what it is important to have theories about. And even that does not exhaust how they ought to function. But their functioning as control beliefs is absolutely central to the work of the Christian scholar. It is this function that I shall concentrate on.

III

To carry the discussion further I must at this point explain what I shall mean by "authentic Christian commitment"; and I must state, at least in skeletal fashion, what I regard as the content of such commitment. I begin, though, with a characterization of *actual* Christian commitment.

To be a Christian is to be committed to being a Christ-follower. From the very beginning that has differentiated Christians from others. To be a Christian is also of course to belong to a certain community, a community-with-a-tradition. But what identifies this community-with-a-tradition is that its members are those who are committed to being Christ-followers.

Crucial to the character of this community-with-a-tradition is the fact that it has certain sacred scriptures, those of the Old and New Testament. On the one hand these are expressions of the religion of ancient persons and peoples. But they have also been judged, by the community of Christ-followers at large, as authoritative guides for thought and life. They have been judged as proper guides for him who would be a Christ-follower. On the issue of the fundamental nature and basis of biblical authority, Christians of course disagree. But on the *fact* of their authority they do not.

Anyone who is committed to being a Christ-follower will of course do and believe certain things by virtue of his fundamental commitment. One cannot have that fundamental commitment without its being realized in some specific and definite complex of action and belief. Henceforth, when referring to some specific person, I shall call that complex of action and belief in which his commitment *is in fact* realized, his *actual Christian commitment*.

But to commit oneself to being a Christ-follower also presupposes some conviction on one's part as to the complex of action and belief that one's following of Christ *ought* to be realized in. On the matter of what that is, Christians disagree widely; as they do on the issue of how one should go about finding out. But every Christian, whether liberal or conservative, has some notion of how his commitment ought to be realized. That complex of action and belief in

122

which a person's commitment to Christ ought to be realized is what I shall call his *authentic Christian commitment.*

For what follows it will be important for me briefly to describe the shape of what in my judgement constitutes your and my authentic commitment. From times most ancient man has departed from the pattern of responsibilities awarded him at his creation by God. A multitude of evils has followed. But God was not content to leave man in the mire of his misery. In response to man's sin and its resultant evils He resolved to bring about renewal. He has already been acting on that resolve, centrally and decisively so in the life, death, and resurrection of Jesus Christ; but more generally, by calling out a people to be witness, agent, and evidence of His work of renewal. *Witness,* in that this people is called to proclaim that God is working in the world to bring about an order of things in accord with the goals that He had when He created them. *Agent,* in that this people is called to do what it can to bring about such an order. And *evidence,* in that this people is called to give indication in its life of what such an order would be like. Your and my following of Christ ought to consist in taking up God's call to share in the task of being witness, agent, and evidence of the coming of His Kingdom.

In committing themselves to share in the work of being witness, agent, and evidence of God's work of renewal the members of God's people constitute themselves a band of disciples of Jesus Christ. For he it was who was the principal witness. He it was who was the decisive agent. He it was who gave the most lucid evidence.

This, expressed in the briefest fashion, is what in my judgment constitutes the structure of what our following of Christ *ought* to consist in. It is to be noticed that on this view authentic Christian commitment is not to be identified with subscription to dogmas. Indeed, it is not to be identified with the believing of propositions, whether dogmatic or otherwise.[8] But notice also that though it is not to be identified with this, yet it *incorporates* this. It does so in a couple of ways.

The people in whose work one is committed to share is called to proclaim certain things, to make certain pronouncements, to tell-forth what is taking place in history. And of course it is presupposed that they believe those things. That is one way in which belief is incorporated within authentic Christian commitment. There is a second way. The people is called to give evidence of the new life. That involves such things as worshipping God, treating nature with delight and respect, and acting in solidarity with the socially op-pressed. But equally it involves *believing* certain things — among others, those taught in the creeds. Thus though authentic Christian commitment is not to be identified with the believing of certain things, yet it does in fact have a belief-content.

For the purposes of what follows it is important to notice that the propositions included within the belief-content of authentic Christian commitment are not just about 'the supernatural'. They are as much about this world and its inhabitants as they are about God. If that is not already evident it would be fully so if we elaborated *what* it is that God calls us to say and do and be.

Authentic Christian commitment as I have explained it is relative to persons and to times. For authentic Christian commitment is what one's Christ-following *ought* to consist in. And that varies not-only from person to person but also from time to time within a given person's life. What I ought to be doing by way of following Christ differs from what someone else ought to be doing and from what I ought to have been doing when younger. Likewise what I am obliged to believe differs from what someone else is obliged to believe and differs from what I as a child was obliged to believe. Thus not only authentic Christian commitment as a whole but also the beliefcontent thereof, is relative to persons and time. One might insist that there are certain propositions which belong to the belief-content of all authentic Christian commitment whatsoever. Probably so. But certainly they will be few and simple.[9]

IV

I said that the religious beliefs of the Christian scholar ought to function as *control* beliefs within his devising and weighing of theories. I can now put my point more accurately thus: The Christian scholar ought to allow the belief-content of his authentic Christian commitment to function as control within his devising and weighing of theories.[10] For he along with everyone else ought to seek for consistency, wholeness, integrity, in the body of his beliefs and commitments. As control it ought to function both negatively and positively. Negatively the Christian scholar ought to reject certain theories on the ground that they conflict with, or do not well comport with, the belief-content of his authentic commitment.[11] And positively he ought to devise theories which comport as well as possible with, or are at least consistent with, the belief-content of his authentic commitment.

For example, the belief-content of our authentic commitment incorporates the belief that one of man's fundamental uniquenesses among earthlings lies in the fact that he and he alone has been 'graced' by God with responsibilities. And that in turn presupposes

124

that man was created *free* to carry out or not to carry out those responsibilities. Accordingly for those of us who are Christian scholars these propositions ought to function as *control* over the sorts of theories that we are willing to accept. Now to my outsider's eye a good many of the psychological theories and claims characteristic of behaviourists and Freudians are incompatible with the proposition that man has responsibility and freedom. Accordingly we ought to reject such theories. But equally we ought to develop theories which comport with, or are consistent with, this belief-content of our authentic commitment. In this way the belief-content of our authentic Christian commitment ought to enter into our devising and weighing of psychological theories. Only when it does thus enter will he who is a Christian scholar be fully serious both as scholar and as Christian.

Several corollaries of this way of seeing the matter should be highlighted.

(1) By and large, the belief-content of his authentic commitment will not actually contain the theories of the Christian scholar. It can and ought to function as a control within his theory devising and theory weighing. But the theories are not already there, just waiting to be extracted. The same holds when we consider the scholar's *actual* rather than his *authentic* commitment. That particular version of Christian commitment exhibited by the 17th century Congregation of the Italian Inquisition incorporated the geocentric theory of the motion of the heavenly bodies. But even *it* did not include more specific theories concerning the paths of specific heavenly bodies, nor indeed a more general theory of motion (a mechanics). So it is in general: The belief-content of a scholar's actual Christian commitment will normally not contain those propositions which are his theories. It sometimes happens that the belief-content of a scholar's actual commitment *suggests* a theory to him. But often not even that is the case. Then the Christian scholar will have to obtain his theories by using the same capacities of imagination that scholars in general use.

This point is connected with the fact that the Bible cannot function as a black book of theories for the Christian scholar. That man is a free and responsible being is indeed a philosophical theory, and perhaps also a high-level psychological theory; it is also something contained within the biblical teaching. But the *detailed* psychological theories which fall under this high-level or philosophical theory are not to be found therein.

(2) With respect to many matters, especially matters of detail, there are alternative theories satisfying the belief-content of a

125

scholar's authentic Christian commitment. Two alternative theories of musical harmony, two alternative theories of mathematical sets, may each comport well and be consistent with a scholar's authentic commitment. The conviction is often expressed that Christians by virtue of their common commitment *ought* to share all their scientific theories in common. Part of the reason for this not in fact being the case is that people's actual commitment falls short of their authentic commitment, plus the fact that authentic commitment differs from person to person. But even a person's *authentic* commitment allows scope for alternative theories. The presence of some theoretical dispute among Christian scholars is not, by itself, sufficient as proof of deficiency in the character of their commitment.

(3) The belief-content of a scholar's actual Christian commitment is not, by and large, the *source of the data* for his theory weighing, and the belief-content of his authentic commitment *could not* be, by and large, the source thereof. For example, the data which some person has for his weighing of a theory of poetic metaphor will consist of beliefs concerning some of the world's poetic metaphors. If he has acted as a responsible scholar he will have acquired most of these by taking careful note of the poetic metaphors that came his way. He will not have gotten them simply by extracting them from the belief-content of his actual commitment; and he *could not* have gotten them by extracting them from the belief-content of his authentic commitment. They are not there to be extracted. But there are exceptions to our generalization. Certain data-beliefs may be gotten both by extracting them from the belief-content of one's authentic commitment and by observation of the world. Experience may confirm what one already believed. In other cases a body of data-beliefs relevant to the weighing of a given theory may be such that some of its members were gotten by extraction and others were gotten (and could only have been gotten) by observation. For example, some of the data-beliefs against which one weighs some theory of human aggression may be taught in the Scriptures, and on that account incorporated within one's authentic commitment; while others were gotten, and could only have been gotten, by one's own observation of living human beings. It is even possible that, for certain theories, all of one's data beliefs are gotten solely from the belief-content of one's authentic commitment. But by and large the Christian scholar arrives at the data for his theory weighing by using the same strategies as everyone else — by observing and reflecting on the world about him.

(4) It is especially important to notice that on this view of the matter one's authentic Christian commitment ought to function

126

internally to scholarship. It ought to function in the search for and the weighing of theories. Christian scholars have classically attempted to relate their commitment to their theorizing in one or the other of three ways. They have repeatedly tried to *harmonize* the belief-content of their Christian commitment with the results of theorizing by introducing one or another revision in their view as to what constitutes authentic commitment. This is what took place, for example, in the eventual acceptance among various Christian scholars of the heliocentric theory of planetary motion, of the evolutionary theory concerning the origin of species, of the documentary hypothesis concerning the origins of the Pentateuch, etc. Secondly, Christian scholars have repeatedly tried to *set* the theories and data of science within a *larger Christian context.* They have tried to discover some pattern into which the theories and data of some particular science along with the belief-content of what they regard as authentic commitment all together fit. Thirdly, they have repeatedly tried to offer distinctively Christian *applications* of the results of scientific theorizing to the problems of human life. *Harmonizing, setting within context,* and *applying* — these, I say, are the classic ways in which Christian scholars have attempted to relate their Christian commitment to their theorizing. Let me say emphatically that these strategies all have their place. Yet what is common to all of them is their *conformism* with respect to science. They all take for granted that science is OK as it is. In none of them is there any *internal* relation from the side of Christian commitment to what goes on within the sciences. In none of them does Christian commitment enter into the devising and weighing of theories within the sciences.

So these strategies cannot constitute the totality of the Christian scholar's program. For the person who exhibits authentic Christian commitment cannot take for granted that the data beliefs and theories of contemporary scientists are true. The most obvious reason is that contemporary scientists *as* scientists disagree. One has to choose. But even if that were not the case within some branch of contemporary science, even if all those who were experts in some field agreed, why should the Christian — *or anyone else* — surrender all his critical faculties in the face of this fact? For those experts in the field will have practised their science with their control beliefs. Why should I assume that mine are theirs, or that a science in accord with theirs will be in accord with mine?

(5) Rare will be the Christian scholar whose only control beliefs are beliefs contained within his actual Christian commitment. And not only is this in fact the case. It is justifiably the case. The

reasons for a medical researcher's rejection of the Chinese theory lying behind the practice of acupuncture, as not even being the sort of theory he will entertain, will usually have little if anything to do with his religion. It will have to do rather with his being imbued with that whole orientation to disease developed in the Western world within the last century. For no one is just a Christian. He is also, say, an American, a caucasian, a member of the middle class, of somewhat paranoid personality. And all of these appellations indicate characteristic sets of beliefs which, in the appropriate circumstances, may function as control within his theory devising and theory weighing.

(6) A Christian scholar and some non-Christian scholar may each justifiably accept some given scientific theory. For the theory may accord with the control beliefs of the non-Christian scholar and also with the belief-content of the authentic commitment of the Christian scholar. That there is this sort of convergence seems to me obvious. The point is worth making only because of the rampant notion that if some theory acceptable to a Christian is also acceptable to some non-Christian scholar, then the claim that there is such a thing as Christian scholarship is absurd. What is absurd, rather, is any concept of Christian scholarship leading to such a conclusion. On the other hand, there may be less of such 'shareability' than one might at first glance suppose. One is inclined to think that low-level theories will especially exhibit it. But low-level theories in science often presuppose high-level theories. And it may well be, in many cases, that unnoticed features of these high-level theories, or of complex hierarchical theories, make them in fact unacceptable either to the Christian scholar or to some non-Christian scholar. What should also be noticed is that a theory in accord both with the authentic commitment of some Christian scholar and with the control beliefs of some non-Christian scholar may not be in accord with the control beliefs of some other non-Christian scholar. Likewise, given that authentic commitment differs from person to person, it may not be in accord with the authentic commitment of other Christian scholars.

(7) If we were foundationalists we would insist that nothing may be used as a control on our weighing of theories unless it itself either belongs to a fund of foundational certitudes or can be justified thereby. But we have found foundationalism untenable. Accordingly any such insistence would be out of order. Neither the data against which we weigh our theories nor the controls that we lay on our weighing of theories can be gotten from a foundation of certitudes.

What happens when a person becomes convinced that within the body of his belief incompatibility has emerged — whether this incompatibility be logical contradiction or the weaker relation of lack of comportment? Well, the actual responses are varied. But the responsible course is to seek to revise one's beliefs in some such fashion as to make the incompatibility disappear. As we saw earlier such revision can in principle always occur at a number of different points. It may be a long time before a firm conviction emerges as to the best point of revision.

A special case of the above question to which we must address ourselves is this: What happens when incompatibility emerges for the Christian scholar between what he regards as the results of science and what he regards as the belief-content of his authentic commitment? Here of course the possibilities of revision are broadly speaking two: He can either revise his scientific views, even to the extent of setting out to reconstruct some branch of science; or he can revise his view as to what constitutes the belief-content of his authentic commitment, thereby also revising his actual commitment.

In fact Christians have repeatedly chosen the latter recourse. Developments in one and another science, including theology, have produced incompatibility in the beliefs of Christians between what they regard as the results of science and what they regard as the belief-content of their authentic commitment. And to resolve them Christians have repeatedly adopted the strategy of revising their view as to what constitutes authentic commitment. They have followed the course of *harmonizing* their commitment with the results of science. In the extreme case they have given up their Christian commitment entirely. In less extreme cases they have resolved the incompatibility by some revision internal to the content of their commitment.

That, I say, is how things have gone. I wish to add my conviction that sometimes at least that is how they should have gone. Sometimes when incompatibility for the Christian scholar emerges between what he regards as the results of science and what he regards as the belief-content of his authentic commitment, the best recourse for him is to revise his beliefs on the latter. For sometimes Christians are mistaken as to what constitutes the belief-content of their authentic commitment.

Up to this stage I have pressed the point that the Christian in the practice of his scholarship ought to let the belief-content of his authentic commitment function as control over his theory-weighing. My point now is almost the opposite: Sometimes he should allow scientific developments to induce revisions in *what he views as* his authentic Christian commitment. For example, the Congregation of the Inquisition viewed the geocentric theory as belonging to authentic commitment. I think they were mistaken, and virtually the entire community of Christians now thinks they were mistaken. We have all revised our beliefs, though we have by no means all revised them at the same point. What originally induced the revisions were developments in astronomy and physics. Thus it must be concluded that developments in science have induced at least some of us to move toward a better view as to what constitutes authentic Christian commitment — assuming as I do that at least some of the revisions do constitute a better view.

On occasion the relation between theory and commitment has been described in such a way as to make it appear impossible that one's devising and weighing of theories would ever have an influence on one's commitment. It is said that religious belief is *pre*-theoretical. Though it can shape our devising and weighing of theories they cannot shape it. This seems to me just factually mistaken. The history of thought is replete with cases in which someone's view as to what constitutes authentic commitment was revised in the light of theoretical developments.[12]

The fact that scientific developments have repeatedly induced revisions in the views of Christians as to what constitutes their authentic commitment has proved profoundly alarming to many Christians. Many accordingly have sought for ways to prevent such developments from occurring in the future to them and to their particular sub-community. I regard such attempts as futile. There is no way of preventing such occurrences. I also regard them as misguided. For though I would be among the last to minimize the dangers to a person's commitment to Christ in such developments, we must also humbly admit that sometimes the revisions were justified. Sometimes Christians have been mistaken in what they thought constituted authentic Christ-following; and sometimes they were made aware of the mistake by developments in science.

I have spoken thus far of revisions induced in our actual commitment, and in our views as to what constitutes authentic commitment, by scientific developments. And I have said that some such revisions are justifiably induced. A question which naturally comes to mind is whether scientific developments can produce changes in one's authentic commitment. Can it be that scientific developments change what one's following of Christ *ought* to consist in — change what one ought to be doing and believing? This, I suppose, is the *ultimately* alarming possibility. But I think the answer must be Yes. As a result, for example, of what we now know about man's effect on his environment it is probably the case that if we as Christians are to be consistent in our beliefs we must treat nature in ways significantly different from those of the past. It is probably the case that if we fail to do so, we are defecting from our authentic commitment.

The scholar never fully knows in advance where his line of inquiry will lead him. When the Christian undertakes scholarship he undertakes a course of action that may ultimately lead him into the painful process of revising his actual Christian commitment, sorting through his beliefs and discarding some from any longer functioning as control.[13] It may even lead him to a point where his authentic commitment has undergone change. We are, all of us, profoundly *historical* creatures. We can't leap out.

VI

There are a great many important matters pertaining to our topic that I have not been able to discuss. In particular I have not been able to discuss how the Bible ought to function in the scholarship of the Christian.

Let me simply observe in conclusion that the task of implementing the vision of the Christian scholar which I have been espousing is not a job for "hacks". It requires on the contrary all the qualities of the competent, imaginative, and courageous scholar. To contribute to the development of theory, sometimes in defiance of the academic establishment, obviously requires such qualities. But equally, to discern that some part of the belief-content of one's authentic Christian commitment ought to be functioning as control within some particular piece of theory development requires such qualities. For the connection does not always leap out. The belief-content of one's authentic Christian commitment is a wonderfully rich and complex structure, and ever again one discovers that some connection of commitment to theory was missed by oneself as well as by one's predecessors.[14]

---

1 There are a certain number of variants on the formulation I have given above of *foundationalism*. The reader who is interested in these variants can consult my forthcoming book: *Reason Within the Bounds of Religion* (Eerdmans Publishing).

2 They are developed in detail in my forthcoming *Reason Within the Bounds of Religion.*

3 Devising a theory obviously presupposes an act of *abstraction* on the part of the person who devises it. It presupposes that he has focussed his attention on a certain limited range of some entities' properties or relations, to the ignoring of others. But it would be a mistake to conclude from this that abstraction is an identifying characteristic of the devising of theories, or even that it is an identifying characteristic of the devising of *scientific* theories. For one thing, abstractively attending to some limited range of some entities' properties or relations does not yet give one a theory — does not yet give one a generalization. But also, abstraction can occur when theories are not even in view. It occurs when, in listening to a musical work, I focus my attention on a certain limited range of the work's features and allow others to recede into the penumbra of my attention. Indeed, no one could, even if he wished, focus his attention on all the properties of the music that he is listening to. It may well be that what differentiates one science from others is that it deals with only a certain limited range of the properties of those entities which fall within the scope of that science's theories. If so, then abstraction is at the basis of our differentiation of sciences. Yet it remains true that the devising of theories does not *consist* in the abstraction of properties, and that the abstracting of properties does not occur only in the devising of theories.

4 See Imre Lakatos: "Falsification and Scientific Research Programs" in Lakatos and Musgrave: *Criticism and the Growth of Knowledge* (Cambridge, 1970). See also Thomas Kuhn: *The Structure of Scientific Revolutions* (Chicago, 1962).

5 One can weigh a theory with respect to other of its features than this. One can weigh it, for example, with respect to its aesthetic qualities — say, its elegance or inelegance.

6 Just what this last relation may be, that of *comporting as well as possible with,* I cannot explain. But it seems to me clear that often we demand more than logical consistency between theory and control belief; and it seems to me that sometimes at least that "more" can be aptly described with these words. Also, sometimes the situation is not so much that *we* search *for* a theory consistent or comportible with some control belief of ours. Rather, our control belief *suggests* such a theory to us. The searching is at a minimum.

7 For a somewhat different perspective on the function of what I call "control beliefs" in theoretical activity, see "A Defense of the Logic of Discovery" by Gary Gutting *(Philosophical Forum,* IV, 3). Gutting distinguishes between the logic of confirmation and the logic of discovery. He holds that *regulative principles* (as he calls them) function in the latter but not in the former. They function as premisses in arguments whose conclusions are of the form 'It is plausible to think that T can be confirmed'. My doubts that a satisfactory concept of confirmation can be framed have led me to pursue a different approach. I speak only about weighing a theory as to its acceptability, not about weighing a theory as to its *promise for* proving acceptable. And what I call *data beliefs* are, strictly speaking, a subset of what I call *control beliefs.* P's control beliefs for the weighing of theory T are beliefs which P requires T to be consistent with (or to comport well with) if he is to accept T. Among these will be certain singular propositions about the entities in T's scope. And

these are P's data beliefs for his weighing of T.

8　By a *proposition* I just mean something which can be asserted. Propositions are thus true or false. Cf. my *On Universals* (Chicago, 1970), Chap. I.

9　It should be noticed that the belief-content of my authentic Christian commitment will differ from those beliefs which it is necessary for me to hold if I am to be a Christian at all. This latter is *minimally necessary* for my being a Christian. The former is what is *maximally obligatory.*

10　Note: I do not say that he ought to allow the belief-content of his *actual* Christian commitment, but rather the belief-content of his *authentic* commitment, to control his devising and weighing of theories. For if the former diverges from the latter, then his prior obligation is to bring it into conformity with his *authentic* commitment.

11　To reject a theory is not necessarily to be done with it. Often when confronted with a theory which one knows to be unacceptable the best strategy is to pursue various research programs suggested by the theory, in the hope that along the way some clues will emerge for the construction of an alternative and better theory.

12　For a discussion of some historical examples of changes induced in people's actual commitment by developments in the sciences see Richard Popkin's "Scepticism, Theology and the Scientific Revolution in the Seventeenth Century" in Lakatos and Musgrave (ed.): *Philosophy of Science* (Amsterdam, 1968).

13　What often happens, as part of this process, is that a scholar is forced to *structure* the belief-content of his commitment in terms of what is more essential and what is less essential, what is nearer the core and what is nearer to the periphery.

14　Substantial portions of this lecture will appear in my forthcoming book: see note 1 above.

Our Christian calling of doing science

Prof. Dr. H. G. Stoker

A. *Prolegomena*

1.0.1. 'Science' we take in the wide sense of 'Wissenschaft' (See Appendix A).

1.0.2. What we mean by 'our Christian calling' needs no elucidation at this meeting.

1.0. Doing science is one of the specific callings of man. Our Christian calling of doing science includes complementarywise (a) the Christian performance of science (specifying the human, personal and social factors of science) as well as (b) the practice of a Christian science — "Christliche Wissenschaft" — (specifying the achievements or results of doing science).

1.1. Several arguments stressing the necessity of our Christian calling of doing science (see Appendix B) hold not only for doing science, but for realising other callings as well; for instance that we should do science to the honour and glory of God. These arguments may not be underrated. But besides these types of argument we need — in view of our subject — arguments specifically holding good for doing science. And again several arguments state the necessity of our scientific calling, but do not tell us nor allow us to infer *how* (in what ways, according to what guiding principles or rules) this calling should be specifically realised.

2.0. But before going into this, we have to distinguish between doing science and doing our other callings.

2.1. Science is a type of knowledge. Knowledge is constitutive of, as well as a *means* for realising man's diverse tasks (resp. callings). But only in the case of doing science is the forming and furthering of knowledge the specific *purpose* of the task. Wherever man (responsibly, systematically, justifyingly and technically methodologically) forms and futhers *knowledge* as the specific *purpose* of his undertaking, science appears.

2.2. The question of what doing science is could be approached in another way. Science is a type of knowledge. The other types of knowledge we take together under the umbrella-term of *'usual'* (sometimes called 'naive', 'everyday', 'pre-scientific', 'non-scientific') knowledge. Life and world view (including religious faith) provides a comprehensive unity of usual knowledge. Usual knowledge is — without a special and specific stress — interwoven with everything man does. But in the case of doing science the forming and furthering of knowledge acquires a selectively relevant purpose and accordingly a specific stress, implying in view of this purpose that science be done systematically, justifyingly and in a technical methodological way. Yet *usual* and *scientific* knowledge cohere in various ways, not only because they both are knowledge but especially because science has (principially, actually and historically) its roots in usual knowledge, being basically as well as in its outlines co-determined by the relevant convictions of whatever life and world view plays a role. That 'part' of usual knowledge that co-determines the doing of science we call *'prescientific'* knowledge.[1] The prescientific convictions of the particular life and world view may be taken as the context (Kuhn would have called it 'paradigm') within which science is done. On the rebound, scientific achievements may become integrated with usual knowledge *(vide* e.g. the Copernical view of our stellar system) and many new scientific discoveries and insights correct in some way or other our usual knowledge, and may even effect changes in life and world view convictions. Yet of the two, usual knowledge is not only the more original but also has a depth and a comprehensive scope that surpasses scientific knowledge; the humanly creaturely limitations of scientific knowledge being in fundamental respects greater than those of usual knowledge. To this may be added that the doing of other tasks than that of science may make use of scientific results and methods (as e.g. in the case of scientific farming) as a means to fulfil their respective purposes.[2]

2.2.1. The above provides us already at this stage with an argument for the necessity of fulfilling our Christian calling of doing science, we being committed to do science within the context of (especially the fundamental convictions of) our Christian life and world view — and in accordance with the relational demands of the various fields of research of the various sciences.

3.0. At this stage the question arises, why should man form and further knowledge (do science) as a specific calling? This question is often answered: in order to explicitly disclose the ordered structure of laws God has laid down for the cosmos as a whole and for all its coherent articulations. But to this should be added: in order to explicitly bring out the *polupoikilè sophia tou theou* (the many-coloured wisdom of God — Eph. 3 : 10) of which the cosmos and all its coherent diversity testify — thereby exhibiting God's honour and glory. Subordinate to the above, knowledge (science) should be formed and furthered on the one hand in the interest of the enrichment of man himself — wisdom (resp. knowledge) being better than rubies (cf. the basic sciences); and on the other hand it should be of service to man's realising his other callings (cf. the applied sciences — the application itself of scientific achievements being done by the others).

3.1. In order to understand *how* we should realise our Christian calling of doing science, we should beforehand investigate knowledge — usual and scientific knowledge both being knowledge.

3.1.1. Knowledge is unique, irreducible to anything else of and within the cosmos. Accordingly it cannot be defined but only indicated and identified by ostention (i.e. by pointing at or by naming it). With an apology to Heidegger "you do not learn to know what knowing is by reading a treatise on knowledge; you learn what knowing is by knowing".[3] Accordingly every definition of knowledge is circular and so is the following description of knowledge should it (wrongly) be taken to be a definition. "Knowledge is the result of the knowing exploitation of the knowable by man the knower".[4] This description of knowledge is but a distinction between, and a relating of the components of knowledge (cf. *accompanying figure on next page)*. Of these the term *'the knowable'* needs special elucidation.

The knowable (whatever can be known) is that to which the knowing activity attaches itself, that about which knowing is concerned and in the case of doing science its fields of research. For instance physical entities, plants, animals, human beings, the cosmos are knowable; their knowability is an ontic characteristic; in other words God has created the cosmos knowable (and man with his abilities and capabilities to know). Also knowable is the revelation of God in his Word (and in creation — to be understood in the light of his Word-revelation) about himself and his relation to all 'things'.

3.2. Arguments for our Christian calling of doing science can (a) *contextually* be attached to the whole knowledge concern and its radical and absolute dependence on God, to its place and role within the cosmos (knowledge belonging to the cosmos as do an atom, a cell, an animal instinct) and to its place and role within the human realm (e.g. concerning the mutual relations between science on the one hand and the church, the state, industry, society, etc. on the other); and (b) *analytically* also to any of the components of the knowledge concern (i.e. to A, to Aa, to B, to Bb, to C and to D of the attached figure). Of *all these we will subsequently restrict the exposition of our subject to the argument as attached to C, the knowable.*

Knowledge

(Scientific results, achievements)

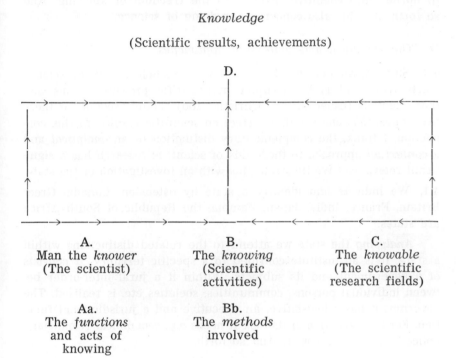

D.

A.
Man the *knower*
(The scientist)

B.
The *knowing*
(Scientific
activities)

C.
The *knowable*
(The scientific
research fields)

Aa.
The *functions*
and acts of
knowing

Bb.
The *methods*
involved

3.3. Another exposition of knowledge is also relevant to our subject. Knowing is a unit.[5] Observation (taken in a wide sense) is a partial-act of knowing; genuine observation is a knowing observation. Thinking too is a partial-act of knowing; genuine thinking is a knowing thinking. Thinking at the same time is a means in the hands of knowing. But within the unit of knowing, memory and (intellectual) imagination too have their functions. And so forth. But special mention needs to be made of faith (taken in the wide sense in which Bavinck takes it). Without faith (faith in the know-able, faith in the capability to know, faith in reason, faith in the presuppositions according to which, and faith in the prescientific contextual views within which science is done) science is impossible. And of fundamental significance in this context is religious faith. When exploring knowledge we should start with knowing as a unit

137

and not with a dichotomy of independent observable 'neutral' 'facts' and an independent autonomy of 'neutral' thought.

3.3.1. We should, of course, delve deeper into what knowing is. Into the mysterious revelational character of knowing. Into the mystery — to borrow a term of Blondel — of the symbiosis of man (the knower) and the knowable;[5a] into subjectedness of knowing to norms; into cognitive truth; into the freedom of knowing. And so forth. All this also concerns our doing of science.

B. *The analytical and contextual approaches*

4.0. Since A. Kuyper and H. Bavinck we have held that doing science starts from and is based upon prescientific pre-suppositions and that scientists (especially the Christian too) should account for these presuppositions and for their effect on scientific results. In this connection, I think, the complementary distinction of an *analytical* and a *contextual* approach to the fields of scientific research has a significant relevance.[6] We illustrate this with an investigation of the state.

4.1. We indicate and identify a state by ostension: Canada, Great Britain, France, India, Japan, Zambia, the Republic of South Africa are states.

Analysing the state we attend to the related distinctions within a state. It is an institute confined to a specific territory. It consists of a government and its subjects. Within it a jural inter-order between individual persons, communities, societies etc. is realised. The government has a legislative, an executive and a jurisdictional function. For the execution of its task it needs e.g. economical (financial), police and military power. And so forth.

4.2. The *contextual* approach concerns the diverse contexts within which the state has its function, place and role. These contexts (can) form a progressive series of scope or of comprehensiveness and can be illustrated by means of a set of concentric circles. Firstly there is the place and role of the state within the human realm — Dutch: 'samenleving' — sometimes called 'society at large' and sometimes 'community at large'. In this respect e.g. the liberalistic, communist, Roman Catholic and Calvinist contextual views of the state differ. Secondly the state can be viewed within the context of man and his place and role in the cosmos. Here e.g. naturalists, humanists, Roman Catholics and Calvinists have different contextual views of the state. Thirdly within the contextual view of the cosmos materialists, idealists, Roman Catholics and Calvinists view the state differently. Fourthly the state can be viewed within the context of God (or whatever is taken as the absolute instead of God) and his relation to the cosmos and to man. In this connection the views of the state held e.g. by Roman Catholics and Calvinists or by theists, penantheists, pantheists, cosmists, panecosmists etc. differ too. Fifthly (within the former context) the investigation of the state could contextually be approached within the distinction of good and evil (including sin) and the victory of good over evil — of which I especially mention the Christian truths concerning the fall of man and his redemption in Christ. Also in regard to the prescientific contextual view of evil, scientists differ. Other contextual views concerning the state — intersecting the above series — are e.g. the view of the jural function of the state within the context of culture at large and the state contextually seen within its history and within the history of mankind.

4.3. The cosmos and everything within it has inseparably and at once its analytic and contextual 'meaning moments'. A scientist when exploring the cosmos or something within it cannot evade the prescientific contextual views concerning the matter being explored; they are — even if tacitly, implicitly, inarticulately — present in his research; and they basically and in outline influence his view of whatever he investigates. It is of interest to note that the contextual views tend to guarantee the unity of science; that in the measure that scientists explicitly try to exclude contexts when doing analysis, science is fragmented. But in the measure that scientists explicitly stress their respective contextual commitments, science is disrupted into conflicting stands, tendencies, currents and schools.

This seems to me by and large to be the basic dilemma of doing science within our dispensation of fall and redemption: the dilemma of fragmentisation and/or disruption of science.[6] To this overall dilemma we should tie the justification as well as the realisation of our Christian calling of doing science, thereby implying our strategy of co-operating with other-minded scientists without suppression of the relevant antithesis and of maintaining the antithesis without excluding the relevant co-operation. For the calling of doing science goes to man, to (using C. van Til's terms) 'believers' and 'unbelievers'.

4.4. It may be noted in passing that there is a vastly greater measure of agreement between 'believing' and 'unbelieving' scientists in the case of analytic investigations than in the case of contextual approaches to the research fields, keeping in mind, however, that the contextual and analytic meaning moments are inseparable and that even analytic achievements when seen within different contextual views, differ.[7]

4.5. The prescientific contextual view within which the scientist exploits his research field partakes of several characteristics that e.g. Thomas H. Kuhn ascribes to 'paradigm'.[8] It is more than a pattern of a theory, more than a mere set of presuppositions; it is a prescientific view of the research field[9] to which the scientist is committed, a view that tells the scientist what the valid problems, the relevant scientific criteria and the appropriate methods to be used are, a view that leads and directs research, thought and observation and which in itself cannot be proved by logic and experiment. A change of contextual view (or paradigm) is only possible by persuasion and conversion. (In passing I may note that Kuhn's division of paradigms seems to be too historical and somewhat artificial, whereas our suggested division of contextual views according to a ranging series of ever more encompassing contexts seems to me to be more systematic and more appropriate). At any rate the approach to the problem of our Christian calling of doing science according to the significance of our prescientific contextual Christian convictions seems to me more than worthwhile — and, as has been indicated, we will subsequently attach this approach to the knowable component of the knowledge concern.

4.6. One remark is yet necessary. According to Kuhn, paradigm changes occur fundamentally on account of the increasingly critical weight of anomalies present when viewing the research field within a particular paradigm. Also in our Christian exercise of science changes of contextual views (paradigms) occur on account of critical anomalies encountered, of new discoveries and new insights and of the demands of the advance of history. But the very fundamental (and accordingly most comprehensive) contextual views — e.g. the general truths of God's Word-revelation and the light they shed upon the cosmos and its coherent diversity — we will never give up, unless we lose our Christian faith. *Mutatis mutandis* this holds good for all scientists, whatever their most fundamental prescientific convictions may be.[10]

C. *Arguments for our Christian calling of doing science attached to the knowable, specifically to the general truths of the Word of God*

5.0. When I knowingly observe the apricot tree beyond my study window, this tree shows itself to me, tells me what it is, presents information about itself. Believers and unbelievers agree that science should concern itself with the information that the cosmos (the 'world', 'nature') and the coherent diversity within it presents to man, however differently they may understand this information. *But only* the believer holds that the revelation of God in his Word about himself and his relation to all things, also is information, of which science necessarily is in need. He accordingly has more information at his disposal than the unbeliever. Our problem is whether and how difference in acknowledgement of information by believers and unbelievers makes a difference in their doing science respectively.

Of course, Scripture is no textbook, its words no scientific terms, its sentences no scientific propositions; its truths are prescientific truths; and the significance of the prescientific information of God's Word for science is not meant in a biblicistic sense. What we especially have in mind is the significance of *general Scriptural truths* explicit from *Genesis* through *Revelation* and the light they shed on the cosmos and 'all things' within it. We hold that these general truths are relevant for doing science. It goes without saying that scientific research should take all relevant information into consideration; scientists may reject no information relevant to their doing science. But this implies that the believer committed to God's Word-revelation acts unscientifically when he does not acknowledge Scriptural truths relevant to his scientific undertaking. We submit that these prescientific truths offer the scientists new relevant information for doing science; that they concern all science, that they should (even if sometimes only tacitly, implicitly, inarticulately) function as contextual views (or paradigms) within which the diverse fields of scientific research should be explored; that they shed new light on the cosmos and all it contains; that in a fundamental way they lead and direct the scientific enterprise; that they allow us to infer normative guiding lines from them and rules according to which our Christian calling of doing science should be realised; and that doing science in this way differs in fundamental respects and in outline from doing science that does not take these general Scriptural truths into consideration.

5.1. In passing it should be noted — as already intimated — that the contextual approach to science consists of a coherently ranging series of ever more encompassing contexts. Many of these the Christian doing science should discover within the cosmos itself. But our present exposition is restricted to a number of contextual views provided by the general truths of God's Word-revelation.

a. *Out, through and unto God are all things*

6.0. Within this context the believing scientist sees the cosmos and everything within it — *in casu* his research field, himself, his doing science, the methods and tools he uses and the results he achieves — in its creatureliness, in its ultimate self-insufficiency as well as its pointing back to its Origin; he also sees the limitations of his scientific endeavour. From this we may infer normative guide lines or rules: (a) that the scientist see the cosmos and everything within it and especially everything concerned with his doing science in its creatureliness, as ultimately insufficient; (b) that he avoid and reject every '-ism' that absolutises, makes self-sufficient, or independently autonomous, the cosmos or anything within it — *in casu* anything that concerns his doing science. When we muster the history of science, of every science, say from Thales up to now, and pay attention to the commitments of scientists to the '-isms' mentioned, it is obvious that our doing science within the context under discussion does and must make a difference.

b.1. *The radical diversity within the cosmos has its origin in (the creative act of) God*

6.1. There is relative diversity in the cosmos that has come into being during the process of time. But there is also a radical (essential, mutually irreducible) — diversity that has its origin in (the creative act of) God. For instance: man (the creaturely image of God) is radically distinct from animal being, and a living organism from a physical entity; number and space and again the ethical and the aesthetical are mutually irreducible; the structure and task of the church institution and that of the state are essentially different; human history is something radically different from biotic evolution; and so forth. All this implies normatively that the scientist be fully open to and in search of this radical diversity; that he avoid and reject all '-isms' that deny the radical diversity and that reduce whatever is radically diverse (cf. e.g. reductionisms that reduce biotic or physiological processes to chemical processes, jural to logical distinctions, man to mere animal being, education to a kind of animal training and so forth). Again, mustering the sciences throughout the ages it is obvious that our doing science within the context under discussion does and must make a difference. To this should be added that the necessity of doing science within this context reveals the limitations of scientific research in as much as the origin of the radical diversity is scientifically inexplicable. Of course, the believing scientist, who is still a sinner within our dispensation, can and does err, but this does not detract from the necessity of being openminded with regard to whatever is radically distinct. It is furthermore interesting to note that wherever a scientist theoretically reduces the radically distinct, antinomies appear[11] and that

142

whenever he acknowledges the radically distinct within the cosmos, but yet tries to combine them into a unity, paradoxes arise. The Christian doing science and being committed to the context under discussion will reject paradoxes, but at the same commit himself to the hyperdox (that transcends human understanding) of the origin in God of the radical diversity of the cosmos.

Even more fundamental is the radical distinction between God and creation *(in casu* the cosmos), God being in no way whatever creaturely and nothing of the cosmos being identical with God.

b.2. *The coherence of the radical diversity within the cosmos also has its origin in 'the creative act' of God*

6.2. All things within the cosmos cohere in many ways; this especially holds good of the coherence of the radical diversity as well. Above we made mention of the transcosmic unity of cosmic radical diversity in the creative act of God (and this holds good of its coherence as well), but now we meet with the coherence (of the radically diverse), an intracosmic principle of unity (which should not be identified with the cosmic law-order). Referring to examples of the radically diverse given in b.1., it is obvious that they are mutually unisolatable but cohere in many respects. From the above we may infer the norm that the scientist seeks and discovers all the relevant relations obtaining between the radically diverse, but without theoretically reducing or violating anything radically diverse, and without thus falling into antinomies and paradoxes, but admitting the necessity of hyperdoxes. The above also implies the norms that the scientist should avoid and reject all 'isms' that fall prey to making coherence a lever of extrapolation or of totalization, both being forms of reductionism (cf. b.1.). By totalization I mean the error of *pars pro toto*. G. Heyman's psychomonism, Freud's sexualism, the ideal of a unified science of logical empiricism (or logical positivism), psychological and sociological behaviourism, biological evolutionism, causalism (excluding e.g. hermeneutical investigation), the exaggerated or overstressed expectations of the 'Gestalt' — and again of the cybernetic principles, and so forth, are examples of complete or partial totalizations. Totalization and reductionism are two sides of the same coin. It should also be noted that although absolutization implies totalization, the converse does not hold: totalization need not necessarily be absolutization. Again mustering the history of science (of all sciences) it is obvious that the believer's doing science within the context under discussion fundamentally differs from doing science within another context. And here again we come across the creaturely limitations of doing science. We illustrate it with one example only.

Thinking and cerebral processes are radically distinct, mutually irreducible. Yet they cohere and we can investigate their coherence. But *how* it is possible that whatever is radically distinct yet can also cohere surpasses human understanding; it is a hyperdox, scientifically inexplicable. By disclosing the coherence of the radically diverse we are faced with the miraculous structure of the cosmos, of the *polupokilè sophia tou theou* (the many-coloured wisdom of God) revealing his majesty and greatness. The above shows the normative necessity of an openmindedness for all that is radically distinct, yet coheres (which is only possible within the context concerned) and even allows the believing scientist to distinguish moments of truth in all the mutually conflicting '-isms' concerned.

Even more fundamental is the radical dependence of the cosmos (including man created as God's image and called to serve God in all he does) on God.

b.3. *The unity of the coherent (b.2.) radical diversity (b.1.) of the cosmos*

6.3. The coherent radical diversity of the cosmos forms a complementary unit; its components may never be bifurcated nor rendered asunder. This truth demands that the scientist does science within the context of both principles in unison. As an illustration I refer to what I call cosmic dimensions of (a) modalities, (b) events (or the dynamic), (c) idiostant structures and (d) values and what Dooyeweerd calls the dimensions of the horizon of human experience viz. (a) time, (b) modalities, and (c) individuality structures. Each of the four cosmic dimensions divulges the radical diversity within the cosmos as well as their coherence. The *radical diversity* within (a) the cosmic dimension of modalities could be formulated as sovereignty in its proper domain; within (b) the cosmic dimension of events (or the dynamic) as freedom (taking freedom in a very wide sense) according to the proper competence; (c) within the cosmic dimension of idiostant structures as that of the identity of the proper structure; (d) and thus also in the case of the cosmic dimension of values. The *coherence* of the radical diversity within the cosmic dimension of (a) modalities could be formulated as universality in its proper domain; (b) within the cosmic dimension of event as the universal dependence of the proper freedom on other proper freedoms; (c) within the cosmic dimension of idiostant structures as that of universal intertwinement (or encapsis) of the iodiostant structures; and (d) thus also in the case of the cosmic dimension of values.

Again mustering the history of science, of all science, in respect of the contextual view of *coherence* of the radical *diversity* within the

144

cosmos, it is obvious that realising the Christian calling of doing science does make a difference.

c. *The cosmic law order*

7.0. To explore the cosmic law order is one of the major tasks of the scientist, the other being the exploitation of the coherent diversity for which the cosmic law order obtains. The cosmic law order has its origin in God, the Lawgiver, and holds for the cosmos as a whole and for everything within it. It is a coherent diversity of religious commandments, cultural norms and laws of nature; of general laws and universal laws of the contingent; ontic laws (sometimes called law principles) and humanly positivised laws (normatively bound to answer the ontic laws); and so forth. Some of these laws are revealed in Scripture. The scientist has to seek, discover and formulate this God-given (and also humanly positivised) cosmic law order in its cohering diversity. This implies that the believer avoid and reject all '-isms' that deny the law order (e.g. anonism, indeterminism, casualism); that arbitrarily subjectify the law order (e.g. terminism, nominalism); that in some sense or other humanise the law order, making man an autonomous law giver (e.g. conceptualism; decisionism; positivism; conventionalism); that absolutise the law order (e.g. nomism, determinism, law-fatalism); that do not do justice to the radical diversity of the law order (all types of reductionism); that do not do justice to its coherence of a radical diversity (all types of totalization falling into the error of *pars pro toto)*, that tear types of law asunder (e.g. dualisms, pluralism); and so forth. Our Christian contextual view of the God-given cosmic law order accordingly allows the inference of all these guide lines or rules of realising our Christian calling of doing science. Mustering the history of science, of all the sciences, in this respect it is also obvious that our doing science does make a difference.

c. *Man*

8.0. The prescientific contextual view of man specifically concerns the anthropological fields of research. But in a general way it concerns all science.

8.1. Anthropology is virtually a family of mutually related special anthropologies such as theological, philosophical, cultural, sociological, ethnological, historical, educational, psychological, biological, physiological and other anthropologies. The prescientific contextual view within which anthropology is pursued forms a whole consisting of a ranging series of related special contextual views of man, of who and what he is, of his place and role within the cosmos and fundamentally of his relation to God or whatever is taken as an 'absolute' or 'absolutes' instead of God. The whole could be called the master contextual view of man (cf. Kuhn's term 'master paradigm' or 'disciplinary matrix'). When doing one of the special anthropologies some of the special contextual views of man have a more direct and explicit bearing on the research concerned, the other being more tacitly or implicitly present.

8.1.1. The prescientific master contextual view of man, when realising our Christian calling of doing anthropology, sees man *(inter alia)* as a creaturely, self-insufficient, cosmic image of God, in everything dependent on God, subject to God's call and his law-order, divinely appointed as *mandator Dei,* called to serve God in everything he does, in his creaturely mastery of nature, and himself, in his creativity of culture, in his care of man and in his worship of God; man being in all these respects radically different from animal being; but who has fallen into sin and is essentially in need of redemption in Christ; who has to partake in the battle against sin and evil and in the furtherance of the advent of the Kingdom of God.

8.1.2. Two characteristics of our contextual view of man — significant for all anthropology — deserve special attention. Firstly, man basically being endowed with his abilities, capabilities and talents and facing his given opportunities (having to do with all his might whatever his hands find to do) is fundamentally a responder to his calling in everything he does. Not challenge and response (Toynbee) but in a wider and deeper sense: opportunity (i.e. calling) and response fundamentally typify man. Secondly, man is endowed with a creaturely possibility to *choose* and *decide* (by virtue of which he initiates a series of activities, is *accountable* for his choice and decisions, can give and can be called to give an account of his doings) and with *responsibility* (by virtue of being subject to *norms,* of accordingly not being permitted to choose arbitrarily whatever he prefers and of falling into guilt by violating the norms concerned). In these respects too man is essentially (radically) distinct from animal being.

8.1.3. From our prescientific contextual view of man, guiding lines or rules could be inferred indicating *how* we should realise our Christian calling of doing anthropology. Over and against the above we find (when mustering the history of all anthropologies) a host of '-isms' resulting from other prescientific contextual views of man which the Christian anthropologist should avoid and reject. Realising our calling of doing anthropology does make a difference.

8.2. The prescientific contextual view of man is moreover a concern of every scientist, of all science. Saying this we do not have in view the human personal and social factors of doing science (cf. A on p. 137), but still attach our inquiry to the knowable (the reason fields of science (cf. C. on p. 137). Every scientist responsibly knows that it is he that does science and that he has a prescientific contextual view of himself when doing science, a view of who and what he is, of his abilities and capabilities. For example the empirical positivist's faith in the independent autonomy of science, his idea of science, the scientific criteria he posits and his view of his accountability and responsibility implicitly reflect the view that he has of himself. Over and against this the Christian scientist basically has another view of himself doing science. Also in this respect realising our calling of doing science does make a difference.

d. Good and evil (including sin)

9.0. In our dispensation of fall and redemption the distinction between good and evil has a universal range and thrust. We meet it everywhere in our cosmos. Every life and world view (including religion) testifies to it. Are good and evil eternally conflicting forces (Old Persian view), or is evil basically an illusion (Spinoza) or a lesser evil (Leibniz) and how do Christians view this distinction and the victory of good over evil? The answer to these questions too, functions as a prescientific contextual view within which science is done. The rather easy-going (rationalistic and moralistic) optimism of the enlightenment of the 18th century and the somewhat naive trust of logical positivism (resp. empiricism) in the progress of science or the pessimism of a Schopenhauer, a Freud, a Spengler, a Sartre attest to this problem of good and evil. Theologians, philosophers, anthropologists, ethicists, sociologists, jural scientists and even historians etc. cannot avoid the problem of good and evil. Educationists holding to the inborn goodness of the child or those that maintain the necessity of disciplinary education (Prov. 29 : 15) are confronted with this distinction. Many anthropological sciences give mutually conflicting answers to the basic meaning of punishment (reforming of the transgressor, security of society, undoing ((Bonsanquet: nullification)) of evil and so forth).

The late psychiatrist Schoep contends that although the scientist cannot investigate the workings of sin, he can yet discern its effects, as in the case of the psycho-analytic truth that the sub- and unconscious psychical processes are not open to the control of man and influence his activities (especially in psycho-pathological cases) unconsciously; this he holds to be an effect of sin; had man not fallen into sin, his sub- and unconscious psychical processes would have

147

been open to his selfcontrol. We could furthermore refer to plant, animal, and human pathologies. Even Dooyeweerd's principle of God's irony within the history of man attests to our problem. All these and other considerations of the necessity of distinguishing good and evil concern epistemologically the so-called value-judgements. In the case of scientific theories we come across the conflicting ideas of what science is and accordingly of what good and of what bad science is; cf. in this respect, e.g., the conflict between logical positivists (resp. empiricists) and members of the American-English historical school as well as the conflicting views about scientific rationality.

Furthermore it can be shown that the logical positivists have a specific prescientific notion of truth value, whereas the historical school (Kuhn) stresses that within the prescientific contextual view (paradigm) of the research field concerned value has a basic function. After all, is the admittedly (at least partial) incompatibility and incommensurability of scientific results achieved within conflicting paradigms and the resulting (at least partial) talking at cross-purposes of the adherents of conflicting prescientific paradigms (i.e. contextual views of the relevant research fields),[12] virtually not a scientific evil — i.e. the effect of the workings of sin — more fundamental than mere wrong or non-observations and logical fallacies? We can delve still deeper. Is the necessary dilemma of our dispensation (4.3.) of fragmentation and/or disruption of science not also an evil and an effect of sin?

9.1. The above is a rather random collection of illustrations of the universality of the distinction of good and evil — even and especially *in rebus scientiis*. It indicates that this distinction is virtually also a prescientific contextual view within which science is done. The Christian doing science sees this distinction fundamentally according to the general truth of God's Word-revelation, of man's fall into sin, of his redemption and of the recreation of the cosmos in Christ. From the prescientific contextual view of good and evil too, guiding lines and rules could be inferred for the realization of our Christian calling to do science and of avoiding and rejecting all the '-isms' concerned to which doing science within other prescientific contextual views falls prey. Also in this case our doing science as Christians does make a difference.

D. *In conclusion*

10.0. The above approach to our Christian calling in the area of science, although universal in intent, is yet partial and one-sided. 10.0.1. Firstly, because it concentrates on the contention that our

Christian exercise of science does make a difference. It would be rather peculiar if there were no agreement whatever between the believer's and the unbeliever's doing science, considering that God's call to do science goes to both believers and unbelievers, both being human beings of the same make and both doing science within the same world (or cosmos). Restricting myself to the believers' comportment, they often do (and should) acknowledge discoveries made and insights gained by unbelievers — even to the extent of being obliged to change their own views. This holds good notwithstanding the fact that the agreements are to be seen within the prescientific contextual views of the believers, and in this respect they do differ. The nature, the vast measure and the conditions of agreement between believers and unbelievers deserve a penetrating investigation — also in view of the need for our co-operation with other-minded scientists without suppression of our contextual commitments and the need for stressing our commitments without refusing co-operation.

10.0.2. Our approach is partial and one-sided too because we restricted our calling of doing science by attaching it to the knowable, more particularly to the general Scriptural truths. This should be counterbalanced by all the other approaches mentioned in 3.2.; and further more by e.g. the intrinsic connectedness of the history of man (and especially the history of science) — also our doing science necessarily being subject to historic change; by the approach concerning truth and science (truth being more than the validity of the results of scientific investigation); and by the approach concerning the law-order (specifically: the norm-order) holding good for the totality of the scientific concern, for all its components and attachments and for its relation to all other human callings. To this I should add that the very fundamental concern is God and science, whereby the Trinity should be taken into account, science having to be done to the honour and glory of God, by following Christ, and under the guidance of the Holy Spirit — a guidance, as V. Hepp has rightly emphasised, that is not restricted to man's faith in God's revelation nor to the worship of God, but that has a universal value for all man's calling and doing.[13]

10.1. We have restricted our exposition of our Christian calling to do science to the very fundamental contextual views — to the general truths of Scripture — that should lead and direct our scientific enterprise. (Other less fundamental and less comprehensive contextual views — e.g. concerning the cosmos and its coherent diversity — we have to discover in the course of the advance of history). The prescientific contextual views cannot be proven nor disproven by logic, observation or experiment; these latter presupposing and being done within the prescientific contextual views concerned. In the case of the very fundamental contextual truths our only appeal is to God's Word-revelation itself. *Mutatis mutandis* this holds good for every kind of science, whatever the scientist's fundamental commitments and appeal may be. There is no (and especially no religiously) neutral science.[14] Concerning the overall dilemma of doing science in our dispensation of fall and redemption, viz the dilemma of fragmentising and/or disrupting science, we are committed to the conviction that the last ground of the unity of the cosmos and its cohering diversity — and accordingly of science itself — is God's revelation concerning himself and his relation to all things, which is a theocentric transcosmic ground of unity. This ground of unity cannot be found within the cosmos, nor within man, nor within human science.

10.2. It is on account of this theocentricity of the cosmos and of everything within it — also of doing science — i.e. on account of the revelation of God in his Word concerning himself and his relation to all things — and more specifically on account of the Christian scientist's commitments to the general Scriptural truths concerned, that the Christian realizing his calling of doing science can in principle see the cosmos as it really is. 'In principle' because yet being a sinner in our dispensation of fall and redemption he can and does err. This implies that God's revelation and the light that the Scriptures shed on the cosmos and its coherent diversity and especially on man, his nature, place and role or calling within the cosmos, make the believing scientist in principle openminded, genuinely open to whatever his research field relevantly bids him. To this the sections C.a.—C.e. testify. This furthermore allows him in principle a balanced view of the fields of research as well as of his task and avoids all the onesidedness or extremes to which the '-isms' concerned fall prey. In addition to this, his fundamental contextual commitments make him aware of his creaturely limitations and of the significance and weight of his scientific calling — the latter being God that calls him to do science. Over against this the unbelieving scientist — although holding that he is openminded and fully open for his research field concerned — is closed and closed-minded in his research to the measure and extent that his fundamental contextual commitments pertain e.g. to the cosmos, to something within the cosmos,[15] to his so-called 'experience' or to some superstition or other; in other words, to the 'isms' concerned. The choice between the '-isms' is manifold, on account of the radical diversity within the cosmos. And it is understandable that the unbelievers' doing of science falls apart into conflicting fundamental commitments (e.g. schools). All this does not imply that there is no truth in the unbeliever's doing science; for no science can be done that is wholly based on the lie. What is relevant is the falsification of the research field concerned by the unbeliever, falling prey to his '-isms' on account of his invalid fundamental prescientific contextual commitments. And it does imply that whatever measure of truth there be in the unbeliever's scientific achievements, the believer has to accept it, but freed from its false foundation.

10.3. Since Thales up to today[16] a host of mutually conflicting views of what science, scientific criteria, scientific methods and scientificity are, have been, and will be promulgated. It is obvious from all the above that the Christian realizing his calling in science, may not evade the task of forming his proper Christian view of science and all this implies. Furthermore, he should avoid all kinds of syncretism, i.e. of fusing fundamental Christian contextual commitments with those of non-Christians — an error to which many Christians in many respects have fallen and do fall prey.

11. Appendices

11.1. Appendix A — On the division of Science
(Cf. my 1961, 1970 and 1971).

a. Francis Bacon, August Comte, Wilhelm Windelband and Heinrich Rickert, Becher, Hegel, Külpe, Mill, Wundt, Johannes Heesen, Abraham Kuyper, Herman Bavinck, Herman Dooyeweerd etc. submit different divisions of science in accordance with different principles of division. The following division of science according to a division of the knowable (or the fields of scientific research) seems to me to be the most appropriate. According to the Scriptures the first distinction is (the revelation of) God the Creator and creation; creation again can be subdivided into heaven (with its angels) and earth (or cosmos). Within the cosmos again we can distinguish its diversity (its 'parts', its facets, 'aspects' or particular groups of entities, processes, etc. belonging together). All these distinctions cohere (are mutually related). Accordingly we submit the following division of science into special sciences.

A. *Theology* — The science of the revelation of God (in his Word and in creation to be seen in the light of his Word-revelation) about himself and his relation to all 'things'.

A.a. *Ouranology (with Angelology)* — to be entrusted to the guardianship of Theology.

B. *Philosophy* — the science of the totality of the cosmos (as distinct from God — totality in the primary sense); of the radical diversity within the cosmos; of the universal coherence of the cosmic radical diversity (totality in the secondary sense); and of any original (i.e. irreducible) distinction within the cosmic radical diversity and its place, function and role within the totality of the cosmos.

C. *The* (natural, cultural, social and other) *Particular Sciences* ("Fachwissenschaften") each having a relevant "part" of the cosmos ("part" taken in a wide sense) as its research field.

D. *The Intermediary Sciences* (such as Chemical Physics, Physical Chemistry, Biochemistry, Chemical Biology and so forth).

E. The *Transversal Sciences* (Theory of Knowing or Epistemology, Theory of Knowledge or Gnoseology and the Theory (or Science) of Science).

b. The subject of this paper belongs to the Theory of Science. The theologian, philosopher, particular scientist ("Fachwissenschaftliche") and the intermediary scientist each has his relevant field of research, but at the same time knows (and should know responsibly) what he is doing; that it is he that does science and how he does it, what his view of science and of his research field is, what the appropriate methods are and how he uses them, *et cetera.* All this *(and more)* belongs to the research field of the theory of science and this implies that this field intersects the other fields of science transversally.[17] It implies too that each of the other sciences does contribute to the theory of science. Although the theory of science has its field of research (i.e. science itself) in its own right, each of the other sciences can and should contribute to the theory of science. It is accordingly wrong to reduce theory of science to philosophy of science, although philosophy of science[18] (on account of philosophy's field of research) can contribute a much larger share than the other sciences, whereas — as I see it — theology can and should give the deepest contribution.

c. As a last remark I only mention the necessary interrelation of and interaction between all sciences, the one needing — because all 'things' cohere — achievements of other sciences that it cannot investigate in its own research field. This, of course, in addition to each scientist's falling back on the usual (prescientific) knowledge concerned.

11.2. *Appendix B*[19] — *Arguments for the necessity of "Christian science"*

From among the many proofs or arguments for the right of existence

152

or for the necessity of "Christian science" we indicate the most important, without further clarification or commentary; keeping in mind that the list is yet incomplete.

(a) There are the proofs from inclusive perspectives.

(i) The believer has to do whatever he does or does not do — including the exercise of science — for the sake of the coming of God's Kingdom.

(ii) Christ has been given all authority in heaven and on earth and He is King of all things, also of the exercise of science.

(iii) The battle between the Kingdom of Light and the Kingdom of Darkness must be waged in every area of life, also that of science.

(iv) In all things done by man, also in his exercise of science, he faces a divine calling to which he has to respond to the honour and glory of God.

(v) Etcetera.

(b) There are the proofs from the prescientific world and life view.

(i) Historically and principially, science finds its origin in a world and life view and is in its main lines determined by it. The Christian, i.e. the Calvinist, has to practise his science from out of the presuppositions of his Calvinistic world and life view.

(ii) All practice of science is fundamentally based on religious ground motives. The Christian has to practise his science from out of the Scriptural religious ground motive of creation, sin and redemption.

(iii) Etcetera.

(c) There are proofs from out of the world of science seen as coming from the scientist as a human being, from out of science as knowledge, faith, thought, etc.

(i) Man practices science as a total person. In all formation of science the human and also the personal factor necessarily plays its role. The Christian scientist must also build his discipline as a total person.

(ii) There are those people who have been born again and those who have not. Those who are born again, face reality in a different fashion and in their exercise of science they are directed differently from those who are not born again. This means that those who are born again must build their science in a fundamentally different way.

(iii) Knowing and believing are not contradictory. All knowing is based on faith and in all practice of science faith and basically religious faith are at the foundations of such practice. This concerns faith in the very fundamental presuppositions which are co-determinative for the formation of science. A Christian scientist must practise his science responsibly from out of his Christian religious faith and the presuppositions that come along with this faith.

(iv) Christian faith reveals the horizon of reality and this horizon gives meaning and direction to science.

(v) Religious faith as such makes the practice of science possible. If there were no religious faith attitude, it would not be possible to exercise scholarship. This is of fundamental importance for the practice of christian scholarly activity.

(vi) By virtue of his being a christian, the christian meets fundamentally different problems from the non-christian. A different way of viewing our problems implies different kinds of research. Different kinds of research have different results at least in general.

(vii) A transcendental analytic investigation of thought demonstrates that it is the human self, his heart, which distinguishes between the logical and non-logical and ties them together. Such a self is either directed to God in faith, or in idolatry to something else. The believer must practise his science from out of being directed in his heart by God.

(vii) Etcetera.

(d) There are proofs from out of the knowable.

(i) Not only reality or the cosmos are knowable (matter, plants, animals and man —, nature, culture and religion), but also God's revelation in His Word concerning Himself and His relationship to all things. The christian scholar has to find in God's Word the principles that direct him in his scholarly activity.

(ii) God's Word-revelation sheds its lights on reality, that is the cosmos, and consequently casts its light on all fields of scholarly research and shows us the cosmos as it truly and really is. In a fundamental way this state of affairs brings new light to the matter, which our ordinary research of the cosmos outside of God's Word-revelation could not bring about. It is necessary that the Christian scholar give an account of this light because it is the Word of God which casts its light on the various fields of science.

(iii) The Christian scientist must practise his scholarship from the perspective of a reality that has been saved by Jesus Christ and from the perspective of a christian total view of reality.

(iv) Etcetera.

(c) There are proofs from science as result. No science can be completely selfsupporting. Every science needs to go to other

154

sciences, and to relate their findings to its own experiences in its own proper field. Precisely because of the unity of scholarship and the unity of scientific truth, we must promote a universal inter-action between the sciences, for borrowing and lending of discoveries and experiences, not merely between the various particular sciences ("Fachwissenschaften") amongst themselves, but also between the particular sciences and philosophy and between theology and the particular sciences as well as philosophy. The exercise of christian scholarship requires mutual interaction between christian particular sciences, Calvinistic philosophy and reformed theology. The most fundamental interaction required is that between theology and the other disciplines.

This is not the place to critically test the validity of all the arguments above, and many more. We simlpy direct attention to the following. Some of these proofs will only speak to the Christian believer. Others of these proofs may make critical dialogue with others possible. It is also true that we have to pay attention to the different contexts within which proofs may be valid. For example, proofs from the perspective of regeneration are directed to the actual existence of christian scholarship and not immediately to its truth. The proof which is based on the fact that all sciences must be practised in the light of God's Word, is directed to the truth requirement of christian scholarship. For scientific truth means that scientific knowledge corresponds to what is scientifically knowable. In fundamental respects the light of God's revelation on all the fields of research is necessary for this kind of truth. Several of these truths show a religiously neutral kind of scholarship is im-possible. From this point onward we can discover indirect proofs for christian scholarship. For example, the demonstration that in fundamental respects also, other ways of doing science are not religiously neutral and in addition end in dialectics and antinomies.

---

l   The acknowledgement of 'usual' knowledge and of 'prescientific' as that 'part' of usual knowledge that co-determines basically and in outline the results of science, obviates on the one hand Popma's objection to the term 'prescientific' knowledge (a term that according to him underrates what I call usual knowledge and exaggerates the meaning of scientific knowledge) and at the same time my objection against substituting for 'pre-scientific' knowledge the term 'non-scientific' knowledge, because a negative predication should be avoided and Popma's distinction of 'non-scientific' and 'scientific' knowledge is too much of a bifurcation, not doing justice to the mutual relation of usual and scientific knowledge. Kuhn on the other hand acknowledges prescientific knowledge in the sense I use 'usual' knowledge (in which science has its roots), but also in the sense of his paradigm as an exemplar, the latter being genuine scientific achievements presupposed by the actual doing of science. This justifiable distinction I can meet by using the term 'prescientific' for the former case and 'pre-scientific' for the latter.

2 The succession (as well as the intermediate stages) of usual knowledge, prescientific knowledge, scientific knowledge integrated within usual knowledge, popularized scientific knowledge and scientific knowledge could be illustrated by a continuous colour strip, the one end being e.g. blue and the other green.

3 "Man lernt nicht was Schwimmen heiszt durch eine Abhandlung über das Schwimmen; was Schwimmen heiszt sagt uns der Sprung in den Strom".

4 I use both the terms 'knowledge' and 'knowing' on the one hand in the sense of the whole knowledge concern (A—D); but on the other hand, 'knowing' as the activity and 'knowledge' as the result of this activity. According to the syntactical context within which these terms appear, it may be clear in what sense the term concerned is used.

5 See my 1961, 1970, 1971. The wide sense of 'observation' includes *inter alia* observation by means of the senses, psychical introspection, psychical extrospection, experience of resistance, instuition of the selfevident (e.g. principles), religious faith in God's Word revelation and so forth. This is only meant as an incomplete illustrative summary of types of observation.

5a See my 1961, 1965, 1970, 1971.

6 See my 1967, 1968/69, 1971.

7 The terms 'space', 'time', energy, mass velocity of movement have different meanings within the contextual views ('paradigms') of the Newtonian and the Einsteinian mechanics — as Kuhn and others have pointed out.

8 We may substitute our term 'contextual view' for Kuhn's term 'paradigm', considering that the term 'paradigm' has become a standard phrase in e.g. the physical, biological, psychological, sociological sciences, in economics, in the theory of arts etc.; but then it should be kept in mind that our term 'conceptual view' does not coincide with Kuhn's term 'paradigm' in every respect.

9 Kuhn says of his 'paradigm' that it allows us to see how nature is populated and how the populations behave. But he also speaks of anomalies observed that do not fit in the paradigm. Our contextual view (as well as Kuhn's paradigmatic view) is taken in a complementary inseparable double sense of a. the view that the scientist has of his research field and b. the view that the research field presents to the scientist.

10 Even for Popper, I contend that he will never genuinely try to falsify his principle of falsification nor his commitments to critical relationalism and inter-individual humanism.

11 Antinomies occur and paradoxes arise, also e.g. in the case of reducing one cosmic dimension (of e.g. modalities, of events, of idiostand structures, of values) to another (Cf. my 1961, 1970).

12 Restricting myself to the contribution of Calvinists to philosophy — and this holds, I think, for other sciences as well — how many polemical discussions between the older and current generations and again in our time between adherents to a cosmonomic, a suppositionalistic and a cosmoscreatic philosophy in Holland, Northern America as well as in South Africa testify to an imcompatibility and an incommensurability of the views concerned as well as a speaking at cross-purposes, the one misunderstanding what the other contends, notwithstanding that they all commit

themselves to the same fundamental faith in the Word-revelation of God.

13 Cf. V. Hepp — his 1937.

14 Cf. my 1965; 1970 and 1971. There are even no neutral methods, because each presupposes that which is manipulated by it and the purpose for which it is used; whereas the view of the manipulated and that of the purpose are always seen within principially distinct contexts.

15 Secularization, i.e. doing the cosmos (and man within it) justice but without excluding God's revelation of himself and his relationship to all things, we may not oppose. Secularism excludes God's revelation and views the cosmos (and man within it) as independent of God or absolutises it; and this is unacceptable.

16 Currently there is a veritable crisis of the foundations of science. After logical empiricism (logical positivism) has had an almost monopolistic dictatorial sway over the theory (philosophy) of science during the first 50—60 years of our century, an extensive and intensive reaction (I may almost say: revolution) has set in during the past one to two decades. The new opponents of logical empiricism — each developing science-theory in a new way — include inter alia Popper and the Popperians (especially Lakatos), the American-English Historical School (Hanson, Toulmin, Kuhn and Feyerabend, to whom we may add Polanyi), the Frankfurt school (e.g. Habermas, Apel), the Neo-Marxists, the Göteborg School (e.g. Törnebohm, Radnitzky); furthermore contributions of individual scientists (e.g. Husserl, Scheler ((especially his socio-theory of science)), Heidegger, Bertalannfy); and many science theorists trying to intermediate between the schools concerned, especially between logical empiricism and the historical school. Striking is the basic disagreement on the nature and the foundation of science, its presuppositions, its criteria, its justifiability, its rationality, its historicity and so forth. Moreover the majority of science theorists acknowledge the necessity of presuppositions (foreknowledge, precognitions, paradigms, etc.) when science is done. During the monopolistic reign of logical empiricism our view of science was simply ignored as fundamentally unscientific and prejudiced. In current times there is a better chance of coming to grips with otherminded science theorists.

17 Formerly I called theory of science an 'interscience'; the term 'transversal science' seems to me to be more appropriate.

18 More than a decade and a half ago I became convinced that theory of science should not be restricted to nor equated with philosophy of science. It was an encouraging experience to find that e.g. Popper, Toulmin, Kuhn, Radnitzky and others also claim that science theory is a science in its own right and neither reducible to nor wholly equatable with philosophy of science.

19 This is a translation (not by myself) of my 1969, p. 244—7.

SELECTED BIBLIOGRAPHY

Hepp, V. (1937): *De basis der eenheid der wetenschap.* Kok, Kampen.

Kisiel, Th. and Johnson, G. (1974): *New Philosophies of Science in the USA;* in: Zeitschrift für Allgemeine Wissenschaftslehre; V/1.

Kuhn, Thomas (1961): *The function of Dogma in Scientific Research;* in: Scientific Change; Ed. A. S. Crombie.

Kuhn, Thomas (1962): *The structure of scientific revolutions;* IEU, II, 2.

Kuhn, Thomas (1970): Reprint with *Postscript.*

Kuhn, Thomas (1970a): *Reflections on my critics,* in: Criticism and the Growth of knowledge; Eds. Lakatos/Musgrave.

Kuhn, Thomas (1970b): *Notes on Lakatos;* in: Boston Studies in the Philosophy of Science; VIII.

Kuhn, Thomas (1974): *Second Thoughts on Paradigms;* in: The Structure of Scientific Theories; Ed. F. Suppe.

Lakatos, Imre (1970): *Falsification and Methodology in Scientific Research Programs;* in: Criticism and Growth of Knowledge; Eds. Musgrave/Lakatos.

Lakatos, Imre (1970a): *History of Science and its Rational Reconstructions;* in: Boston Studies VIII.

Musgrave, A. E. (1971): *Kuhn's Second Thoughts;* Br.J.o.Ph. Sc.

Polanyi, M. (1958/62): *Personal Knowledge;* Harper Torchbooks.

Radnitzky, G. (1968/73): *Contemporary Schools of Metascience;* Henry Regnery Coy., Chicago.

Scheffler, I. (1972): *Postscript on Kuhn;* Ph.o.Sc. 39/3.

Shapere, D. (1964): *Structure of Scientific Revolutions;* Phil. Review.

Shapere, D. (1967): *Meaning and Scientific Change;* in: Mind and Cosmos; Ed. Colodny.

Shapere, D. (1971): *The Paradigm Concept;* Science (American Ass. for the Advancement of Science); 172 (3894).

Stoker, H. G. (1961/1969): *Beginsels en Metodes in die Wetenskap;* De Jong, Johannesburg.

Stoker, H. G. (1962): *Eenheid en Differensiasie in Wysbegeerte en Wetenskapsleer;* in: Koers, Universiteit, Potchefstroom.

Stoker, H. G. (1965): *Outlines of a Deontology of Scientific Method;* in: Dooyeweerd's Festschrift 'Philosophy and Christianity'; Kok, Kampen.

Stoker, H. G. (1967): *Die eenheid van die wetenskap;* in: Referate — die S.A. Akademie vir Wetenskap en Kuns.

Stoker, H. G. (1968/9): *Die eenheid van die wetenskap;* Philosophia Reformata, Jrg. 33/4, Kok, Kampen.

Stoker, H. G. (1969): *Christelike wetenskap — 'n noodwendigheid;* in: Die atoomeeu — 'in U lig'; Universiteit, Potchefstroom.

Stoker, H. G. (1970): Diverse artikels in Oorsprong en Rigting, II; Tafelberguitgewers, Kaapstad.

Stoker, H. G. (1971): *C. van Til's Theory of Knowledge;* in: Van Til's Festschrift 'Jerusalem and Athens'; Presb. and Ref. Publ. Co.

Stoker, H. G. (1970/71); *Een en ander oor metode;* Bulletin van die S.A. Vereniging vir Christelike Wetenskap; Ed. University, Potchefstroom.

Toulmin, S. (1967): *Conceptual Revolutions in Science;* Synthese 17 (75—91).

Toulmin, S. (1970): *Normal and Revolutionary Science;* in: Criticism and Growth of knowledge; Eds. Lakatos/Musgrave.

Toulmin, S. (1971): *Rediscovering History;* Encounter 36.

Toulmin, S. (1972): *Human Understanding;* I; Clarenden, Oxford.

Christian scholars and Christian science

Prof. Dr. J. Chris Coetzee (Sr.)

1. Any scholar or learned man professes a certain field of knowledge or a specified science. He studies and investigates, develops and systematizes his particular field of knowledge. He "creates", so to say, a science, and in one way or another he proclaims his field of knowledge, its development and expansion. The more he develops his field of knowledge, the closer becomes the association between himself and his science. There is a decided, unmistakable and indissoluble association between scholar and science, they belong inseparably together. This is so because the scholar is the maker of a science, and the science is his "creation".

And a Christian scholar also professes a certain field of knowledge. And he, like every other scholar, has a particular approach to this field of knowledge. The Christian scholar alone studies and investigates, develops and systematizes his particular field of Christian knowledge. He can not decide for a so-called "pure" science, he can not maintain his Christian faith in professing such a non-Christian science. He can not even come to the aid of such a non-Christian science with any tactical means, apologetic subterfuge, theological sophistry. Scholar and science once again condition each other, they run, as it were, together.

There are fundamental and existential problems facing the Christian scholar in his study of a Christian science.

2. The Christian scholar is a scholar but at the same time a Christian. He believes in the fact of the creation of man and his world by an Almighty God, of the fall of man through disobedience, and of his redemption by a Saviour Jesus Christ, the Son of God, and by the Holy Spirit — that is, he believes in the Triune God, Father, Son and Holy Spirit. He believes that God created man in His image and after His likeness, that God gave man at his creation life-long dominion over His other creatures: world, plants, animals, and that God gave man also the ability to rule over His creation. This ability consists mainly in knowing the other creatures: man must and can know creation to exercise dominion over it, and this only to the

greater glory of God, the Creator. Man is called upon to strive after knowledge, to increase and develop it to the utmost extent. The Christian scholar then is a scholar who pursues and practises his profession as a scientist in order to know God's creation and thus to honour his God.

He believes that God has revealed Himself in His Word to man, that is in the Holy Bible, but also in nature which is also God's creation. The Christian scholar is therefore a scholar of God's Word and of His creation: he must and can be a student of God's Word as His special revelation and of God's world as His general revelation.

3. Science is knowledge with certain special qualities: it is clearly defined and limited to a specific area of knowledge, systematic and logically structured, proven and verified, verifiable and valid, reliable and applicable. Science is in fact a mental structure, an intellectual building with a fair and firm foundation and a solid consistent superstructure. The foundation on which the building is erected, is a firmly formulated word system of basic ideas or thoughts. The superstructure, i.e. the building itself, is erected with certain material, and according to certain clearly defined, principles.

The actual foundation of any science is a clearly defined philosophy of life or a fixed belief. Hence we have in fact different schools of science. A Christian science then is a science with God's Word, the Bible, as its sound foundation or basis, in other words, based on Jesus Christ as the Saviour of a lost mankind and of nature, and to the glory and honour of God Triune. A non-Christian science has then a non-Christian foundation: a Jewish, a Greek, a Mohammedan, an evolutionistic or an idealistic, or realistic or humanistic basis. On this foundation then is erected either a Christian science or a non-Christian science.

For the erection of the mental structure or building, the science, there are at least the following guiding principles and material:

(a) A special life and world view — Christian, non-Christian, idealistic, realistic, humanistic, evolutionistic;
(b) a specially gifted and developed mind (high intelligence, love, will, etc.);
(c) the writings or work of other scholars in this particular field and one's own previous study and investigation;
(d) command over a scientific method of study and research — the application of trained mental qualities such as observation, perception, imagination, memory, thinking, and also clear aim(s) for the mental structure: immediate, intermediate, final aims.

Sciences are usually classified into two large groups: mental-moral sciences and physical-natural sciences. The first group gives special attention to matters of the mind, the second to matters of physical nature. But this distinction is only relative: some sciences are equally well mental and physical (Mathematics, Psychology) and all sciences are in fact products of mental activity. The distinction is sometimes qualified as humanistic and naturalistic: the first has to do with man as creature, the second with nature as created.

But these distinctions are actually only an aid for convenience of reference. And both groups are equally the field of research and study for Christian and non-Christian students. In the Middle Ages when universities arose the distinction was made between the *artes* (linguistic studies: grammar, dialectic, rhetoric; and mathematical studies: arithmetic, geometry, astronomy and music) and the *scientiae* (theology, law, medicine). A curious modern problem for the Christian scholar is the classification of theology (a science, an art, or . . .), because all the other *artes* and *scientiae* (mental and physical) are concerned with God's creatures, (inanimate world, plant, animal, man). All *artes* and *scientiae* are fields of study for the Christian scholar.

4. In conclusion I may say that there must be and there are Christian scholars, side by side with non-Christian scholars. The Christian scholar is fully a scientist with the Word of God as the foundation of his science, with a Christian life and world view, Christian aim(s) in study and research, and also a Christian special methodology. The Christian scholar is in all respects the equal of the non-Christian but has a Christian foundation and a Christian life and world view, whereas the non-Christian scholar has a non-Christian foundation and life and world view.

Therefore, I know and posit the Christian scholar

(a) has a special calling to know God's creation,
(b) has been given by God the mental and physical ability to fulfil his calling, and
(c) has one final aim: to know, to love and to serve the Creator and the creation.

Therefore the Christian scholar must, can, and does profess a Christian science. For, His is the Kingdom, and the Power, and the Glory, for ever.

What are the problems affecting the development of Christian science in the modern world, specifically in the case of non-Christian countries?

Prof. Dr. Ryuzo Hashimoto

I would like to present some problems which I have had in mind for some time. My presentation will be mainly from a practical point of view.

1. *Introduction*

According to the statistics recorded in the *Britannica Book of the Year* (1974), the percentage of Christian people on the six continents is as follows: Europe 51.6%, South America 87.3%, North America 41.4%, Oceania 77.7%, Africa 12%, Asia 4%. These statistics show that Asia has become the most un-Christianized area of the world. The percentage of Christian people in Asia is somewhat different from country to country. The *Japan Christian Year Book* for 1975 gives the statistics of the percentage of Christians in South East Asia as follows: Philippines 90%, Sri-Lanka 8.6%, Hongkong 8%, Indonesia 8%, Korea 7%, Taiwan 5%, Burma 3%, Malaysia 2.5%, India 2%, Pakistan 1.4%, Bangladesh 1%, Japan 1%, Thailand 0.5%. Unlike some countries in Asia where Christian mission activities are to some degree restricted, there is complete freedom for mission activities in Japan; and yet the percentage of Christians in this country is the smallest in Asia today. Japan may be considered a typical non-Christian country.

I have had the privilege of visiting some of the churches in other Asian countries in the past, and I was able to discover many problems common to these countries, problems which I did not find when I visited the churches in the United States and Europe. But on the other hand, I must confess that these common problems vary so greatly from country to country, that it seems impossible to generalize about them. Dr. Harvey Smit, one of my colleagues at Kobe Reformed Seminary, writes as follows: "Another common misconception in the West is that there is an oriental mind or way of thinking shared by all the people of the East: Indian, Chinese, Korean, Malaysian, and Japanese. But anyone who has carried on a discussion with an Indian and a Japanese cannot help but realize how completely different their ways of thinking are, and anyone who has lived for any time in China or Japan recognizes the basic differences of social attitude and the ways of thinking between these two cultures. Dr. Hajime Nakamura in his important study, *Ways of Thinking of Eastern Peoples,* finds, on careful examination, 'no features of the ways of thinking exclusively shared by East Asians as a whole but rather very distinct and differing cultures'." ("The Meeting of the Japanese Mind with the Christian Faith". *International Reformed Bulletin,* No. 43, 1970.) This is a precise analysis of the Asian situation. It is not possible therefore for me to point out common problems shared equally by all of these Asian countries. Instead, I will try to present some of the problems which have hindered the development of Christian science in Japan. When I speak of the development of Christian science, I am not thinking of the development of Christian science in general, but science as understood from the Calvinistic point of view.

2. *Problems which have hindered the development of Christian science in Japan*

The Japan Calvinist Association holds a national conference once each year. Last year, the theme of the conference was: *Is Theistic Culture Possible in Japan?* and this year's theme was: *The Cultural Task of the Calvinists in Japan.* There is a reason why we selected such themes for two successive years. The Reformed Church in Japan, to which I myself belong, at its Constituting Assembly in 1946, delineated two objectives which it would seek to carry out in Japan. The first one was formulated as follows: "Henceforth, for the reconstruction of a better Japan, we must in all sincerity subject ourselves to the will of the omnipotent and righteous God who rules history. In obedience to His commands we must respect God and love our neighbours as ourselves. We must make the Glory of God our highest end, not only in the field or spiritual culture but even in such mundane matters as in 'Whatsoever ye eat, or drink, or whatsoever ye do'. That this theistic life and world view is the only sure foundation on which a new Japan can be built is *the First Point* zealously maintained by the Reformed Church in Japan". The second objective was expressed as follows: "It is our firm conviction that the Oneness, or Unity, of the 'Invisible Church' should be made concrete on earth as the one 'Visible Church' with provisions of One Confession of Faith, One Church Government and One Good Life. This is the *Second Point* maintained by the Reformed Church in Japan". These are the two objectives which we resolved to carry out in our nation. As far as I know, the Reformed Church in Japan is the only Reformed body in Asia which has stated such a cultural task in its official church declaration.

We believe that the second task was partially carried out during the first twenty years following the establishment of our church through preparing a Confession of Faith, a Form of Government, a Book of Discipline and a Directory of Worship. But upon self reflection, we have become aware that the first task has not yet been fully discussed by the church. Concerning this objective, Prof. Shigeru Yoshioka, the former president of Kobe Reformed Seminary, writes in his recent book, *The Tradition and the Faith of the Reformed Church in Japan* as follows: "In our declaration, this theistic world and life view is comprehended in three points. The first point is to worship only one true God rejecting all kinds of idol worship in the religious field, the second point is to establish the theistic culture in the cultural field, and the third point is to assert the principle of separation of church and state in the political and social fields".

We carried out this first point by confirming our Church Motto which says: "To build the church as the pillar of truth destroying every kind of superstition and atheism in thought and life". Like the peoples in Athens of Paul's day, Japanese are very superstitious. It is said that the religious population of the Japanese nation is two or three times larger than the real population. Dr. Prunner of Vienna University once spoke of Japan as the Exposition of World Religions. Therefore, the Japanese Government was shocked by the results of its nation-wide investigation (1972) of the religious consciousness of youth between the ages of 18 and 24. Only 18.9% gave affirmative answers, 5,8% denied religion and 74% were indifferent to any kind of religion. Reformed Christians in Japan are strongly opposed to superstition and atheism. The task which is expressed in the third point is to be further explicated in our thirtieth anniversary Declaration of Faith concerning the Church and State. In this declaration, to be issued in April 1976, the Lordship of Christ over church and state and in every field of society is stressed. Concerning the second point we understand that this kind of task should be carried out, not through the institutional church, but through a non-ecclesiastical organization like the Japan Calvinist

Association. This is the reason why the Japan Calvinist Association has been the agency through which we have been trying to accomplish this task; trying to meet the calling of our Lord as expressed in our Declaration. Since its start as the Calvinistic Students' Movement in 1950, this organization has been dedicated to the task of developing a Christian science in Japan. This association has a membership of 170. Numbers are still small but, fortunately, 34 members are professors or instructors in colleges, universities or institutions. I have tried to discuss with some of these professors, men in different fields of study, what problems they are facing as Christian scholars.

3. *Christianity and oriental philosophy*

First, I would like to consider the problem of Oriental Philosophy. Modern science was born in the Christian Occidental World. Science was possible only in a framework which presupposes the God of Creation, a God who rules over all of creation by means of laws which He has ordained. These scientists had the common conviction that there are universal laws in the natural phenomena which man must discover. But as Prof. Tetsuo Tsuji showed so clearly in his book, *Scientific Thought in Japan,* there is no such awareness that there are universal laws in nature in the traditional thought of the Japanese people. Therefore, it is said that there was a kind of technology in Japan, but no science before Western science was introduced. It has been a common opinion that oriental philosophy was incapable of developing modern science. But recently a kind of nostalgia has been felt toward Oriental philosophy not only in the field of religion and philosophy but also in the field of science. Prof. W. K. Heisenberg, a world famous physical scientist, writes in his book, *The Revolution in Modern Science,* that the great contribution to theoretical physics made by Japanese scholars after World War II indicates some relation between traditional oriental philosophy and the philosophical substance of quantum physics. This opinion has been supported by many Japanese scientists. Dr. Hideki Yukawa of Kyoto University, a Nobel prize winner who proved the existence of the mesotron, says: "Oriental philosophy has been connected very closely with top knowledge of physics". Others say that only Oriental philosophy surmounts the difficulty of the Occidental science. Thus Oriental philosophy has been re-evaluated even in the field of science in Japan. The Soka-Gakkai (Creation Value Association), whose adherents increased very quickly after the war, up to seven million families, established its own university last year. A Symposium of the members of the faculty has been published recently, in which one scientist mentions that the Idea of Mu (Nothingness) of

Buddhist Philosophy will prepare the way to solve the limitation of modern physics. "The Universe itself is a being without beginning. As Buddhist terminology MUSHI-MUSHU (No Beginning-No Ending) shows, the Universe itself were not created by someone supernatural. The absolute one God as Creator of the Universe, which Christianity has taught, does not exist anywhere". A naked challenge to Christian theism!

Recently, the Christian view of nature has been charged with responsibility for the disastrous air and sea pollution in Japan. There have been some strong opinions that the destruction of the environment has come out of the Western view of nature and science, a view which has its roots in Christianity. They say that in Western thought there is good humanism in the injunctions to love all men but that there is no love towards nature. Such critical opinions even come from outside Japan. Prof. Lynn White of the University of California, seems to support such a view. In his article entitled: *The Historical Roots of our Ecology Crisis,* which is contained as an appendix to Dr. Francis A. Shaeffer's book: *Pollution and the Death of Man,* he writes as follows: "We would seem to be headed toward conclusions unpalatable to many Christians. Since both science and technology are blessed words in our contemporary vocabulary, some may be happy at the notions, first, that, viewed historically, modern science is an extrapolation of natural theology, and second, that modern technology is at least partly to be explained as an Occidental, voluntarist realization of the Christian Dogma of man's transcendence of, and rightful mastery over, nature. But as we now recognize, somewhat over a century ago science and technology — hitherto quite separate activities — joined to give mankind powers, which to judge by many of the ecologic effects, are out of control. If so, Christianity bears a huge burden of guilt ... What we do about ecology depends on our ideas of the man — nature relationship. More science and more technology are not going to get us out of the present ecological crisis until we find a new religion, or rethink our old one. The beatniks, who are basic revolutionaries of our time, show a sound instinct in their affinity for Zen Buddhism, which conceives of the man-nature relationship as nearly the mirror image of the Christian view. Zen, however, is as deeply conditioned by Asian history as Christianity is by the experience of the West, and I am dubious of its viability among us". Thus the Christian view of man and nature has been much challenged in many areas. There is an urgent need for us to have our own philosophy of nature and culture. Buddhist philosophy of nature is incapable of giving due appreciation of nature. By eternalizing nature, Japanese people posit an infinite restoring power of nature. And this is at least one reason why they have let their natural environment become extremely polluted. It is a Calvinistic view of nature, I believe, that offers the solution in this ecological crisis. For, as A. Kuyper pointed out: "Thereby of course Calvinism puts an end once and for all to contempt for the world, neglect of temporal and undervaluation of cosmical things. Cosmical life has regained its worth not at the expense of things eternal, but by virtue of its capacity as God's handiwork and as a revelation of God's attributes" ("Calvinism and Science" in *Lectures on Calvinism*).

4. *Christian science as a bulwark against pagan philosophy*

To confront pagan philosophy, it is necessary to develop a true Christian science. Without undertaking this task, Gospel Evangelization will achieve only half measures. This has been one of the big shortcomings among the so-called Evangelicals in Japan. Dr. Yoshitomo Yamanaka, president of the Japan Calvinist Association, pointed out that the biggest hindrance to the development of a Christian science is the Dualism deeply rooted in the Japanese mind and so prevalent among Protestant Christians. He discussed this point in his book: *Religion and Social Ethics*.

His analysis is very interesting and highly esteemed even by non-christian scholars. He complains that many evangelical Christians hate philosophy. This antagonism toward philosophy invited a simplistic separation between faith and science, theology and philosophy, religion and culture, gospel and theism. According to Prof. Yamanaka, this dualism was planted in the Japanese mind by Dutch merchants in the seventeenth century. Western science was first introduced to the Japanese people by Roman Catholic missionaries in the latter half of the 16th century. Roman Catholicism is dualistic but not a dualism. They did not separate their religion from their science, trade and policy. Though the Japanese rulers were eager to trade with the Roman Catholic countries, they feared the religion which was behind them. Then came the Protestant Dutch merchants who persuaded the Shognate rulers that in order to avoid invasion they should not trade with the Roman Catholic countries. The Dutch merchants agreed with the Shognate not to bring their religion to the Japanese people. Thus the Roman Catholics were banned in 1641 and only the Dutch people were allowed to continue trading. And Japan closed her ports to all foreign countries for two hundred years. Prof. Yamanaka pointed out that this same dualism of faith and trade can be seen in other fields. Ran-Gaku, meaning Dutch science, taught the Japanese people to separate science from faith and religion. But is was difficult to develop science without having some kind of philosophy, and consequently, they put Confucianism in the place of Christianity. This was known as Wakon-Yosai (Japanese Spirit — Western Skill). This prevailing type of dualism has been a great hindrance to the indigenization of Christianity in Japan.

Prof. Toshio Satoh of Tokyo Union Seminary complains that he could not find any distinctively Christian approach in the articles of some Christian scholars in the field of social science, which he collected for a Christian encyclopedia. Still, he writes: "Faith is faith, science is science" *(Faith and Social Science)*. This type of dualism naturally results in an idea of neutrality in science. And this idea of neutrality separated from faith is in agreement with the common Japanese feeling about religion. Dr. Harvey Smit pointed this out by saying: "Common among most Japanese is the view that religion is a matter of individual feeling and emotion rather than of rational teaching, and the adoption of a religion is strictly individual, emotional matter. Christianity is also conceived as an individual religion in Japan". Therefore, they stick to this dualism. Their faith, if it is to remain a pure faith, must stay away from science, and science must remain a wholly neutral zone protected against any invasion by faith. Irrationalism in religious feeling and rationalism in scientific thought have lived together in Japanese minds. If we connect our faith with science, we are accused of being fanatics. Still those who say this feel no problem in building a snake-worshipping shrine on the roof of a wholly computerized factory.

What should we do in this situation in order to develop a Christian science? The most effective step would seem to be to establish a Christian university. But this is very unrealistic in contemporary Japan. It seems to me rather that it would be harmful to establish a Christian university where there are no strong churches capable of furnishing competent, confessing Christian professors. Also from a financial point of view it would seem to be impossible to establish a new Christian college or university in Japan. Modern science demands a huge amount of money if it is to maintain high academic levels. Prof. Halacy once illustrated the modern flood of information as follows: "A four inch high graph paper is enough to express the technological progress from the dawn of civilization to 1945 but a thirteen story building's height graph paper is necessary to express its progress from 1945 to 1960" *(Nine Roads to Tomorrow)*. The computerization of information is indispensable. Moreover, the rapid development of group research or group projects has made the scale of such types of research much greater than before. In the case of what we call big science, the Government or huge enterprises set up the project, direct the research, and make use of the results. Dr. Yukawa warned that this situation resulted in a loss of subjectivity amongst scientific researchers. What can Christian scientists do in such a time of crisis in the field of science?

Dr. Stanford Reid once wrote in an article on *The Christian Professor in the Secular University,* that the best witness which the Christian can give through his publications is to show that Christians have the ability to do both scholarly research and analysis. But I think Christian scholars should do more on the basis of their research, that is, they should give new direction or change the stream of scientific thought. Dr. Yukawa pointed out that the most serious development of science has been seen in the field of molecular biology which is almost able to control the life phenomenon. He says: "We must control the development of science or else mankind will be destroyed". This is one of the most dangerous fields in science today. Prof. Munemitsu Tomoeda of Kanazawa State University, a professor of molecular biology, warned about the same dangerous tendency in the field of chemical biology in Japan *(Faith and Science,* no. 5). In this article entitled *Life Seen Through Molecular Biology,* he describes how he, as a scientist, came to confess the God of the Bible. One of the Japanese papers reported the decisive influence exerted by Prof. Reiji Okazaki of Nagoya State University. He was also a Christian belonging to a conservative group. Unfortunately, he died this month of an A-Bomb disease with which he was infected in Hiroshima thirty years ago. In the countries where Christians are in the minority, it is very important to produce such academics, who can act as good Christian witnesses in their own field.

5. *Christian and non-christian scholarship*

We must always remember that from the beginning of our human history the sons of Cain produced more cultural products than the sons of Abel. We know that we are not capable of keeping up with non-Christian levels of scholarship. But the valuable results of the scientific enterprise of non-Christians are based on the reality of God's creation and this is not destroyed by the false interpretations of man. Therefore, the results which are obtained by all scholars may be accepted. However, this does not change the fact that the Christian principle is the real foundation of these results. Only Christian eyes can see this situation and the real meaning of these results. By Faith we understand what nature means to all mankind and the true position of man in nature. Only Christians can show the real purpose of science and thus save science from its suicidal secularization. As Dr. Herman Dooyeweerd has said: "It is forgotten that the secularization of life would have been impossible apart from the secularization of science, and that this scientific secularization has taken place under the overwhelming influence of the religious secularization" *(The Secularization of Science)*. Our task is important, urgent and unrewarded in this world. But we must perform this task with all our powers because we know that our sovereign Lord commands us to do so. "Wherefore, my beloved brethren, be ye steadfast, unmovable, always abounding in the work of the Lord, forasmuch as ye know that your labour is not in vain in the Lord" (1 Cor. 15 : 57).

Problems affecting the development of Christian education in non-Christian countries — Indonesia

Prof. A. H. Nichols

I. *Indonesia — an orientation*

Indonesia, formerly known as the Dutch East Indies, is a farflung archipelago whose people insist that its 3 000 islands are united, not divided, by water! Out of a total population of 130 000 000 the fertile island of Java alone sustains 80 000 000 inhabitants. Like other countries of Asia, Indonesia is caught in the throes of drastic economic, social and cultural change. The resultant tensions are heightened by very real ethnic, linguistic and religious differences. In fact the nation's present condition, and main problems, are symbolized by the national motto: "Bhinoeka Tunggal Ika": Diversity Becoming Unity.

Although 85% of the population are Muslims the constitution gives freedom to the other religious groups: Christians, Hindus and Buddhists. This religious pluralism is guaranteed by the state ideology known as Panca-Sila, the five principles promulgated in the 1945 Constitution. They are:

1. Belief in Almighty God.
2. Humanitarianism based on justice and respect.
3. National Unity of Indonesia (nationalism).
4. Democracy wisely guided by means of representation and mutual agreement.
5. Social justice for all the people of Indonesia.

Until now the Pancasila Ideology has survived despite the opposition of both the Communists and the advocates of an Islamic State.

The first "sila" is increasingly emphasized in the nation's schools. From one point of view this government policy protects the rights of the Christian minority. From another point of view it strengthens the tendencies to syncretism already inherent in Indonesian (or more particularly Javanese) culture.

After the abortive Communist coup in 1965 and its bloody aftermath, Christianity enjoyed a period of swift growth. Now there are over ten million Christians, three quarters of whom are Protestants. That number, however, includes many thousands of new converts whose understanding of the gospel is inevitably shallow.

The oldest form of Christianity in Indonesia is Roman Catholicism. Francis Xavier and other Roman Catholic missionaries laboured in the Moluccas during the early sixteenth century, under Portuguese protection. Today, due largely to its impressive educational work, the Roman Catholic denomination is vigorous, widely dispersed, solidly rooted and actively engaged in national life.

But it is the Protestant churches that constitute the largest segment of the Christian community. They are the fruit of Dutch, German, Swiss and American Missions and the majority could be said to stand in the Reformed stream (e.g. the Heidelberg Confession is still widely used). Most are strongly traditional without however necessarily being biblical. In recent years there has also been fast growth of churches outside the Reformed family — for example those of Pentecostal and Mennonite background. These latter groups tend to be much more flexible. However, it is no doubt a tribute to the dominant Calvinist strain that Indonesian Christians have shown an exemplary awareness of their prophetic role in the nation's life, not least in the field of education.

Thus Dr. O. Notohamidjojo, first Rector of "Satya Wacana" Christian University has sought to encourage the development of a Christian mind which would understand and conquer both traditional monism and Western secularism.

Before we consider the legacy of the traditional culture which conditions the way in which all outside ideas (Western and Non-Western) are received, it might be helpful to remind ourselves of certain Biblical teachings whose familiarity unfortunately obscures their startling implications.

II. *What were the Biblical truths which historically promoted the development of science and culture in Europe?*[1]

Although in the contemporary modern world discussions about the relationship of Science and Religion assume that the two are irreconcilable antagonists there is no doubt that modern science is largely a product of the impact of the Bible on Western thought.

While it is true that we owe to the Greeks the mental tools of our science e.g. logic, mathematics and experimentation, their conception of the world as a living organism, the divine source of all living being (including their Gods!) was totally incapable of producing the scientific development we have inherited.

Despite faulty exegesis by church leaders who resisted new scientific theories (e.g. about the movement of the earth or the age of the world) it can be argued that it was the triumph of a biblical worldview that made possible the rise of modern science particularly after the reformation. This is all the more remarkable because the Bible itself gives us no scientific data which could provide the basis for the amazing scientific progress we have witnessed.

What were the relevant Biblical truths which dawned afresh on Western civilization in the sixteenth century after some centuries of obscurity resulting from an unholy matrimony with Platonism and Aristotelianism?

1. *God.* Firstly there is the doctrine of the sovereign almighty creator of the Old Testament whom Paul proclaimed to the Athenian philosophers. His powerful word has brought all things into existence from nothingness and he still rules and sustains all creation.

2. *Nature.* The Bible knows no "Nature" with a capital N. The "Nature" of paganism and of Greek philosophy has been de-deified. It is no longer feared or adored but simply regarded as the handiwork of God to be admired, studied and managed.

3. *Man* is no longer merely an integral and insignificant element of the cosmic totality. He is the unique image of God who is set in the world to investigate and rule it. In the Bible, God and nature are no longer both opposed to man. On the contrary God and man together confront nature.

4. *History.* There is no longer an eternal cycle of nature or cycle of history. Time and history are, like the universe, created by God and therefore completely determined and governed by His Will. Thus the history of the world moves towards its appointed destination and in every detail reflects the out-working of God's foreordination.

5. *Work.* In Greek thought leisure was the virtue to be sought and manual labour was considered appropriate only for slaves. How different is the Biblical attitude! Even before the Fall man was entrusted with the care of the garden and after his rebellion it was the fatigue of labour, not labour itself which was his punishment. In the Scripture all labour is considered holy to the Lord and is sanctified by the example of Jesus the carpenter. This follows from the Biblical witness that the material creation is in no way intrinsically inferior to the spiritual.

III. *What is the indigenous frame of reference confronting Christian educators in Indonesia (especially Java)?*[2]

Firstly it must be immediately admitted that Java's subjection to Western political, economic and cultural domination has in the last hundred years set in motion an irreversible process of disintegration of the indigenous world view. Contemporary Javanese culture is therefore an heterogeneous, disjunctive and internally contradicting complex of traditional and Western elements. For the vast majority of those over 40 years of age the old world view still prevails. For the younger generation, some of whom enter Christian tertiary institutions, there is no neat evolutionary process from tradition to modernity but rather the daily clash of two rival systems of thought. Bavinck's illustration[3] of the Indian villager who felt like a man sailing down a river in two canoes, standing with one foot in each and alternately shifting weight from one craft to the other, could be aptly applied to the conflict experienced by Indonesian youth.

Despite the incoherence and complexity of the present situation I shall concentrate here on sketching an ideal type of precolonial Javanese thought. I do this partly because I assume that the international secularising forces that are corroding a traditional world view will be analyzed and discussed by speakers from other countries, and partly because it is impossible to understand the modern situation without taking seriously the tenacity of the traditional perspective. Perhaps too, we must note that while in their totality Javanese concepts form a unique amalgam, in their individual elements they are probably parallelled in a wide range of Asian and Non-Asian traditional cultures.

In traditional Javanese culture an indigenous matrix was imperfectly compounded with heterogeneous Hindu, Buddhist and Islamic elements. Throughout the centuries prior to the "coming of the West" there ensued a slow process of absorption and synthesis which resulted in the crystallization of a world view which possessed a high degree of internal consistency.

How then can we characterize the indigenous faith which constantly thwarts all national aspirations to become a modern democratic state enjoying economic prosperity and social justice? What is the basic attitude to reality that has been disturbed by the rude invasion of the West's secular, scientific and industrial culture? This is an important question because at the centre of every culture stands man and his beliefs about what things are really like at bottom. These beliefs will, of course, determine the type of culture he shapes.

The basic outlook of Javanese culture can be described as one of *cosmic monism*[4] or what Van Leeuwen calls the "ontocratic pattern",[5] that is the tendency to reduce the manifest plurality of the cosmic totality to one principle. In cosmic monism man himself is a transitory product of the undifferentiated divine unity which we call nature. This is a long way from a Biblical teaching on man as God's viceregent, and even further away from the secular version in which man is exalted to become the proud creator and determiner of all things. Rather in cosmic monism, man has no qualitatively different place of his own. He just revolves like all the elements of the cosmos along with the seasons and follows the cyclical course of birth, life and death. Man's basic attitude to the world then is one of adaptation. Not surprisingly a key concept in Indonesian culture is that of harmony.

For an outsider, the Javanese "Weltanschauung" can most easily be approached through the traditional medium of the *Wayang*. The wayang are Javanese shadow plays based upon adaptation and developments of the Indian epics Mahabharata and Ramayana. These wayang plays, performed with flat leather puppets which throw their sharply etched shadows against a screen which is viewed from the other side, preserve and transmit a religious mythology which commands an undiminished, deep emotional and intellectual adherence. These beloved shadow plays offer an explanation of the universe and explore poetically the position of Javanese man, his relationship to the natural and supernatural order and to his fellows. In contrast to Christianity and Islam, the religion of the wayang has no prophet, no Bible, no Redeemer, no absolutes, and no linear concept of history moving towards its predestined goal. The Javanese world view has been epitomized as "a stable world based on conflict" and "a wheel spinning eternally on a fixed axis". So the wayang conveys the inexorable flux of things, and the endless variety and sharp individuality of its characters reflect the variegation of human life experienced by the Javanese. But this teeming multiplicity is ordered by clearly marked dichotomies which reflect the dualities of the Universe: male and female, sun and earth, mountain and sea, night and day, etc. But all are, at bottom, necessary and complementary to one another. Day is not day without night, youth is not youth without age peering over its shoulder. Anderson[6] points out that the harmonious tension and energetic stability of this weltanschauung are in essential opposition to the cosmologies of Christianity and Islam in which the Supreme being is quite unambiguous, representing only one set of poles (maleness, godness, light and truth).

Again whereas Islam and Christianity present a stark contrast between man and God, wayang cosmology offers a world not only teeming with life and living energy but also *elaborately ranked and ordered.* We find the ancient Southeast Asian concept of the God-King by which the temporal ruler represented divine power incarnate and the king's subjects partook of this power in exact proportion to their proximity to the throne. Each level of the hierarchical social order has its own peculiar function within the total structure. If one order fails to function all the others suffer the consequences. Thus the *king* communicates with the supernatural powers and secures their good will; the *brahmana* performs the rituals of the state, the *satrya* must administer the government and defend the state; the *traders* and the *artisans* have their obvious roles. *Morality* is related to one's function in the social order. In Western culture, as a consequence of long centuries of Christian influence, the same ethical criteria are applied to the business executive as to the labourer (in theory at least). But this is foreign to the Javanese culture where social approval depends on how adequately one fulfils the tasks of one's class. There developed a stratification of moralities according to caste, each of which may often conflict with the others. The ideal mode of behaviour is *to acquit oneself appropriately* according to the rank which one is *fated* to have. No permanent importance is attached to that lifestyle, however.

Such is the universal knowledge and affection for this wayang mythology that Javanese children from their earliest years come to know the different heroes of the drama, not merely the names of the characters but also their physical, psychological and ethical traits. Each village has a set of rough wooden or cardboard wayangs. Frequent performances mean that the child learns from these mythological models the philosophical teachings which will later orient him to the outside world. This education moulds not only his religious and moral sense but also his aesthetic awareness. As in ancient Greece, there is no line dividing the idea of the good and the beautiful. The same word is used for both *(sae)*. Both can be seen as aspects of the more basic concepts of appropriateness or harmony. Javanese dancing is taught to children to develop physical grace and harmonious personality.

Foreigners who fall under the spell of Javanese culture often speak of the "tolerance" of the indigenous people as their most salient characteristic (in earlier decades it was dubbed "syncretism" or "relativism"). Anderson argues[7] that this virtue (as he would see it) is not an innate quality of the Javanese, but something which results from the pervasive wayang mythology whose rich multiplicity of concrete models legitimizes a wide variety of social and psychological types.

Another consequence of this mythological outlook is that man sees life and the flow of events as a process beyond human control and therefore beyond human responsibility. "The only thing he can do is play out the part assigned to him in accord with that station in the order of things into which he is born and with the inner detachment which is the precondition of his spiritual salvation ... His freedom as well as his assessment of his own value as a human being, lies not in influencing or directing the predetermined course of events but in transcending it, through selfknowledge and identification with the essential unity of the permanent order beyond time and transient things (or, less nobly, in trying to secure his personal safety through magical manipulation of the cosmic relationships affecting his life i.e. by fasting and meditation or black magic)".[8]

There is one other element in the traditional framework that I would like to touch on and that is the idea of "Power".[9] In Western cultures power is just a term, an abstract concept used to describe observed patterns of social interaction. The sources of power would include weapons, wealth, organization and technology and hence theoretically there is no limit to its accumulation. As a Westerner (and more particularly as a Christian) one would be concerned with such questions as the legitimacy of power and how it should be rightly exercised. In Javanese culture however one finds a completely different concept of power which helps to explain for instance why in modern Indonesia aspirations of social justice, responsible leadership and public service are frequently unrealized.

In Javanese monism the first assumption is that power is a concrete reality and no more an abstraction. "Power is that intangible, mysterious and divine energy which animates the universe. It is manifested in every aspect of the natural world, in stone, trees, clouds and fire but is expressed quintessentially in the central mystery of life, the process of generation and regeneration. In Javanese traditional thinking there is no sharp division between organic and inorganic matter, for everything is sustained by the same invisible power".[10] Because in the Javanese view, the quantum of power in the universe is constant, then the increase of power in one person or place unavoidably necessitates a proportional diminution of power elsewhere. What is more, since all power derives from a single homogenous source, power antecedes questions of good and bad. To the Javanese way of thinking it would be meaningless to claim that power based on electoral success or wealth is legitimate whereas power based on guns is illegitimate. Power is neither lawful or unlawful. Power is. Accordingly traditional literature is not concerned with the exercise of power but with its accumulation. It could be mobilized by yogaistic and ascetic practices, or by verbal magic. In the old kingdoms the ruler would also concentrate around himself any objects or persons held to have unusual power. His palace would be fulfilled not only with such paraphernalia as krisses, spears, carriages etc. but also with unusual human beings such as albinos, clowns, dwarves, and fortune tellers.

The idea of power had ethical consequences. The chief virtue valued by the "priyayi" ruling class is that of being "halus", a concept which covers qualities of "smoothness, refinement, calm and subtlety".[12]

The opposite quality, that of being "kasar", is regarded as the natural state of man in which his energies, thoughts, and behaviour lack all control and concentration. To be kasar, no effort is required. On the other hand, "being halus requires constant effort and control to reach a reduction of the spectrum of human feeling and thought to a single smooth, white, radiance of concentrated energy".[13] Thus in the minds of traditional Javanese, being halus is in itself a sign of power, since halus-ness is achieved only by concentration of energy. In the typical battle scenes of the wayang plays the slight, halus satria almost invariably conquers the demonic giant or wild man from overseas. The contrast between them is striking. The satria hardly stirs from his place and when he does he moves smoothly, impassively and elegantly. But the demonic opponent uses acrobatic leaps, lunges and shrieks. The clash is especially well symbolized at the climatic moment when the satria stands perfectly still, eyes downcast and apparently defenceless while his formidable adversary repeatedly strikes at him with dagger, club or sword — but to no avail. The concentrated power of the satria makes him invulnerable. This quality of halusness which marked the life-style of the traditional aristocracy continues to have extraordinary attraction in Java to this day. The man of real authority should have to exert himself as little as possible. The slightest lifting of his finger should able to set in motion a chain of actions. The man of real power does not have to raise his voice and does not have to give overt orders. The ethics of halusness are basically the ethics of power.

If halusness is the hallmark of the priyayi, the focus of his ethics, and the expression of his power, how is it obtained?

Here we see the importance of *knowledge*. Power and the halusness which adorns it can only be achieved by spiritual discipline passed on initiation into certain specific forms of knowledge. The education of the satria is seen as a long process of moving closer to the ultimate secrets of the cosmos, which is finally attained only through illumination. It is worth mentioning here, too, the special status enjoyed by literate men in a largely illiterate traditional society. Again this is illustrated in the wayang plays where the single most powerful weapon in the hands of the favoured Pandawa is not an arrow, club, or spear, but a piece of writing.[14] The traditional attitude to knowledge as a key to power continues to exert a powerful influence. The priyayi life style is concerned with the ideal man. This man proves his inner nobility by what he is, by his position and prestige, not by what he does, i.e. not by his skill and ability to perform.[15] This prestige ideal comes to expression in the aspiration for white collar jobs. Educational diplomas are sought not so much as certificates of skill or as preparation for future tasks but as gateways to high social position.

IV. *Further problems affecting the development of Christian scholarship*

1. *The problem of Islam*

When we pause to reflect that 85% of Indonesia's population is Muslim the question that obviously arises is "Why have all attempts to make Indonesia an Islamic State failed?"

Any explanation of that extraordinary fact would no doubt include mention of the following:

a. The tenacity of the indigenous Javanese world view — a description of which has been the burden of this paper — its remarkable tolerance and ability to accommodate new ideas into its own framework.
b. The type of Islam which entered Indonesia was one which had already undergone basic modifications during its passage through Persia and India. These modifications made it more congruent with the traditional Javanese matrix.[16]
c. The penetration of Islam in Indonesia as a whole was more assimilative than revolutionary because it came on the heels, not of conquest, but of trade.[17]
d. Finally we should not underestimate the role of the Christian minority whose schools and political party helped create a climate favourable to the concept of a pluralist society.

However, since the end of the nineteenth century an Islamic reform movement has with increasing vigour sought to eradicate heterodox accretions and to regain an uncorrupted orthodoxy. Dr. Bakker[18] has documented the resurgence of Islam in Indonesia and in particular its intensive pre-occupation since 1967 with the expansion of Christianity. Recent events leading to the changing of the venue of the W.C.C. congress from Jakarta to Nairobi illustrate the more aggressive attitude of certain Islamic groups.

Such Islamic groups are increasing their pressure on the Government to compel Christian education institutions to admit Islamic religious teachers to protect the convictions of Muslim students. Perhaps with some justification, they view Christian schools as thinly disguised instruments of evangelism rather than the natural and legitimate expression of Christian educational assumptions.

2. *The practical problem — How to survive?*

A Christian university such as "Satya Wacana" receives practically no financial aid from the government nor has it yet found rich Christian benefactors in Indonesia. In 1975 student fees accounted for nearly 40% of Satya Wacana's budget (i.e. 40% of 400 000). A further 40% of the annual budget comprises donations from foreign agencies including Christian churches.

This dependence on foreign donors is always a potential problem especially if the donor does not share the convictions of the University. The Indonesian churches themselves until now, have not given substantial financial support partly perhaps because of their own slender resources and possibly because of lack of communication with those in remote areas. Of course the University could always raise fees to such an extent that it became self-supporting. However, this would make it an institution for the rich only. In addition to donations one fifth of students' fees are currently set aside for aid to poorer students.

Then there is the problem of staff. At present the indigenous staff consist of 100 full-time lecturers and 93 part-timers. The present Rector, Dr. Sutarno has stressed the need to build up a team of dedicated Christians who are also academically well equipped. But in practice the Christian universities do not have the financial resources of their State counterparts nor can they match the high wages paid by international combines to scientific personnel.

3. *Problems in theological training*

There is an obvious relationship between the quality of theological education and of the pastoral ministry on the one hand and the production of Christian thinkers on the other. Here I can only

180

touch on a few problems that impress the foreigner.

The past two decades in South East Asia have seen an emphasis on academic excellence reflecting an understandable desire to match standards in the West. However, the "scientific study" of theology pursued in artificial isolation often seems to destroy Christian piety and to engender intellectual arrogance.[19] This problem like many others is not unique to Asia. It is, of course, exacerbated if the "scientific theology" is conducted on unbiblical presuppositions. For instance there is a lack of theological literature in Indonesia (e.g. commentaries) which is intellectually respectable but does not regard the Bible as a fallible human response to God's revelation. Moreover few of our students have the critical capacity to lay bare methodological principles underlying a commentary. What is printed is regarded as "gospel".

The current stress on "contextualization" of theology, not invalid in itself, in practice tends to unduly exalt the criterion of relevance with the result that theological curricula exhibit a shrinking biblical core and downgrading of biblical languages.

Finally, there is the problem of financial viability of the seminaries which have hitherto been supported by foreign mission agencies. Few local congregations yet see a responsibility to give financial support for theological training.

4. *Problems concerning the Basic Aims of Christian Education*

Indonesian Christians have a strong awareness of their calling to be the "salt of the earth". They are proud of their own contribution to the struggle for independence from the Dutch. They are proud of the fact that although Christians comprise not more than 10% of the population their representation in the national leadership is proportionally greater.[20] Their network of Christian schools, maintained despite difficult circumstances, bears witness to their awareness of the vital role of education in shaping the future of their nation. They live in a revolutionary situation and desire to give a clear lead in the struggle for "The realization of a just and prosperous society".[21] To achieve this hope a revolution of attitude and mind is necessary. The old, cosmic, monistic world view is inadequate. That passive, subjective, participatory outlook ever seeking harmony with nature spells doom for every five year plan and frustrates every effort to utilize modern technology. Christians know that the Biblical doctrines of creation and redemption deliver the world and the social order from sacredness and encourage that ability to think rationally, objectively, critically and in terms of the future, which are the pre-condition for modernization. Moreover it is the Gospel of God's salvation in Christ which alone changes man's heart and motivates him to serve God by serving his fellow man. What do Indonesians see as the fundamental aims and raison d'être of Christian educational institutions? The older generation of Christian educationalists seemed to have emphasized evangelism, constructing a Christian science, training Christian leaders and service to the larger community. One senses that a reassessment is in progress. It is the last two aims which are seen as priorities now. The times are critical and urgent practical answers are required for pressing problems. There is no time for ivory tower theorizing. The key words are modernization, creativity, development, humanization, liberation and community service.

In so far as these new emphases reflect a desire to come to grips with the real and to provide unselfish service to the nation as a whole they must be welcomed. But there is a problem. A small amount of reflection makes clear that none of them are self-explanatory ideas. For instance development is not a self-defining concept. We must ask development for what? in what direction? of what capacities? The term development does not supply the norms we need nor do any of these terms which pop up in all contemporary discussions. On the contrary they must be evaluated and given a content in the light of more fundamental criteria derived from the Bible's teaching about the nature and destiny of man.

Conclusion

Earlier in this paper we saw the liberating influence that the Bible once had on Western science and culture. We then examined at some length the indigenous world view still exercising tremendous influence on the minds of Indonesia's millions. But we recognize that however powerful its hold, the traditional mythology will not be able to withstand the onslaught of Western secularization. Furthermore, there is a real danger that the ensuing spiritual vacuum will be filled by the worship of science and technology and with a false faith...in human progress.

However, Christian educational institutions still have a wonderful opportunity to present a true understanding of the Universe based on God's Word. Please pray that God's Spirit may bless and guide our Indonesian brothers that they may be faithful to that Revelation and be enable to integrate that faith and learning. Pray, too, that the Word of Truth may transform the values and attitudes of both staff and students giving sanctity to all their endeavours and producing a spirit of sacrificial service. In this way they will be a blessing to the nation they love and bring praise to our

Lord and Saviour.

---

1 This section is a simple summary of a position ably expounded in such books as Malcolm A. Jeeves: *The Scientific Enterprise and Christian Faith,* 1969; and R. Hooykaas: *Religion and the Rise of Modern Science,* Grand Rapids, Eerdmans, 1972.

2 The writer of this paper would like to stress that he is *not* an authority on Indonesian culture. He has served in South East Asia for 5 years, only the last 3 of which have been in Indonesia.

3 *The Impact of Christianity on the Non-Christian World,* Grand Rapids, Eerdmans, 1949, p. 60.

4 See O. Notohamidjojo: *Attitude dalam Pembangunan,* Jakarta, 1974, ch. 2.

5 A. Th. van Leeuwen: *Christianity in World History,* London, 1964, p. 158.

6 Benedict R. O'G. Anderson: *Mythology and the Tolerance of the Javanese,* Cornell University, New York, 1965.

7 Op. cit.

8 Soedjatmiko: *An Introduction to Indonesian Historiography.* New York, Cornell University Press, 1965, p. 410.

9 Again I am in debt to an essay by B. R. O'G. Anderson: "The Idea of Power in Javanese Culture", *in:* Claire Holt (ed.): *Culture and Politics in Indonesia,* New York, Cornell, 1972.

10 Anderson: ibid., p. 7.

11 See C. C. Barg: "The Javanese Picture of the Past" in: *An Introduction to Indonesian Historiography,* Soedjatmiko (ed.), op. cit., p. 89.

12 Clifford Geertz: *The Religion of Java,* New York, Free Press, 1960, p. 232.

13 Anderson: *Idea of Power,* op. cit., p. 38.

14 Anderson: op. cit., p. 47.

15 S. de Jong: *Een Javanese Levenshouding,* Wageningen, 1973, p. 200.

16 Anderson: *The Idea of Power,* op. cit., p. 58.

17 C. Geertz: *Islam Observed,* New Haven, Yale University Press, 1968, p. 12.

18 D. Bakker: *The Struggle for the Future,* a paper on The Christian Faith in the Modern World, R.E.S., 1970.

19 Koyama: *Reflections on the Association of Theological Schools in Asia,* ATSEA, 1974.

20 Raden Soedarmo: *The Christian Calling in the State,* R.E.S. Gotemba Conference, Japan, 1970.

21 Quoted from the preamble to the 1945 Constitution of the Indonesian Republic.

The challenge to reformed higher education in the Latin Third World countries

Prof. Dr. Sidney H. Rooy

The challenge to the Reformed faith in Latin America is a unique one. Not that it is not so in other continents. You recall no doubt Goethe's claim that every generation must write its own universal history. I believe that applies to culturally and religiously different peoples as well. Or to put it more forcefully, the context to which the message comes determines the specificness of its content.

Nowhere is this clearer than in the Biblical message which assumes different forms and words in changing times and places. The basic unity of the message is often hidden behind the priestly and prophetic mask of a specific *kairos*. A transverse section of history reveals conflicting and paradoxical theological formulations that have consistently caused headaches for systematic theologians.

One might take the idea of God, the concept of salvation, or the doctrine of eschatology as examples. To refer briefly only to the first, myriads of definitions bombard our theological schemes. To say that God is the father of our Lord Jesus Christ is already to adopt a certain epistemological approach.

Three examples follow:

1. In the words of a literary evangelical in Latin America (Alberto Rembao):[1] "I have Christ. I do not know God, but I am willing to risk my destiny and my soul's salvation that He must be like Jesus of Nazareth himself, in whom the eternal Christ emptied himself, as the Scriptures say, and which I believe worthy of faith. I do not say that Christ is like God, but that God is like Christ ... from the known to the unknown.
   "Lord? God or Christ? Better Christ, because with God one might err, because God can be a philosophical matter, but Christ, no Christ is exclusively a religious matter ... my Christ, veteran of the three-day war."

2. An eleven-year-old Latin American child of Protestant parents was asked to give the name of the first person to occur to him on hearing certain words. He reacted as follows:
Death: "Jesus".
Liberation: "Ché".
(Ché Guevara, a popular Argentine hero of revolutionary and student groups, who fought in Cuba and who was killed by the military forces in Bolivia a few years ago.)[2]
3. Missionaries working with the Guarani Indians in Paraguay translated the word "God" to the highest tribal God — *Tupá*. Many years later anthropologists discovered that there exists in tribal folklore an unnamed God who is the eternally present One behind all the vicissitudes and changes of the named ones, — including *Tupá*.

In these examples we see diverse interpretations of the reality of God and how He is to be known. To regret that the "pure" and "true" definition of God was not first given by Reformed missionaries, does not eliminate the basic problem. What is the Biblical concept of "God" for our situation and our need? Is He Moses's God of fire and smoke, is He the shepherd of the Davidic Psalms or the divine Vindicator of others, the Comforter of Isaiah or the righteous judge of Amos? Is He the "daddy" (Abba) of Jesus, the Unsearchable One of Paul, or the essence of the love-deed in John? Or is He the father in the Nicean Trinity, the *summum bonum* of the scholastics, the mysterious presence of Tauler, the *Deus Absconditus* of Luther, the moral governor of Kant, the Transcendent one of Barth, or the "object of theology" in Berkhof? And if one responds that He is all of these and unspeakably more one would no doubt be approximating the truth.

All that I am trying to emphasize is that it is psychological, theological, and sociological impossibility to say that *one* theology is to be preached to the nations. This is possible only on a terribly superficial level in which common terms may be used but which inevitably take on different meanings in changing times and places.

It must be emphasized that the constant and essential factors in the Christian message are not relativized through their historical incarnation. Rather these factors are determining and active agents; they are not themselves being formed.

Nonetheless it must be maintained that the manifoldness of God's dealing with man, the reality of His active intervention and participation in history, and the ever-new constellation of human possibilities, constantly give new meanings and understandings to the Christian community. This must be recognized in order to understand on the one hand, the tragedy that has been caused by the exportation of static occidental theologies to the missionary situation, and on the other hand the urgent need for profound reflection and the birth of creative theological formulations in the new world situation which relentlessly imposes itself upon us. Which means simply that having taken seriously Barth, Berkouwer, and Berkhof, different as they may be, we must press on. Black theology, Asian theology or Latin American theology should be encouraged and expected.

This lengthy introduction is an apology for what I want to say. My thesis is this: the uniqueness of the Latin American context reveals certain universal human needs and hopes which when properly analyzed and formulated may inspire an equally unique contribution to the world church. This contribution we shall call Latin American theology. This is a claim to originality, but not to pride. Each people and every time may claim originality and shares the duty to formulate its own response when the new *kairos* challenges.

Which leads to the question: what is the uniqueness of the Latin American situation? The history of the pre-columbian Indian cultures of the Aztec, Maya and Inca empires and many hundreds of other tribes, of the cruel destruction by the Spanish and Portuguese crusades, and of the greatly diverse mosaic that remains is, I trust, known to you.

Long and arduous debates continue about the nature of the evangelization that accompanied the process of colonization. There are two legends, as the Spanish have it. The white legend, defended by traditional Catholic historians, puts the blame on the *Patronato Real* (Royal patronage) which not only tied the church's hands in its evangelistic task, but made it the arm of the Spanish crown. This ecclesiastical dependence subsequently extended to most of the Latin American countries; it was accentuated by an acute lack of priests and an anti-ecclesiastical masonic liberalism. The concomitants of the new liberalism included the opening of doors to free-thinkers of all sorts, romanticists, positivists, protestants, and later socialists and communists.

The black legend is the traditional Protestant interpretation. I heard it repeated three weeks ago in Chile by Joaquin Vasquez, pastor of the new metropolitan Pentecostal tabernacle (which seats 14 000) in a Sunday morning message. According to this view, the present Latin American situation would be totally different if only the Indian empires had been conquered by Protestants. With the new world crusaders came a medieval feudal system, an autocratic government and a hopelessly corrupted superstitious form of Christianity. The process of evangelization is thus a syncretism of the

186

animistic pagan belief and the semi-pagan idolatry of medieval catholicism.

Both positions are basically wrong insofar as they do not deal integrally with the past and present crisis of the Roman Church in Latin America. As Miguez rightly observes, a few attempts were made, not to syncretize, but to integrate certain traditions and rites into the conquering ecclesiology (the Aztec, Inca imperial centres in Mexico, Peru, and especially in the Jesuit villages in other Latin American lands.) This attempt, however, was a complete failure.[3] Rather, a totally foreign religion was imposed with Latin terminology for doctrines and ceremonies. "Baptism" to this day in Guarani means "become Spanish".

The evangelistic attempt to erase the primitive religion by destroying its art, literature and customs was sociologically and psychologically impossible. So there grew a sort of counter-culture of popular religiosity independent of Catholic piety. The Catholic rites are accepted as a sort of religious imposition, but when they are fulfilled, the people turn to their own meaningful customs. Catholicism, according to Columbian sociologist Fals Borda, created "anti-norms", that is, norms of conduct antithetical to indigenous ones. For example, European norms gave the rules for marriage, commerce, and law, but the static nature concept of the indigenous peoples tended to be reinforced by Constantinian Catholic values. Thus, though the family structure be changed, traditional value patterns continue. There is no "theology of the transformation of nature",[4] only its acceptance and that of traditional society patterns.

Protestantism's entrance to the Latin American scene was as dependent upon external factors as was Spanish Catholicism. The British commercial enterprise broke the Spanish monopoly. The imported liberal, masonic and positivistic intellectualism sought non-Catholic support in its anti-ecclesiastical stances. The Europeanized bourgeois aristocracy in Latin America found more profitable the industrialized markets of the Protestant North than those of Southern Europe.

The arrival of the Dutch and South African Reformed, German Lutherans, Waldensians, Welsh Congregationalists, Scotch Presbyterians, and many more, is due to these external factors. After the first World War came the flood of predominantly North American missionaries. The Colonial Protestant groups founded social islands and the missionaries formed spiritual ones. Only the third group of Latin Protestants are really indigenous — the Pentecostals. They grow on the "popular religiosity" soil mentioned above and use the church as an escape from their hopeless poverty and futile sense of dependence. Their churches become the "refuge of the masses" to use the phrase of a Reformed sociologist.[5]

I think enough has been said, to make clear that neither the Catholic nor the Protestant churches have become integrated into the Latin American reality. Christianity has rather remained an ethnic religion — and there is reason to believe the same is true in Asia and Africa.

As José Miguez has said: "Neither Catholicism nor Protestantism, as churches, is rooted deeply enough in Latin American human reality to produce creative thinking: In other words, both churches have remained on the fringe of the history of our people".[6]

Strange as it may seem, three congruent strains dominate Protestant and Catholic ecclesiastical types in the present. In both groups a traditional *conservative* strain resists change and adaptation to their social context. In their doctrine of creation, the Catholic concept of natural law, and the Protestant concepts of providence and sin, combine in a unique way with the natural fatalism of the aborigines. The status quo is divinely ordered and we are to accept our destiny passively. "Qué va a hacer?" and "mala suerte" are its confession, and worship at the lottery altar its rite. Neither the traditional Catholic structure, nor the other-worldly pietism massively imported by would-be non-theological evangelists from North America, cares to trouble itself about the abject poverty, prison tortures, and hopeless injustices of our Latin American lands.

The common point here is a convergence in the Catholic, Protestant and Indian mind of a static view of the world and of history. Here all share a sort of fatalism that resolves itself in an indifferent acceptance of the present and a futuristic Christian hope that waits for the roll to be called up yonder. The only roll call at our moment of history is at Sunday worship, in the sacraments and in individual acts of piety here and there.

Whereas in the conservative group the majority of Christians may be found, relatively few are to be found in the second strain, in the more *radical* and *progressive* groups. The third world priests and the ISAL Protestant theologians share a common theme: God is active in human history, and through Jesus Christ is incarnate in its development. The name that suits God best is Liberator, through him the great transformation of society is promised. But as Christ emptied himself and became poor we must identify ourselves with the poor and afflicted. An optimistic anthropology sparks a Christian activism that must stop at nothing in the great crusade for justice.

Opinion divides sharply on the question whether "reform" or "revolution" is necessary to bring about healing to oppressive structures. However, evil tends to be seen in global and social terms. The individual finds his authentic role only in the service of the whole. The "reformists" believe that traditional churches can be challenged and changed by a lively prophetism, while the "revolutionaries" judge that violence is inherent in the structure of the prevailing societies. Thus the churches, identified as they are with these structures, offer more resistance than hope. The revolutionaries find not Marxist religion but Marxist social categories most adequate as a basis to challenge the status quo. Accordingly violence comes not by chance to any man, it is inherent in the present order. Changes within an oppressive order are always partial, therefore a radical (root) transformation is required.

Here comes the great problem. Most are agreed that neither U.S. and European capitalism nor Russian imperialism is desirable for Latin society. The first creates a fundamental economic dependence that enslaves whole groups of people in peripheral lands. The second marshalls an unlimited political power centre, as dependent upon romantic liberalism as the naive capitalism that dominated much of the occidental world, a power centre which has no way to escape the power — justice dilemma. Their romantic concept of human nature gives birth to the millenial hope of a classless society. Only Christian realism can provide valid correctives to such unjustified faith in human nature.

In the context of these generally rejected options, was born the theology of liberation. This group of mainly Roman Catholic theologians (Gustavo Gutierrez, Hugo Assman, Juan Luis Segundo, and others) have tried to give theological formulations to the existential needs of a continent in crisis.

As personal faith characterized the early church, and reason the higher middle ages, so in our contemporary world "come of age", "liberation" should characterize the Christian community. According to Gutierrez, the theology of liberation is the critical reflection in the light of the Word of God of each new generation of Christians on its own spiritual experience and faith consciousness in concrete-historical situations.

This reflection on the single integrated process of liberation occurs on three levels; the Pauline ones of love, hope and faith. The first lies on the level of a love for one's neighbour which only becomes realized in real and effective transforming power on the economic, social and political levels of human existence.

"It is at the level at which nations and classes fight to break the bonds of oppression which have unjustly enslaved them. In as much as the world today is experiencing unprecedentedly rapid cultural change, coupled with the existence of instant communication in a 'global village', the poor and oppressed have, at last, become *aware* of the fact that they are poor and oppressed; in fact, they have come to realize what the *cause* of their oppression is — namely, the capitalist system. This awareness has given rise to a deep-seated yearning (aspiration) to be free. In fact, "this aspiration to liberation is beginning to be accepted by the Christian community as a 'sign of the times', as a call to commitment and interpretation", (in particular, by the CELAM conference, Medellin, 1968).[7]

The second level is the eschatological hope for the liberation of man throughout history, the dream of utopia coming true, the coming of the kingdom. On this level Gutierrez introduces his philosophy of history in which an optimistic and evolutionary progress requires that man participate consciously in the "continuous creation, never ending, of a new way to be man, a permanent cultural revolution".[8] Man becomes liberated through "the conquest of new, qualitatively different ways of being a man in order to achieve an ever more total and complete fulfilment of the individual in solidarity with all mankind".[9]

The third level is that of faith, a "liberation from sin and entrance into communion with God and with all men".[10] Here not political revolution, (as on the first level) nor cultural evolution (as on the second), but personal conversion from sin through the grace of God in Jesus Christ is central. This conversion from concrete historical and social wrong alone provides healing for man's "interior personal fracture".[11] Nothing less than a radical liberation from sin will root out injustice. Such liberation Christ alone offers us through his Spirit.[12]

For the theology of liberation, what is crucial to the Latin American situation is the relation of sacred to secular history, of the church to the world, of the history of salvation to universal history. In Latin American church history the relation of the church to the world can be diagrammed as follows:

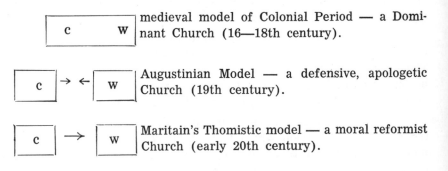

medieval model of Colonial Period — a Dominant Church (16—18th century).

Augustinian Model — a defensive, apologetic Church (19th century).

Maritain's Thomistic model — a moral reformist Church (early 20th century).

190

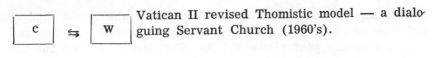
Vatican II revised Thomistic model — a dialo-guing Servant Church (1960's).

Liberation model — a politicized Church, increasingly taking the side of the oppressed. (1970's).

John Tuinstra sums up Gutierrez's position as follows: "Thus, the church at this point of history in Latin America, and elsewhere, can most effectively be involved in the world's struggle for liberation through unabashed solidarity with the oppressed — denouncing injustice, announcing the Kingdom, while conscienticizing with a view to the creation of a new man in a qualitively new society".[13]

Or, in Gutierrez' own impassioned style: "Every attempt to evade the struggle against alienation and the violence of the powerful and (the struggle) for a more just and human world is the greatest infidelity to God. To know him is to work for justice. There is no other path to reach him".[14]

This brief touch of "liberation" theology introduces us to a third congruent strain of Catholic and Protestant perspectives in Latin America. It is the level most difficult to define. We might call it the restless, uncertain and undefined group. A growing sociological and anthropological awareness of the complexity of the modern world is upon us. The third world priests, ISAL (Iglesia y Sociedad en América Latina) and the Theology of Liberation have deciphered religiously the results of modern science. What concerns them is the perspective of half the world's 3.9 billion people with per capita incomes of less than $200 annually, the stark failure of so-called loan and development programmes,[15] the increasing indebtedness of third-world lands, the rapidly widening gap between the rich and the poor nations partially due to rapid price increases of factory goods and nearly static primary resource prices, the unchanged internal social imbalance of the Latin American nations where 2% of the people often own more than 50% of the lands and leave them relatively unproductive, the unholy alliance existing between the national oligarchies and multinational interests, and so one might continue.

The basic question is whether the people of God must be concerned about such matters. Are they primary or secondary? The answer is not easy to give. What would Old Testament prophets do, were they here, men like Moses who carefully stipulated jubilee year equalization laws, like Isaiah who clamoured for orphan and widow care, like Amos whose liturgy was justice in place of solemn church services and righteousness in place of the weekly budget envelope (5 : 24). What about Jesus with his woes to the rich and blessings to the poor (Luke 6 : 20 ff.)? And his desire for the more important matters of the law: justice and mercy.

We have noted that the conservative ecclesiastical groups have a static concept of creation, of natural law and of providence. This results in a sacralization of the status quo. On the other side are those who radically reject matters as they are. For them creation is a dynamic concept. Man as God's partner has come of age and must create a new corporate man in a qualitatively new society. The third group are those of the uneasy conscience. They constitute a growing section of the evangelical catholic and Protestant churches who are deeply concerned about the inhumanity of the gross injustices under which half the world population subsists. The tragedy is not lessened but deepened by the ignorance in which the majority live. Moreover the material blessings of the first world have soured into a practical materialism little better than the theoretical materialism of the second world.

The great challenge, as I see it, to Reformed higher education in the Latin third world countries lies within the uneasy conscience group mentioned above. Here the Reformed understanding of the Scriptures has significant contributions to make, certainly in theology, but perhaps even more in the other sciences. Without the contribution of Reformed sociologists, economists, political scientists, anthropologists, psychologists, and others, any theological formulation will be as limited as a second grader's analysis of aerodynamics. Theology is no longer the queen of the sciences, it can only aspire to be a humble companion on the road to understanding.

Let me suggest a few concepts which demand the attention and the co-operation of all the sciences. Let us consider them in pairs, concepts which are complementary but whose reality must be held in healthy tension. The first pair is creation and salvation. The conservative strain (of both Catholics and Protestants) emphasize the static concept of creation. The sin of man brought the curse upon the world and the dimension of God's wrath upon it. Creation structures continue in weakened form, while the added new structures are necessitated by sin. Governments have a more controlling and limiting function than a moulding and creative one. Salvation is both an escape from the world of creation and the strengthening means to endure its sinful flesh. Salvation has no definitive word to speak about creation, rather salvation is itself God's chief interest in our historical moment.

The disease of fatalism is no recent newcomer to the third

192

world scene. It is but a true reflection of cyclic concepts of nature religion reinforced by static Catholic natural law and Protestant asceticism.

The other side of the creation — salvation tension is taken, as we have seen, by progressive liberation theology. Here creation is dynamized by active human participation in the historical process. God Himself is, as it were, incarnated in man's calling to create new men in a new society. The tendency here, in reaction to traditional ecclesiastical staticism, is to glorify human possibility. Creation must be seen in eschatological perspectives, it is more present and future than past. The challenge is to make real the kingship of Christ now.

The original creation and its past processes are a sort of evolutionary mass whose progress has meaning to the extent that its inherent limitations are suppressed. Once again, as in conservative theology, there is a basic dualism to be overcome. Either creation and salvation remain isolated from each other, or the one is absorbed into the other. As Lambert Schuurman puts it: "In ethical terms, conservative theology believes that moral men can organize a moral society; progressive theology holds the opinion that a moral society will produce moral men".[16]

Before this impasse, it seems to me that Reformed thought has a real contribution to make. One of those contributions can be a deeper understanding of the Kingdom-Church tension which is almost wholly lacking in the Latin American context: either the kingdom is spiritualized or entirely secondary and the individual churches become redeeming agents in the world, or the kingdom is the world in which the church is not qualitatively distinct. On the one hand, the conservative tradition believes ingeniously that a fantastically growing number of individual christians and churches is the best solution to present world injustices, while on the other hand the liberation school preaches the kingdom in basically political and social terms and the church becomes instrumentalized as the agent for change. Both under-emphasize the terrible power of human sin: the one forgets the social blindness and limited vision of christian individuals and groups, and the other puts its faith in human revolutionary projects.

These deficiencies are related to a third pair of terms that need to be held in a healthy tension. Neither the conservative tradition nor the radical finds room for a theology of the covenant nor for a proper understanding of God's election. The lack of an election-covenant consciousness in the individualistic imported Protestant theology both among conservative pietists and liberal "civilizers" is notorious. Equally is this so in the Catholic structure. The radical reinterpretation of traditional concepts treats the Latin American reality far more realistically probably because of the incorporation at long last of the social, economic, and political sciences. But the universalization of the covenant and election categories empties them of their dynamic Biblical content. The kingdom becomes the better social and economic life realized by Christians, Marxists, and humanists — but little of divine grace remains.

These brief references are meant to be only suggestive in character. What is so sorely needed are reformed specialists who are willing to identify themselves with the third world situation. We need no more imported solutions, the massive missionary force from pietistic and liberal circles is enough evidence of that. We also do not need theoretical and dogmatic theologies from serious reformed circles abroad. What we do need is a really profound dialogue with men of learning and science in all fields, but especially in the humanities, in order to understand the complexities of the third world situation. Sometimes we feel like a few men on a small raft on a stormy night when only the brightness of the stars assures us of one whose creative will still rules the destinies of men. Creation, we know, is real. Again we feel like wanderers among men who are dying for lack of subsistence elements and then we know that salvation is more than words, kind wishes, and charity.

It is not that nothing is being done. We must work unitedly with all who share the biblical vision of a dynamic creation — salvation, kingdom — church and election — covenant faith. Ecclesiastical names and membership numbers are of little importance to us. There are more biblically reformed people outside our historical pigeon-holes than is often realized. The fact that we are so few in number and the need is so great gives us a different perspective on ecumenicity, experimental forms of theological education, non-professional pastoral roles, extra-ecclesiastical and cross-denominational agencies (such as the Fratermidal Teológica Latino-americana), incorporation of sociologists and economists as regular members of our theological faculty, the role of women in the churches, and the like.

Let me conclude by saying in a different way the thesis with which I began. Long ago we thought the Bible was the Word of God applied unilaterally to our present situation. Later we learned that for proper hermeneutics we had to take seriously the Semitic and Greco-Roman cultures. More recently we have learned that our own attitude is decisive in the process of interpretation. Perhaps recent analyses of language and communication have taught us that the angle from which we experience God, salvation, or love is essentially partial and reductive in character.[17]

This may seem to be negative, but really it is not. What it does is force us to confess the wonder of God's working in His world. Not only does it drive us to our knees in humility, it reminds us that God has much more to teach us in each new context. For that reason we must speak of a living and vibrant covenantal response in the totality of the life of every culture. Asian theology, African theology, and Latin American theology ought to be only suggestive of the many diverse theologies that grow spontaneously in the Kingdom of our Lord when His Word and Spirit become incarnate in our historical experience.

1 "Mi Christo", Alberto Rembao, cited in: *Certeza*, No. 47, 1972, p. 207 (Buenos Aires).
2 José Mignez Bonino tells the story in: "Theology and Liberation", *International Review of Missions*, Vol. LXI, no. 241, p. 67, January 1972.
3 José Miguez Bonino: "Cristianismo en América Latina", *En Marcha*, No. 20, 1974.
4 Ibid., p. 8.
5 Lalive d'Epinay: *El Refugio de Las Masas*, Ed. del Pacifico, Santiago de Chile, 1968.
6 *Fe Cristiana y Latinoamericana*, ed. C. René Padilla, Ed. Certeza, Buenos Aires, 1974, p. 119 ff.
7 Summarized by John K. Tuinstra: "Gustavo Gutierrez: *A Theology of Liberation*, An analysis and appraisal". Mimeographed, Amsterdam, 1974.
8 *Theology of Liberation*, p. 32.
9 *Ibid.*, p. 32—33.
10 *Ibid.*, p. 235.
11 *Ibid.*, p. 175.
12 *Ibid.*, p. 176.
13 *Op. cit.*, p. 32. This is a concise and worthwhile introduction to Gutierrez' position. I am especially indebted to Tuinstra in this section for the summaries and quotes since I had no English translation available.
14 *Op. cit.*, p. 272.
15 "The investments that are made and the credit that is given by the great capital investments in Latin America, constantly draw interest in their favour, in such a way that in the period 1955—69 for each dollar invested in Latin America $4 have been obtained, while still maintaining the original investment". Document of ISAL, 1971. Unpublished. See also *Aid as imperialism* by Theresa Hayter, Penguin Books Middlesex, 1972; and: *World Development: An introductory reader*, ed. by Heléne Castel, MacMillan, New York, 1973.
16 *Lutheran Quarterly*, Vol. 22, pp. 77—91, Fall, 1970.
17 See Juan Luis Segundo: *Liberatión de la Teologiá, passim;* Edit: Carlos Lohle, Buenos Aires, 1975.

Problems affecting the development of Christian learning or Christian scholars: disunited and without a common base

Prof. Dr. Gerard van Groningen

"... people and nations fumble in confusion about new technologies and what they will do the world" — is the opening sentence of a report on the second assembly of the World Future Society.

The two thousand men and women comprising this society which seeks to guide the world into the future, found that the only real conclusions they could agree on were those that drew attention to present problems. There was no agreement on what to do for the future except to come to a general concensus that although the future "will be bothersome, sometimes dangerous, yet embodying humanity's historic will to cope with perils", it will somehow survive.[1]

Voices varied at that assembly. They were heard to say the following: "We can ward off the doomsday syndrome if we understand that human decisions determine human conditions". "We are about to enter a not-so-brave new world that will require accommodation to a less affluent and simpler way of life". Referring to the world today, one said, "It's like ten Industrial Revolutions and the Protestant Reformation rolled into one ... all taking place in a single generation". "It's naive to deny the necessity for some kind of competent elite to participate in the government decision-making process". (This sentence was used to sum up the discussion of entertaining the desirability of working out for the future the old ideas of the philosopher — kings and the benevolent dictators). And the last voice we quote said "Lets keep our hands off the future ... man is in little danger of going under ..."

The assembly of the World Future Society, comprised of social

196

scientists, many of them academics, looked at the present world and were deeply troubled.[2] They looked to the future but they had no prophetic word. So it has always been when men and women, educated and experienced though they be, speak as sociologists, as scientists, as politicians and as philosophers who do not acknowledge God the Lord of Creation, man, history and culture.

What is it that causes the modern world to miss the mark? Why is it that all the learning, practice and resultant experiences of humanity have not enabled mankind to cope with itself in this cosmos in which it has been placed to be at home? The simple — possibly we should add and simplistic — answer that can be given is *sin*. If we do insist on centring our thoughts on *sin* as *the* problem, then we are confronted by the following questions: Is redemption, God's answer to sin, of no effect? Is not redeemed humanity, freed from the power of sin and free in Jesus Christ, able to speak meaningfully and helpfully to the modern world? If you say "Yes, it should and can", the questions that then focus with burning intensity on our consciences are, but why is it then that we speak of our western world as the post-Christian world? If the reborn, converted, justified, sanctified saints should and can speak meaningfully, why is it that in that part of the world that was once considered Christian, people and nations now fumble in confusion?

Let me sum up my introductory statement as follows:

The unbelieving, unredeemed part of humanity in our post-Christian world is fumbling in confusion as it admits its failures past and present. But it continues to refuse to listen to the only Sovereign Triune God (because the Scriptures as divine revelation are unacceptable). Adding to the tragic situation is the fact that the masses of humanity, along with the scientists, cannot hear much, if anything, from the redeemed part of humanity. Why not? Because a babel of voices arises from within it. The fact of the matter is: the redeemed are tragically divided. Some speak only of redemption; some speak of the divinely redeemed part of humanity *and* of a secular world; some speak of redemption in the setting of a mechanistic (somehow evolving) world. Some major on this world as our home and a weak minor is heard on the theme of redemption. Still others take a very one-sided or single-eyed view. There are those who see and stress the philosophically discerned dichotomy in life; others stress, without the seeming awareness of other basic problems and motifs, various types of synthesis and accommodations that have plagued the Christian world. Still others stress sociological factors, e.g., political or civil religion, consumerism[3] or the imbalance

197

between the rich and poor. Each one claims to speak for Biblical Christianity. The result is that neither unredeemed nor redeemed man is doing much other than fumbling in confusion. This is certainly the case in most of the academic world, in the "Christian" as well as in the "secular" academic area.

How desperately necessary it is for the western countries, where Christianity was once a recognized influence, to face up to the fact that these very countries are "dechristianizing". And even more tragic is the fact that when these countries should be looking expectantly to the educated and educating communities within them, they have little reason to do so. The fact is that there is little done to develop Christian learning in such a way that it can, will and actually speak meaningfully, helpfully, fruitfully, hopefully to the de-christianizing masses. It is not that there are no scholars, specifically, Christian scholars. It simply is not because there are baffling problems arising from within our contemporary "post-Christian" world. It is, and I believe fundamentally so, because of the lack of solidarity among Christian scholars. Even more basic and fundamental is the inability of the Christian scholars to recognize and adopt a mutual meeting, starting and controlling point. As I develop my trend of thought, I trust this main factor will emerge clearly and that in the process subsidiary aspects will also come to the fore.

Permit me to make an explanatory statement before I proceed. When I began to consider what to include in a paper in which I was to discuss problems affecting the development of Christian learning/scholarship/science in de-christianizing countries of our modern world, I found that I had to either briefly mention factors in two specific areas, or deal with problems fundamental to the two areas. Let me briefly explain.

The option before me was to address myself first of all to the various forces coming from outside and impinging upon the Christian academic community. I chose not to spend much time on these; I did include references to some of these, cf. footnotes 1 and 2.

The second option was to address myself to the actual problems within the Christian community. I would have dealt briefly with the synthesis in thought patterns, accommodations in philosophies and theologies, political and social influences upon and the implications of our Christian academic task in the world. I am thankful that some papers have amplified this area.[4]

The third option, and this is the one I chose to develop, is what I consider to be the basic and fundamental aspect of our

Christian challenge in the rapidly de-christianizing modern western world.

I. *How did we get where we are?*

A review of the course of the historical development of intellectual activities, its major motifs and emphases can be found in numerous writings.[5] Let me try to give a brief statement. I begin with the earlier Christian era.

St. Augustine and co-labourers were controlled by a theological motif. To be a theologian was to be intellectually respectable. God, as revealed in the Scriptures, and man's relationship with God were their major themes. The *City of God* is basically a treatise on the God-man relationship. Thomas Aquinas had God as his major subject. The "Prime-Mover", the "First Cause" were phrases employed to keep theology foremost even when the created world was the subject of attention. C. Westermann states that the major emphasis of the theologically dominated thinker, teacher, writer was the *Who*, the Person, i.e. God as He is and acts.

Then the philosophical emphasis became dominant. The emphasis was shifted from the *Who* to the *What*. The key words were no longer "Person-person" but "Existence-reality". It was intellectually respectable to analyze and to speak of this world's meaning, its purpose, its integral relationships. As philosophers concentrated on the *What*, God as Person, and personhood as such, became either mere things, or part of the *What*, or they were ignored as not too relevant. In fact, God as person was removed increasingly in philosophical thinking from any meaningful relationship with existence. And one is amazed in reading the record to note how many theologians followed the dictates of the philosophers.[6]

The development in philosophical thinking, i.e., the movement to the *What*, and the ignoring or removing of the *Who*, led to the question — *How?*[7] Thus the scientist came to the fore. Scientists basically deal with methods, control, development and with products and their use. But when the scientists voluntarily, or when asked to, give answers to the questions relating to the *Who* and the *What*, we have *Scientism*. Then the scientists no longer concentrate on scientific activity but have placed theology and philosophy under its dominance and speak on their behalf.[8]

The era of *scientific* emphasis and of *scientistic* dominance can be divided, roughly, into two parts. At first the naturalistic, inorganic, materialistic scientist had dominance over the minds and attitudes of men. However, when the scientists uncovered and unleashed the terrifying power (especially the nuclear) in the *What* by developing their *How,* without reference to the *Who,* humanity became terrified. Minds were concentrated on humanity's existence, interrelationships and future. Then, the social scientists came into prominence. Today we have the social scientists, frantically trying to deal with the after effects of the naturalistic — inorganic scientists' discoveries and products. Now, in this our post-Christian western world, people are assembling in conferences, thinking, talking, discussing. A deep concern for the future of humanity is expressed. Having moved from a dominance in thinking about God, (there was then little of the necessary emphasis on God's relationship to the *What* and *How)* to a dominance of the *What* (which was isolated increasingly from the *Who)* and on to the dominance of the *How,*[9] men and women today are asking: *Why? Why* are we where we are? And *Where? Where* are we and *where* are we going? As these questions are asked, the concentration point of man's intellectual activities is not God; it is not being, existence, reality (the cosmos); it is not methods and products. It is mankind itself. And the admission is: we are fumbling in confusion in this highly developed technological world, which has become a dehumanized, terrifying place. Indeed, if it was Christian once, it certainly is post-Christian now.

Is it not sad that the theologian, the philosopher, the scientist, unredeemed and redeemed alike and together, have brought in so much chaos and are continuing to add to it with their fumbling?

But, the question which is before us and is to be answered is not: What is the actual situation? Rather, it is this: What is at the root, at the basis of all this chaos, fumbling, confusion, uncertainty and fear? Why is it that the Christian Western world of yester-century has become the post-Christian western world of the 20th century? And why is it that Christian scholarship seems so ineffective in the midst of it? Could it be that they are unjustifiably ignored because they have learned from past failures? Should we look to them again? The very fact that we are gathered in conference suggests that we believe we deserve another opportunity. But, the question before us is: What can be expected of us scholars?

II. *Shall we repeat the Past?*

Shall we repeat the past? Shall we give each of the three another try? The theologians? Or the philosophers? Or the scientists? The very fact that that thought is entertained could indicate that we have not learned from the failures of the past. Or is it that we are witnessing this ill-fated effort to set up one as basic, primary? It can be shown that that is the case. Let us, indeed, become aware of what the situation is in the western world today.

As stated in the introduction, humanity of today cannot cope with the very problems it has brought upon itself. So, what are we the Reformed, the Calvinists, redeemed servants of the Lord, to do? The answers vary, but, in fact, the answers I hear in the United States are the ones of the past. There are those who say, "return theology to its regal position of the past".[10] Rhetorical questions, in some cases, are deemed satisfactory support for this dogmatic statement. Should all of mankind not acknowledge, know and worship God? Is the study of the Scriptures and its message of redemption in Jesus Christ not the key to all solutions? Is it not proper that we again emphasize the all important Who, He Who is the First and the Last, and continue to? Having asked the questions, the theologians turn to their Bibles, their Biblical Theologies, their Dogmatic Theologies, their Systematic Theologies, their Confessional Theologies. Many of these Theologies are well-developed. Intricate nuances are explored. Meanwhile, philosophers become annoyed because of the theologians' interest in setting up their disciplined studies, and their refusal to seriously consider, let alone interact with, the philosophers. Especially bothersome is the theologians' insistence that the philosophers have to listen to them. Meanwhile the scientists go on their way adding to the confusion and pessimism so prevalent today.

The philosophers, annoyed because they are expected to listen to the theologians, do much in the same manner. Although philosophy has lost its intellectual prestige to science, philosophers are hardheaded enough to ignore that. They continue to philosophize, analyze, theorize, formulate hypotheses and speak with a tone of final authority. They may incorporate some theology into their philosophy and then are quick to speak of philosophical theology (the emphasis is on the adjective).[11] Or, they may relegate theology to a position of one of the many sciences and claim the Royal servant's (emphasis again on the adjective) chair for the philosophers. Meanwhile, they continue to theorize and opinionize. They delve into the intricate abstractions of reality, of structures, of thought processes. Some can be heard to hurl anathemas at the theologians who hound them. Others rail at the scientists and masses who, of late, by and large, ignore them. But really, why shouldn't the scientists and the masses do so? Do they want to be caught up in the awful abstract world, the world of philosophy — in which God is not given His rightful place (His Word, especially the Written Word, is not given due recognition); where man is not seen in his proper covenant relationship with God and the practical problems of life (natural sciences) are not given their proper due?[12]

As the theologians, stressing *Who,* and the philosophers, stressing *What,* go their separate ways, except to remind each other that they each have the right to be considered prior, first, queen, royal, the scientists continue to work on their own platforms with their methods. They develop new techniques and they uncover new potentialities in the cosmos. They enhance humanity's fears. They compound the present chaos as they blindly grope onward seeking new powers, methods, new products. And as they grope, they talk to each other. They do not limit their talk to methods, raw materials, products and their use. Ignoring the isolated theologians and abstract philosophers, they try to give answers to questions which arise as they work, which the believing theologians and believing philosophers together with the believing scientists should answer. But, woe is humanity! The scientists have no message !

Another factor that should be mentioned is that too many of the evangelical, Reformed theologians and philosophers, embarrassed by past failures of their disciplines, but awed by the scientists' tremendous advances in methods and products, join the scientists in their scientism! It is most difficult to explain. It is a fact nevertheless. As scientists of all beliefs and ideals increasingly admit that they have produced confusion and fear, a roadway to a possible dead end, the theologians and philosophers continue to follow the failing scientists in their scientistic talk.[13] Is it a wonder that the social scientists, speaking for themselves and possibly for the masses, are beginning to say, "will everyone please keep their hands off the ship of humanity's future?" Surely drifting at random can not be worse than having three ship's officers, one of whom may know how to read the charts, another may know something of the sea and the third one may understand something of the mechanics of steering, but who refuse to properly acknowledge each other and the strategic importance of each one's role.

It is clear, is it not? We should not repeat the past. There is no hope for escape from our fumbling if the theologian remains isolated, the philosopher abstract and the scientist feverishly busy producing and talking scientism's language but rushing humanity ever more deeply into confusion and despair.

III. *What should be done?*

It would seem to be quite easy to solve the problem. Accepting that the situation has been diagnosed correctly, all we have to do is select recognized representatives from among the theologians, the philosophers and the natural and social scientists and lock them in a conference room and keep them there until they agree to work together!

Indeed, it is high time that the thinkers, preachers, teachers, technicians begin to talk to each other more freely, more openly. Doing so, let them honestly and sincerely seek to learn from each other, to help each other and together grow and develop as servants of God and fellowmen in this cosmos. Is it not true that the fragmentation among the various workers (interdisciplinary as well as within the disciplines) has not only prevented unity, harmony and mutual development, but has also led to distrust, uncertainty, anger and fear? Is it not true that each discipline claiming priority, basic importance (be it said to be in a janitorial, regal or dictatorial role) has led to pride and self exaltation and simultaneously to disrespect, disdain and even rejection?

Today is the time to join forces and break down the barriers between the disciplines.[14] If we are to find the answer to the spiritual and moral problems facing man in the modern world which has been turned into a "closed world", we must have the *Who* recognized, heard and obeyed. And more, if we are to find the answer to the intriguing questions of what is reality, existence, knowledge, we must have the *What* before us as a necessary object for concentrated study and understanding. Simultaneously, if man, the covenant creature, created in the image of God, is to obediently serve the *King of Creation,* he must learn the *How* within this cosmos. In addition, the *Why* and *Where* asked by the masses, must be seriously studied by *all* — and not just by the social scientists. How important it is that humanity, led by Reformed believers, begin to demonstrate the Wisdom of God revealed to man. Is not that man wise who can and does answer the *Who? What? How? Why? Whereto?* in a supplementing and harmonious way?[16]

It has become quite clear that it will not do merely to place the theologians, philosophers, scientists and representatives of the fearful, confused, pessimistic masses of humanity together in a locked conference room. However, they must meet, talk, plan and work together. But where do they begin? What is a common starting point and a common basis on which all depend, rest and from which meaningful action can spring forth?

It has been said that the Scriptures, the doctrine of the Word of God, is the key and central factor for all to consider. Let no one deny the importance of the Holy Scriptures. All men need it desperately. It reveals God as man's personal God, and the only way of redemption. The goal of life is spelled out in it. But, the Scriptures do not specifically and pointedly serve as the focal point for the various disciplines.[17]

Others have insisted that the plan or way of salvation is the focal and all embracing factor. Again, it is very true that all of humanity, sinful by nature and lost, is in desperate need of salvation. But, as with the Scriptures held up as the focal factor of orientation, so with the plan of redemption; we find that it does not serve directly, specifically. Indeed, people as individuals require salvation which is revealed in the Scriptures. But, how many millions of people do read the Scriptures, are saved through faith in Christ but do not speak directly and meaningfully to the trembling and fearful world of today. Is it not a fact that in spite of forty million evangelicals (Bible believing and saved people) in the United States, the life of the country, as much as that of any other western nation, proclaims the sad fact that it is caught up in a post-Christian era? Can you imagine: all the attention the forty million saved people give to the Bible has not stopped (possibly in some ways abetted) the rush into our post-Christian conditions!

Is there then no answer to our post-Christian problem? Is there no solution? Is there no basic central factor that can be pinpointed as crucial to our present situation? I am not prepared to say that there is no answer. In fact, I am prepared to say, and will say, emphatically and persistently, that there is. The all important fact on which we must concentrate to arrive at an answer, a solution, and at the same time, an orientation point which will serve as a starting point for all, unitedly and simultaneously, is the *Fact, Truth, Doctrine* of *Divine Creation.*[18]

IV. *Creation: The crucial factor in our post-Christian era*

It can be truthfully said that theology in isolation leads to and abets irrelevance in our post-Christian western world. Philosophy in isolation creates deeper dimensions of doubt. Natural science has opened the way to the reign of pessimism.[19] The social sciences are leading people at an even quicker pace into deep despair. But the divinely revealed truth of creation, clearly spelled out in the Scriptures,[20] repeatedly referred to as a direct starting point and basis for life and activity here and now[21] and for eternity is the focal point calling for immediate attention. Indeed, if theologians, philosophers, scientists, yes, all men, are to be used to reverse the onrushing tide of post-Christian living in the western world and to prevent the slide from relevant contemporary Christian life to a post-Christian era in the Third World, the fact and doctrine of divine creation must be seriously considered.

It is very heartening to hear voices calling for a serious consideration of the doctrine of creation.[22] Increasingly one can find recent writers referring (some with urgency) to the necessity of returning to an acceptance of and a working with the fact of creation.[23] However, it should be acknowledged immediately that, as in the past, so the present invitations and demands for a renewed consideration of the fact of creation open the doors to much confusion, distrust and division which is fostered by the discussions concerning creation itself.

Consider briefly for a moment what the case is presently. The doctrine of creation is not interpreted by some in terms of *beginning* but in a Christological manner.[24] Others suggest a soteriological interpretation or application is to be preferred.[25] Some recent writers have given a very existential interpretation.[26] Others deal with the Scriptural text (Gen. 1 & 2) in such a way that literalism could become a real problem.[27] Still others, particularly those deeply interested in philosophical studies, are in danger of over-emphasizing the work, word and product of creation in relation to other truths revealed in Scripture.[28] Still others have spoken and written in favour of interpreting creation in terms proclaimed by science.[29] Finally, there are those who would reread the Scriptural account as given in Genesis 1 and 2 as a revelation of God's grace, reflecting a tendency to restrictively "theologize" the concept of creation.[30]

The differing approaches and emphases in regard to the fact and doctrine of creation indicate a number of things. 1) The Biblical teaching of creation has become a reason for fumbling and confusion. 2) Serious work must continue to be done on this Biblical doctrine. However, it would seem that as scholars and students involved in the various academic disciplines took this fact and doctrine of creation seriously, and agreed that its neglect serves a vital role in the movement into post-Christian living and activity, a unity and consensus could be expected slowly but really to emerge.[31]

The vital and crucial role of the act and doctrine of creation can be seen quite readily if we stop to reflect on the following: In a serious consideration of creation, the Creator receives the prominence He rightly requires.[32] Creation answers the basic question *Who*. The Scriptures identify Him specifically and reveal His inner Self to an extent. In addition, as God the Creator is acknowledged, mankind created in His image also comes into proper focus. Thus the Person and persons involved in the drama of modern life are immediately and properly placed before us. Since the doctrine of the fall and re-creation is intimately associated with the doctrine of creation, these very necessary doctrines cannot be excluded. The theologian should give leadership in this area.[33]

205

In a serious consideration of the fact and doctrine of creation, the created cosmos is placed in proper focus. The question of the *What* is thus given its basic answer. The related aspects: existence, being, reality, knowledge, relationships are unavoidably seen in their divinely placed context. In a serious consideration of the fact and doctrine of creation, man's role and task is placed before him/her. The cultural mandate is the starting point of all scientific, natural and social studies. Thus the setting for finding the answer to the HOW is before us. In this context, methods, developments, products and their uses do not come into an unfocused scene. The philosophers have their necessary role in this area.

In a serious consideration of the fact and doctrine of creation we find that the answer to the *Why* arising from restless masses as well as from a reflective thinker, is found. God created in His good pleasure for His glory. Humanity's purpose is revealed as that of being vice-regent, co-worker with God and to share His glory forever. The theologian, the philosopher and the ethicist should work side by side on this facet of life.

In a serious consideration of the fact and truth of creation, the answer to *Whereto?* is uncovered. The Creator, who is the originator of all things, created for a purpose. He had a goal in mind. Thus, life is not to be seen as an aimless drifting but as a controlled process moving onward to a determined goal. The answer is: to Eternal life — a life of blissful existence through and with God, life which involves unending joyous service for God. The theologian, philosopher and specialist in humanities (especially historians) should work together in this area.

We see then that the fact and doctrine of creation reveals the Wisdom of God for our day by day life, study, activities, play, work, rest — yes, for every facet of life.

We see also that the fact and doctrine of creation, properly and seriously considered, requires the theologian, philosopher and the humanities specialist to seek each other and demands that these three urgently request the scientists to join them so that together the *How* can be readily discussed, in the context of a mutual discussion of the WHO, the WHAT, the HOW, the WHY, and the WHERETO.

Conclusion:

The basic factor involved in the de-Christianizing process in the western world is that, whether we look to the theologians, the philosophers, the scientists, the specialist in the humanities, or the masses of humanity, the first act of God is not given sufficient or proper

206

recognition. Since this act of God, which reveals Him, which produced this cosmos and placed tremendous potentialities within it, is ignored, our various disciplines, specifically, our academic disciplines, are not orientated, they are not mutually supportive of each other. They tend to work at cross purposes and in contradiction to each other. In fact, they operate too much as if they were wholly oblivious of each other. And the masses of humanity are caused to suffer unmercifully because of the fumbling, the confusion, the uncertainty and chaos caused by a divided work force which was intended by the Creator to be united force in His service, and as such a force, to be the means of an ever richer, fuller, blessed life of joy in the fellowship of God.

---

1 "U.S. News and World Report", June 23, 1975, p. 64, 5. Conclusions which "attracted much support" were
   a. "Effective leadership will be hard to find ... the world will lurch from crisis to crisis until political systems can deal with dangerous trends before they get out of control".
   b. "A second tower of Babel has been erected because of the dominance of television, the computer and other electronic technologies. The psychological effect of T.V. — instant outrage, instant imitation and instant demands — increases the tension because problems confronting the world today and tomorrow require time for proper solution".
   c. "The core issue ... is to strike a balance between ... population and ... shrinking resources ..."
   d. "... global crises that may include nuclear terrorism, oil wars, widespread famine and political revolution are almost certain to occur before the end of the century".
2 The World Future Society is joined by others who have looked at our modern world and who have found additional serious problems and mentalities affecting it. E.g. Dr H. O. Brown, formerly of "Christianity Today", in a series of lectures given at the Reformed Theological Seminary's Mid Winter Theological Institute, pointed out along with other binding and crippling forces, the serious debilitating effects that modern bureacracy exercises in life. The human spirit is increasingly bound and burdened by bureaucrats safely situated in the political area of life. Rule upon rule, law upon law, regulation upon regulation, many inherently antithetical to each other, are issued from bureaus. The effect of this type of bureaucracy is, as a rule, twofold. Either a hard mentality is developed: everyone must do it, everyone does it; and thus, individual privileges, initiative, and responsibilities are removed or repressed. Or, the spirit of rebellion and resistance comes to expression, fostering an increasing disrespect for ordinances and laws including, and often singling out, the necessary and abiding God-given ones. Thus bureaucracy is a definite cause of anarchy.
3 The inconsistency of many stressing this is seen in the manner they themselves consume — using automobile and air travel extensively, placing

the finest of foods and drinks on their tables, filling their wardrobes with clothes featuring the latest fashions.

4 Cf. e.g. the papers of Dr S. Rooy and Dr P. G. Schrotenboer.

5 C. F. Henry refers to it in his article "The Bible and Modern Science" in the Holman Study Bible, A. J. Holman Co. Phil. Pa 1962, pp. 1184—1194. Various essays on Science and Religion in Encyclopedias survey the field. In studies on Creation, such as Claus Westermann's *Creation,* Stuttgart, 71, translated by J. J. Scullion S.C., SPCK. London, 1974, it is mentioned in various settings.

6 Voices are heard at times, as was the case at the Conference during a discussion period, that theologians as a rule, have introduced the major problems into the Christian world — especially into Christian thinking. It seems that the general pattern has been as follows: When theology was confronted by social, political, philosophical and/or cultural influences, in an effort to speak meaningfully to these influences, theology permitted itself to be influenced by them. Obvious contemporary illustrations are the existentializing of Biblical hermeneutics and theology under the influence of existential philosophy and social forces (e.g. women's liberation movement).

7 If there is not a *Who* present as originator, controller, provider, *How* then does this universe operate? More importantly, the question becomes: How can man control today and guide into the tomorrow?

8 It would be very incorrect of me to give the impression that the movement from the theological to philosophical to scientific dominance can be clearly traced and neatly blocked out. It should be pointed out, and that with emphasis, that the philosophic and scientific elements were always present, as the theological also were. In fact, aspects of these have been present at all times. Early Gnosticism, e.g., was a primitive attempt to combine the theological and philosophical motifs with a dominant scientistic emphasis. Cf.: *First Century Gnosticism,* Brill, 1967, in which I have discussed these factors at some length.

9 This statement does not deny that scientists do not have and are not controlled by a basic philosophy of their own. And, it should be added, the scientists, wittingly but possibly more unwittingly, have adopted much that the philosophers have presented as truth.

10 This is a direct quote from a source I deem wise not to specify. The fact is that there are a number of sources that can be quoted.

11 Time and space will not permit me to develop and establish my proposition that the effort to combine modern philosophical thinking with theology is the main source of contemporary Process Theology — a theology which is having many, yet as a whole disastrous, effects on the Biblical message of creation, fall, redemption and Christian witness and service in the world today.

12 This paragraph is not intended to suggest that there is no place for the philosophers or that all they say is to be ignored. E.g. the paragraphs on p. 329—330 of Prof. J. Van der Stelt's address must be taken seriously. I refer especially to those beginning with "This near total blindness to the need for an integral Christian education..." and "failing to see the need..." "The sad, also ironic, effect". In fact, many theologians and Christian scientists agree with the concepts expressed. However, it does not follow that because philosophers have pinpointed a problem that they alone have produced, or basically, primarily, can produce the solutions to these problems

cited. Thus, the burden of my paper is at a deeper level than the various problems cited, and others could be added to those referred to. Specifically, if the Christian community is to agree on what the problems are, what the unique character of each problem is, and the approach to and method for solving these, each *area,* each discipline, each servant must be given his/her rightful and necessary place in the Christian community of scientific scholarship.

13 It seems that real cases to point to are the theistic evolution proponents and situation ethics proponents and counsellors, who in turn are among the most vocal supporters of liberalized abortion laws, removal of restrictions against the use of drugs, and of the restructuring of the family life and the roles within it.

14 Should we not give serious consideration to the problems caused by having Seminaries isolated from other institutions of learning? Of having specific science departments which operate in a world of their own, isolated in different buildings, and even on different campuses, virtually sealed off from the religion, philosophy and humanities departments? A. A. van Ruler speaks to this problem in the context of his discussion on *The Christian Church and the Old Testament,* Eerdmans, G. R., 1971. He wrote that theology has a role in relation to the other sciences, e.g. the problem "on the relationship of the theologian and that of the philologist can be solved", and consequently the question of theological scholarship and the theological faculty — only if one realizes... "it has to set an example for all sciences by understanding the words in terms of the theme, and man and the world in terms of God, which it can do because it is acquainted with revelation and therefore with truth. This observation presupposes, however, that theology, scholarship, and the university are seen in the context of the *corpus christianum.* The theocratic concept is a necessary presupposition for theology as a science", p. 23.

15 The "closed world" of the scientists is the world in which the supernatural, the spiritual and divinely revealed morality has no place. The "closed world" has God shut out, spiritual aspects of life declared unknowable and it holds revealed morality as an impossibility. This closed world concept is a basic presupposition in most, in fact, nearly all science text books used in controlled and supported high schools, colleges and universities. Recently, voices from among a few disturbed thinkers have expressed doubts and reservations about the "closed world concept". They have had little effect to date.

16 When we consider the wisdom of God in regard to redemption, we hear God saying that Jesus Christ is the wisdom of God (1 Cor. 1 : 31). Jesus Christ, the God-man answers the WHO. The plan of redemption for man and the cosmos answers the *What.* The crucifixion, resurrection and ascension to the Father's right hand answers the *How.* The sin of mankind and God's intent to glorify Himself nevertheless answer the *Why.* The final consummation (1 Cor. 51 : 21) answers the *Whereto.*

17 In circles where men insist that the Scriptures are the central, originating, orienting factor for all disciplines, one finds that philosophers are either theologians, (concentrating on the Bible because it basically is the sum total of reality), or limit philosophy to apologetics, or have no use for philosophy at all. In a similar way, scientists find that they either have to live a compartmentalized life if they are to be genuinely at work as

scientists, or as another way out of their problem, they theologize their science.

18 I repeat — the truths concerning the Scriptures and redemption are very important to all of mankind. I also insist that the fact of creation cannot be properly known and it will not serve its basic function in peoples' thinking and lives if God's redeeming Word has not been applied and realized.

19 J. L. McKenzie: *A Theology of the Old Testament* wrote: "Pessimism reigns in the sciences. Creation breathes hope", p. 195.

20 The fact and truth of creation is referred to at least sixty-five times in the Scriptures. The verbs used to speak of creation are usually create, make, form. The context, however, makes it very clear that these terms are used to refer to divine creation, *ex nihilo* and by divine fiat.

21 Consider how Isaiah, calling men to hope and assurance, repeatedly refers to creation: Is. 40 ff. Paul began his missionary messages to the Gentiles by appealing to the fact of creation — a fact common to the lives and experiences of all people. It is of interest to note that Dr R. de Ridder, in his *Discipling the Nations,* Baker Book house, 1974, sees the foundations for the church's discipling task in divine creation.

22 During the 1974 Winter Theological Institute (held annually at Reformed Theological Seminary) Dr H. O. J. Brown, then associated with "Christianity Today", spoke of the various forces binding the human spirit: technology, mass media and bureaucracy. He called for a serious consideration of the doctrine of creation because it provides the basis from which to counter these enslaving forces. Note also that Dr Rooy called for renewed attention to this doctrine; specifically he called for a living dynamic conception, rather than a static one. Undoubtedly, this call must be heeded, but carefully analyzed and applied in terms of Biblical revelation as well as of the revelation which comes to us through His handiwork.

23 Cf. C. Westermann, J. L. McKenzie: Ibid.

24 Cf. E. Brunner: *The Christian Doctrine of Creation and Dogmatics,* Dogmatics, Vol. II, Lutterworth Press, London, 1949—64. Cf. especially chap. I.

25 Karl Barth gives the impression that creation is another way of saying God was freeing the good from the evil, according to G. C. Berkouwer: *De Zonde,* Kok, Kampen, 1958.

26 G. Widengren: *Creation and Law,* Edinburgh, Oliver and Boyd, 1961. J. L. McKenzie: Ibid. C. Westermann wrote that the question of existence is older than the question of who created. Ibid., p. 71. Man was initially not theoretically interested in creation but, threatened in his existence, developed the concept of creation.

27 E.g. The Creation Research Society includes some writers who may cause some problems in this area.

28 Some voices representing the A.A.C.S. in Toronto have been interpreted in such a fashion — and one hesitates to add — possibly with some justification.

29 Various "Neo-Evangelicals" have been quoted as supporting these positions. J. W. Klotz, in: *Why Not Creation,* edited by W. E. Lammert, Presby. and Ref. Pub. House, 1970, quotes Dr E. Carnell as saying that certain traditional Biblical interpretations have to be given up out of respect for geology, paleontology etc. He also stated "... evangelical scholars are increasingly surrendering to the theory of evolution" and quotes from the "Journal of the American Scientific Affiliation" to prove his point.

30 T. R. Ingram: "The Grace of Creation". W.T.J., Vol. 37, No. 2, p. 206 ff. Grace is defined by Ingram as the showing of love, favour when it is not merited. Since the created world did not merit existence, its presence is evidence of grace. It seems that Ingram is not too far removed from some Neo-Orthodox thought when he expresses himself in such a manner. It would seem to be more consistently Biblical to limit the use of the term grace to favour, love shown to the *offending, rebellious* and therefore *undeserving* man. In distinction from this, we find the Scriptures speaking of God's good pleasure, His desire, His joy in regard to His creating work.

31 When the sentiment was expressed in a discussion recently, a recently converted young adult commented: "We can never expect this to happen in the world we live in today!" This sentiment may prove to be correct in the final analysis, this lack of expectancy and hope may be the main reason why redeemed men and women will not make a serious effort to deal with this root problem in our de-Christianized Western world.

32 At this point cf. Dr J. Kromminga's paper in which he discusses the threats to the Christian character of the Christian institution. The first threat he analyses and correctly so, is "a shrinking God concept". Of interest is the fact that he also spoke of a unified world view which is required in our modern world.

33 A. A. van Ruler wrote: "Once it is perceived that the task of theological scholarship is to take seriously God's revelation in the world, one simply cannot ignore the problem of how the Word of God, the inner Word (what is in 'God's mind and heart') is expressed toward the children of men in outer words in the context of all historical reality". He added that regeneration is necessary for the theological task. Ibid., pp. 61, 62. This is not to be construed as a subtle plea to re-enthrone theology as the queen of sciences. It is, however, intended to be a plea to all those who in one way or other, for one reason or another, have depreciated theology and its vital role for all the sciences, to desist from doing so.

The position of the Christian lecturer, teacher and student at a Christian institution with specific reference to the educational task

Prof. Dr. J. A. Heyns

So far two central themes have been discussed: the Christian institution and Christian science. Today we are going to deal with the Christian scholar and by doing so, anthropology immediately becomes the focus of attention. Aspects of anthropology have of course been discussed in previous lectures. But then they were discussed in a rather sporadic and unpremeditated way. The Christian scholar and his educational task at the Christian institution, also when he studies and lectures on science, cannot be discussed meaningfully unless it is borne in mind that he does it as a human being. After all, it is as a human being that the lecturer educates the student towards complete adulthood. And as fellow human beings they are in a relationship which has no parallel at any other institution.

Our present theme will therefore be treated according to the following outline:

1. *The Christian scholar as a human being*

1.1. As a being of the Kingdom of Heaven
1.2. As a being in relation to others
1.2.1. In relation to God
1.2.2. In relation to his neighbours
1.2.3. In relation to himself
1.2.4. In relation to nature
1.2.5. In relation to his culture
1.2.6. In relation to structures

2. *The Christian scholar as one who educates*

2.1. Education

2.2. Educational aim

2.3. Educator

2.4. Educand

3. *The Christian scholar as one who educates through science*

3.1. The aspect of a life and world view of science

3.2. The ethical aspect of science

3.3. The futuristic aspect of science

1. *The Christian scholar as a human being*

Education as an interaction between two people, having as its object the richfulness of man, cannot be understood without a clear picture of man himself. It stands to reason, however, that all of Biblical anthropology cannot be treated in this paper. Only those aspects which are of importance for our topic will be discussed. For our purpose two statements about man are of importance: he is a citizen of the Kingdom and he stands in relation to others.

1.1. As a citizen of the Kingdom of Heaven

God is Creator-King, i.e. He is the author of all creation and preserves the continuation of the entire cosmos. God reigns supreme and His subjects: dust, plants, animals, humans and angels are subjected to His reign — that is the Kingdom of God. The subjection of man to the reign of God is his obedience to God, and therefore we can say: where and when man is obedient to God, something of the Kingdom of God breaks through into this sinful world. Where and how does God reign over man? He reigns over man — to begin with the central message of the *Holy Word* — in and through Jesus Christ. He who accepts Him in true spiritual belief becomes a citizen of the kingdom, and he who is a citizen of the kingdom discovers the kingdom not only within himself but also outside himself. The deepest Biblical truth about man is, therefore, that he is called to be obedient to God in all spheres of life and by doing so to strive for the coming of the Kingdom of God.

If we say that man is a member of the Kingdom of God we profess that God through Christ not only reigns in the church, but also within the family circle, the school, the university and the state; not only in theology, but also in politics, science and art. It is also accepted that man is called to obey God not only in church but also in the university; not only in theology, but also in politics. The church is not the only holy sphere opposed to the

213

rest of the world which is then thought to be profane. Theology is not the only science which serves God. He who has listened to the Word of God in church and who has accepted it, knows that the entire universe belongs to God and that He wishes to be served and glorified in that universe. Man not only answers God directly in his personal religious service or in church on Sundays, but in his entire being-in-the-world he is an addressed being and for that reason man is, at the deepest level, an answering being. Man knows that the *one* call, namely to listen to God and to obey him, is concretized in various careers and that to work at a vocation means to be man with God in this world. Man cannot escape the call of God's Word, because he is by nature a listener to the Word.

If man is a citizen of the Kingdom, then education at a Christian institution is the work of the Kingdom; i.e. work done in obedience to God with the aim of leading man to obedience to God in all spheres of life. But because man is a being of the Kingdom he is also a being in relation to others.

1.2. As a being in relation to others

The various relations of man to others are not merely additions to his being, but are in fact the measure by which we judge him as man.

1.2.1. In relation to God

To be man is to be with God. The Christian scholar should not only know this but should prove it by his deeds. Man is created and sustained by God. Man is dependent on God whether he knows it or not. This truth also qualifies man as an answering being — not only the positive answer but also the negative one remains an answer. It is for this reason that man is a religious being and can never be neutral.

According to Scripture man was created in God's image. That is to say, man, in distinction to all other creatures in created reality, is indicator, representative, ambassador and envoy of God on earth. He must mirror God in what he is and in what he does. From the very first moment of his being, i.e. from the moment of conception in the womb, man is an image of God. It is obviously impossible for him immediately to take up his representative task functionally and actively, *but his status* before God, as distinct from that of other creatures, he has already received. It is the task of education to allow man to achieve this status and to lead him towards his destination as man.

1.2.2. In relation to his neighbour

Being human is also being with one's neighbour. The Christian scholar at the Christian institution must give reality to this ideal. He does not choose his neighbour, but he is called to be a neighbour: the knowledge and insight, greater experience and wisdom which he possesses he has to make available to others. Neighbourship begins there where I — and then as lecturer — recognize the other man as a man of God; and vice versa, where I — as a student — allow myself to be seen. This visibility presupposes an alignment and openness to each other through which true communion will be created. Education can only flourish where this communion is based on true, warm neighbourliness — and this again is based on the assumption that they see each other with love, and that each allows the other to be seen with love; that each will talk to the other with love and that each will listen to the other with love; will receive and grant assistance with love. This love is the result of man's creation as an image of God. Man's togetherness with his neighbour is an image of his togetherness with God.

1.2.3. In his relation to himself

Being human is also being and remaining one's self. The Christian scholar who lives in relation to God and his neighbour is also himself somebody, because if he were nobody, he would not be a suitable candidate for the achievement of his task and calling. To be somebody means to have selfknowledge: to know oneself as a creature of God, to know one's potentialities and limitations. He who knows himself does not fall victim to personal overrating or underrating. A realistic self-knowledge leads to self-acceptance. He who accepts himself completely accepts God's work in and around himself. He is completely content, because he knows he is the result of God's work. From this naturally flow *self*-accountability, *self*-critique, *self*-development, etc. He who lacks these characteristics cannot educate, and cannot be educated.

1.2.4. In his relation to nature

To be human is to be busy with the world. Man and his world belong together. They are committed to each other, they are meant for each other and are in many ways closely interrelated. Nature was given by God to man to subject and control, to develop and to conserve. Labour in general and therefore science specifically, is a God-given calling. By his labour man proclaims the glory of God and proves that he rules this world in which God has placed him. The man who in his labour realises and actualises the possibilities of creation is a co-worker of God. We can therefore say: In and by his labour man proceeds with God's creation. Even more: labour has a healing and reconciling perspective. Man combats natural disasters; he alleviates pain and in this way continues Christ's redemption. Labour — and therefore science as well — is Kingdom work. Through it man acts with nature in directing the future of nature: a completely recovered nature, and a nature completely in accordance with the will of God. And man acts with nature and the things of nature according to their destiny: to give a home to man. From this aspect of making nature hospitable to man it is clear that labour is not merely subjected to norms, but that labour itself is an order — creating activity of man. In this spirit the Christian scholar will himself labour and attempt to educate the Christian student towards this view of labour.

1.2.5. In his relation to culture

Being human is to be culturally creative. By and through his labour man transforms nature into culture. Man has to be educated for the creation of culture — this has to be done by someone who is not only able to create culture actively but who is also civilized, i.e. who in his cultural creation can also fulfil his God-given call as man. The dynamic character of culture means that man can never remain in what was given historically but has to look for revision, change and renewal. Inherent in the social character of culture is the fact that men are not only individually creative in culture but that they are engaged communally in this activity. The *ethical* nature of culture means that man creates culture with others for others. The Christian scholar, therefore, is someone who, while labouring at science together with others, educates students to become ambassadors of culture.

1.2.6. In his relation to structures

Being human is to live in structures. Apart from personal relationships man also has a supra-personal relation which may be called the structural aspect of the community. The structure is not only the outward form of a situation but also the inward characterization of the form, viz. its imperative nature. Not all structures are changeable. There are God given structures and structures created by man which one cannot ignore. Responsibility for these structures and their christianisation must not be ignored by the Christian lecturer in his attitude to his students.

216

We have now come to the conclusion of our discussion of Christian anthropology. Within this elementary framework we then have to view the educational process of the Christian institution.

2. *The Christian scholar as one who educates*

2.1. Education

Education, we may say, is the directed leadership and deliberate forming by one man of the other to lead him to the realization of his destiny. When two people reach a point where the one requires aid and the other provides that aid — the one at the starting point and the other past that point — the education which the latter provides is not something which happens involuntarily but is indeed a calling and an order. It is for this reason that education should not be neglected and that the very best manpower and dedication are needed. Education will have to be accounted for not only to humanity, but to God Himself. It is precisely this close connection between education and God which makes education a religious affair.

The necessity of education can be considered from two angles. The first may be called a perspective of creation. It is true that we read that although God created man as a consummate being, it does not mean that man was a complete being. God placed man at the starting point of a long journey and not at the point of culmination. Similarly each child is also placed at a point of departure. Although God's divine judgement of man was that he was good, that did not exclude the possibility of development which again includes education in principle. Therefore education is not strange to the nature of man. Secondly we also have the perspective of sin. Man who was created as a consummate being fell into sin and by doing so opposed himself to God and his neighbour. Sin in its ultimate form means that man has missed his aim of being man. He refuses to accept exterior norms, because he wishes to create his own norms, and be his own authority.

It is for this reason that education can never accept that man is a *tabula rasa* which simply has to be inscribed. Education continuously has to destroy that which has been erected by sin. It will have to erase what has been written by sin before it can write its own message. No educational occurrence can succeed if it doesn't take the sinful nature of man into account. It stands to reason that such education cannot succeed unless it accepts the radical change in the nature of man through the act of belief in Jesus Christ.

2.2. Educational aim

Education as directed guidance and deliberate moulding cannot exist without a specific aim. To state that man's personality is to be developed, or that he has to be led to moral independence, or that he must be selfsufficient in his own freedom are true guidelines in themselves, but they are incomplete. The most complete aim for education is guidance towards an acceptance of man's ultimate destiny. And the content of this destiny will not be found in an existentialistic or humanistic anthropology but in Holy Scripture. Certain of the aspects of man's destiny on earth have already been indicated. Man is destined to be a citizen of God's Kingdom and that means that in all spheres of life he is required to obey the norms and laws created by God for that Kingdom. But it also means that one has to find one's destiny in all the various relationships in which man finds himself; in his relation to God, man's destiny is to be His servant; in his relation to his neighbour man's destiny is to be available in service to his neighbour; in his relation to himself his destiny should be self-development; in his relation to nature his distiny is to be a responsible ruler; in his relation to culture his destiny is to be a responsible user; and in his relation to structure his destiny is respectively obedience and responsible creation.

Education which does not permit man the achievement of becoming a complete being within these relations cannot be regarded as successful. The crisis of education in our time is that the utility aspect has become the criterion of all thinking and action. There is no greater aim than the optimum development of the latent powers of the individual or the human race in toto. But that these developed powers should be in service to God is often disregarded. It is for this reason that we hear of human rights — including the right to education. But the fact is often disregarded that these rights become meaningful only when they are coupled to duties which must be executed.

2.3. The educationist

Education proceeds from the educationist (parent, teacher, lecturer) and is aimed at the educand (child, scholar, student). It stands to reason that the educationist must satisfy extremely high requirements in order to succeed in his aim. Without belief in God and love for his fellow-men; without knowledge and wisdom; without experience and authority; without tact and insight, no education can succeed. He who is not himself an integrated being, cannot attempt integration in the lives of others. He who is not himself an intelligent adult, cannot lead others to adulthood. The aim of the Christian educationist at the Christian institution is for several reasons much more difficult than that of the educationist at a secular institution. Why? Because he has to provide a unique content to the *Christian* concept. For the same reason, however, it is much more rewarding.

2.4. The educand

With the verbal transfer of the educational truths and their practical realization in the life of the educationist there are corresponding agreement and imitation in the life of the educand. The educand is first and foremost a human being. And as such he is an unfinished product, a man-in-genesis. A part of his unfinishedness and incompleteness is that at a certain stage he knows less than the educationist. For this reason he cannot be regarded as permanently inferior to the educationist, because if that were true it would not only be a negation of his value and meaning as man, but his being is lowered to a static size and he would be denied the possibility of full development. The fact that the educand acts on a lower level — which also is no static situation — does not imply that he cannot progressively, with the extension of his own education, play a more important rôle in the educational process. After all, education ought to result in the educand finally becoming the educationist.

3. *The Christian scholar as one who educates through science*

In conclusion a few remarks about science. Science is taught at a university; that is, the university as academic institution deals with the different aspects of scientific labour, with research and lecturing. But the university, and the Christian university specifically, must be more than merely an academic institution: it must produce people for this world. Mere transfer of factual knowledge is no substitute for a way of life. And the fundamental question is: how can the university execute its task to prepare the student for a way of life? Various possibilities can be investigated — and are in fact being investigated at certain universities. One of these is to introduce a special course such as *studium generale* in which students receive instruction in a life and world view. Such an approach has great advantages undoubtedly and must be recommended. But that is no adequate answer to the problem. To the contrary, it evokes the question whether an additional course to the science being studied is really necessary to bring home to the student the Christian principles underlying his philosophy of life? Shouldn't every science itself provide these principles? It is for this reason that we can conclude: only then is a university Christian, and its education Christian, when each science is taught as a Christian science.

True Christian education necessitates a special view of science and this science the Christian lecturer will have to present to the Christian student. Like the university, science also has a twofold character: one internal and the other external. The internal objective is the act of obtaining knowledge which obviously has to meet certain requirements. The external objective is to proclaim the Glory of God and to serve man and his community. The university also has a twofold destiny: to develop science as science and to allow students (as scientists) *to take their place in the community* and so to fulfil their rôle as leaders. The university is concerned with the whole student, not only with his intellect, and therefore the whole student should be involved in his education by the university. The major task of the university, namely the intellectual development of the student, may not be divorced from the development of his personality and character. Much more than in the past the university will have to study ways and means for introducing a complete educational aim in which the cultivation and motivation of the student as a whole being are involved. But this will have to be done from within science itself. What are the most important aspects of science? I suggest the following as of greatest significance for our purpose:

3.1. The life and world view aspect of science

The viewpoint that the so-called pre-scientific phase (where the life and world view is usually placed) as well as the post-scientific phase does not belong to science as such, cannot be accepted. When you say science, you say life and world view. No science is divorced from that, whether it is explicitly rejected or not. And when you say man, you say life and world view, because every individual has a total complex of answers to fundamental questions, considerations and reflections. For that reason education will always be looked at from this point of view. There is no such thing as neutral education even though it may be defended very strongly. It is precisely the task of the educationist, therefore, to be aware of the intrinsic nature of the framework within which he operates. Indeed, education may be called the conquering and establishment of a responsible life and world view.

3.2. The ethical aspect of science

The university, which is responsible for scientific teaching, will point out to its students that it is concerned not only with the acquisition of knowledge but also with the implementation of such knowledge. Each science — the one more so than the other — has an ethical perspective and with this the university of our time will have to acquaint its students. Therefore, the students should be intimately and responsibly integrated with the community in which they live and which they will later have to serve. Science may not sit on the balcony and as a spectator view the world drama which is being enacted. Such a balconized science, though it may answer to its internal objectives, is a sterile science and not worthy of being called a science. Similarly a student may not excuse himself from or be kept in ignorance of the practical implications of science for daily life. It is precisely because scientific knowledge and technology have advanced so rapidly that the question of what the student is going to do with his science, has become so important. Indeed, the ethical relevance of science in our times has become of the greatest importance. Certain experiments may be acceptable considered from the point of view of the accumulation of knowledge, but from an ethical point of view they may be completely unacceptable. This situation will have to culminate in and be closely guarded by a finely developed sense of ethical responsibility in the student. More than ever the function of science as the conscience of culture will have to be brought home to the student and lecturer and must be kept alive.

3.3. The futuristic aspect of science

The student's involvedness in and responsibility to the present community as well as to the future can not be over-emphasized. He must be taught responsibility, but from within, i.e. from that with which he is busy, namely science. The modern university will have to lecture on science in a futuristic perspective. Science is specifically concerned with the future for two reasons. Firstly, science is very intimately bound to life, and life as such is an anticipation of the future. He who lives and works in the present orientates himself to and prepares himself for much more, labours for the future. Science which directs the community of today, is therefore at the same time constructing the community of tomorrow.

The second reason why science, especially in our time, is so intimately concerned with the future, is due to the almost indescribable powers of science and technology today. Science with its applied results can catastrophically destroy all life on earth and can also execute qualitative changes in the history of this world of ours.

If mankind is to survive, it will not merely be because people are born but because they decide to prolong life on earth, and for instance banish the use of the atom bomb, the hydrogen bomb and the germ bomb. In this way man receives life from his own hand. These are the considerations which suddenly force man to realize his responsibilities for the future. And it is these considerations which give modern university students their unique, even dramatic opportunity to be involved in the community of the future. The shape of the future is determined by man, obviously not exclusively, but at least in a co-determining way. And the student is included in this activity.

The study of and projections as to the future are not the task of a single science, but every science has a teleologic, i.e. futuristic dimension. And no science may regard this task as a mere accidental annexe to its main task of getting on with the work. The teleological perspective teaches the student who is fully aware of his limitations that he may not just passively await the future and that he may not waste his powers on inconsequential matters, but that he must actively plan for the future; that he must theoretically assimilate the latent possibilities of the present in their significance for the future and in so doing help to build the future, well knowing that the true future, in contrast with the designed future, will be eventually a gift of God.

In the light of the importance of a future dimension coupled to the implied general changes in the accepted ways of life, a well-planned future will have to form an integral part of a Christian educational programme. If not, the result may be people educated for a world which will no longer exist when they are grown up. It is for this reason that the Christian educationalist, who comprehends the future events within the framework of a Christian eschatology, has to express his prophetic voice more clearly than ever before. Modern man, who in many ways has fallen a prey to his own cultural and structural creations, will have to be feed from them on the one hand and have to be prepared to master them and to remain master of them on the other hand.

True Christian education will therefore have to be neither conservative nor progressive but allow both accents to harmonize evenly. Someone rightly said: There are only two lasting bequests we can hope to give our young. One is roots, the other wings (Hoddling Carter). What is needed, therefore, is to have the educand firmly anchored in lasting principles, on the one hand, and the opening of a perspective to a meaningful future on the other hand; a future which is in the hands of man yet remains a gift of God; a future towards which he may work with joy and thankfulness, and a future for which he may wait hopefully and faithfully.

The position of the Christian teacher at the Christian university — with special reference to the situation in Japan as a non-Christian country

Prof. Dr. Takeshiro Kodera

1. *Christians and the Christian universities in Japan*

I work at a Christian university as a Reformed Christian teacher. But it is a Christian university located in a non-Christian country. Japan is not a Christian country, but rather a gentile country. The percentage of Christians in Japan's total population is very low. The total number of Protestant Christians in Japan was 773 598 in 1974, as shown in Table 1. Japan's total population is approximately 110 million. Therefore, the percentage of Protestant Christians in the total population is only 0.7%. Even when we include Catholic members, it becomes only 1%.

Table 1: Number of Ministers and Church members in 1974:

	Ministers	Members
The Reformed Church in Japan	106	5 798
Church of Christ in Japan	147	12 750
United Church of Christ in Japan	2 270	194 059
Others (including more than 100 denominations)	19 347	560 991
Total	21 870	773 598
Catholic Church	9 400	383 934

But with the educational institutions, the scene is a little bit different. Christian schools in Japan have organized the Education Association of Christian Schools in Japan. The membership of the Association numbers 91 schools. Among them, 30 universities (four year colleges) are included.

There are three kinds of universities in Japan: National, Local, Municipal and Private universities. The number of each in 1974 was 80, 32 and 298 respectively. Therefore, the number of Christian universities represent 10% of all private universities. Christian universities in Japan generally have a good reputation. But this is mainly because Japanese people expect that the education offered by these institutions has a moral foundation which comes from Christian belief. And they seem not to expect the education itself to be Christian.

Most Christian schools in Japan were founded in the last part of the 19th century by American missionaries. At that time, Western civilization was not yet widely prevalent in Japanese society. The Christian schools, which were called Mission Schools, were the important route through which Western culture was introduced into Japanese society. And many missionary teachers were admired not only as evangelists but also as bringers of the new and higher civilization. This role which the Mission Schools had achieved is surely one of the reasons for the good reputation which the Christian universities are enjoying today.

But the cultural situation in present day Japan is quite different from that of the era when most of the Christian universities were founded. Western civilization and technology are widely prevalent in Japan and they are no longer a novelty. The role of Christian schools has necessarily changed. They are no longer major importers of Western culture, but are expected to be educational institutions in the real sense. The Christian schools were called Mission schools in the past, but some say that they should be called schools with a mission: an educational mission.

What then is education? This is a topic about which many discussions are going on at present in Japan. Especially with respect to higher education, such discussions are very lively, because many universities have been thrown into disorder in recent years. Radical students criticised their own universities. They often violently occupied the buildings of the university, and erected barricades to prevent teachers from coming to teach. The purpose of their movements seemed not to be based on penetrating thought and well articulated theory. Their movements had no specific relations with any established political parties including the communist party. Sometimes, they were called new leftist movements but they simply originated from vague dissatisfactions they had against the established form of the university and more generally against the rigidity of the existing social order. They insisted that these firmly established structures were oppressing their freedom. Therefore, their movements were very destructive and had no constructive goal.

This disorder in the universities came to a head several years ago, and now the situation seems to be cooling down. But the many questions raised by them are left unanswered. One of them is the question: what is education?

I am not a specialist in education, but I had to think it over and over again as president of a university during this uncertain period. When I was appointed President, the campus of Kwansei Gakuin University was completely occupied and blockaded by radical students, and we could not enter our own campus. It seemed to me that the situation could not be relieved without having clear notions about education, especially higher education.

There was a tendency in post-war Japan for education to become rather a highly technical matter. The pressure to teach scientific knowledge to as many as possible and at as high a level as possible was strong. But the disorder in the universities brought some reflection, and it has become a more and more acceptable idea that education must be a matter of promoting the formation of personality, to build up character, and to nurture human nature. Education does not mean only to impart knowledge to younger generations and train them technologically, but this must be done on the basis of some human morality. Education must be human education. In my case, it was fortunate that Kwansei Gakuin University is a Christian university. Human education could be fostered by strengthening further Christian education.

Japanese people in general had been under the strong influence of Confucianism (the thought of Confucius). But after World War II, Confucianism was criticized as a teaching which supported a feudalistic society, and has been rejected as a moral foundation for education. But because the Japanese people have not come up with a moral foundation which could serve as a substitute for Confucianism, they find themselves in a chaotic spiritual situation.

Christianity is not accorded the popularity which Confucianism traditionally had, but I think it has in essence a property which can serve the same role that Confucianism did. This consideration seems to point to the importance of Christian education in present day Japan.

Again I would like to say that education must be based on some human morality and so human education is a fundamentally different matter from the training of animals, for example, for a circus.

2. *Problems which the Christian universities in a non-Christian country have to face*

From the preceding consideration, it will naturally be understandable that a Christian university in a non-Christian society such as Japan has an important role just because it is in a non-Christian society. But at the same time, because it is in a non-Christian society, it has to face some specific problems.

Here I consider two aspects. One is the problem of how to firmly maintain and continue Christian education. The other is the evangelical responsibility of the Christian university.

I have here some statistics about my school, Kwansei Gakuin University, showing the number of Christians among teachers and students. (See Table 2).

If we compare this with the percentage of Christians in the total population of Japan, we find that these percentages are strikingly high. But at the same time, this table shows that it is impossibly hard to get Christian teachers, especially in higher education. In this situation the problem of how to maintain and promote Christian education becomes important.

The so-called Christian code is one of the devices available for such a purpose. Different Christian schools have different codes. The most severe code requires that all teachers must be Christians. Universities which have such a severe code are few. Two universities which were established after World War II, that is the International Christian University and Shikoku Gakuin University, are examples.

Table 2: Number of Christians in Kwansei Gakuin:

Teachers	Total	Christian	% of Christians
University	264	83	31.44
Senior High School	36	15	41.67
Junior High School	21	10	47.62
Office Clerks	246	39	15.85
Students			
University	14 267	216	1.51
Senior High School	999	20	2.00
Junior High School	559	3	0.54

As to Kwansei Gakuin University, its original constitution when the school was founded prescribed in its second article that "The object of this institution is training of chosen young men for the Christian Ministry, and the intellectual and religious culture of youth in accordance with the principles of Christianity", and this prescription has been taken over in the present constitution. But its Christian code is a very limited one. Only the Chancellor (the Chairman of the Board of Trustees) and the Principal of the High School must be Christians. Even the President of the University and the Deans of Departments need not be Christians.

Of course, this does not mean Christian education in Kwansei

Gakuin University is not active and effective. Our Christian education is widely supported by almost all members, Christians and non-Christians, of the University. But we have offices which specifically work for Christian education. One of them is that of the chaplain. The University and every Department have a chaplain who works exclusively for Christian education. Another example is the Christian Activity Committee which was at first voluntarily organized by Christian teachers and now has become an official organization of the University and is playing an important role in Christian education.

It seems to be very important that the attitude of non-Christian teachers is, in general, highly supportive. Most of them seem to be aware of the necessity of a moral foundation in education, though they themselves do not specifically advocate any particular morality or religion. Of course, scholars who oppose Christianity do not get appointed at the Christian university. But, in fact, the public in Japan has rather vague sentiments on the various religions. For example, most Japanese perform their marriage ceremony according to Shinto rites and the same people have funeral rites according to Buddhism. They seem not to distinguish clearly between morals and religion. Such a vague notion of religion makes the activity of the Christian university easier, but at the same time it makes evangelical activity harder. I think this vague attitude is one of the reasons why Christians in Japan easily entertain heretical thought, departing from true Biblical faith.

Another problem which the Christian university in the non-Christian country experiences lies in its evangelical activity. As already mentioned, Christian universities in Japan were mostly established by foreign missionaries. Some foreign missionaries worked for churches and some for schools. Many churches and schools were founded by them. But schools eventually outgrew churches. At present, Christian churches can not financially help Christian schools at all. Most Christian schools are now independent institutions. As to Kwansei Gakuin University, it was founded by the missionaries of the Southern Methodist Church of the U.S.A. and afterwards the United Church of Canada joined the work. But it has no constitutional relationship with any specific Church at present, though we still have missionary teachers from America and Canada. It is an independent educational institution.

But the Christian schools in a non-Christian country can not escape from evangelical activities beside their educational functions. And evangelical activities must mainly be carried on by Christian teachers. Activities of the Christian teachers are many-sided. Not only do they teach their specific subjects, but they also serve as speakers in Chapel, which is maintained in every Department. Some Christian teachers gather students voluntarily and have a Bible class. As a group, they are organized into the Christian Activity Committee, which not only organizes but also carries on evangelical activities.

Of course, there is no difference in salaries and other conditions between non-Christian teachers and Christian teachers. The evangelical responsibility is naturally born by Christian teachers as an additional task. The fruits of evangelical activities in Christian schools should not be evaluated only by the number of students who have been converted to Christianity during their school days. Many who are not converted at school seem to be very much influenced by the education which is offered according to the principles of Christianity. I think that the Christian teachers at Christian universities are rewarded from heaven. Table 2 shows the number of Christian students at Kwansei Gakuin University. We see from this table that the number of Christian students increases at higher ages.

The evangelical activities at the universities should, in principle, be carried on in close co-operation with churches. But many Christian schools are now hesitant to co-operate with churches, because many churches are in a state of disorder. In many churches the word of men, not the Word of God is spoken. I remember Chapter 2, verse 13 of the First Letter of Paul to the Thessalonians: "And we also thank God constantly for this, that when you received the word of God which you heard from us, you accepted it not as the word of men but as what it really is, the word of God, which is at work in you believers". We are earnestly anticipating the development of churches where only the Word of God is spoken, as the Reformed Church is trying to do. I can point out the fact that membership of the United Church of Japan decreased by 1 912 during 1973. The decrease is about 1%. The Reformed Church in Japan is still a very small Church, but its members increased by 698 during the same year. The percentage of the increase is nearly 14%.

I myself as a Reformed teacher at Kwansei Gakuin University, one of the most important Christian universities in Japan, think that what I am doing is of the utmost significance for myself. I have been studying economics as a social scientist, I have been teaching economics to our students as a Christian teacher, and for a five year period I had assumed administrative responsibility at the University as President. All these jobs seem to me not to contradict my faith at all, but rather to promote my faith profoundly.

3. *Possibility of a Christian social science, especially Christian economics*

Lastly, as a Reformed social scientist, I would like to consider briefly the possibility of Christian or Reformed sciences.

I would not deny the possibility of a Christian science, but at the same time, I do not think that Christian science is a matter which should be made up intentionally. We should not try to construct it artificially. Such an attempt will not be rewarded. For example, economics has its own method. We have to study economics according to the methodology of economics. But who studies economics is an important matter. In my case, it will be a Reformed scholar who is studying economics. I think it makes a difference whether a Christian studies economics or a non-Christian studies it. Economics has many aspects. It varies from pure theory which is predominantly logical, to economic policy which inevitably has close relationships with value-judgements. This is the reason why economics can have different features, according to who is the economist who studies economics. I think this can be said not only about economics but also about social science in general.

The object of economics is man. And man in economics is defined as economic man, who wants to pay the least cost and tries to get as much as possible. An economic man is very rational in his behaviour, but is also purely egotistic. This definition of an economic man reminds us, Christians, of a sinner. In a society where no individual has the power to affect others, in other words, in a society which is composed of equally small individuals (which seems to be what Adam Smith had in mind) the egotistic behaviour of each individual will tend to bring the optimum well-being for all, through the guidance of an "Invisible Hand".

But in our society at present, some individuals or organizations do have the power to affect others. In such a situation, it will be very important to realize that man is a sinner. If a sinner as such gets power as a dictator or a monopolist, the social situation will become critical. We can not be so optimistic as Adam Smith was two hundred years ago. We have to consider and analyse economic society from a different point of view. We can not be so optimistic as Adam Smith was, but we are fundamentally optimistic because we know that the world is still under the control of our Lord. But this does not mean that we need not study our economy objectively and try to find the most suitable economic policy. This becomes rather critically important, because if we fail to find the way according to which we should live, this world in which we live would then be turned into a state of confusion.

Our day-to-day life is subject to the exercise of the power of some individuals, that is, the influence of politicians who decide economic policies, of monopolistic entrepreneurs who decide the prices of commodities, of labour union leaders who decide the level of wages, etc. When we think of these tendencies in the present world, it is understandable that some economists say that economics is a normative science. For example, Professor Roelf L. Haan, who follows the thought of Professor Herman Dooyeweerd, has written in his book *Special Drawing Rights and Development* (Leiden: Steifert Kroese, 1971), that "As economic science studies human behavior according to economic norms, economics is *per difinitionem* a normative science, in contrast with the study of the 'laws of nature' ". We have to recognize that the normative aspect of economics is increasing in weight because of the current tendency of society. But at the same time it seems to me very important to recognize that economics has in part also a similarity with the study of the 'laws of nature'. Human desire could not be satisfied without human effort, which is accomplished in accordance with the laws of nature. For example, the most fundamental law is that "we can only use things which we have manufactured with our labour". When we consider our economic policy, we have to find some ways to mitigate the conflicting interests of individuals or groups of individuals which have some social power. To realise such mitigation, I think, two things become important. The one is the normative attitude of the person who is in power. The other is the knowledge of natural laws in economics, which makes it possible for people to understand what will be the inevitable consequence of some one's economic behaviour.

In all cases, the personalities of individuals who have power over other individuals become critically important. If such an individual is a sinner who behaves egotistically, the society which is affected by him will not be a stable and satisfactory one. The important matter here is that every individual should know that he is a sinner in his nature and has to be generous to others. But this is not a matter which is easily realised. I think that here again the importance of Christian education is clearly shown.

An economist who studies the economy of the present world must know that he himself is a sinner. I remember a sentence written by Professor Bent Hansen. He wrote about Professor Jan Tinbergen, the first economist who was awarded the Nobel Prize, "he (Prof. Tinbergen) has always felt that in working on development problems in poor countries and devoting his life to improving economic conditions in such countries he would help to repair some of the evils of colonial oppression and pay off some of the debts of the old colonial powers — including his own country" *(International Trade and Finance: Essays in Honour of Jan Tinbergen,* London: Macmillan, 1974, p. 10—11). From this sentence, we can learn about the generosity which an economist must have. Holy Scripture tells us that "Judge not, and you will not be judged; condemn not, and you will not be condemned; forgive, and you will be forgiven" (Luke 6 : 27). Especially we should be generous to the non-Christian world. Paul writes to us, "Who are you to pass judgement on the servant of another? It is before his own master that he stands or falls" (Romans 14 : 4) and "For what have I to do with judging outsiders? Is it not those inside the church whom you are to judge? God judges those outside" (1 Corinthians 5 : 12—13). Though we are saved by the Saviour, we can not act as if we are an agent of God.

Professor Jacob Viner wrote on Adam Smith that he "ridiculed those who attributed to man's wisdom what is really the wisdom of God, or nature". As already said we can not be optimistic in the same sense as Adam Smith, but we know the verse of Holy Scripture that "the foolishness of God is wiser than men, and the weakness of God is stronger than men" (1 Corinthians 1 : 25). It is important to realize that we are weak. We, as weak men, should try hard in our vocation in which we see value. I myself am satisfied with my job of teaching students and of studying economics at a Christian University, which seems to be very important especially at the present stage of the world in which we have to live.

The Christian in the secular university

Prof. Dr. W. Stanford Reid

WHEN the writer of this paper was first asked to present it to the Conference of Christian Scholars, he was at first somewhat puzzled as to how he should deal with the question. Should this be a paper which discussed abstract philosophical principles or problems, or should it deal with the present realities of the situation as he knows them. After considerable thought, being an historian trained in empirical investigation, he decided on the latter procedure, trusting that his philosophical position would become clear as he set forth what are primarily reflections on his own experience in three universities both as a student at undergraduate and graduate level and as a teacher for the past thirty-five years, during eighteen of which he was also an administrator.

No doubt the situation of a Christian within secular institutions of higher learning may differ from place to place. The writer, therefore, whose experience extends primarily to three North American universities, will tend to think primarily in terms of the situation in the United States and Canada. He has had some experience, however, as a visiting lecturer in Europe, the British Isles and the West Indies which, he trusts, will prevent his remarks from being too provincial. It is necessary, nevertheless, to give some idea of the background against which he sets forth his views of the situation of the Christian in the secular university.

The university in North America as in Europe and Great Britain had its origins in the desire of Christian people to provide an education for the rising generation. Roman Catholics, whether in the Spanish colonies or in New France, established universities at a very early date, and Protestants followed the same practice, with the result that down to 1850 one might say that most of the North American universities still had what might be called a basically Christian orientation, although by that date many of the leading Protestant institutions had become largely secularized in fact. The Roman Catholic colleges and universities have been able, largely because of direct church control, to maintain their Roman Catholic character down to the present time although even now they are succumbing to the same process which has come to dominate what were once Protestant institutions.

While there have been many factors involved in the gradual secularization of formerly Christian schools of higher learning, one of the most important has been the gradual flight of Christians from the classrooms. Yale, for instance, was founded as a result of the predominance of rationalism at Harvard. Then, after Timothy Dwight's passing from the presidency of Yale, the same process took place there. Other Christian institutions were founded as a result, but repeatedly they have become infected with unbelief and instead of the Christians staying to do battle in the intellectual forum, they have moved to or established new Christian colleges. The reason for this may have been that which was given to me by a Christian Ph.D. student who stated that he wished to teach in a Christian college. When asked why, he replied "Because I shall be in an environment where I shall not have to battle for my faith all the time". While this may be true, he will also find out that in a Christian college he will be so loaded with teaching responsibilities that he will find little opportunity for research and writing. Further-more, he will have little opportunity to exercise an influence on the field of scholarship as a whole. Some Christians have seen this, we may thank God, and are returning to the secular university to maintain a witness as Christian academics. This may well mean the one hope of the secular university which is increasingly finding that its materialistic-positivist-idealist philosophies do not work.

1. *The Christian teacher in the secular university*

One finds today little or no worked-out philosophy of education in the secular university except that of "objectivity" and "freedom" of thought. As Marc Zamansky, Dean of the Faculté des Sciences at the University of Paris, pointed out in 1969, the French universities have very little integrated coherent thought about their purpose and methods, and much the same can be said for the secular universities generally in the non-Communist world.[1] True, many of those teaching in these universities have now come to doubt the validity of any claim to pure objectivity in their work, but they still insist that there should be complete freedom of thought for all points of view. Indeed, the very decline of faith in the possibility of objectivity has reinforced the idea of freedom which is really a total relativism and a denial or ignoring of any idea of absolute truth.

While this attitude is true for the university as a whole, it is most commonly expressed in the disciplines embraced by the Humanities and Social Sciences. In the physical or natural sciences, however, there are still many faculty members who have not gone along with this relativism, nor have they taken to heart the ideas of such men as Max Planck or A. S. Eddington who speak of metaphysics or mystery as being behind the work of the chemist, the physicist and the biologist.[2] The physical scientist frequently adopts the attitude that what he has discovered in his laboratory or on his field trips is absolute and final truth. The present writer remembers when as a junior member of his department he had an argument with one of the discoverers of DDT who tried to have him fired because he refused to accept his evolutionary ideas. In the face of this situation, the Christian scientist has problems not faced by his colleagues in other faculties. And yet, after many conversations with both Christian and non-Christian — one must come to the conclusion that the desire for academic freedom is still very strong even in physical science faculties.

Because of this situation in the average secular university, the Christian teacher usually has complete liberty to teach as he sees fit. He is of course bound, by virtue of his Christian pre-suppositions, to take a position different from that of his Marxist, his positivist or his idealist confrères. But if he can support his point of view with sound evidence he seldom has any trouble. He does not need to stand up and commence his course of lectures by proclaiming that he is a Christian. As one university chaplain said to the present writer at the beginning of his academic career: "Go ahead and teach your courses as you feel they should be taught, with your own emphases and presuppositions, and your students will soon know exactly where you stand". If the Marxist, the materialist or the idealist has the right to teach from his point of view, surely the Christian can claim no less freedom to teach as he sees and interprets his material.

In his teaching and his academic work generally, however, the Christian's attitude is important. He will soon discover that among his colleagues and students there are always some who are hostile to him and his views. On the other hand, he will also find those who ignore and disregard his ideas. In fact they may even regard him as somewhat eccentric and strange. As one colleague put it to a Christian professor: "How can you have the brains to obtain a Ph.D. and still accept Christianity?" In this situation, which is common in the secular university, the Christian has two alternatives. He can by a rigid and censoriously dogmatic attitude alienate and antagonize both colleagues and students, so that he only increases their hostility. In so doing he may of course feel that this is the cross he must bear. Yet he may adopt another attitude, that of good humour and friendliness which attracts rather than repels people. Indeed a sense of humour may in this situation be counted as one

234

of the gifts of God's sanctifying grace, for it is basically a sense of proportion which enables one to see himself and those around "in the light of eternity", so that he does not take himself or his problems overly seriously.

At the same time, the Christian teacher must be what Cornelius van Til describes as epistemologically self-conscious. He must see the importance for his own work of his fundamental pre-suppositions, and how in differing from those of the non-Christian they influence his point of view and so of his interpretations of the factual content of his scientific knowledge. He must recognize in this the noetic influences of both sin and regeneration. This will enable him to understand why, although he may buttress his position with all kinds of evidence, others who may never have experienced the regenerating power of the Holy Spirit cannot see eye to eye with him. When he sees and understands this, many of the problems which seem to force themselves upon him will tend to be resolved. Yet so often this is exactly where the Christian teacher fails, for he has not sufficiently studied and understood his own position and how it differs in the field of scientific study from that of the non-Christian.

This takes us back to the question of the Christian teacher's own spiritual life. In a secular atmosphere such as is common in most non-Christian universities and colleges, it is very easy for a Christian to "let down his guard". He can become slovenly about his own private Bible study and prayer, he can become very casual in his study and reading of Christian literature. He may not give it up, but he may content himself with superficial Bible reading, a hasty prayer here and there and the reading of a few popular and superficial pamphlets or magazines. It would seem, therefore, that the Christian teacher must devote the same sort of attention and hard work to his spiritual life as he should to his academic work. This will mean that he should also be closely involved in the work of the church not only passively, but actively, for helping with the teaching function of the church he will find it necessary constantly to clarify his own thinking as a Christian academic.

Another aspect of his Christian nurture is his spiritual life within the university community. He will soon find that there are other Christian faculty members and also Christian students with whom he can have fellowship. Indeed, such contacts can become extremely stimulating as they may well result in the exchange of ideas, particularly if faculty and students can come together to discuss how their Christian faith gives them an orientation to their particular disciplines. Co-operation with organizations such as the

Inter-Varsity Fellowship, and the leading of discussion groups, will often give to the participating faculty member as much as the students receive from him. Coupled with this are the opportunities which the Christian academic has to write popular articles, particularly in relation to his own field of interest in the university. While these articles may not be the type which he will report for the university president's annual list of publications, they can be of very great help to the Christian layman who is sometimes overwhelmed by the views and ideas expressed in the secular press. Also, again such activities force the Christian academic to formulate his own ideas and thoughts more clearly.

These endeavours, however, are in a sense merely the background to the Christian's responsibility to relate his faith to his academic discipline. Some Christian teachers in secular universities never attempt this feat. They are content to adopt a kind of nature-grace dichotomy in which never the twain shall meet. It may be that intellectual laziness is one cause. But it may also be that the individual is working in a field where such an integration of his faith and his discipline is difficult, perhaps impossible in the light of the teacher's lack of Biblical and theological knowledge. The present writer has always been thankful for his time of study at Westminster Theological Seminary and particularly for the guidance of men such as Cornelius Van Til and for the opportunities which he has had to read the works of and have discussions with Herman Dooyeweerd of Amsterdam, both of whom opened up this whole matter for him. It would seem clear that the Christian academic in the secular university must know his own position and its implications if he would be able to relate his faith to his scientific studies.

That this is no option which the Christian can take or leave as he likes should be clear from the Biblical injunction that we are to bring every thought into the obedience of Christ (2 Cor. 10 : 5). This will not be a simple matter nor an easy one, but will require intensive and hard work which will never end. As the Christian academic increases in the knowledge of his own field he will find that new phenomena appear which he must seek to subsume under his Christian interpretation. At the same time, as he increases in knowledge as a Christian he will find new aspects of his faith which he must apply. Thus he will never be able to say, I have made the final and ultimate Christian interpretation of my field. For as John Robinson, the leader of the Puritans who migrated to New England, said: There will always be new light springing forth from the Word of God.[3]

Basic to his thinking are the fundamental doctrines of the

Christian faith. Controlling all his thinking is the basic pre-supposition of the biblical doctrine of the Tri-une God, who is sovereign over all things. This in turn involves the pre-suppositions of creation, providence and redemption. But it also brings into focus something which Christian academics often ignore, the doctrine of Common Grace which makes it possible for the Christian to communicate with the non-Christian not only on the religious, but also on the scientific level.

This brings us to the fact that the primary activity of the Christian academic is that of teaching. In this connection it should be emphasized that he is not conducting an evangelistic campaign or service. He is employed by his university to teach a specific field in a specific discipline. This is his responsibility, and while he teaches from his own Christian perspective, his work is not to preach sermons but to instruct the students in the particular science which they are supposed to be studying. He may very well bring out the differences in pre-suppositions with which men approach the subject, indicating that he prefers the Christian approach. In fact he may not even have to do this as his emphases in the course may well show this. But as in the case of the work of any Christian, in the final analysis he must leave all results in the hands of the Holy Spirit. It may be, as the present writer has found, that the result will be that students will come privately to ask questions, but that is something which the faculty member must leave to the care of Providence.

Another aspect of the Christian's work in the secular university is that of research and writing. This is of very great importance, for it not only enables the Christian scholar to present a Christian interpretation in his own field, but it also brings prestige to those who hold the Christian position. This is not a matter of private satisfaction, but has as its effect the encouragement of the Christians, both faculty and students who are in the university. Furthermore, it may well lead non-Christians to consider more carefully the claims of the Christian position. The writer of this article has found a good instance of this in his own experience. Teaching a freshman course on *Science and Society since 1500* he discovered that quite a number of the students each semester have been checking his monograph *Christianity and Scholarship* which they have then proceeded to take out and read. He has even had it quoted to him in class discussions and referred to in essays. True, this may have been a form of "apple-polishing" but at least they had read the book!

One other aspect of the Christian teacher's activity in the secular university is that he may well find himself placed in a position of administrative responsibility as a departmental chairman, a dean of faculty or in some other capacity. As a Christian he has an opportunity to manifest the Christian graces in his conduct of his office — and those graces may not always be sweetness and light but may require firmness, exactness and the assuming of responsibility. But such a position enables an academic who is a Christian to show his Christian faith and faithfulness most clearly and publicly. This can set the tone for a department, indeed for a whole faculty as he seeks to do all things to the glory of God.

In academic circles outside the university the Christian teacher in the secular university also has a peculiar opportunity. If he has done his work well in the field of both teaching and writing, he will have the opportunity to present papers and lead discussions at both Christian and non-Christian institutions and conferences. It may be that he will be faced with the necessity of dealing with topics far beyond his own field, but partially because he comes from a secular university, partially because he has shown himself to be a good researcher and writer, he will have the opportunity to wield an influence within the academic community far beyond the boundaries of his own university or college.

All these activities involve the Christian teacher's witness. True he does not preach from his podium, but as he sets forth his own views whether by word or by pen, he is still bearing his witness in one of the most crucial areas of contemporary culture. But this also means that he must be constantly open to discussion and criticism. It will be of little use if he seeks only to set forth his views dogmatically and fails to show himself willing to consider other ideas and alternative interpretations. He may well subject them to rigorous criticism, but he must be willing to give them a hearing. In so doing he may well help to straighten out some of the thinking of his colleagues, but may also have an effective impact on his students, particularly his Christian students who are looking for guidance in orientating their thinking to their academic studies. This brings us to the problems of the Christian student.

2. *The Christian student in the secular university*

When a Christian student comes to a secular university he may, depending upon his background, enter a world which is entirely new. He will find faculty members who are generally indifferent to the Christian point of view, regarding it as irrelevant. He will encounter a few faculty members who, positively antagonistic to the Gospel, take every possible opportunity to denigrate it. And he will also discover a number of the faculty who are Christians, some of

238

a fundamentalist stripe and others more theologically oriented who are Reformed in their thinking. As a student in the 1930s, the present writer found very few of the last group but there are many more in the American universities at the present time.

What is the student's reaction to this situation? Much will depend upon his own home and school training. Some may well have been antagonized by the Christian home background from which they have come and are only too anxious to find an excuse to reject the parental teachings. Others may well arrive at academy with Christian convictions, but are not trained and perhaps not anxious enough to think through their problems and so succumb to the general secularism. Others will register for courses which they feel will not cause them religious problems, while others, usually a minority, enter the university with a sense of calling to study God's handiwork in all its aspects to the glory of his name. But much of the attitude will depend upon the milieu from which the student has come.

Another factor will be the students with whom he consorts and the friends he makes at the university. If he seeks out and makes contacts with other Christians he will soon find that there is a mutual fellowship which brings mutual help in times of difficulty. Another factor provided by the university is that of the courses and program in which the student works. Very often if he concentrates in a rather narrow field, so that he thinks only in the terms of that field, he may well develop a dichotomy in his thinking, enclosing his religion in one water-tight compartment and his academic work in the other, without attempting to relate the two. A certain type of anti-intellectual fundamentalist thinking very often follows this pattern.

One help to the Christian student is the student Christian society. In North America we find at least three groups working on the campus. Although it might be better if there were only one, they nevertheless do help to give the Christian student an anchor and guidance. One cannot help but notice, however, that such groups, unless they have some form of permanent leadership, tend to vary from time to time, sometimes becoming strongly fundamentalist, emotional and anti-intellectual, and sometimes Reformed, intellectual and even philosophical depending upon the student leadership involved.

In helping and strengthening such students Christian faculty members can play an effective role. Students may not always feel that they need such help, nor may they agree with the professors' ideas and points of view, but in many cases they will recognize that Christians are present, holding important academic positions, and to them they can turn in case of need. The faculty members in turn can give their assistance by helping students in extra curricular activities such as Bible study groups of various kinds. More important, however, is their function as personal advisers, particularly when the student comes up against another faculty member who denies specifically the Christian position. The believing teacher is able to indicate to the student the noetic impact of regeneration which enables the Christian to see matters in a different light from that of the non-Christian. Once this idea is grasped, it makes all the difference in the world to a student's understanding of his own position as well as that of the non-Christian.

Probably the most important part which the Christian professor plays, however, is simply as a teacher. The Christian who attends his classes soon discerns that here is a teacher who approaches his subject from the same perspective or angle as he does. This not only enables him to look at his subject from a truly Christian point of view, but also encourages him, particularly if his teacher is known as a sound scholar, to realize that the Christian faith is entirely in accord with true scholarship. The author has also had the experience of students from other faculties coming to him to say what an encouragement it is to them simply to know that a Christian is teaching and writing effectively in his own field. Thus in many different ways the Christian teacher helps and encourages the Christian student on his way.

The question may then be asked: If the Christian student needs such help, why does he go to a secular university and not to a Christian institution? This question has been put to a number of students with varying results, but one underlying reason given is that they feel that they will have to come to grips with the secular world at some point in their lives, and the sooner they do it the better. While they recognize that Christian colleges and universities have their point and purpose, they feel that they should come to grips with the opposition as soon as possible, and that learning in university what the non-Christian thinks will be of the greatest help. They appreciate their home and church training, but feel that they must now apply it in everyday life in the secular world. They frequently feel that the Christian institution tends to be a sort of hothouse, while it is only in the chilly blast of the secular world that they will grow strong to bear an effective witness. One other reason for their attending the secular university is that they feel that they there receive a wider and better education in terms of their interests and disciplines.

While some students coming from Christian homes and even

from Christian schools may fall by the wayside, those who survive, and they are numerous, usually come out stronger and more effective Christians than if they had not been obliged to struggle for their faith. Moreover, they probably understand the non-Christian points of view far better than those who have only heard of them second hand from Christian teachers, or have read of them in books without having to answer the unbeliever's arguments.

3. *The challenge of the secular institution*

The secular institution of learning presents today a direct challenge to the Christian academic community. It is a challenge to action, not just to talk. Our institutions of higher learning have often been founded by Christians but they have been taken over by unbelieving secularists. The challenge is, therefore, to go back in and take over, not by force of arms or political manoeuvrings, but by the sheer weight of Christian scholarship. Not an academic Anabaptism which forsakes the world, but a thoroughgoing Calvinistic "world-conquering" vision is what is needed.[4]

Indeed, it may be that only if this takes place will the university world itself be saved from disintegration. Secular university thinking is today becoming schizoid in that while it talks of reason and personality, it is also talking of pure chance as behind everything, a chance which has hardened into an unbreakable determinism. Herman Dooyeweerd believes that this is characteristic of eighteenth century thought, but it is just as true today.[5] The result is, as Jacques Ellul has pointed out in his *The Technological Society*, that everything has now been reduced to a technique,[6] including even the technique of making love. The result is that except in the purely professional or technical fields, both professors and students are at a loss to find meaning even in their own studies. As more than one secular writer has pointed out recently the result may well be total scepticism which results in an acceptance of the mystical or the occult as the only hope, for real scepticism has in history usually led to superstition.[7] If this wins the day, the universities are finished and as Malcolm Muggeridge has indicated a new Dark Ages will be upon us.[8]

In this situation the Christian perspective seems to be the only answer to the questions raised by secular thought. Taking seriously the sinfulness of man, the Christian holds that education is what might be termed training in discipline. Such training is not merely for the purpose of learning some new techniques, but has as its basic aim the training of man in order that he may understand and use God's creation, thus equipping him to fulfil his culture mandate

241

upon earth. By this means he will "glorify God and enjoy him forever".

Yet when we turn to this question of education, we immediately find that the Christian and the non-Christian come to their work with different approaches, and in many ways reach rather different conclusions. The reason for this lies in their different pre-suppositions, for while they may have exactly the same facts at their command they have different interpretations of the facts very frequently, because they begin from different starting-points.

The non-Christian assumes from the beginning the autonomy of the human mind and usually the autonomy of the phenomenal universe. Though he may speak of a god of some sort, he still insists upon the independence of man, particularly the scientist, from all divine control. If, however, he follows this train of thought to its ultimate conclusion he ends with an ultimate chance, which makes all his systems incomprehensible. As R. R. Thompson has put it concerning the atheistic evolutionist:

> The doctrine of evolution by natural selections as Darwin formulated it ... has a strong anti-religious flavour. This is due to the fact that the intricate adaptations and co-ordinations we see in living things, naturally evoking the idea of finality and design, and therefore of an intelligent providence, are explained, with what seems to be rigorous argument, as the result of chance.[9]

The only thing which saves the atheist or the agnostic from intellectual disintegration is his inconsistency which is a gift of God's "common grace".

The Christian scholar on the other hand, pre-supposing the Biblical doctrines of the Tri-une God, creation and providence finds himself in a somewhat different position. He recognizes that this is a complex but coherent universe whose laws he is able to discover and whose phenomena he can use for the support and enjoyment of life. He recognizes also that he has come to this knowledge only by the redemptive work of Jesus Christ applied to him by the Holy Spirit, and that therefore when he fulfils his calling as a scholar and teacher he is helping to open up this universe to greater understanding and comprehension even by those who do not accept his pre-suppositions.

The Christian perspective, in this way, with its stress upon the sovereignty of the Tri-une God, his creatorship, his providential governing "of all his creatures and all their actions", and his redeeming grace, provides a framework in and by which the rationality of both the universe and its human interpreters is assured. In the

242

final analysis it is the spacio-temporal universe seen in the light of eternity which alone makes sense. At the same time, it is this perspective which enables us to see and understand personality as being framed in the image of the creator and sustainer of all things, which enables us to realize that man is not just another product of physical and biological nature, but rather a unique being created to rule over and use the earth and its fruits to the glory of God. Christian understanding thus places both science, in its broadest sense, and technique in their proper positions while at the same time guarding the humanity of the individual.

Christ in his parables of the salt and the leaven (Math. 5 : 13; Luk. 13 : 21) indicated what this means for the Christian and, in the present university situation, the Christian scholar. Salt and leaven are effective only as they are mixed in with the other ingredients. Placing them in a cellophane bag in a pile of dough would be of absolutely no use. It would seem, therefore, that for Christians to act effectively as both salt and leaven, they must enter into the world, rub shoulders with the non-Christians and in the market place, reason and argue with the passers-by. It may be that if they do so, they will like Paul be invited to speak in the Areopagus concerning the "strange" god which they set forth (Acts 17 : 16ff). This is the work of the subjects of the Kingdom of Christ in this world. While the Christian academic is a member of the Church, the representative of Christ's Kingdom to the world, as a citizen of the Kingdom, his responsibility is to make Christ's rule effective, if you will, by infiltrating the Kingdom of this world. He does so, however, not in a disguise which hides his Christian identity, but as a Christian who seeks to indicate that all things, in every sphere of human thought and activity, belong in the Kingdom of Christ who is lord over angels, principalities and powers. It is when the Christian sees his work as his responsibility as a citizen of the Kingdom which "is not of this world" but which is "in" this world, that he recognizes his position and seeks to be at least 10% better than those who live solely for this world.

At the same time, the Christian academic who is called to work *in* the secular university, will have to recognize that his pre-suppositions are different from those of his non-Christian colleagues. This need not bring him into conflict with the conclusions to which his colleagues come in their scientific studies, since at "ground-level" God in his benevolence to all men, enables even the unbeliever to reach the truth. It will be at ultimate level that the conflict will arise. Yet it may be that even at the ultimate level he will receive a hearing if he has shown himself to be a good teacher and a competent scholar.

In one of his addresses on the subject of education, the late Dr. Gresham Machen made the statement that one thing which we need is that the attitude of the world should be changed in regard to Christianity.[10] It should be willing to listen to and hear what Christians have to say about their faith. If a Christian teacher does a good job as a scholar in the secular university, while his views may not be accepted, at least they will be listened to. This was Paul's experience in Athens, and it may be ours also, even though we see only a few really accept the Gospel. Furthermore, the Christians will have the opportunity to indicate that Christian pre-suppositions not only provide a framework and a base upon which to build sound scientific knowledge, but that in the final analysis, Christianity alone supplies the necessary foundation. The Christian teacher should seek to open up the way for both his colleagues and his students to see that Christianity is not anti-scientific, but is, with its doctrines of the sovereign God, creation, providence and redemption, the one system of thought which makes science possible.

In all the foregoing no mention has been made of Christian institutions of higher learning. It should not be thought, however, that they are of no importance or are superfluous. They should be the seed bed from which will grow strong Christian plants. They should be institutions which prepare and train men and women to go into the graduate schools and then on to the faculties of the secular universities. Unfortunately many graduates of Christian institutions seem to think only of how quickly they may leave the secular graduate faculty to return to the warm and comparatively safe environment of the Christian college. If this is the general attitude of many Christian scholars, and I am afraid it is, there arises the danger that instead of being the light of the world, they will simply spend all their time lighting each other's lamps. They will devote themselves to talking to themselves. They will not be in the position to give the leadership which the academic world needs so much today.

Christians today must move into the secular institutions if they would bear their witness in one of the most important spheres of our western culture. Christ gave his marching orders to his church to go into all the world and preach the Gospel to *every* creature. Unless the Christians do this in the secular institutions of higher learning, they are neglecting their responsibilities. The university today, with the large numbers of young people who are seeking entrance to it, is one of the most important places of Christian witness. It is there that we must claim all things for Christ, that in them also, he may have the preeminence.

---

1 M. Zamansky: *Mort ou Resurrection de L'Université?* (Paris, Plon, 1969), pp. 15ff.
2 Max Planck: *Scientific Autobiography and Other Papers*, F. Gaynor, tr. (New York, Philosophical Library, 1944), pp. 90ff. A. S. Eddington: *Science and the Unseen World* (1929).
3 J. T. Adams: *The Founding of New England* (Boston, Little, Brown, 1949), p. 96.
4 J. Tonkin: *The Church and the Secular Order in Reformation Thought* (New York, Columbia, 1971), pp. 93ff; W. S. Reid: "The Christian in the World: a Facet of Calvin's Thought", *The Gordon Review*, III (1951), pp. 40ff.
5 H. Dooyeweerd: *A New Critique of Theoretical Thought*, D. H. Freeman & H. de Jongste, trs. (Philadelphia: Presbyterian & Reformed, 1955), II, 354ff.
6 J. Ellul: *The Technological Society*, J. K. Wilkinson & R. K. Merton, trs. (New York, Knopf, 1965).
7 Cf. two articles in *Time* (New York): "Astrology: fad and phenomenon", March 1969, 93: 47—48; "The Occult: a substitute for faith", June 1972, 99: 62—68.
8 M. Muggeridge: "Living through an Apocalypse", *Christianity Today*, August 1974, 18: 4—8.
9 R. R. Thompson: "Introduction" to Charles Darwin, *The Origin of Species* (London: Everyman's Library, J. M. Dent & Sons, 1956), p. xxiii; cf. also J. Jeans: *The Mysterious Universe* (Cambridge, University Press, 1944), pp. 1ff.
10 J. Gresham Machen: "Christian Scholarship and the Defence of the Faith", in Machen: *What is Christianity?* (Grand Rapids, Mich., Eerdmans, 1951), p. 129.

ANNOTATED BIBLIOGRAPHY

W. F. Buckley Jr.: *God and Man at Yale* (Chicago: Henry Regnery & Co., 1951). An analysis of an American university and its faith in "Academic Freedom".

J. Ellul: *The Technological Society* (New York: Knopf, 1965). A somewhat Barthianleaning analysis of modern society, as background to an understanding of the modern secular university.

R. H. Gabriel: *Religion and Learning at Yale* (New Haven: Yale University Press, 1958). A study of the change in outlook at Yale over the period 1757—1957, with an insistence that a liberal education and Christian faith do not collide or coincide.

E. H. Harbison: *Christianity and History* (Princeton: Princeton University Press, 1964). Essay no. 5 "Liberal Education and Christian Education" sets forth a plea for the view that Christian faith really floods a liberal education with a new and true light.

A. S. Nash: *The University and the Modern World* (New York: MacMillan Co., 1944). While the author of this work is not entirely committed to a Reformed position, his analysis of the contemporary situation on the university campus is good, and his proposed "reconstruction" is one of the most positive suggestions yet made.

J. G. Machen: "Christian Scholarship and the Defence of the Faith", *What is Christianity?* (Grand Rapids: W. B. Eerdmans Co., 1951). In this address Dr. Machen shows the importance of presenting a logical and well-reasoned statement of the Christian faith to the unbelieving student.

J. Tonkin: *The Church and the Secular Order in Reformation Thought* (New York: Columbia University Press, 1971). A good analysis of the Reformers' view of the secular order, which helps to form a background to the Christian approach to secular education.

E. A. Walter: *Religion and the State University* (Ann Arbor: University of Michigan Press, 1958). A symposium which attempts to analyze the situation on the state university campuses in the United States, but it really provides no answers.

The medical school — secular or Christian

An examination of relationships facing the Christian teacher

Dr. D. R. Hanson

1. *Introduction: The medical school in a secular university*

Whilst the salient feature of the modern university will appear to many of us to be its secularisation, its inability to look at itself or its work *sub specie aeternitatis* (in the light of eternity), it has to be noted that interesting and significant vestiges remain of the Christian orientation with which many European universities began. It is possible to appeal to many features of the older universities, ceremonial, organisational and curricular, to demonstrate the comprehensively christian outlook assumed at their founding and thought essential to be propagated by their teaching. Therefore it is not as a complete alien, that one teaches christianity in the university — howsoever the times seem out of joint and the character of the institution seems secular.

A fortiori, the Medical School (in which the speaker's teaching experience has lain) exhibits traces of christian motivation. Not solely by virtue of the disproportionate strength of numbers of christians on the staff, but also having regard to the character of medical training as the bringing of care to those in need. Explicit statement of christian convictions in the classroom is not impossible and at numerous points within the teaching of medicine will be highly relevant.

Demands upon the medical school

An expanding curriculum — answering the advance in medical technology, asks for constant pruning of the older wood, if annual harvests of graduates are to be gathered. The de-humanising influence in the more technical branches of medical learning accumulates: statistics, cybernetics, computer studies appear now alongside the biochemistry and biophysics which I remember finding so far removed from people, their sicknesses and needs. An anatomist (and the learning of human anatomy in the cadaver can be a singularly humanising experience) recently bewailed the fact that it became almost impossible to learn the name of a single student in his classes — their contact has so declined.

In this curriculum, what time can be found for Man, our very proper study as potential doctors ?

It used to be possible to teach some courses on history and philosophy of science but the sciences themselves, and their technical applications, progressively oust such old fashioned luxuries from the time table. No wonder that the medical student, on completion of preclinical studies, enters the hospital for his clinical training abundantly receptive to any teaching that places the care of the sick within a framework, a worldview of christian principle. But more of this later.

Interfaculty communication within the university is a very tender plant indeed, and few are the skilled cultivators of it. Certainly the lot of the medical school is to find its own way within the university. The university as such becomes more and more identifiable with its management functions, its attention to finance, its employment of staff, its distribution of necessities and so on. The heart seems empty.

The community wants something of us too — it asks for doctors who will service it — as cars are taken to be serviced (or rather better!) so that its life is freed from discomforts, uncertainties, disagreeable discoveries of truth. Among the many demands from the community are heard, of course, the appeals for relief of suffering, anxieties about ability to go on working despite handicap, fears of dying and fears of bringing to birth, fears for children, for partners, for parents. But there too one hears the call for experts — isn't the technological apocalypse, the consultation of intra cellular, or radioactive, or computerised oracles, so much more gratifying (like Abana and Pharpar, the rivers of Damascus) than the facing of a turbid reality. An investigative technique gives the doctor something more to shelter behind, also. How impressed patients are with the recitation of a few laboratory measurements and how easily may one be tempted to pass such off as the answer to his question. Scientific abstraction, having lifted our feet thus off the ground, contrives to maintain a state of affairs in which it becomes impossible to return to the real — not the pretended question — "Will I — or he, or she, get better?"

But the community which places demands on us is not only the affluent and sophisticated consumer society of the West. Many of our graduates will find their way eventually to the places where poverty and hunger are the rule. Where death in infancy is expected and a man of fifty years is thought very old. Have we trained them in such a way that the needs of these communities can be met ?

Professional demands are placed on the medical school — demands to maintain an elite solidarity within Medicine (the initial capital indicates an idolatry at work). The approved qualifications have to be jealously guarded, approved methods perpetuated, however recently established. How can these demands upon medical training prepare tomorrow's doctors for their task in the undernourished, unemployed, disaster-ridden world to which they may go?

Not least of those who place demands on the university in its training for the practice of medicine is Government. Our secular institutions of higher education relate to the State as to the giver of every gift, however imperfect. A government department becomes the chief (if not the sole) arbiter in the matter of health care. A Secretary of State may claim to be responsible for the nation's health and the secular vision of health and what it entails, impinges without remission on the teaching of medicine.

Let Government declare some new form of "care" permissible at the manipulation of those tireless pressure groups, who, considering themselves enlightened and advanced, nevertheless act only "in the interest of the people". The medical school must oblige by incorporating it in the curriculum. We are expected to make the thing feasible; the pressure groups can be relied upon to make the permissible desirable. Abortion on social (even economic) grounds is such an instance. Legislation has given us a new medical industry — a notoriously expanding one! And already we hear the outriders of the Euthanasia campaign. Of course the feasibility, the technical possibility for these ignoble "advances", is already there. Can the medical school in its secular isolation, its closed universe, train doctors for whom the possible or the permitted or (as in Hitlerian Germany) the demanded actions will still have to be sanctioned by the criterion of true service?

Both Government and the Profession are easily seduced by the attractions of prestige in Medicine. Prestigious buildings, prestigious equipment, prestigious technique and specialisation — all of them place temptation before the teacher and the student of medicine. Self-service as a criterion is easily denied in words, less easily in practice. Can the christian teacher of medicine lead in another and better direction ?

2. *The student in medical school*

It is upon his relationships with students that the teacher of medicine

249

experiences the pressures exerted by those other relationships briefly described above. Who are his students? I speak of my own.

In some respects they are quite unlike the student as he appears in the popular eye. The medical student is already in possession of a number of defined academic goals. Aware of the need for a grasp of hard facts and exact knowledge, he anticipates the testing of his education at both the examination for qualification as a doctor and in his subsequent career. He is often somewhat anxious lest he be weighed and found wanting when it comes to a confrontation with serious sickness. He is remarkably tolerant of, indeed supportive of, an authority structure in his educational environment and in the organisation of hospital life. He has already begun to identify himself with a profession that he believes is both learned and somewhat altruistic. He may believe that his membership of this profession will bring him wealth and respect but he expects that this will involve the keeping of high standards of knowledge and practice on his part.

The medical student, at entry to the university, was qualified by examination results in scientific subjects. His training from the age of fourteen or fifteen years in school has been determined often by the selection of medicine as his career. An indifferent acquaintance with one modern foreign language, a desultory familiarity with elements of history and geography, a complete ignorance of any classical language, of philosophy, theology, art and music, a very inadequate awareness of literature and a frequently appalling lack of fluency in his own language make up his scholastic patrimony.

Thus prepared, he commences in medical school. Before he leaves, he will probably be married and possibly a father. His capacity to absorb data in the classroom, or on the hospital ward, will be sorely taxed by other responsibilities. Even his traditional sporting enthusiasm has been drastically curtailed.

All we have said of him ought to be understood with a further proviso — he is increasingly likely to be a she! Over fifty percent of medical students entering my school are now female.

The selection methods employed ensure a high degree of secularity in the medical student's outlook. It will not be surprising that the student graduates as a radically secularised physician. A positivist without knowing it, he is yet inspired by ideals of classical humanism tinged with christian motives. But he is rootless and sceptical; he expects no answers to ultimate questions and distrusts all that he calls dogma — excepting of course the dogmas of secularism.

3. *The christian teacher in the faculty of medicine*

One hopes that in meeting the christian university teacher, his students, colleagues, patients (in our particular case), subordinates and superiors will have something distinctive to observe. As a man made new, a new creature in Christ Jesus, a real man, it is to be desired that what he shows is not a constrictedness, a privation of character, a negativity, an isolation; rather should it be at each point the reverse. It will profit us little, in this conference as in our respective institutions of learning, to perpetuate the notion that christian scholarship, christian culture, (for that matter christian anything) is possible without in the first place its christian practitioners. Perhaps the time is opportune to re-emphasise that in all we do (and let our lives be as full and varied as they may) the character of a Christian man must be evident, and the fruits of the Spirit of Christ should be at work. Let it be said that christian scholarship pursued feverishly in the ambition of bringing to light a new, a distinctive, a christian interpretation of reality, christian facts unobserved by unbelievers, is a huge folly where love has no place, meekness is despised, joy is only selfsatisfaction and there is no peace. Any prayers uttered there for our work would be better described as propaganda. By contrast, as Reformed scholars, we ought to sense a dependence on the favour of the Lord in our scholarship as in our family or church life. Our good results, our successes are His gifts to us. In connection with the theological topic of Common Grace, it has recently been pointed out among Reformed people that the common-ness of our insight and knowledge, the universal quality of theoretical statements depends upon the fact that there is but *one* reality, and that one created by, through and unto our Lord Jesus Christ. It just will not do to expect of the christian scholar a permanent scientific conflict with his non-christian colleagues, or a sense of guilt in lieu of the same. But we seriously wrong our christian scholar when we fail to expect of him, whether in or out of his classroom, laboratory or clinic, both the bearing of a christian man and a conscious relating of his task to the Lord who has entrusted him with it.

The teacher of medicine has the task of demonstrating before students a relationship with patients. The christian in this position is called to remember the dignity of his fellow man, to respect it in the use of courtesies, to honour it by presenting (in appropriate form) true information for the patient and by offering advice rather than instruction. The office of the patient as the father or mother of a family, his diligence in the service of an employer, his carrying of scars suffered at the command of his country, these should be reminders to us that respect must be shown before it is won. The christian is well placed if he has learned to think little of himself.

His clinical task, and that for which he teaches students, will always be engaged in with the consciousness of limitation. A man's days are numbered; neither physician nor patient nor student is the better for imagining otherwise. The christian medical teacher is very likely to be the first person the student ever met who suffered no anxiety from this very basic realisation. The placing of death is correlate to the placing of life, and the student will appreciate opportunity to discuss the one as much as the other. The christian is called to resist the secularisation of death in medicine with all his strength. It is not without significance that the care of the dying in my own country is a field pioneered and commanded by christians. For the professional physician with lesser motivations it is hard to remain committed to the patient he has no more to offer. The dying insults him as it provokes his own anxiety.

The teaching of technique (in our English sense of manual skills) is involved in our work. The christian will, I hope, be concerned to demonstrate and inculcate the many aspects of (for example, surgical) skill: the economy of movement and of application of a knife, the aesthetic aspect of a surgical manoeuvre, the penalty or reward of a wrong or a right choice, the vital nature of the responses of a patient undergoing surgery and the play of feeling in both patients and surgeon upon the conduct and outcome of the operation. The wealth of diversity and detail in reality can be brought before students standing round an operating table and the atmosphere of the operating theatre (if not always steeped in solemnity — for humour is not without a place in reality) can be most appropriate to the discovery of that wealth.

The scientific standards to be practised and taught are demanding standards. Diagnosis must be painstaking and full of honesty; a little more effort may not always be amazingly rewarded, but is rarely wasted. The use of new drugs and the plethora of advertising concerning them tend to evoke a sceptical reaction in which the christian is perhaps tempted too easily to share. A kind of thriftiness repels him from the lavishly promoted "latest thing on the market"; a strong aversion to the half truths and the meaningless phrases of the manufacturer's "blurb" may leave him with an unjustifiably restricted pharmacopoeia. When he practises research it is to be hoped that what he writes will have the same critical standards to pass before he puts pen to paper.

The guarding of trust between patient and doctor will be a concern he shows and teaches. The so-called "double-blind" trial of pharmaceuticals he will regard with suspicion in that it undermines the confidence of patient in doctor. For the same reason he will respect the judgements of professional colleagues and in Biblical fashion will prefer to keep silent about grievances or criticisms until he can confide them to the colleague they concern. At times he may be called upon to act in a way that his non-christian colleagues will not approve. A christian doctor some three years ago was brought before a disciplinary committee in the United Kingdom, when he informed the parents of a minor that she had been (and was) receiving contraceptive medication from another agency without his consent. But he, it was held, had transgressed the code of confidentiality. Can the christian teacher use such a case to develop the ethical sense of his medical students? He has ample opportunity to do so. He will have no illusions about their narrow horizons in education and experience and if he can sympathise rather than show irritation, his aptness to teach will be enhanced.

The standards by which the christian practises medicine and by which he plans his service of others as a doctor should be made explicit in his teaching. The critical time through which our medical services are passing in the United Kingdom has made many of us conscious of inadequate motives and poor justification for views we had adopted as standards.

How must our service of Christ's Kingdom in medical scholarship react to the financial stringency we face? how to the pressure of socialist doctrine? how to the loss of manpower by emigration (the brain drain)? and how to the depression of medical standards by immigration?

Clearly the maintenance of health and the care of sickness could absorb in any country, the whole of its gross national economic product if no bounds were set to their prosecution. Fundamental strategic choices have to be made. The perspective which Christ's Kingdom gives our lives is surely the source for realistic answers and choices.

4. *The non-christian student in the christian medical school*

What I earlier said of the medical teacher is certainly apposite to the Christian medical school. No matter what the statutory position of an institution, its fruitfulness for the Kingdom of God is bound up closest with the christian character of its teaching members. Perhaps we have so much argued that the christian character of a school, political party or family is *not guaranteed* by its believing membership that we have blinded ourselves to the fact that such a believing membership is the first essential. Certainly the teaching institution that would serve the Lord must be committed (institutionally) to continuing and fervent prayer for the power of the Spirit of God to be shown in the lives of faculty members. That, at least, all heads of departments, and the majority of teachers are "alive in Christ" seems to me a *sine qua non*. If we fail to provide a structure by which such a factual status can be maintained, we have hardly contributed a fresh coat of paint, let alone a bulwark to the Kingdom of God. If the college is to be free from the church's domination, its faith life will have to become the subject of its own examination and continued criticism. No less than in the institutional church, an internal discipline must be supported if the name Christian is not to be ridiculed and the power of blessing to be withdrawn.

The opportunities for medical colleges, Christian in name and deed, are fast diminishing. Some however continue faithfully in their calling and in particular their contribution in the developing nations is now considered. The names of Vellore and Ludhiana Christian Medical Colleges are known world wide for what they represent in India. I know both teachers and graduates of these institutions as colleagues and friends. Certainly, in so far as medical qualifications are concerned, theirs are highly respected, but in fact there is more: of Ludhiana graduates I recently heard a distinguished medical man say "Yes, something of the Christian witness there seems to stick". And so we should hope.

But the problems these colleges face are great. How can they consolidate and perpetuate a Christian faculty when they are expected to take the best qualified local (Indian) candidate for a post whether he be christian or not? And of course such is the expectation.

What chance is there of organising and staffing a Christian hospital in which the training will take place? All kinds of internal discipline are likely to be castigated as colonial traits. One knows of mission hospitals in this continent where the bribe negotiates all the patient's progress to his consultation with the European doctor, and further to the receipt of whatever is then prescribed. Such an institution is failing at the basic level of obedience to the gospel. It is gratifying to know that other institutions will gladly run the risk of governmental displeasure rather than suffer the existence of corrupt practice on their territory.

I wish to sketch some goals and standards which I conceive to be important in the policy of a Christian medical college, chiefly having regard to the missionary situation in a non-Christian environment. (My indebtedness to Dr. Stanley Browne, Director of the Leprosy Student Centre, and formerly Director of the School for Medical Auxiliaries in Yakusu, now in the state of Zaire, has to be recorded.)

The continuing and supreme goal of a Christian Medical College will be, in Word and Deed, to carry the Gospel of the Kingdom of God in Jesus Christ. Its special calling is to wage warfare against sickness and suffering in the strength and love of the Lord by the training of doctors, nurses and auxiliaries who will become the front line troops in the fight.

The teaching of its students raises at once the question whether it is necessary to take as pattern and aim, the practice of professional medicine in the West. How effective in the fight against malnutrition, infant mortality and continent-wide epidemic will be Western-style doctors? How likely are such graduates to give their service to the nations and communities that need them? How long before they seek the natural home for the style of medicine they have learned to practice? I ought perhaps to repeat that much in Western medicine that carries great prestige ought to undergo re-assessment. Here in South Africa already the christian re-assessment is going on in relation to what I will describe as spectacular surgical experimentation. Can we justify the investment of such time, men, materials and funds in a single surgical intervention, that, otherwise deployed (and at no great distance) would bless thousands? Here would be a task for the christian medical faculty — the defining of priorities in medical investment.

The training of students in the practice of medicine does nevertheless mean that we are concerned with medicine rather than magic and that science will be one important tool of this medicine. Our christian mind regarding science will be put to the test. Has any of our christian philosophies yet shown that it can stimulate the development of natural science in a healthy direction? Browne, without (I think) the benefit of a highly elaborated christian philosophy, but prompted by urgent and specific needs, developed a training programme in general and specific natural science in his school for *infirmiers,* that deserves close further scrutiny by those who are concerned over the secularisation of science and its position of dominance in Western culture.* Moreover, in an area of 10 000 square miles for a population of 45 000+

---

* Browne, S. G.: The training of medical auxiliaries in the former Belgian Congo. *The Lancet.* May 19, 1973, pp. 1103—1105.

he was able to develop a pattern of comprehensive medical care by a Church-related medical service. His students, happily, were admitted from schools of Baptist Mission stations and from other Protestant Missions, and were highly motivated for service to their communities and able to share in the evangelistic work which distinguished this medical outreach. However, his experience indicates a style of medical education we must consider in the carrying out of our obligations to our grievously disadvantaged neighbour.

The non-Christian student in our colleges must be our neighbour and the object of our love in a Christian sense. I hold it ludicrous to say that our obligation is limited to his education. In our relationship with him, our hope and prayer must be for his conversion to Christ. If we train him to the passing of a degree examination which gives him a career and a hope for some success in it, we must not allow ourselves to forget that a hope which concerns this life only, is the lot of the most miserable of men. Such a consideration will suggest that a christian school of higher education has certain limits of size. It has to be possible to get to know the student and he to know us. Besides, by keeping the size modest, we are the more able to avoid an authoritarian pattern of conduct, which I think desirable. Perhaps so, we can avoid the uprooting of the student, intellectually and morally, which his rapid transition from a village society to a Western orientated scientific milieu, may otherwise engineer.

His entry into a christian higher education college will give the non-christian student opportunity, not only to discover the Bible which will function there explicitly as well as implicitly, but to embark on a more general form of christian education than his special studies. He will be made aware of a new world-view and its theoretical elaboration as a truly Christian philosophy, if the institution is taking seriously her task in education. Care must be taken that Science does not develop in the mind of the student as the ultimate principle of interpretation. A widening of his horizon must be attempted and with it we must show that life can only be opened up under the direction of a faith.

The existence of a faith community that transcends nation, language and race (yes, time as well) must be shown in the teaching and in the organisation of co-operation among christian scholars for the purpose of education. The powerful motivation of "Christ in us — the hope of glory" must appear in the science we teach. Says Browne: "The value of example is nowhere more apparent than in the realm of medical ethics". Where better than in a Christian Medical College can that example be observed and followed ?

May I express the hope that the Reformed, both here in South Africa and elsewhere, will seize what opportunities are granted them by God, to bring the newness of life which characterises his Kingdom into the task of medical higher education.

The status of the Christian teacher in a secular educational institution and the status of the non-Christian student at a Christian educational institution

Prof. Dr. Jong Sung Rhee

1. *Introduction*

The Korean peninsula is located between three strong countries, namely China, Russia and Japan. Because of this geographical position Korea has been the centre of an international political and cultural conflict. At the same time the country has played an important role as the transmitter of civilization between these three countries. At the turn of this century a fourth country came into the picture and has become very influential. That country is the United States of America.

Culturally speaking Korea is the centre of multi-cultural interchanges between these four countries. Among those the Soviet Union has the least importance to Korean culture; China has been the fountain and main source of Korean culture for many centuries; Japan was dominant for nearly half a century (1900—1945); and the presence of the United States of America has increased her influence since the turn of the century.

Because of political and cultural influences on the country from outside there have been two notable reactions: one a strong nationalism and the other a kind of flunkeyism which is found among the upper class people and high ranking officials. Nationalism is more evident among Christians and in Christian educational institutions. This is perhaps the main reason that Christian higher educational institutions have been very important centres for modernization of the nation for the last three decades. These institutions have been the bulwark of nationalism and the anti-communist movement.

With this very brief introduction one can easily perceive the

258

issues and problems that Korean Christians are struggling to solve to-day, particularly in both Christian and secular educational institutions.

2. Facts concerning Christian institutions in Korea

2.1. Number of Christian higher educational institutions

Yonsei University (1886) Presbyterian and Methodist.
Ewha Women's University (1910) Methodist.
Soongjun University (1905) Presbyterian.
Keimyoung College (1955) Presbyterian.
Seoul Women's College (1958) Presbyterian.
Sogang University (1958) Roman Catholic.

2.2. Total number of students in those six schools

Christian students	8 827	40,6%
Non-Christian students	14 740	59,4%
Total	23 567	

2.3. Total number of professors

Christian professors	983	80%
Non-Christian professors	246	20%
Total	1 229	

2.4. Number of students who have become Christians after entering the Christian schools

Though there are no accurate statistics it is estimated that about ten percent of the non-Christian students become Christians during their matriculation.

3. The status of Christian teachers in a secular university based on a study at Korea University

3.1. Professors and students

Total number of professors	307	
Number of Christian professors	82	28%

(No statistics on the number of Christian students available.)

3.2. Activities and programs for non-Christian students

3.2.1. There are no evangelistic activities carried on by Christian professors on the campus. Some of the Christian professors, however, are very active outside the campus in church work, and some of these are working for religious freedom and human rights.

3.2.2. The entire campus was open for various Christian student activities such as the Student Christian Association, Campus Crusade for Christ, University Bible Fellowship etc. These groups were very active and appeared to carry out effective programs.

3.2.3. There was no limitation of Christian activities until last May. In May the school authorities were told by the government to dissolve all of the student organizations on the campus. Therefore, at present no Christian activity of any kind, including evangelistic efforts, is permitted.

3.2.4. Korea University is one of the oldest private universities and is the third best educational institution in Korea. It was founded by a famous Korean patriot in order to train future Korean leaders with a strong sense of nationalism. The university is a non-Christian institution, because at the time of its founding Christianity was misunderstood as a religion for Westerners only. It is very important, however, to note the fact that there are now 82 Christian professors out of 307 full-time teachers. This fact implies or at least suggests two things: (1) that the Korean church has produced many of the intellectual leaders in the past, and (2) that Christian professors are apparently performing a kind of evangelism by simply being present on the campus of this non-Christian university. Koreans as a whole have been under the influence of Buddhism and Confucian culture for many centuries, and therefore they are in general antagonistic to other religions and cultures. This fact, more or less, compels Christian professors to be very cautious about Christian witness on the campus. As a result Christian professors do not engage openly in any Christian activities on the campus.

3.3. A few observations

3.3.1. The university does not have any courses on religion whatsoever. Though the government does not prohibit the teaching of some religious courses, the secular colleges and universities seldom offer any religious courses.

3.3.2. Recently the government declared a ban on all sorts of student extracurricular activities on the campuses including Christian student programs. This automatically shuts the door against Christian activities on the campus.

3.3.3. In the past Christian professors were well respected by their colleagues as well as by their students, but recently that popularity has fallen off.

3.3.4. In general, Christian professors and students, in recent years, have had little concern for evangelism and not much confidence in Christian doctrines and teachings because they are told by some Christian theologians that this is the age of secularism and that even God is dead. Such radical theologies have affected the average Christian laymen as well as Christian intellectuals causing them to be lost in doubt and frustration.

4. *The status of non-Christian students in a Christian institution, based on a case study at Yonsei University*

Yonsei University is the oldest Western type of a Christian educational institution in Korea, founded by an American medical missionary in 1886. The American missionary was a Presbyterian and a physician, and became the court physician in the Yi dynasty. In later years other departments of studies were added and now this institution is the second best university in the country. Yonsei graduates have become distinguished leaders in various fields of national life, and the university was for many decades the most popular channel through which western civilization was introduced to Korea. This university was founded for the purpose of training Christian leaders both within and without the churches. At present students and professors of the university are actively engaged in social and political issues.

4.1. Number of Christian students at Yonsei University

Total number of students	7 728	
Number of Christian students	3 019	39,1%
Number of students of other religions	409	5,6%
Number of students without a religious affiliation	4 300	55,3%

4.2. Number of Christian professors

Total number of full-time teachers	594	
Number of Christian professors	492	82,8%
Number of non-Christian professors	102	17,2%

4.3. There are two courses on Christianity offered in the university giving four credits. These two courses are required of all students. They are basic introductory courses.

4.4. There are several groups and associations which engage in evangelism among non-Christian students on the campus

The Yonsei Christian Student Association, Intervarsity Fellowship,

Agape Fellowship, Y.M.C.A., Y.W.C.A., the English Bible Study Group, University Chapel and the Day-break Prayer Meeting are the activities which attract non-Christian students to Christianity. All of these groups are now dissolved by the new Government law.

4.5. According to recent statistics, 10,4% of freshmen students have been converted to Christianity after entering this school, and 5,7% of the Christian students rededicate themselves to Christian work during their study at Yonsei University. These statistics indicate that this university is quite successfully performing its purpose which is to bear witness to the Gospel of Jesus Christ as it trains both church and national leaders.

4.6. There has been a rather strong resentment and opposition to Christianity among both students and professors, because Christianity is often understood to be an agent of westernization and capitalism introduced and maintained by Americans. However, in the past year, much of this resentment has disappeared because many Christian professors and students were expelled from the university because they actively engaged in street demonstrations, anti-government action and in various efforts for social justice. About 90% of the students who were taken into prison and released last year were Christians. Given this high percentage of Christian students struggling for human rights and social justice, many non-Christian students have come to understand Christianity as a religion for such a time as this. For many students Christianity has now become credible.

4.7. Unfortunately there are no special efforts among the Christian professors in the university for non-Christian student evangelism. Occasionally some of the Christian professors speak at the chapel. Or they may take responsibility as student advisors, but they do not take positive action for campus evangelism.

4.8. A few observations

4.8.1. Most of the Christian colleges and universities were started with a common purpose, that is, to train Christian church and national leaders in the context of clear Christian principles.

4.8.2. This purpose was not altered until recent years. However, in the last few years this principle has been weakened by college and university administrators and most of the Christian schools tend to become non-Christian schools, or to become neutral as far as religious commitment is concerned. Many Christian theologians and professors in these schools, particularly in Protestant schools, have been influenced by radical theologies and the so-called theology of secularity and they feel no urgent effort to do evangelistic work on the campuses.

4.8.3. Non-Christian students in a Christian school tend to look at Christianity not as a religion of human salvation, but as an organization with particular social functions; and they judge Christianity on the basis of its capacity to achieve social reform and to secure social justice, human rights, and religious freedom.

4.8.4. Some of the Christian schools have in the past accepted baptised Christian students only. But now none of the Christian schools maintain such policy because there are not enough Christian students to accept. And so about one half of the entire student body are non-Christian students. When Christian colleges and universities accept non-Christian students they do so hoping to change them to committed Christians and to educate them as national leaders and some as church leaders. But that hope becomes dim as time goes by. It is therefore very urgent that Christian educators rethink their policies and re-establish a firm conviction and principle of operation in this time of secularity and materialism.

5. *Possible solutions of the problems in Christian educational institutions in Korea*

5.1. The Korean church, like many other Asian churches, is in a missionary situation, or as I term it in "an island situation". Asia is still under the domination of non-Christian religious cultural influence, and in recent years has come under Communist influences with the exception of a few countries. In such a situation the Christian churches are minority groups surrounded by satanic powers of non-Christian forces. Therefore, all the churches must band together closely in order to survive. If one church were to step out and be cut off from that togetherness, she would then become an orphan and be swallowed up by the non-Christian powers.

5.2. All Christians, including students and professors in their respective schools, must have a strong sense of missionary vocation and seek to evangelize their colleagues and students through the testimony of their faith in Christ on the campus. As I already pointed out many Christian professors and students are becoming less confident in this aspect of their Christian vocation. In Yonsei University, for instance, the chapel service three times a week has been the centre of spiritual nourishment and of warm fellowship, and therefore it has been the centre of important and effective evangelistic efforts of the university. However, for the last few years the chapel hour has become a time of cultural activities and of recreation with the support of the university president.

5.3. We are living in an age of secularity. Everything tends to become non-religious. Social activities, patterns of life, government policies, education, music and even religious practice are becoming more and more secular. Is this a correct trend? Is this in accordance with God's providence? For me the answer is obviously negative. Therefore, we must retain what God has taught us to keep. And particularly we who are Christian intellectuals in higher educational institutions must retain our God-given duty on the campus and perform our function to witness Jesus Christ as our Saviour.

5.4. We as Christian intellectuals have a dual responsibility: one is to teach and to train men and women in the knowledge of human affairs so that they become good citizens in their respective positions; and the other is to give testimony that Christ is our Saviour so that the same students can become citizens of the Kingdom of God and co-workers in building His Kingdom in this world.

5.5. How can we perform this dual responsibility? Many contemporary, leading theologians and church men seem to conform themselves to this world in their theological thinking, Christian life and their social practice. It is true in Korea, too. When radical theology, theology of secularity and the Death of God theology were introduced to Korea many leading theologians accepted them in haste and transmitted them to Korean Christians without appropriate comments and very necessary evaluation. The result amongst average Christians, lay leaders and many pastors was deep frustration, doubt in their traditional belief and discord among themselves. I believe that Christian intellectuals must first be transformed themselves by the Word of God as the Apostle Paul says in the Letter of Romans: "Adapt yourselves no longer to the pattern of this present world, but let your minds be remade and your whole nature thus transformed" (12 : 2, N.E.B.). It is the God-given responsibility of every Christian institution and of every Christian, and, I believe, of Christian intellectuals in particular, to cause the minds of natural men to be transformed and to make them the ambassadors of Christ, and to create a new world according to the pattern of God's providence. In order to perform this sacred duty we who are Christian professors must affirm the Christian heritage in our daily life, re-commit ourselves to this duty in the institutions to which we are sent by God, and re-order, in the pattern of God's will, this world where secularism, materialism, this-worldliness and atheism are dominant. We who are Christian instructors must regain our firm conviction in Christian principles and our faith in God, and teach the non-Christian students the gospel of salvation revealed in the life, death and resurrection of Jesus Christ. It is becoming clearer and clearer as time goes by that the teachings of secularism, materialism, and atheism cannot solve the complicated problems of the time in which we live; and even they themselves do not know how to handle those problems. Hippie-ism, amoral behaviour of young people, ever increasing antagonism between nations and the class struggle in some countries are the outcome of lawless minds of the time derived from the lack of knowledge of the Truth. We must take some positive action in order to solve these problems and reorient the course of modern human history.

5.6. In this situation we who stand in the Reformed tradition must realise again our responsibility to the modern world. There are many similarities between the time of Calvin and our time. He was able to solve the problems of his time and gave the right instructions to the people to have a true Christian life by reaffirming the living Word of God which is Jesus Christ and the written Word of God which is the Holy Scripture.

So we as Reformed theologians and instructors here should adapt his methods and philosophy of education in order to solve our own problems so that we can give glory to God who made this world. We Christian intellectuals must discern and interpret the signs of the times (Matt. 16 : 3) lest we are flung out into the dark as the useless servant by our Lord. There are many signs of the times and he who has an eye to see must see them now.

Authority and discipline at institutions for higher education

Prof. dr. S. C. W. Duvenage

1. *Orientation*

Human society is unthinkable without authority and discipline. Authority is, as a matter of fact, a *sine qua non* for every form of society. Wherever human beings come together or live together in groups, this phenomenon appears as a matter of course. This phenomenon undoubtedly is related to order and peace. If it functions correctly it promotes security and trust. If there is no authority or if authority is handled irresponsibly, lack of order, chaos and even anarchy will appear. The relationships of human beings to one another are determined in a significant way by the authority factor. In every institution existing among men, there are tasks to be fulfilled, roles to be played, rewards to be given, management to be exercised and decisions to be taken and executed. These events occur in such a multiplicity of ways that this appears to be the most natural thing in our world. However, in all of these events appearing to take place so spontaneously, the authority factor is presupposed.

There is always one person or a group of persons in control or exercising leadership, and others who follow. The entire structure of human society, no matter what form or shape it exhibits, is subject to this phenomenon. The political organization of a country may be communist or democratic, it may be a monarchy or a fascist regime, it may even be patriarchal in the way of primitive tribes, but in every case the factor of authority is fundamental. And the same holds for other areas of our societies. Whether we are confronted with ecclesiastical-religious, cultural-social, economic or educational relationships, nowhere will it be possible to get things done without our acknowledgement of authority.

Throughout the ages the patterns of authority have not been uniform. Every age in history has exhibited different forms of authority. Almost continually the pendulum has swung between two ultimate poles of authority, namely that of hard, unlimited, dictatorial and repressive authority — and that of uncontrolled libertine anarchism.

This difference of form is found not only in political situations, but in every form of society: in the home, church, industry and educational institutions.

It is not necessary to enter further into this matter of different forms. It is necessary, however, to pay attention to what has happened to institutions of higher education throughout the world in recent times. For it is evident that the university is in many respects the mirror of society at large, so that crises that occur in society and presently exist there, are first of all experienced at the universities. In more than one respect the university has become a duplication of society at large. To no mean degree this is the case with respect to our present subject. For it appears that one can with justification speak about a crisis in authority at many universities. We shall return to this later.

2. *Origin of authority*

In order to determine what the character and function of authority and discipline at Christian Institutions for Higher Education is, it is necessary first to make a number of principial distinctions with respect to the origin of authority. There are two possibilities. In the one case the point of origin is man and in the other the point of departure is found in God. In the one case we only operate along horizontal lines, in the other case a vertical dimension is also acknowledged and is even given priority. In short we can refer to these two possibilities as the humanistic and the Christian views of authority.

2.1. The humanistic view

In the humanistic view man sees himself as autonomous, i.e. he posits his own law. In his life and in that of society he does not acknowledge, whether overtly or covertly, the word, law and hand of God. In a paper on *State and Authority* Belifante declares at a conference of the Humanistic Institution in the Netherlands: "It is clear that the founding of authority in God cannot be very strong, since His existence can be accepted only subject to so many dubious proofs, that it is hardly believable".[1]

And Charles W. Hendel declares just as blatantly: "The rational position was this: authority is a great universal fact of creation, with God's will the ultimate originative power ... Except in traditionally religious circles, this view has virtually disappeared from philosophy. We see now only man and the world, with nothing beyond. Man claims moral and metaphysical freedom, the world exhibits an inexorable necessity, and the system of nature, man-and-the-world, is without a reconciling ground in God".[2]

It is remarkable how, in the course of centuries, the humanistic ideas have had a number of results for the authority relationships of human society. We would like to point out two typical results, both very evident consequences of humanism, both very visible in Western cultural patterns. Both of these consequences of humanism show that authority relationships run the danger of not having enough room to function. In one case this results in totalitarianism, that is, an absolutisation of authority; and in the other case it results in the other extreme, liberalism, which is a lack of acknowledging authority. A run-down democracy has enough room for both of these outgrowths.

In the first case we can think of bureaucracy in its ultimate consequences. This is the organisation of society according to the model of a number of large corporations which have drawn all power into their own hands. This is the complex of industrial, military, educational and state institutions, which in an impersonal and bureaucratic manner, without fear of losing power, can provoke left and right and cause the so-called freedom of the individual finally to disappear. At no other point does pragmatistic humanism appear in such a futile and self-destructive manner. In the final analysis this is a concentration of power. More and more power is centralised in a number of large corporations or other institutions and in the central government.

In this way humanism reaches its ultimate consequence, namely a totalitarianism which arbitrarily has as its result the destruction of the individual and society. The other outgrowth of humanism in Western culture is a reactionary phenomenon. This is the swing of the pendulum to the other extreme. It is remarkable that this comes to expression most strongly among students.

In response to the bureaucratic domination of the system and of the establishment, man started to look for self-identity, creativity, and realisation of his humanistic ideal of autonomy and total freedom. The most important representative, if not the most important instigator, of revolutionary thinking in our times, is doubtless Herbert Marcuse. It is a well-known fact that the revolutionary powers which come to the fore in various areas of our contemporary society, have been influenced by this neomarxist thinker and author.

Marcuse states that with respect to our society, the status quo needs to be revealed for what it truly is behind its mask. This will mean a revelation of the fact that domination or repression is the actual essence of our contemporary highly developed industrial society, as a political authoritarian system which does not acknow-

ledge and even frustrates the actual essence of man, namely his autonomous self-determination, the determination of his own course of
life, his happiness and his joy. Taking off this mask must simultaneously become a liberation: " ... a liberation from the repressive,
from a bad, a false system — be it an organic system, be it a
social system, be it a mental or intellectual system: liberation by
forces developing within such a system".[3]

Marcuse regards such a stance as especially decisive. In the
first place this has to come about by the total refusal to accept
the system.[4]

By such an absolute refusal, man can deliver himself from
his chains. Our theoretical consciousness must be translated into
political terms, and after we have acquired insight, this has to be
expressed in society. Reason, the *ratio,* must become revolution. A
transformation of consciousness must take place. For Marcuse therefore, it comes down to this, that we not only need protest, but as
we become aware of the situation and as we follow this up with
protest, this also has to determine the direction of the revolution.

The calling to revolutionary protest and to revolutionary acts,
becomes an inner necessity. Just as in Marx's case, so also in the
case of Marcuse there are strong revolutionary aspirations. With
powerful words he challenges us to act in a revolutionary manner.
In his essay *Re-examination of the Concept of Revolution* he leans
strongly on Marx and on the Marxist view of revolution.

In the final analysis, reactionary student activism, based on
Marcuse's philosophy, is an attempt to realise completely the humanistically founded concept of freedom.

Allowing the pendulum to swing to the other side, changing the
accent, absolutising the ideal of freedom, do not bring a solution.
On the contrary, it causes the radical students of necessity to land in
a marsh of permissiveness and nihilism, which are blood relatives
of anarchism.

In this process of radicalisation, the revolutionary student lands
in the other extreme of consistent humanism, namely extreme individualistic liberalism. As he turns his back on the bureaucracy, his
inherently humanistic attitude does not save him from the danger
of getting stuck in this liberalism. The final consequences of this
are lawlessness in the area of sex, drugs, and the rejection of all
authority.

2.2. The Christian view

The Christian rejects in the light of the Word of God, both the
preceding extremes with respect to authority relations. Both of these

extremes operate with exclusively humanistic tools. They only move horizontally and therefore, sooner or later, end in a *cul de sac*. However, there is an alternative which the believer in the Scriptures accepts and proclaims, namely that the source of all authority is from God. If we ask for proof, we can in the first place point to the cultural mandate which man has received in paradise. Already then, in the very beginning, man was placed by God in a position of authority. But in many other places in Scripture, the matter of authority is dealt with. With respect to worldly authorities it is underlined in Romans 13; with respect to the relationship of parents and children, as well as that of employers and employees, Ephesians 5 and 6 and 1 Peter 2 : 13 deal with the matter and even refer to every kind of human order. In John 19 : 11, Jesus expressly comments on Pilate's belief that he had authority over Christ: "You would have no authority over me if it had not been given you from above". In all these expressions we find that authority is not exclusively a horizontal matter, nor a matter merely between one person and another, but that there is also a vertical line. In all these expressions it clearly appears that there is only one author of all authority who is the authentic bearer of all authority and this is God. Among people, authority is always delegated authority. Among people, one can never speak of absolute authority. Only God is the absolute bearer of authority.

2.2.1. Office and service. To understand the matter of authority and authority relationships more clearly in the light of Scripture, it is necessary to draw into our discussion a concept which in humanistic circles has totally disappeared, namely the concept of office.

H. van Riessen stresses that bearers of authority in any form of society do not have their competence in themselves, nor are they in every respect the link between the original Mandator and the subjects, but that they are in an office. Along this road people can, in the different kinds of social groups, arrive at the fulfilment of their cultural calling in a direct, free responsibility before God, who calls them to His service.[5] Paul says about the public authorities in Romans 13 : 4 "For it is God's servant, for your good". In Greek the word for servant here is *diakonos*. In the time of Paul this term was also used in the church. It indicates an office. The deacon has to serve at table during the love meals. This is the liturgical side of his office. But there is also a social side, namely in that he has to take care of the needy and the ill. Paul here takes the ecclesiastical concept of service and applies it to as "profane" a phenomenon as civil authority. Civil authority is a *diakonos*. It is in God's service for the sake of justice and righteousness, peace and order.

Paul expressly states the purpose of this service: "For your good". Civil authority is called to promote the prosperity and well-being of the citizens and society. Civil authority serves God when it works for peace, for the sake of and among His subjects, peace especially in the deeply serious Biblical meaning of the word, namely that all things must bear proper order before the sight of God.

In his brochure: *Man in God's world,* Paul G. Schrotenboer very clearly points out the Biblical idea of office.[6] He analyses another Greek word, which is especially relevant for our understanding of authority relations. This is a word and a matter used by Peter in 1 Peter 4 : 10 and 11. "In the measure in which each of you has received a gift of grace, you have to serve one another with that gift, as good servants of the manifold grace of God. If someone speaks, let it be as though he speaks words of God; if someone serves, let it be God who gives him the power, so that in all things God can be glorified through Jesus Christ, to whom belongs all glory and power in all eternity". The Greek word that is here used for servants, namely *oikonomoi,* points to a service or office or even a managerial task, which is related to management or administration, that has been given to this servant. This has been entrusted to him. No matter whether this occurs in the family, or in business, or in whatever relationship, it always means that a person is called to serve. He possesses delegated authority. He represents the actual bearer of authority, God.

Schrotenboer arrives at the following penetrating proposition. "The office of man is his position in relationship. His position, as it relates to God, constitutes him a servant who is called to obedience. As it relates to fellow men it makes man a guardian, who must bring his charge to maturity. As it relates to the world it constitutes man a steward who must faithfully exercise dominion in the name of God".[7]

For our discussion it is especially important that we pay attention to man's relationship to his fellow man, in which he stands as one who is called, as a bearer of an office, as a guardian. He is placed in a position of authority over others. We therefore have to acknowledge, even though all men are equal before God as men, that on earth we cannot simply talk about a total equality in our relationships. There are mutual relationships which God has established as superior and inferior, as subjects and authorities. Some of us have to accept the responsibility of a position of authority and others of us have to follow. But the secret is not to let the

271

position of authority degenerate into tyranny and this secret is found in the acknowledgement that every bearer of authority only has representative authority and that in the final analysis he is a servant of God. Only God has absolute authority.

With respect to these principal points of departure we can conclude that man never has authority in himself. He represents an authority. He is a bearer of authority and the command of the actual author of all laws and of human existence, God. To have authority on earth is to take part in creation in the name of the author, so that His word can have dominion. Where the author and his word disappear, there we find the destruction of the structure of authority. Where it is acknowledged, man acts according to the source of authority in his life. This source is the Word itself. When this source disappears, authority as such becomes empty and insignificant.

2.2.2. Authority and insight. We must clearly differentiate between authority and power. In order to understand this distinction clearly, it is important to understand the concepts of insight and knowledge. If somcone has been given authority, but he does not excercise his authority with insight, knowledge, and judgement, then his authority is misplaced. Then we get simple exercise of power which calls for opposition and which causes irritation.

When persons in positions of authority do not succeed in exercising their authority in the right manner, they cannot expect respect, but rather rejection, hostility and an attitude of contempt. We can compare this to a machine which is handled with brute force or with violence. Just think about an ice-breaker in the North or South Pole. This is a powerful instrument to break the oceans of ice and to make them accessible to ships. But this has to be done in a controlled manner. The inherent power of the machine is power without judgement or knowledge. In the case of man this is different, or at least, it should be different. When a person is placed in a position of authority and he combines this with insight and knowledge, he can indeed act with great power. Authority and power then go together legitimately, but only when there is insight and knowledge. Power without insight is as destructive as a machine can be. It sometimes happened that kings who sat on thrones simply because of monarchical laws of succession, abused their position of authority in weakness and foolishness. In such cases there is indeed an exercise of power. But because insight, wisdom and competence are not present, this exercise of power violates the position of authority.[8]

In this respect we can look at the reign of Solomon who

reigned with wisdom. He prayed for this and he received it (1 Kings 3 : 9, 4 : 20). The correlation between true authority and insight or knowledge is a principle which is thoroughly rooted in Hoy Scripture. For example, there are many expressions in the Gospels which deal with the authority of Christ and which relate it to his wisdom (Luke 2 : 47; Matt. 7 : 28, 29; Mark. 4 : 32, 36) or which relate it to his obedience to the word and the will of God (John 5 : 30; 12 : 49; 14 : 9—11). Also in the case of the disciples, they could only go around as witnesses with authority after Christ had opened their minds to understand the Scriptures (Luke 24 : 45). Insight into the Scriptures, speaking and acting in conformity with the Scriptures, always bear authority. The same principle is valid in the pedagogical situation. Paul admonishes parents to educate children "in the discipline and instruction of the Lord" (Eph. 6 : 4).

3. *Authority relationships at institutions for higher education*

In order to further qualify the phenomenon of authority as it is supposed to function at the institution for higher education, it is necessary to analyse the various types of authority in line with what we have stated so far.

3.1. Various types of authority

The current distinctions in sociology come from Max Weber. In the past he came with the apparently obvious and logically justified division of charismatic, traditional and legal authority.[9]

Charisma means grace and charismatic authority means the authority of the leader who has been given a special dispensation of grace. Those over whom he exercises his authority, accept this leader because of his excellent qualities and they follow him so long as he reveals his qualities.

The foundation of traditional authority is the acceptance of the legitimacy of a tradition while the foundation of legal authority is found in the belief that a certain office is legitimate. In the latter case it is not a matter so much of the person, but of the office, which calls for obedience. In line with this there is usually also the acknowledgement of definite rules and a precise division of tasks.[10]

Next to these three different kinds of authority, we today differentiate two other types, which are not so much based on some *a priori* of belief, but on empirical grounds. The new types of authority are usually not seen as totally divorced from any of the other types, but more as their completion. The first of these additional types can be called rational authority, in which the aspect of expertise is dominant. Of course, this expertise is exercised by the bearer of authority in the interest of those who have less influence or who are his subjects. In this case we especially meet the aspect of insight, ability and even responsibility.

The last kind that is acknowledged, is called functional authority and signifies the legitimising of exercise of power through the agreement of those who are subject to this kind of authority.[11]

The latter is a typically humanistic description of authority. Here it appears to be exclusively a matter of relationships between people that are totally taken care of by people. Authority in this case is simply human power that is acknowledged and accepted by those that are subject to it.

In this case the subjects of authority must first declare: I acknowledge this authority because I agree with its purpose. In this way authority is made dependent on the acceptance of the object of authority.

In this case we have to do with a form of conditional authority. The subjects are prepared to legitimise it, when and so long as the goals of the bearer of authority can be accepted.[12] This is purely humanistic and in the final analysis is the measuring stick of our modern permissive society in which the refusal to acknowledge any other form of authority opens the road to anarchy.

3.2. Crises in authority

Already at the end of the last century, history teaches us, traditional forms of authority were being challenged. During the second half of the 20th century, however, we experience a process of the actual breaking-down of authority everywhere. This is related to the equalising and democratising trends. The crisis in authority is even noticeable in such apparently untouchable bulwarks as the Roman Catholic Church and the authorities in countries behind the iron curtain. Furthermore, it can also be seen in proven institutions such as the family, home, school and institutions of higher education.

In a democratic society the questioning of authority is not wrong. For it is possible to ask questions about the manner in which authority is being exercised. This is inherent in the nature of democracy. But what happens today, is that not the how, but the why of authority is being questioned. The crisis of authority is a crisis of legitimacy.

Probably the universities today are the most vulnerable with respect to the undermining of authority, especially because the intelligentsia throughout the ages, in all countries, to a greater or lesser degree, have been in the forefront of revolutionary movements. And if our age is really an age of denial of authority, this will become visible in the first place among the intellectually advanced. John R. Searle concludes: "The dominant tradition in our high culture is one of being against authority. We celebrate the rebel but not the bureaucrat, the revolt but not the institutions".[13]

Richard E. Peterson is of the opinion that radical youth movements in the entire Western hemisphere and Japan can best be understood in terms of a loss of trust in traditional forms of authority. In the United States, where radical youth movements are primarily composed of students, and where in 1969 5% of the total population consisted of students, this certainly is the case. The mass media and the teachers have taught these students that contemporary human existence leaves much to be desired. They accuse the older generation of causing this situation or of being complacent about it. Thus they have arrived at the point where their authority is being rejected because, in the words of Paul Goodman, the authority is not only immoral but functionally incompetent. And in order to give shape to their lack of trust some of them have become student activists in the "New Left" and others have become pacifists in the Hippy-culture.[14]

Richard Flacks stresses the same truth. He is of the opinion that there is a strong antipathy to arbitrary control and to centralised and manipulative processes of decision. He regards the anti-authority sentiment as a fundamental motive for the campus protests of the last few years. Writing in 1969, he looks back on 5 years of student protest and comes to the conclusion that in most cases they had been accelerated by administrative action that was interpreted as arbitrary. He concludes that these protests received their impetus from administrative activity that continued to be one-sided and compulsive.

The matter can also be viewed from another point of view. Many of the protest activities at universities reveal a search for new forms of power by those who feel that they are powerless. This means that protest is a way in which students want to make their presence felt. Some of these forms are more cultural than political. Style of clothing, music, language, and even drugs become weapons of provocation and challenge, not only so that certain people can distinguish themselves from the rest of society, but also to gain influence and authority for themselves. The more politically motivated protest activities, such as mass protests, sit-ins, student strikes, destruction and even violence, which in the final analysis come down to politicising of the campus, are also a method to acquire authority and to compel change.[15] From this point of view the protests take on the form of rebellion, if not revolution. Sheldon S. Wolin and John H. Schaar typify this process as follows: "On the political side, what has taken place on the campusses is best described as rebellion against the established forms and holders of authority and a search for new modes of authority".[16]

The lack of respect for rules and authorities on campus therefore has to be seen as a delegitimising of authority, a characteristic of our culture in general.

The student rebellions in the sixties and early seventies often revealed a revolutionary character in more than one respect. One of the most important background factors in this connection is the questioning of the legitimacy of authority, the deliberate undermining of authority and the continual challenge of those who are in control. Student activists have acted in this way verbally as well as in action; sometimes peacefully and sometimes blatantly violently. They have directed their arrows at the entire establishment and all its institutions, not least of all the university.

The ceaseless attacks on the university as an institution have undoubtedly undermined the authority of the academy and the trust in the authority of the university officials. In time, academics themselves started to doubt their own moral and legal authority. "Many academic men no longer really believe they have a right to define a curriculum for their students or to set standards of performance, much less to prescribe the modes of thought and feeling appropriate to 'an educated man' ".[17]

The question arises whether the phenomenon of students' rebellion and revolution, which in many Western countries seem to be something of the past, has resulted in significant changes in authority relationships in institutions of higher education. We can answer that to a greater or lesser extent, kinds of change have occurred. We notice increasing democratisation, increasing rationalisation and increasing functionalisation of authority relationships. These tendencies are noticeable not only in educational institutions, but also in other sectors of society, such as industry and the state.[18]

The idea of democratisation has been adequately expressed by Robert Paul Wolff as follows: "Characteristically it emphasizes decentralization of decision making, community control, local initiative, and a willingness to substitute *ad hoc* procedures of maximum responsiveness for the rigid patterns of traditional politics".[19]

More than in any other area, the university has seriousiy entertained these ideas. Up to the beginning of the sixties there was no question of student participation in the control of the different departments of the university. As a result of student activity on campusses and of the many demands of students at many foreign universities and even some South African universities this pattern has changed. Students have demanded the right for themselves to acquire co-determination in all branches of the university of which they regard themselves as an intrinsic component. Students have received the right of representation in controlling bodies at virtually every level of some universities.

It stands to reason that along this road, students not only acquired determination with respect to matters directly touching them, such as curricula, housing, regulations for student life, but also in academic matters, such as the granting of degrees and even the appointment and promotion of staff.

The second result of student revolts, in so far as this affects authority, is the increasing rationalisation of authority relationships. This process of rationalisation has come along with the process of democratisation. This type of authority places the emphasis on the factors of insight, expertise and personal competence in inter-human relationships. In the academic situation this means that the authority of the teacher over the student cannot easily be manifested any longer without competence of the teacher. The student of today looks for expertise and insight.

As a matter of fact, in any pedagogical situation, whether this is at home when children have arrived at the stage of more or less independent thinking or whether it is in school, we can no longer depend solely on an appeal to legal authority. If a parent or a teacher wants to defend his point of view against a child simply with the statement: "This is so, because I am your father or your teacher", then he is very vulnerable. This is even more the case in the academic world where the teacher has to give leadership to the student in the process of acquisition and cultivation of knowledge.

In the third place the result of student demonstrations and of the questioning of authority at institutions of education, is the functionalisation of authority. Stronger and stronger the demand occurred that authority must first be accepted by the subjects before it can be acknowledged in any way whatsoever. Within the humanistic patterns of thought this is the final outcome of liberalism.

So it appears that the winds of revolution that have blown across the campusses of institutions of higher education during the last decade, have resulted not only in negative fruits in the area of authority relationships. On the one side they have done away with the Biblical principle of office in which the office bearer has been placed by God. The humanistically orientated principles of the ideal of democratisation simply do not know such a principle.[20] Legal authority is not only questioned in this way, but in many ways it is simply removed and in its place we get functional authority. This fits completely within the framework of the process of democratisation.

On the other side, we can view positively that rationalisation of authority has received stronger emphasis. But because this has been propagated and applied without acknowledging its necessary companion, legal authority, it cannot yet be regarded as a basis for the solution of the authority crisis.

4. *Authority relationships at the Christian institutions for higher education*

Without entering as such into the proper character, structure and function of the university, it can be said that it is a unique, irreducible, differentiated structure of society. It exists and functions together with other structures of society, but it is itself independent and the principle of sphere sovereignty can be applied in this case. In other words, the university does not receive its authority from another social institution, for example not from the state or from the church, because it receives its authority directly from God. As soon as its independence as an institution is threatened or relativised, and as soon as its position of equality with other social institutions becomes one of subjection to them, the principle of sphere sovereignty is crowded out. But, just as little as the university can tolerate control by another institution, such as the state or industry, just as little can this be allowed within the university, so that teachers or students or the administration become the main controlling body. If either society or the members of the university themselves are allowed to transgress border lines, and if it is possible for all kinds of foreign activities to be pushed into the university, then the university becomes a political or economic institution, then the unique structure of the university and its own sovereignty are undermined.

With respect to the other institutions in society the university has the calling of standing in inter-relationship with them. This requires co-operation with acknowledgement of equality, inter-relationship with acknowledgement of sphere sovereignty, mutual support with acknowledgement of mutual independence, and interdependence without the disappearing of the proper identities.

In addition to this, the university also has a calling in connection with the intra-university relationships related to its internal composition. With respect to its internal composition the university, of course, exhibits various components. The most important internal component is the council and the administration, the body of teachers with the senate as its representative and the student body with its student council. In all cases the rector is related to every component because in a peculiar measure he is the central authority figure in the university.

Between the diverse components which each possess relative autonomy, there are many relationships as a result of the diversity of functions, but all are drawn together by a common purpose and by a determined pattern of authority.

The question which interests us is which pattern of authority really belongs to a christian institution for higher education? We can determine this as follows. In the light of our earlier thinking about the matter as founded in Scripture, and remembering the different types of authority, we can characterise authority at the christian institution as a combination of legal authority and rational authority.

This pattern of authority belongs to the university in its totality, as well as within each one of the relatively autonomous parts of the university. But it is also valid in all the relationships between the various components.

Let us take one of the most important relationships at the university, that between student and teacher, and extend our views of authority within this relationship.

The typical structure and peculiar character of the university is that it is an academic community of teachers and students. That kind of community has need for a pattern of authority in which both the legal and rational aspects of authority can find a place.

The teacher is in the first place called to an office, that of instructing and forming the students. In addition there is the task of research and of preparation for the professions. With respect to the exercise of these four tasks the teacher has been appointed by the council and he has had to sign several conditions of employment. Without doubt therefore, he has a certain office and is therefore in a position of authority with respect to those who have been entrusted to him, the students. By virtue of his office the teacher bears great responsibility, primarily toward God but in the second place also toward the council of the university. In this respect too, he is a servant *(diakonos)* of God. And he is there for the good of those who are subject to his authority. As a good servant *(oikonomos)* with gifts of grace which he has received, he has no absolute authority, but he does have authority. He is guardian over those that have been entrusted to him. He has a cultural task of moulding the students that have been entrusted to him. He has to lead the student in a certain direction until the student can develop independent scientific thought. And in the exercise of this task each teacher is directed from the centre of authority of his life. In the case of the humanist this centre is man himself, in the case of the Christian it is the Word of God. If it is the Word of God, then in the exercise of his authority, the teacher is controlled by the norms of the Word of God.

In all these things we are dealing with legal authority. The official character of it is primarily stressed.

The student also has an office, and the student also has a specific task at the university which has to be carried out responsibly, *coram Deo*. In the office of the student we also find activity and its own dynamics.

The exercise of scholarship in unbelief does not acknowledge the author of all authority and does not operate out of the true centre of authority of human existence, namely the Word of God. Whoever does acknowledge these points of departure, will also be able to give a rightful place to authority in the process of education. In the process of education and pedagogy the aim is to lead the student to intellectual independence and cultural maturity. He must be led and formed in order to respond from out of his heart to the centre of authority in his life, namely the Word of God. Only in this manner can one arrive at true self-discipline. The objective norm is determinative for both teacher *and* student. The exercise of authority in Christian education relationships is qualified by the calling of the teacher to lead students to an independent, responsible response to the norm according to the Word of God.

On the other hand, there is also the point of departure which we discussed earlier, namely that authority has to go hand in hand with insight, with knowledge, and with expertise. Since everything in the academic institution centres around insight and knowledge, this will be especially weighty in the exercise of authority in this kind of situation. The legitimacy of the authority of the teacher will become apparent the more his knowledge becomes apparent. One can even speak here of a process. The student can grow in knowledge and finally he can be the equal of the teacher. The teacher must acknowledge this by giving the student co-responsibility and by giving him the position of a colleague. "A pupil is not above his master, but everyone who is fully trained will be like his master" (Luke 6 : 40).

This aspect is that of rational authority and it is the necessary correlate of legal authority. In this respect we must remember that the student is in his adolescent or even late adolescent years and that the teacher does have to be aware of this. Tyranny, dictatorial procedures, rule upon rule, rigorous do's and dont's, sarcasm, and childish treatment are to be rejected and do not fit in this situation. We are indeed not talking about compulsive, judicial exercise of authority. Rather, we are talking about moral, spiritual, inner, educational, academic authority which needs to argue and to convince, which needs to reveal understanding and interest, and which must inspire and forgive in terms of openness and empathy. In this way teacher and student can truly be responsible servants of the gifts of grace that have been entrusted to them.[21]

We can learn a lot from the oldest and first situation in which there was real Christian education, in which real Christian moulding was done and in which the pupils were prepared for their future profession in a Christian manner. This was the relationship of Jesus Christ himself to his disciples. For three years he, the rabbi of Nazareth, taught his disciples. Just before the end of this three year period of instruction, he taught them a lesson about the question of authority. But he did this in a unique way. He had washed their feet and after that he said the following to them: "Do you understand what I have done to you? You call me master and lord, and right you are, because that is what I am. But now, if I who am your lord, and master, have washed your feet, then you should wash one another's feet. Because I have given you an example and therefore you must do as I have done to you. Truly, truly I say to you, a servant is not greater than his Master, and an envoy is not greater than the one who sent him".

An institution of higher education that is called Christian, is placed every moment before the immense and glorious challenge to let Christ give shape more and more to its relationships and to take His Word seriously.

All students are primarily to a greater or lesser extent involved with the typical structural function of the university. They are not merely objects or phenomena within the university context. They are subjects. They subjectively share in the exercise of science, both in its teaching (acquisition of knowledge) and in its research (cultivation of knowledge). In like manner their subjective and individual involvement in their vocational preparation and shaping stands fast. The moment a student's individuality is at stake, the moment he is degraded to a single unit in a vast set of numbers, or a cog in an enormous machine, the essential nature of his existence is involved.

281

This premise determines more than anything else the true position of students at the university. It nullifies the notion that students are merely clients restricted to an act of purchasing the fare being offered by the university as a market place. Indeed, thinking of students as "raw material" to be manipulated and moulded, is irreconcilable with the structure of the university.[22]

Students must be seen as genuine members of the university community, clearly distinguishable from mere clients of a business enterprise. The Latin word from which "student" derives contains the pregnant meaning of "dedication with interest" or "participation with diligence". This not only implies membership but also active participation. As members of the community subjectively involved in the multiple activities of the university they possess without doubt not only privileges but also rights. They share in academic freedom, they possess a limited authority as a differentiated community within the university as a societal structure, and congruent to other constituent members. In short, they fulfil a material function in the exercise of the university's vocation of intrarelationship.

On the other hand there are indeed differences between student and lecturer as well as between teaching staff and student community. Therefore, there are also differences in their respective rights and responsibilities. The student is not a member of the university in the same sense as the lecturer, and indeed cannot be. For instance, though the student is a participant in the exercise of science he in no way shares the responsibilities of the lecturer vested in the latter by virtue of his office. The student is still in the process of development towards adulthood and maturity. This does not apply to the lecturer. Furthermore, the student voluntarily joins the university community, while the lecturer is appointed due to his specific qualifications. In essence, therefore, there are tremendous differences in the legal position of the lecturer and student.

By virtue of his appointment, the lecturer holds a specific office and therefore stands in a position of authority, a position the student cannot claim for himself. Should he do so, it cannot be with legal sanction.

The proponents of student co-authority appeal to an equal basic right which the student is deemed to possess by virtue of his freedom of scholarship. Geck recognizes a constitutional freedom for the student. He does not study in response to civic injunction, but due to his highly personal interest.[23] His scholarly freedom gives him the right, within the context of valid contemporary custom and legal precepts, to select freely the university, course of study, professor, and even certain academic arrangements within the confines of the specific institution. However, it becomes problematic when acceptance of the student's specific constitutional freedom of scholarly pursuit transcends the rights just mentioned above. Should the student demand co-authority, then his right to scholarly freedom is altered to one of co-authority, and against this grave doubts must be raised.[24]

To this must be added that students are not compelled to participate in the primary tasks of the university, i.e. teaching and research, while the teaching staff is compelled to execute these tasks. Co-authority and direct control of teaching and research matters must therefore be disqualified as inadmissable control.[25]

With this conclusion we have arrived at the heart of the matter at hand, namely the position of the student in the university structure. The student is a member of the community, but in academic and administrative matters he has no authority over policy decisions or the exercise of control. He is co-practitioner of science, he shares fully in academic freedom, but as the fourth constituent in the composition of the university, he possesses limited legal jurisdiction, jurisdiction which does not include control. The other three constituents viewed in their historical principial context do possess such jurisdiction.

Therefore, the student could not by virtue of his academic freedom claim equal jurisdiction with lecturers for example. Such a pretence is based on false assumptions. The superiority and office of faculty and senate members must be respected.

Talcott Parsons very strongly stresses the factor of superiority: "We have stressed that students are, by definition of their roles, participating members in the academic system. But, the justification of the student's obligation to recognize faculty precedence remains. The matters of competence and of commitment and responsibility cannot simply be declared irrelevant; long training and experience and previous achievement, as well as career commitment, must 'count'... In this setting, the academic freedom of the student, properly subclassified for the immense variety of different classes of students, appears to be part of the academic freedom of the system as a whole, and is entirely consistent with faculty precedence.[26]

The legal jurisdiction of the student does entitle him to have his voice heard in academic matters. Should the university be a *universitas magistrorum et scolarium,* then the student may not be treated merely as a spectator, client, object, beggar or immature ward.

Should this be the case, it would affect the student's academic freedom. Maciver penetrates to the core of this issue when he declares: "Whatever the system may be, the breath of life dies within it unless the student is freely permitted, indeed encouraged, to think for himself, to question, to discuss, and to differ. This statement covers the essential freedom the student needs... He should be thought of as the subject rather than the object of education... This, then, the freedom to express and to defend his views or his beliefs, the freedom to question and to differ, without scholastic penalization, is the academic freedom the student particularly needs".[27]

Based on the preceding, a plea has to be submitted for greater scope to be granted to the student's voice at all levels of the academic enterprise. This voice must not be limited to the lecture halls, but should extend to the department, faculty and senate of the university and could conceivably be effected by means of thoroughly prepared memoranda on the contents of the syllabuses and curricula, on test and examination procedures, on methods of evaluation, on academic standards etc.[28] Of course here is no question of agitation, demonstration or any such non-academic display. This would already constitute a serious violation of the student's academic freedom.

The accommodation of authority in the contemporary university demands great wisdom. Each of those concerned — students, lecturers, alumni and administrative staff — have their own separate interests and therefore must have their own institution or organization. But there are many decisions affecting various of these interested parties. Evidently there are numerous levels of interest that overlap and where joint decisions could be taken provided this were done in the proper manner.

To the extent that each of these interest groups has to consider a specific matter this can be done while eventually assigning such a matter to the final instance where it belongs. It is therefore unnecessary to accommodate students at faculty, senate or even council meetings. On the other hand, a minimum code must be found for the rights and responsibilities of the students too. They have indeed freedom and responsibility as constituent members of the university — a freedom and responsibility that ought to be taken seriously.

Participation in university activities ought to incorporate all interested parties. Firstly through direct consultation, secondly through application of general rules prepared by representative bodies. But the application of these rules must follow two precepts. It must be fully decentralized so that not all matters are voiced at

284

the highest level where relevant decisions then have to be taken. What can be completed at lower levels, must be completed. Here committees may play an important role. Secondly, care must be taken that these committees are representatively constituted taking fully into account their competence and responsibility. In such a manner partnership may be reconciled to leadership.

Partnership as the realization of the typical structure of the societal concept of the university is necessary because future universities cannot be built without the commitment of all those who share this common interest.

1 Belifante, A. D.: „Staat en gezag". In: Het Gezag, W. P. van Stockum & Zn., 1968, p. 10.

2 Hendel, Charles W.: "An Exploration of the Nature of Authority". In: Friedrich, Carl J. (ed.): Authority, Harvard University Press, 1958, 7.7.

3 Marcuse, Herbert: "Liberation from the affluent society". In: Hamalian and Karl (eds.): The radical vision, essays for the seventies. New York, Thomas Y. Cromwell Com. Inc., 1970, p. 90.

4 Marcuse, H.: *An essay on liberation.* Boston, Beacon Press, 1969.

5 Van Riessen, H.: *De maatschappij der toekomst.* Franeker, Wever, 1953, p. 89.

6 Schrotenboer, Paul G.: *Man in God's world, the biblical idea of office.* Toronto, A.R.S.S., 1966, p. 3 v.

7 Ibid., pp. 5, 6.

8 Cf. Schouls, Peter: *Insight, authority and power.* Toronto, Wedge Publishing Foundation, 1972, pp. 4, 5.

9 Weber, Max: *Wirtschaft und Gesellschaft.* Tübingen, Mohr, 1922, pp. 157 v.

10 Cf. Van Zuthem: *Gezag en zeggenschap.* Kampen, Kok, 1968, pp. 38—40. Cf. Conner, A. M.: "Gezag". In: Christelijke Encyclopaedie III, Kampen, Kok, 1958, p. 221. He differentiates two types of legally official, or statutory authority and personal or internal authority. This is correlative to our distinction of legal and charismatic authority. The former is based on a certain legal ground and the latter on personal characteristics.

11 Ibid., pp. 42—44; Peper, Bram en Wolters, Willem: *De lastige universiteit.* Rotterdam, Universitaire Pers, 1970, p. 25.

12 Cf. Van Zuthem: op. cit., p. 44.

13 Searle, John R.: *The Campus War.* New York, The World Publishing Co., 1971, p. 169.

14 Peterson, Richard E.: "Reform in Higher Education — Demands of the Left and Right". In: Brickman, William W. and Lehrer, Stanley: Conflict and Change on the Campus: The Response to Student Hyper-activism. New York, School and Society Books, 1970, pp. 83, 84.

15 Flacks, Richard: "The liberated generation". In: McEvoy and Miller (eds.): Black power and student rebellion. California, Wadsworth, 1969, p. 359.

16 Wolin, Sheldon S. and Schaar, John H.: *The Berkeley Rebellion and beyond.* New York, The New York Review, 1970, p. 17.

17 Trow, Martin: "The transition from mass to universal higher education". In: Graubard and Ballotti (eds.): The embattled university.

18 P. Smits: "De functie van het samelevingsgezag". In: Het gezag, Verslag

van twee conferenties georganiseerd door de Humanistische Stichting Socrates. W. P. van Stockum & Zn., 1968, p. 34.

19 Wolff, Robert Paul: *The ideal of the university*. Boston, Beacon Press, 1969, p. 123.

20 Cf. Duvenage, S. C. W.: *Die opstandige student*. Potchefstroom, Pro Rege, 1973, p. 257, 296.

21 Cf. Duvenage: op. cit., p. 405, 406.

22 McGrath states it succinctly: "The traditional concept of a student as a supplicant, as an immature ward, as a mere client, cannot prevent turmoil: indeed, it will only stimulate increased resistance". McGrath, Earl J.: *Should students share the power?* Philadelphia, Temple University Press, 1970, p. 50.

23 Cf. Geck, in: Rupp, Hans H. and Geck, Wilhelm K.: Die Stellung der Studenten in der Universität. Berlin, Walter de Gruyter, 1968, p. 44.

24 Ibid., p. 47.

25 Geck, in: Rupp und Geck: op. cit., p. 60.

26 Parsons, Talcott: "The academic system: a sociologist's view". In: Bell and Kristol (eds.): Confrontation. The student rebellion and the universities. New York, Basic Books, 1968, p. 172.

27 Maciver, Robert M.: *Academic freedom in our time*. New York, Columbia University Press, 1955, pp. 206, 207. Cf. Geck in: Rupp and Geck: op. cit., p. 64.

28 Van Peursen, C. A.: *De toekomst van de universiteit*. Utrecht, Uitgave van de Christen studenten associatie, 1967, pp. 28, 29: „De hoogleraar verstrekt informatie aan de studenten en traint hen om zelf informatie te verwerken, te integreren en later te verstrekken. Maar het omgekeerde — de ‚terug-koppeling' — is ook onmisbaar. Deze vindt op allerlei wijzen reeds plaats — men denke aan de studieraden, die overal aan het ontstaan zijn en aan de mogelijkheid door de wet vermeld, dat vertegenwoordigers der studenten aan een deel van het faculteitsberaad deelnemen (een wets-bepaling die echter in de practijk aangevuld blijkt te moeten worden in de zin dat hiertoe niet slechts de hoogleraren, maar ook de studenten het initiaitef moet kunnen nemen). Toch dient ook hier een verdere ontwikkeling gestimuleerd, zodat wensen en adviezen omtrent te behandelen thema's en onderwijsmethodiek regelmatig van de zijde der studenten binnen kunnen komen. In breder verband dienen de organen van overleg tussen studente, en die van de wetenschappelijke staf director uit te monden in de centra, waar het wetenschapsbeleid tot stand komt".

SELECTED BIBLIOGRAPHY

Belifante, A. D.: "Staat en gezag". (In: *Het Gezag. Verslag van twee conferenties georganiseerd door de Humanistische Stichting Socrates*. W. P. van Stockum & Zn., 1968).

De Graaff, Arnold: *Get the Word*, Christian Labour Association of Canada, Ontario, 1967.

Duvenage, S. C. W.: *Die opstandige student*. Potchefstroom, Pro Rege, 1973.

Duvenage, S. C. W.: *Gesagsverhoudinge, prinsipieel belig en toegepas op die akademie*. I.B.C. studiestuk nr. 60, Potchefstroom, P.U. vir C.H.O.

Flacks, Richard: "The liberated Generation". (In: McEvoy and Miller, eds.: *Black Power and Student Rebellion*. California Wadsworth, 1969).

Friedrich, Carl J. (ed.): *Authority*, Harvard University Press, Massachusetts, 1958.

Friedrich, Carl J.: *Tradition and Authority*. London, Pall Mall, 1972.

Marcuse, Herbert: *An Essay on Liberation*. Beacon Press, Boston, 1969.

Marcuse, Herbert: *One-Dimensional Man*. Beacon Press, Boston, 1964.

Marcuse, Herbert: "Liberation from the affluent society". (In: Hamalian and Karl (eds.): *The radical vision*. New York, Thomas Y. Cromwell Comp. Inc., 1970).

Marsal, Maurice: *Gezag*. Utrecht, Het Spectrum, 1958.

Nash, Paul: *Authority and Freedom in Education*. New York, John Wiley & Sons, Inc., 1966.

Peper, Bram & Wolters, Willem: *De lastige universiteit*. Rotterdam, Universitaire Pers, 1970.

Peterson, Richard, E.: "Reform in Higher Education — Demands of the Left and Right". (In: Brickman, William W. & Lehrer, Stanley: *Conflict and Change on the Campus: The Response to Student Hyper-activism*. New York, School and Society Books, 1970).

Schouls, Peter A.: *Insight, Authority and Power*. Toronto, Canada, 1970.

Schrotenboer, Paul G.: *Man in God's World*, A.R.S.S., 1967.

Searle, John R.: *The campus War*. New York, The World Publishing Co., 1971.

Skolnick, Jerome H. (ed.): *The Politics of Protest*, Sixth Printing, Ballantine Books, New York, 1970.

Smits, P.: "De functie van het samenlevingsgezag". (In: *Het gezag*. W. P. van Stockum & Zn., 1968).

Taylor, Harold: "Freedom and Authority on the Campus". (In: Stanford Nevitt (ed.): *The American College*. New York, John Wiley, 1967.)

Trow, Martin: "Reflections on the transition from mass to universal higher education". (In: Graubard, Stephen R. & Ballotti, Geno A. (eds.): *The Embattled University*. New York, George Braziller, 1970.

Van Riessen, H.: *De maatschappij der toekomst*. Franeker, Wever, 1953.

Van Zuthem, H. J.: *Gezag en zeggenschap*. Kampen, Kok, 1968.

Weber, Max: *Wirtschaft und Gesellschaft*. Tübingen, Mohr, 1922.

Wolff, Paul Robert: *The Ideal of the University*, Beacon Press, Boston, 1969.

Wolin, Sheldon S. & Schaar, John H.: *The Berkeley Rebellion and Beyond* New York, The New York Review, 1970.

Authority and discipline at Christian higher educational institutions

Dr. P. G. Schrotenboer

THE paper of Professor Duvenage "Authority and Discipline in Christian Higher Educational Institutions" provides an excellent basis for a discussion on authority and discipline in the university. I for one find little in it with which to disagree outright. In true Calvinian fashion, the paper lays bare the basic philosophic roots of the diverging ideas on authority in human society today and exposes the regnant idea of human autonomy as basically humanistic and incompatible with the biblical idea of authority among men.

In seeking to describe the biblical idea of authority Prof. Duvenage rightly 1) stresses the derived nature of human authority, 2) relates authority directly to man's cultural mandate and 3) makes authority commensurate with the gifts (insight, competence) of the office bearer. Since authority as the right to order is derived from God, and the mandate for which man needs authority is from God, and the gifts to exercise the authority are also from God, authority in its origin, its task and its operation all put man *coram Deo*.

One will likely want to affirm with Prof. Duvenage also that the university is a unique, differentiated life zone, not reducible to any other sphere, such as state, industry or church. And, as a unique societal structure, it requires its own kind of authority: derived from God, determined in its nature by its specific contribution to the cultural mandate, and dependent in its exercise on the competence of the persons holding authority.

We welcome the emphasis that the paper has put on the *communal* character of the university. This we believe has much to say about the nature of the authority that the university has and how it should be exercised (discipline). This is especially pertinent in that the task of the university is to lead the student to "intellectual independence and cultural maturity". Prof. Duvenage is right on target when he states, "The exercise of authority in Christian educational institutions is qualified by the calling of the teacher to bring the student to an independent, responsible response to the norm, in accordance with the Word of God".

We may also want to agree with Prof. Duvenage that deep-going differences in authority, both in idea and in practice, have gone far to precipitate the crisis in which the modern university finds itself. We question, however, whether the blame rests entirely on the humanists who champion human autonomy and deny that authority derives from God. Let us grant that the humanist, who denies the transcendent norm that guarantees both order and freedom, has no effective way to avoid both totalitarianism and anarchy. Nevertheless the recognition of the existence of the transcendent norm is in itself no guarantee either. It is only in the diligent and wise exercise of authority as given by the Lawgiver for human affairs that authority in the university finds its rightful place and produces its wholesome results.

Part of the problem of authority in the university in our judgment stems from the malfunction of those schools which do acknowledge the transcendent norm and so seek to implement the biblical idea. We shall return to this later.

Another factor in the crisis of authority is the fact that the school is not really a *uni*-versity, but a *multi*-versity. Its 'multi' character derives not only from the proliferation of departments caused by the expanding tasks, but also by the multitude of basic viewpoints on what a university ought to do.[1] With the great influx of students after World War II, given the existing differing ideas of what a university is, all that was needed was a number of gut causes to move the students to rebel. Vietnam was the spark that ignited the fire.

It is instructive to note that the crisis in governance has left few universities in the West untouched. As Stanley Hoffman has written "The diversity of Institutions has been enormous, whereas the similarity in the students' revolt has been remarkable. Every kind of university government has been in difficulty".[2]

The event that epitomized the crises in the university was an ironical incident at Berkeley in 1964. Here the Free Speech Movement staged a student sit-in that resulted in the arrest of 800 students. The President of the University, Clark Kerr, called for an extra-ordinary convention on the Campus' Greek Theatre on December 7 and a crowd of from 15 000 to 20 000 convened. Mario Savia, principal spokesman for FSM, asked to speak. His request was denied. He asked tó announce that FSM would hold a rally elsewhere. This request was also denied. Savia attempted to make the announcement anyway, but was dragged by police from the microphone and other FSM leaders were dragged to the floor. First the

289

crowd was stunned, then pandemonium broke loose. Understandably Berkeley became almost synonymous with student revolt.

It is significant that this incident occurred against the backdrop of the dissatisfaction with the involvements of the universities in the nation's defense research. ROTC, and counter insurgency research — all this in the frame of Vietnam. In other words, it was a complaint that the university had involved itself in non-academic affairs of a political nature.

One final comment on the crisis; it is one of *governance*. In previous decades the shape of the crisis was set by the uncertainty about basic goals and curriculum. These have not been resolved and are with us yet. They have, however, receded to the background in the face of a *force majeure*, the governance of the school.

We would note that in so far as the universities in North America are concerned, there has been less unrest during the 70's than there was during the 60's. This is due not just to the fact that students don't as easily find causes to rally behind as they once did (Vietnam, integration, minority rights). It is due also to a change in the constitutionally regulated structures of the university to allow for a greater sharing of authority. This does not mean that universities have become more attentive to the message of the Word of God written, but it may well mean that the common creation reality as this is normed by God, and upheld by God's Word, forces man, in spite of his predominently humanistic stance, to recognize certain essential elements of true authority in the university.

I cannot judge whether, and if so, to what extent the ideas of Prof. Duvenage are practised by the universities of South Africa, or whether the university at which we are gathered itself observes all the implications of his position. I do know that there is within the international Reformed community much difference on how authority in the university should be exercised. And in some of these institutions this exercise of authority is considerably different today from what it was a decade or so ago.

Therefore it is of great importance that at this international conference we discuss this topic, perhaps compare the one institution with the other and herein subject ourselves to a biblically informed critique of our ideas and our institutions.

As we seek for a biblical perspective it should be kept in mind that the Scriptures give us no illustration or precept of authority in the school. In other words, they do not do for this institution what they do for the home and the state. The obvious reason for this omission is that the school as a societal institution did not yet exist when the Scriptures were written. There was education in Bible times, even some schools, such as those for prophets and rabbis, but human society had not yet differentiated into institutionally recognizable spheres of life that included the school.

One must therefore press behind the institution to the task for which the institution has historically come into being, namely the educational side of man's comprehensive life assignment to rule the world in the name of God, through the redemption Christ gives in the power of the Spirit according to the Word of God.

A passage which makes pertinent reference to this educational task is Romans 12 : 6—8.

> *The gifts we possess differ as they are allotted to us by God's grace, and must be exercised accordingly; the gift of inspired utterance, for example, in proportion to a man's faith; or the gift of administration, in administration. A teacher should employ his gift in teaching, and one who has the gift of stirring speech should use it to stir his hearers. If you give to charity, give with all your heart; if you are a leader, exert yourself to lead; if you are helping others in distress, do it cheerfully. (NEB).*

In this passage we would note the prominence given to ministry *(diakonia)* teaching *(didaskalia)* and ruling *(proistamenos)*. All three are essential components of university life. Moreover, these are all set within the frame of the one body, the many members and the diversity of gifts. In other words, the people of God are all u *united task force* to carry out the work God assigns. The university then is or should be such a united task force in education.

Another key passage is found in the Gospel that records words of Jesus to his disciples concerning the exercising of authority in the Kingdom of God (Matt. 20 : 20—28). The citizens of the Kingdom are not like the rulers of the world who are called 'benefactors' and exercise authority over men and are considered great. Kingdom citizens follow the beat of another drum, one that calls men to recognize that the person who would be most worthy of esteem is the one who serves the most and takes the lowest place. "For the Son of Man came not to be served but to serve and to give his life as a ransom for many" (v. 28).

The authority of the university, we would suggest, concerns these two principles, 1) The authority of the university is subordinate to and its nature is determined by its educational task, 2) Authority of the university, which is a community of scholars and students, must be shared. In explaining both principles we, rather than go another way than Prof. Duvenage has pointed out, would go farther down the road than he has gone, without, we hope, coming to a parting of the ways.

Educational authority

Restrictions upon the proper authority of the university can come from many quarters; industry, state, church. In Russia science is by government order put in the service of atheism. Calvin College in Grand Rapids, Michigan is controlled by the Christian Reformed denomination. The Netherlands' Department of Education has required of all its universities that they be democratized. In South Africa the government imposes entrance requirements upon the university that are set by its racial policy. The question arises whether the university, if it is to carry out its unique educational task, should allow *any* other societal structure than itself to determine its academic affairs.

It should not need to be argued that a considerable amount of the unrest in the universities of recent years has come from their being too closely allied to a political position, party or government. It is an essential part of academic life to take an academically critical stance regarding policies and rise to the defence of its own unique area resisting every intrusion, from whatever quarter.

Unrest in the university has come also from crossing the line from the other side, this time by the university itself. Here I refer to that use of the idea that the school functions in *loco parentis*. This has meant that the school takes the place of parents to impose family standards of morals upon student life on campus making the school a guardian of family morals. Our point is that both the intrusions from outside into the school and the excursions by the school to the outside should be resisted in the name of the educational enterprise.

Sharing authority

One of the most significant changes in university administration in recent decades has been the sharing of authority by various divisions: trustees or regents, administration, faculty, and especially by students.

This democratizing trend has had a two-fold effect. In some instances it has given so much say to students that the work of the university, viz., education has suffered. In other instances the sharing of power has led to a somewhat more stable university life and has enhanced the education.

We would suggest a number of guidelines for effective sharing of power — all within the frame of a Christian view of the university.

Principles of sharing university power

1) The communal nature of the academic enterprise (not the democratic idea that governments rule by the consent of the governed) provides the basis for a sharing of power. In other words, the sharing of the task requires the sharing of control. Authority is for the sake of cultural obedience.[3]

2) The nature and the extent to which one shares authority is determined by considerations such as these:

a. The *trust obligation* by the founders and supporters. Ultimate authority should remain with the regents (trustees) whose task it is to serve the interests of the association that founded and supports the university.

b. The *academic competence* (commitment, dedication, training, talents) of the curators and faculty would indicate that the academic control should lie with them. Curators, as distinguished from trustees, should no less than the faculty, be persons of academic training and competence. It is the academic nature of the university's task that requires that policy be determined by curators and faculty jointly. The other side of this consideration is that students, who have little training, and are as yet but partially tried and trained, should not be given decisive authority in the university.

c. *Devotion and degree of personal involvement* should figure as a factor in the sharing of authority in the university. This means that the academic staff, whose life career is at stake, should have much more say than the students who may not be associated with the university for more than a number of months. By the same token, inasmuch as students are also greatly influenced for better or for ill by their stay at the university, they should be co-determiners in the life of the school.[4] They may not be treated as purchasers of products or services which can be tested and approved before participation. Drugs and articles offered for sale can be tested for safety by some government body for the protection of the public before they buy. But the value of an education can only be determined by the student while he is in the process of receiving training.

d. The purpose of the university, namely to bring students to academic excellence and cultural maturity, would mean that there should be an increasingly greater sharing of authority as the student matures. The extent of co-determination should be set by the degree to which the student attains the qualifications mentioned under 'c' above.

It will be readily seen that participation in control should take into account whether or not, and if so to what extent, the student shares the stated goals of the university. To neglect this factor, would be to deny the communal character of the university.

Another argument for student participation is that in a real sense the student, who has been exposed to the teacher's influence, is in a unique position to determine the competence and effectiveness of the teacher. This factor may, however, be offset by the lack of maturity on the part of the student. In any case it would seem to argue for some say by students in the reappointment of academic staff members.

A model ?

One might wish for a tried and well-tested model which recognizes the communal character of the university, one in which the sharing of authority is regulated according to the varying responsibilities, interests, competences and commitments of the different groups (regents, curators, administration, faculty, and students). Perhaps such a model does not exist. Nevertheless we believe that it is a step in the right direction to involve the students in the making and implementation of policy. It is significant that three Reformed colleges in the U.S.A. (Calvin College, Dordt College, and Trinity Christian College) have recently granted some student participation in the governance of the school.

The recently established and still small Institute for Christian Studies in Toronto has sought to put a plan of participatory governance into effect by distinguishing between directors who manage the non-academic side of the institution and curators, academically qualified persons, to manage the academic affairs. This allows for a 'separation of powers' and for co-operation between curators and the Institute Council in determining and supervising academic policy.

The Institute Council is comprised of fulltime permanently employed Senior Members (faculty) chosen by the Senior Members, and Junior Members (graduate students) chosen by the Junior Members at a ratio of 2 : 1. The officers of the Council are appointed by the Curators.

Among the items of business of the Council is the drafting of policy proposals and the reviewing, together with the Curators, of the work of the Senior Members at times of reappointment and of periodic review of Senior Members with a continuing appointment. In this way students are drawn into the important affairs of the school but they do not play a decisive role.

Conclusion

When the Christian university views a crisis in the university world and finds itself drawn irresistibly into it, it must resist the temptation to think that its troubles are due solely to the intrusion of ideas from outside. The crisis should rather move us to engage in true and deep self-crisicism.

In this criticism our cherished unity between knowledge and outlook will stand us in good stead. For we can engage in self-critique on the basis of our deepest convictions and then proceed to reform ourselves and our institutions in true Calvinian fashion according to the Word of God. In other words, a true Calvinist cannot be a defender of the status quo any more than he may be the runner after the latest academic fad. He will have to be governed by his loyalty to the mandate of his Lord.

In short, the call of the hour is to make concrete in the academic enterprise the fundamental Christian confession that Jesus is Lord. In this confession lie both our mandate and our hope.

---

1 Peter J. Caws in his contribution: "Design for a University" to *The Embattled University* says we should not try to find *the* right solution but agree on *a* right solution (86). There are, he says, too many possible solutions (85). The solution, whatever it is, will have to be accepted by faculty, students, trustees, legislators, and voters. Therefore agreement is the most important consideration. "The curriculum must be interesting, *as judged by the students who are compelled to follow it;* and the government must be fair *as judged by the faculty and students* who are ruled by it" (86, italics in original). The 'principle' operative in this rejection of specific and necessary principles is the democratic idea that universities, like governments, rule by the consent of the governed.

2 "Participation in Perspectives?" in: *The Embattled University,* p. 179.

3 We would not say, as Prof. Duvenage has stated, that authority is 'the foundation stone of society'. It is rather the intrinsic component, correlative to man's mandate. The mandate is primary, the authority is secondary, necessary for the exercise of man's life assignment. Because God gave man the mandate to exercise dominion he has the right to command. Without authority the mandate remains ineffective, without mandate the authority is misguided.

4 In the U.S.A. it is scarcely a question anywhere whether students should share in managing the school. The only question concerns the extent of their sharing and the force of their influence upon policy and appointments.

Academic freedom in Christian

perspective

Prof. dr. W. van 't Spijker

THE concept of academic freedom is largely determined by the historic context in which it is used and by an actual situation within which it functions and which can be quite different from place to place.

1. *Historic overview*

A short overview of the history of the concept is useful.

1.1. One of the first documents which must be mentioned in this connection is the law decreed by Frederik I at the diet of Roncalia in 1158, incorporated in the "Corpus Juris Civilis" (Cod. Lib. IV, Tit, XIII), which gave to professors and students who because of their study had to be in a foreign town, guarantee of freedom and of protection.[1] Motivation for this was the great respect of the emperor for those who with their scholarship enlightened the entire world unto obedience to God and to the emperor as his servant. "Who would not be moved by the fate of those who went into exile from their countries out of love for science, and who without the possession of riches exposed their lives to many dangers?"

In this imperial constitution the "universitas professorum et scholarum" is guaranteed freedom of justice subject to a jurisdiction proper to themselves or subject to the bishop for the area concerned.

This protection made an autonomous body of the university, with its own laws and freedoms which found their meaning in a deep respect for scholarship and in the expectation that God and the emperor, church and state, would later be able to profit from this. It is in this atmosphere of autonomy and freedom that university life could develop in the Middle Ages: free, but bound to ecclesiastical (papal) and state supervision.

It would last up to the reformation before the ties between university and papal church were subjected to critical tensions and finally succumbed. The announcement of Luther's 95 theses which gave the impetus to the immense reformational movement, took place within the framework of academic freedom. It intended

296

to be an introduction to a university debate. In fact, it led to a renewal of the university according to a reformational model. The names of Wittenberg, Strassburg and Genève need to be mentioned in this connection. Together with many university towns, they became the centres from out of which the forces of the Gospel went into many layers of European society.[2]

Nevertheless, it would take until the beginning of the 19th century, before the concept of academic freedom became an indication of a total renewal of higher education.

At that time, on October 10, 1810, the Friedrich-Wilhelmus University in Berlin was started.[3] Schelling, Fichte, Schleiermacher, Steffens and Von Humboldt have each pleaded the freedom of scholarship in their own way and have pointed to this freedom as the high ideal for the exercise of scholarship.[4] It finds its ground in the unity of all sciences, the "universitas scientiarum". This needs to be carried out in the "universitas" of "scientia" and "doctrina" (research and education).

It is borne by the vocational awareness of professors and students together. Schleiermacher thinks very highly of the freedom which must characterize the university. This freedom is especially relevant with respect to the state. The natural direction in which the university moves is that it knows how to repress the dominant influence of the state.[5] In the case of Fichte it seems clear that he ascribes a mystical significance to a free exercise of science. On October 19 Fichte delivered a rectoral oration about the only possible disturbance of academic freedom. For him the university is "the visible presence of the unity of the world as an appearance of God",[6] the most holy possession of mankind.

Fichte does not primarily see this freedom threatened by the public authorities, but in the first place by that kind of student who thinks that he is a special class on earth and who because of his arrogance and intolerance destroys academic freedom in every respect and even undermines the essence of the university in its totality.[7] The ideal of Von Humboldt was to exercise scholarship in freedom, that is, in a lonesome separation from state and society.[8] In this manner the concept of academic freedom became an indication of the climate within which the people who exercised scholarship could be busy with their job without disturbance, almost immune to what happened in their environment.

It is exactly this kind of isolation which created the possibility for an alienation of science from society. Especially after the crisis of the last great war, this isolation was heavily mortgaged by the fact that it had not been able to prevent the rise of demonic powers in Hitler's "Third Empire". Was it not precisely because of its pretended freedom, that with respect to the state, the university delivered society to a pseudoscientific demonic world?[9]

All contemporary criticism of academic freedom is concentrated on this point. The problematics of the debate are largely directed to the relation between university and society.[10] Across the entire front we hear about academic freedom with respect to the church, which in a secularized world no longer has any significance. Certainly in Western society, academic freedom with respect to the public authorities, which in most cases are neutral, seems to be well assured. But there is a new dimension to the problem today in the questions about the relationship between a responsible university and a responsible society.[11]

1.2. This does not mean that the problematics around the concept of academic freedom are being dealt with in the same manner everywhere today. For it does make a difference whether we think about the problem against the background of the European continental tradition, or against the background of the Anglo-American world. The problematics in South Africa seem determined by both of these, and in addition we need to see the various tensions which are typical of South African problems of a more political nature.[12]

The European continental tradition has probably conserved the ideal of a free and isolated exercise of scholarship more than others. Academic freedom seemed best guaranteed there by the attitude of professionalism in the exercise of scholarship. Weber's complaint about the absolute "exam-man" of 1919 even now is not destitute of every ground.[13]

Traditionally the Anglo-American customs in the exercise of science worked more in a direction towards the cultural moulding of the personality. For this reason the various colleges rather directed their questions to the problems of society.

But because of this they were also more vulnerable to losing academic freedom in its deeper meaning. In the latter case, economics, politics, and the big social questions determine what is scientifically relevant. In that case there is no question of a free exercise of scholarship. In the case science becomes the "ancilla" of society. By virtue of its history, one finds traces of both traditions in South Africa. Problems which seem to be important in connection with academic freedom, both in Europe and in America, play their role in South Africa, even though the contemporary political situation does give them a peculiar significance.

1.3. A "communis opinio" about the essence of academic freedom which slowly took form, could only be realised by a matter of fact attitude in science, by a neutralising of the truth concept and by the liberalising of the rights and freedoms of autonomous man. In that case academic freedom is seen as being in the same league with human rights.[14]

The crisis surrounding the concept of academic freedom arises because of a positivistic view of science,[15] which divides the scientific enterprise into numberless sub-sciences. In this situation, as Popma remarks,[16] it is no longer important to know "what" is done so long as one knows "how" it is done. This technicistic attitude towards science, which in Popma's language leads to one-eyed speciality-idiotism,[17] is not interested in the question of truth. Under the cover of neutrality and even with an appeal to Christ's saying that the truth makes free, both truth and anti-truth received equal rights. Autonomous man is thought to be quite capable himself to determine what is good and what is evil. Against this background it is clear how controversial the concept of academic freedom really is.

It is the locus of a pitched battle, which is waged around the very essence of the university and of science itself.

Is it possible to speak about a free science, in the sense of a value-free and neutral exercise of scholarship as one's profession, as an objective affair, so that the thinking researcher, ("denkende Forscher") must be distinguished from the willing man ("wollende Mensch")? Weber puts two viewpoints against one another, the one being that practical, ethical, world and life view problems do belong in the lecture hall though they are different matters to be distinguished from empirical; and the other viewpoint is that even when a distinction between these two categories is not logically tenable, we nevertheless need to distantiate ourselves from all practical value questions ("Wertfragen"). Both these points of view have had their defenders up to the present.[18]

This is related to the view of the autonomy of science. In his masterful inaugural oration at the Free University of Amsterdam in 1880, Kuyper identified the sovereignty of science as the characteristic of its scientific intent.[19] Free from the state and free from ecclesiastical supervision, science is a social area of its own, in which truth is sovereign. In his Stone Lectures on Calvinism, he worked out these thoughts and he limited the freedom of science only by a strict relationship to its subject matter and by the requirement of a valid method: "only by those relationships and subject to that law is science free", that is to say, free from the state and free from the church. But the question which remained was this:

is the university itself a part of society? Kuyper thinks that the social situation in the Netherlands during the 17th century gave a strong impetus to science.[20] (See "Calvinisme", Amsterdam, n.y., p. 123). But he did not further discuss the relationship between science and society. And it is precisely these questions which today determine our view of academic freedom by the incisive problematics they pose.

1.4. Totalitarian systems from the right and from the left have militantly rejected the idea of academic freedom.[21] For Hitler science was a social phenomenon which, like every social phenomenon, is limited by its usefulness to or its detriment of society. In practice this means that freedom of scholarship is subjected to a conformity with the prevailing ideology. The objective world of objectivity is made to depend on the actual existential participation in the national socialistic community.

In the Stalinistic era the communist party philosophers delivered to the public authorities the argument that could be used against the autonomy of science. In 1951 Ernst Bloch wrote: "Thinking must be partial... The image of so-called pure science is but a subjective illusion".[22] The only truly objective kind of science is politically biased science. In the case of national socialism the deciding question in science was the race question, while for communism the class question plays this role. In both cases academic freedom is challenged and finally broken. These problematics return in the work of Habermass and especially in the work of Marcuse. The freedom in the university is regulated by social, political and economic considerations. In a technicised and highly industrialised society with a democratic tolerance which works repressively, the university needs to use its freedom to combat the social powers of repression, hard labour, aggression, suffering and injustice. Our only real need is for measures which counteract the domination of the industrial society.[23] This is the origin of protest, which is a politically impotent form of refusal to participate in this kind of society.

This is the origin of student revolts in America and in Europe. Social discontent, along with a critique of the parliamentary system, caused them to grab for extra parliamentary opposition, both in a protest against the isolation of academic freedom and at the same time to find a bulwark within the university itself by appealing to academic freedom. Both protesting against and profiting from academic freedom, they protected themselves by hiding in the privileged protected campus area or university building. In this paradoxical manner they demanded attention for the fact that the exercise of

300

scholarship takes place in the midst of social reality.[24]

Is this, perhaps, not the case then? Is it not true then, that the university finds itself as a free and autonomous body responsibly standing in the midst of a world which is looking for a responsible society?

Does not the freedom of science have a moral or even ethical character? Can the academic, specifically as academic, view himself as free from social and political responsibility?[25] Is it possible for the academic to find his ideal in the pure exercise of science according to Von Humboldt, in whose view loneliness and freedom are the privileged principles in this area ("die in ihrem Kreise vorwaltenden Prinzipien")? Does the academic not have a special responsibility in and for society? Is it true, for example, that the development of atomic power was a neutral scientific achievement? Is biological research in the area of the origin and development of human life really value-free? Do the various behavioural sciences impress us as merely indifferent areas of research? Is all that which is technically possible also possible in terms of its effects? And in that case does it as such fall within the framework of academic freedom?[26]

2. *Academic freedom in christian perspective*

We can answer these questions in a nearly adequate manner only when we place academic freedom within a christian perspective. This does not mean that we develop a christian theory about freedom and then use this as a norm for judging academic freedom. For the christian faith does not live by any theory, not even a theology of freedom. When the christian faith truly is alive, it stands within the freedom with which Christ has made us free. The "libertas christiana" is the room within which a light falls upon the "libertas academica".[27] Academic freedom, i.e. the freedom of choice of area of study, the freedom of choice of area of scientific research, of the method used and the freedom to publicly defend a scholarly conviction must be a part of christian freedom in the broad sense.

2.1. Freedom in the New Testament

Freedom is a central concept in the New Testament.[28] It does not have the political democratic dimension which it had at first, and the world and life view dimension which it later possessed in Greece. It starts with the concrete act of the liberation of God's people from the slavery in Egypt, which is a paradigm for the true freedom from sin, guilt, the law and death.

This freedom is present because of the suffering, death and resurrection of Christ. It is for this freedom that Christ has made us free. It comes to us in the Gospel, and it becomes real through the power of the Holy Spirit. Wherever He is, there we find freedom. And it finds its way in the life of a Christian through love: the perfect law of freedom.

There is a close relationship between freedom and the independent openness of a believer. "Eleutheria" and "parrhesia" are closely related. In the New Testament the latter has been taken out of the political context which characterised it in old Greece. It becomes the invitation for a free and open dialogue of a man with and before his God. It has to do with working in the public area. Paul uses it to indicate christian existence which freely and unashamedly showed its face to all people, fully open, and authorized by God with an authorization which implies freedom from the fear of people.

The New Testament concept of freedom deals with the relationship between God and people and with the relationship between people and the world. Thus, we see that Paul uses christian freedom to indicate all of the christian life.

2.2. Christian freedom according to Luther

In his documents "On the freedom of a Christian".[29] Luther summarized the totality of the christian faith in these two theses: "A Christian is a most free lord over all things and subject to no one; a Christian is a most servile servant of all and subject to all people". Only by justification through faith, faith in the promise, does a human being become really free. He becomes a participant in Christ who is both priest and king. "Through faith every Christian is elevated so highly above all things, that he becomes lord of all through a spiritual power, so that not one thing can be detrimental to him in any manner at all, and all things become subject to him and serve unto his salvation".[30] In paradise Adam had to cultivate and keep the garden. These were labours of freedom, which were done for no other reason than to please God. Only through faith does a Christian receive that kind of dedication to God.

His works do not make him good. But because through faith he is good in his work, his works are good as well. As the man is, believing or unbelieving, so are his works: good as in faith; bad, as in unbelief. The reality of this faith appears in our love towards our neighbour. "Therefore I want to give myself to my neighbour, as in a certain sense being a Christ, just as Christ gave himself to me. And in this life I will do nothing at all except that which

302

I see as necessarily advantageous and salutary for my neighbour, since I have received all things in abundance through faith... Every one needs to become a Christ for his neighbour in a certain sense, in order that we become Christs for one another, back and forth. Only then does Christ live in his people and are we truly Christians".[31] This christian freedom also subjects itself freely to the laws of the public authorities. Everyone needs to do the labour which is proper to his profession and status. The Christian does not merely live for himself, but in Christ he lives for his neighbour, with proper respect for the calling with which he is called. All of life is subject to our calling by God.[32]

2.3. Christian freedom according to John Calvin

For Calvin too, christian freedom is a matter of the main contents of the entire Gospel, an appendix to justification by faith.[33] In Calvin's work christian freedom does not merely function as a means whereby the strong dominate over the weak. On the contrary, it is primarily a matter of conscience "coram Deo", not consisting merely of enjoying all that is possible, but also in freely taking distance from things that in themselves are neither good nor evil. A Christian is also free not to use his freedom. The love command with respect to the weak is fully valid in this respect. Calvin's remark about the two kingdoms is important here: the spiritual and the civil kingdom.[34]

In the case of the latter the main emphasis is on humanity and civility, which can not easily be found wanting among men. Spiritual freedom cannot simply be declared relevant for our political order. Being free before God in our conscience does not mean that we need to exercise less obedience towards external human orders. Calvin takes it that a Christian is free in both orders, subject to our one Lord, Jesus Christ. He frees us from guilt, making us capable of real service to God and our neighbour.

3. *Summary and conclusion*

If we now place this concept of academic freedom in a Biblical-reformational, a christian perspective, then it becomes a part of the christian life, and has to do with christian relations in its deepest roots, that is in its being before the face of God. It becomes a part of life "coram Deo". It will be lived "sub specie aeternitatis". And this implies at least three things:

3.1. Academic freedom doesn't find its ground in autonomous man, not in a liberal view of human rights, but in the gracious liberation through the promises of the Gospel.

When academic freedom is at bottom a matter of anthropology, we find a dividing line here between two views. The one sees science as a means. For the other, science becomes an idol, the university an alternative church and the exercise of scholarship will function as a new religion. In the latter view we find one of the causes for the paternalistic relation of science with respect to society. When scholars claim a special social responsibility by virtue of their specialist knowledge, we get a new form of clericalism, according to professor Rudwick in his inaugural address as professor in the History and Social Aspects of Natural Science at the Free University of Amsterdam.[35]

Whoever makes a new Gospel out of science, will soon experience the fact that it subjects us to a harder and more ruthless law than the one of Moses. It becomes an idol which mercilessly subjects and drives its servants. The exercise of scholarship as a cultural task for man outside of paradise can be carried on only subjected to the Lordship of Christ by virtue of the freedom found in reconciliation. In Christ all things are gathered together, in Him are all treasures, and in Him we find the final ground for the "universitas scientiarum". It may be that the exercise of science takes place in the area of common grace, or whatever other ways we find to deal with this special area after Kuyper; but the exercise of science for the Christian occurs by virtue of the authority which is vested in our having been made free before God. Therefore, stand fast in the freedom with which Christ has made you free. Stand fast and do not subject yourselves again to a yoke of slavery.

3.2. Academic freedom finds its norm in the perfect law of freedom

Whoever meditates about this, does not act as a forgetful listener. He actually does what the law says. Being in Christ, remaining in His Word, makes us understand the truth. In this way truth makes free. Truly and really. In this way we stand before the reality of the antithesis between two kinds of science, not between faith and science. Along with Kuyper, we may say: there is no conflict. All science derives from faith. Faith stands over against faith.[36] Thinking is a matter of the heart. And these thoughts are at bottom made plain before Christ. This particular view does not have consequences merely for formal epistemology, but even more for the direction and goal of our thinking. When scholarly activity must be viewed as a service of obedience to God in Christ, as part of the battle of faith, it is true in this case also that the weapons are not of flesh, but before God able to destroy obstruction, so that any argument or other barrier erected against the knowledge of God, can be overcome and every objection can be made prisoner to obedience to Christ. When we talk about a "scientia regenitorum" over against that of the world of unbelief, it will have to verify itself in the love of our neighbour.[37] In this way the christian does not know any value-free, neutral or objective science. Thus, there will be areas about which the Christian will, as a free lord, say: it is allowed, but not expedient. All things are permitted, not everything is expedient. All things are allowed, but not all things edify. Let no one look out for himself, but for what belongs to others. The freedom of the Christian, of a christian scholar, could consist in this: that, moved by service to his neighbour and possibly to all of humanity, he reserves the right not to make use of his authority to search all things. Academic freedom is not without limit.

3.3. The third and last view on the concept of academic freedom in christian perspective is that it is an aspect of the freedom of the glory of God's children about which Paul speaks in Rom. 8.

Concretely, that means it is a part of our hope. That is, we cannot talk about the free exercise of scholarship merely from the perspective of the mandate which has accompanied us since paradise: to subject the earth and to have dominion over it. All of this will have to be seen in the light of the languishing of all creation which is subjected to sterility. In this case, freedom becomes a promise which derives its power not from the modern science of futurology, but from the biblical message of eschatology. Our freedom always remains "in part". This protects us from scientific hubris. It forces us to look towards a future when perfection will be realized. And it teaches us today to live often by compromise caused by the tension between justification and sanctification, between special grace and common grace, between the spiritual kingdom and the civil. But this tension already receives its resolution today, through faith in the one Lord Christ, and the Christian derives from this hope a power to live in the midst of tensions, free before God and man. Wherever Christian freedom functions in true faith, in strong hope and in fiery love, there we have the best guarantee for maintaining a form of academic freedom, manifest in reality.

---

1 H. Denifle: *Die Entstehung der Universitäten des Mittelalters bis 1400*, Berlin 1885, Graz 1956[2], 48—60; H. Raskdall: *The universities of Europe in the Middle Ages*, new. ed. by F. M. Powicke, A. B. Emden, Vol. I, Oxford 1936, 143—145; H. Grundmann: *Vom Ursprung der Universität im Mittelalter*, Darmstadt 1964.

2 F. Paulsen: *Geschichte des gelehrten Unterrichts auf den deutschen Schulen und Universitäten vom Ausgang des Mittelalters bis zur Gegenwart*, Ed. R. Lehmann, Leipzig 1919, I, 179—275; K. Holl: *Gesammelte Aufsätze zur Kirchengeschichte*, I, Luther, Tübingen 1923, 518—542.

3 W. Weischedel (Herausg.): *Idee und Wirklichkeit einer Universität*. Dokumente zur Geschichte der Friedrich-Wilhelms-Universität zu Berlin, Berlin, 1960.

4 E. Anrich: *Die Idee der deutschen Universität. Die fünf Grundschriften aus der Zeit ihrer Neubegründung durch klassischen Idealismus und romantischen Realismus*, Darmstadt 1964; R. König: *Vom Wesen der deutschen Universität*, Darmstadt 1970; E. Horn: *Akademische Freiheit*, Berlin 1905, 75ff.

5 W. Nitsch, U. Gerhardt, C. Offe, U. K. Preuss: *Hochschule in der Demokratie*, Berlin 1965; 18—27.

6 W. Weischedel: a.a.O., 231ff.

7 W. Waldstein: *Akademische Freiheit und humane Ordnung*, Salzburg/ München 1969, 5, 17 Anm. 4; W. Weischedel: a.a.O., 240ff.

8 W. Weischedel: a.a.O., 193ff.; H. Schelsky: *Einsamkeit und Freiheit. Idee und Gestalt der deutschen Universität und ihrer Reformen*, Düsseldorf 1971[2], 72ff.

9 N. Wolterstorff: Academic Freedom in the Christian College, *Christian Scholar's Review*, 1971, 99—108; p. 103.

10 E. Topitsch: *Die Freiheit der Wissenschaft und der politische Auftrag der Universität*, Neuwied/Berlin 1969[2].

11 W. A. Visser 't Hooft: *A responsible University in a responsible Society*, University of Cape Town 1971.

12 Cf.: "Hoofverslag van die Kommissie van ondersoek na die universiteitswese", Republiek van Suid-Afrika, Departement van nasionale opvoeding *(Kommissie Van Wijk de Vries)*, 60—108; 134—138; *Woord en Daad*, April 1975, 11; H. G. Stoker: "At the Crossroads. Apartheid and University Freedom in South Africa", in: *Race Relations Journal*, Vol. 24, no. 3, 4, July/December 1957, 1—10; I. D. MacCrone: "Racial Ideology and University Apartheid", ib., 11ff.

13 M. Weber: *Wissenschaft als Beruf. Vortrag 1919. Gesammelte Aufsätze zur Wissenschaftslehre*, Tübingen 1968[3], 582ff.

14 H. J. J. Bingle: "Enkele aspekte van vryheid en verantwoordelikheid van die universiteit", *Koers*, Vol. 31, no. 7, 8, Jan./Febr. 1964, 403—425, especially 410; J. A. L. Taljaard: Akademiese vryheid, *Koers*, Vol. 36, nr. 6, 1969, 425—444; P. G. Schrotenboer: "Academic Freedom — A historical sketch", *Bulletin van die Suid-Afrikaanse Vereniging vir die bevordering van Christelike Wetenskap*, vol. 5, 1969, no. 17, 3—22; idem: "The Liberal Idea of Academic Freedom", ibid., no. 19, 13—30; idem: "A Christian View of Academic Freedom", I, II, 1970, no. 22, 18—30; no. 23, 45—63.

15 K. J. Popma: *De universiteit. Idee en practijk*, Amsterdam 1969; J. D. Dengerink: *Deling en heling van de universiteit*, Assen 1974; H. van Riessen: *The university and its basis*, Ontario 1963, 49—53.

16 K. J. Popma: op. cit., 11.

17 K. J. Popma: op. cit., 54.

18 M. Weber: Ges. Aufsätze zur Wissenschaftslehre, 489ff.

19 A. Kuyper: *Souvereiniteit in eigen kring*, Amsterdam, 1880, 19, 22ff.

20 A. Kuyper: *Het Calvinisme*, Amsterdam/Pretoria, 123.

21 E. Topitsch: op. cit., 11ff.

22 Op. cit., 18.
23 Op. cit., 33ff; Schelsky: op. cit., 159ff.
24 T. Regtien: *Universiteit in opstand. Europese achtergronden en de Neder-
    landse situatie,* Amsterdam 1969, H. F. M. G. Coenjaarts: *Buitenparlemen-
    taire oppositie en de universiteit,* Meppel 1972; C. Troebst: *Studium oder
    Klassenkampf? Bericht eines betroffenen Vaters,* Stuttgart 1973.
25 N. Wolterstorff: op. cit.
26 W. A. Visser 't Hooft: op. cit., 10ff.
27 G. W. Locher: "Libertas christiana en libertas academica", Ned. Theol.
    Tijdschr., 25e jrg., juni 1971, 308—328.
28 *Theologisches Wörterbuch zum neuen Testament,* s.v. eleutheria, II, 484ff.
    (Schlier); s.v. parrhesia, V, 869ff (idem).
29 W.A., VII, 3ff.; Clemen: Luthers Werke, II, 2ff.
30 W.A., VII, 27; Clemen: Luthers Werke, II, 17.
31 W.A., VII, 35ff.; Clemen: Luthers Werke, II, 24f. Cf. Bucer's first book
    (1523), *Das ym selbs niemant, sonder anderen leben soll, und wie der
    mensch dahynn kummen mög.*
32 G. Ebeling: *Luther. Einführung in sein Denken,* Tübingen 1964, 239ff.;
    H. J. Iwand: *Luthers Theologie,* herausg. v. J. Haar, München 1974, 84ff.
33 Calvijn: Institutie, III, XIX, 1.
34 H. J. Iwand: *Gesetz und Evangelium,* München 1964, 390ff.; J. van den Berg:
    Twee regimenten, één Heer, Kampen 1961.
35 M. J. S. Rudwick: *The history of the natural sciences as cultural history,*
    Amsterdam 1975, 22: "The religious analogy is significant, because this
    movement has many of the marks of a secular religion ... 23: We surely
    do not want to be ruled by a new technocratic priesthood — even by
    scientist — priests who claim to be acting 'democratically' on behalf of
    'the people' ".
36 A. Kuyper: *Het Calvinisme,* 124ff.
37 E. L. H. Taylor: *Reformation or Revolution,* Nutley 1970, 49ff.

Academic freedom in Christian perspective*

Prof. Dr. F. J. M. Potgieter

THE phrase: "Academic freedom in Christian perspective" comprises momentous terms. Of these, we who are gathered here will, I take it, be in agreement that "Christian" is the dominant one. Consequently an analysis of "academic" and "freedom" will have to be undertaken in the light of "Christian", in order to arrive at a synthetic whole in its proper immediate and remote context, i.e. in perspective.

As to "Christian": in this paper it is used as synonymous with Scriptural, Holy Scripture being the special revelation of God in and through Christ. Herman Bavinck aptly says that Christ is *revelator* and *revelatio*. Without the Logos there would be no revelation of God. He is the *principium cognoscendi* not only of theology, but of all science.[1]

"Academic" here signifies: pertaining to a university. A typical definition of a university would be that it is an institution or community of academicians, i.e. professors, lecturers and students, intent on study, tertiary instruction, examination, research and education, and in quest of the truth.

From the judicial point of view, it could be defined as a statutory corporation (universitas), vested with authority to confer degrees in various faculties.

These definitions are not mutually exclusive but complementary. And yet they are incomplete, even when considered conjointly. The quintessence of the definition consists in its being an institution or corporation of academicians, bent on study and in quest of the truth. But even this formulation is not beyond criticism from the Christian viewpoint. The objection derives from the expression: "In quest of the truth". The truth in its ultimate form is not open

---

* Although the conference organizers differ from the justification of separate development submitted by the author of this article, they decided not to withhold it from publication in order to preserve the completeness of this Acta.

to research or accessible to human reason, but is *revealed* and as such, the object of faith.[2] This becomes obvious on considering that God is the Truth.[3] Aristotelian metaphysics represents the attempt of the overrated human mind to solve the profoundest questions regarding the origin, being and consummation of all things. It indeed becomes a false substitute for the Word of God, which alone contains the *a priori* truths at the basis of science. Abraham Kuyper does not hesitate to speak of "de valse grondstellingen der dool geraakte Philosophie".[4]

Thus, it is clear that the words: "In quest of the truth" must be circumscribed. But this necessitates a scrutiny of the term science. In his erudite book *Die Idee der Universität* the philosopher Karl Jaspers says: "Um die Idee der Universität und die aus ihr erwachsende Institution zu verstehen, ist daher zunächts das sie tragende geistige Leben überhaupt und vor allem das Wesen der Wissenschaft zu erörtern".[5]

Wat is science — science as pursued at the university — and in how far can man, as its subject, be engaged in the search for truth? Usually it is defined as a body of knowledge, accumulated by deduction or based on observation and strictly controlled experiment, and systematised with reference to general laws.

This definition is subject to criticism, not on account of what it states, but of what it omits. The chief objection against the definition is that it is influenced by the philosophy of Auguste Comte, known as Positivism. This view holds that science has no presuppositions whatsoever. Bavinck exposes the great fallacy of Positivism when he writes: "Deze hypotese (het positivisme — F.P.) is echter niet alleen voorbarig, want welk denker heeft in vroeger eeuwen (vóór Comte — F.P.) aan de mogelijkheid geloofd, dat een wetenschappelijk onderzoeker, zoodra hij de studeerkamer binnentreedt, aan zijn diepste, godsdienstige zedelijke, wijsgeerige overtuigingen het zwijgen kan opleggen? Maar het is met de eigen teorie in lijnrechten strijd, want de erkenning, dat het positivisme het ware begrip van de wetenschap voordraagt, is een Voraussetzung, die het wetenschappelijk onderzoek van te vooren van alle Voraussetzungslosigkeit berooft".[6] Indeed, no one less than Immanuel Kant avers in his "Vorrede zur zweiten Ausgabe" of his *Kritik der reinen Vernunft* that science "muss jederzeit dogmatisch, d.i. aus sichern Prinsipien a priori streng beweisend sein".[7] Also Karl Jaspers includes a paragraph on "Voraussetzungen der Wissenschaft" in his aforementioned exposition of the concept of a university.[8]

Who can deny that even in the case of an exact science like mathematics there are various schools of thought, e.g., the intuitionists, the empiricists and the formalists, who differ with regard to their basic assumptions, which themselves are not verifiable? Or who will contradict that the very foundations of mathematics, which were so securely laid — as men imagined — by Euclid, had to be replaced by those of Riemann and Einstein?

From the above it is evident that the position of a neutral science cannot be defended. Objectivity must, however, be sharply distinguished from neutrality. The truth is objective, but not neutral. Once again, He who is the Truth bears this out. When Ludwig Raiser states that "the search for objective truth... constitutes the true essence of science" [9] one can only assent.

The question arises: does the search for objective truth imply that the subject of science, including us who are Christians, must be open to conviction without reserve? This is not the case. The Christian cannot accept the methodic doubt of Descartes. "Cogito, ergo sum" is not a neutral but a rationalistic standpoint. The Christian believes: "God is, I am created in his image; therefore, I am". His primordial *a priori* is: God is. Having accepted this in faith, he, as scientist, remains stringently theocentric in his approach. And to the extent he adheres to the truth as revealed in Holy Scripture, he is objective.

Of course, the Bible is no textbook for scientific knowledge. It is revelation, written in the everyday language of experience, and consequently does not become antiquated. But it does, as already stated, contain the *a priori* truths, basic to all science.

The object of science is cosmic reality. The nature of science in general and of any science in particular is mainly determined by its object. If it is a created reality, it will intrinsically differ from, say, a reality of fortuitous origin. It belongs to the essence of a created object of science to be *dependent* on the Creator. When the psychologist Leuba, e.g., denies the existence of God, religion becomes an illusion. Prayer would in that case, psychologically speaking, be a phenomenon, which in essence is a delusion. There being no real object of worship, prayer would be fictitious. But if God does exist, prayer would be a genuine experience of communion with God, radically different from anything delusive. To deny the existence of God would of necessity entail the negation of the inherently dependent nature of the object of study and thus invalidate the resultant science. For instance, the educationist who denies that the child is created in the image of God, but that he now is a depraved sinner, cannot present a theory of education which is basically in accordance with the truth.

I bear in mind that Calvin once wrote: "Therefore, in reading profane authors, the admirable light of truth displayed in them should remind us that the human mind, however much fallen and perverted from its original integrity, is still adorned and invested with admirable gifts from its Creator".[10] He holds mathematics, physics, medical science *i.a.* in high esteem by reason of God's common grace, granted also to pagans. Science must be ascribed to *gratia communis,* else the atheist could be no mathematician or lawyer. But the same Calvin also teaches that Holy Scripture or special revelation is the medium by which we obtain a knowledge of the true God and Creator of this world.[11]

Special revelation provides the necessary corrective to our knowledge of the Creator and creation. And this corrective particularly appertains to the basic presuppositions of all science. True science is of a theocentric nature. One's idea of God determines not only one's concept of science, but also one's philosophy of life. This idea is either positive or negative, and, accordingly, his thought will be either theocentric or anti-theistic, allowing latitude for intermediate positions of inconsistent thinkers. In his well-known work: *Education Christian or Pagan* Jeffreys writes (i) "that Christianity being God-centred, is ultimately incompatible with all man-centred views, any superficial resemblances notwithstanding; (ii) that the Christian revelation is alone commensurate with the full dimensions of life".[12]

With regard to the definition of science, we can now, by virtue of the preceding considerations, conclude that scientific investigation can never take place without presuppositions, which are not rationally or empirically verifiable; that all science including the Christian, is a gift of God's common grace; that the distinctive feature and ruling presupposition of the true Christian type is its theocentricity.

The way has now been paved to revert to the definition of a university. What is pertinent to science is *mutatis mutandis* applicable also to the university. No definition of the university is adequate and can be termed Christian unless it accentuates its *a priori* theocentric character.

The definition of the university should also indicate that it is part and parcel of society. There are the three great spheres of life: society, church and state. The cells of the first-mentioned are the families, where children are fostered. In our differentiated society higher education cannot be undertaken by the parents and is delegated to the university, which, as such, is a societal institution.

It is widely held that the characteristic of the university is that it conforms to internationally accredited ideals and traditions and universality. So the conference of representatives of the Universities of Cape Town and the Witwatersrand, held in 1957, declared that all universities "are united in an international fraternity based on ideals and traditions shared in common".[13] And Ernst Anrich states that what constitutes the essence of the university "ist die Wissenshaftlichkeit und ihre Universalität".[14]

The view that the University accepts internationally recognised ideals and traditions, disqualifies itself by its vagueness. No one will deny that all universities should ensure that high standards of learning and research be maintained; but as to ideals and traditions in general: these are at variance and often diametrically opposed to one another, as, e.g., in the Soviet Union, Hitler's Germany and the U.S.A. Neither can universality *in se* warrant the truth which the university pursues. The once universally accepted Copernican world view or the now obsolete atomic theory illustrates this conclusively.

The *character* of a university is primarily determined by the society and the national life from which it derives. It cannot exist in isolation from its societal environment and is thus neither inter- or supranational. Diversity and multiformity within God's creation and societal entities did not come into being casually but under his providence and have to be respected. The closest relationship exists between university and society.

Quoting from "De Wet op het wetenschappelijk onderwijs" in the Netherlands, Prof. Posthumus points out that such education includes "de voorbereiding tot het bekleden van maatschappelijke betrekkingen, waarvoor een wetenschappelijke opleiding vereist is of dienstig kan zijn".[15] Also Gerhard Hess emphasises this affinity, when he says that universities "bilden für Berufe aus",[16] and Hofstadter and Metzger make mention of "the manifold services, aside from teaching students, that are rendered to the community by the great university".[17]

Universities should be founded by like-minded parents within society — like-minded in that they subscribe to a common philosophy of life. Christian parents are responsible to God for the education of their children and are subject to their baptismal vows. Consequently the council of a Christian university should be composed of those members of the concerned society, who hold the theocentric view of life. They must, of course, also be the most competent members, versed in academic affairs and capable of determining the spirit and policy of the university.

The last major term to be considered is: freedom. One of the best known treatises on freedom is that of John Stuart Mill. He waxes eloquent in his: *On Liberty,* and, no wonder, because it *is* a great gift to mankind. His eulogy on freedom, however, is cur-

312

tailed by a depraved reality. Hence the restriction: "So long as what we do does not harm... our fellow-creatures".[18]

In his comprehensive publication: *Are American Teachers Free?*, Howard K. Beale is more outspoken, when he says: "Many believe in freedom in principle, but become alarmed at freedom in practice... Everyone will agree that there must be some limits to freedom, else freedom itself will be destroyed for any one man by unrestrained action of other men".[19]

Von Lübtow specifies these limits with regard to science: "Die in Art. 5. Abs. 3 des Bonner Grundgesetzes verbürgte Freiheit der Wissenschaft in Forschung und Lehre bestet indessen nicht schrankenlos. Zunächt köntte man daran denken, dass sie ihre Schranke an den Rechten anderer, dem Sittengesetz und der Verfassungsmässigen Ordnung findet".[20]

More clarity as to the essential meaning of freedom is imperative, if we are to probe the deepest sense of academic freedom. Prof. Fred Clarke's remark that "there is no freedom which is not, in a very real sense, a kind of obedience",[21] speaks of insight. Frenzel is more definite when he says that freedom in the last resort is "der Beugung vor der höchsten transzendenten Autorität Gottes selbst".[22]

Also with regard to this stubborn problem only the Scriptural, theocentric approach provides the clue to a solution. In his infallible Word, God reveals Himself as absolute Authority and at the same time as being absolutely free. This is the sublime meaning of his selfrevelation as contained in Ex. 3 : 14: *"I am that I am"*. His authority consists in his being the unique Personality, who alone can say: "I" in the absolute sense of the word; and his freedom follows from the revealed truth that his "I" or Self ever is what it is: He remains true to his essence in all eternity, and is, as Creator, limited in no way by any created category of being.

As created in the image of God, man also possessed both authority and freedom. His authority was of the order of creation. By virtue of the miracle of creation, he could also say: "I". Miracle it is, because, according to the principles and categories of human logic, there can be no other "I" alongside of the absolute "I". By reason of the miracle of creation, then, man as "I" also had creaturely freedom. In other words, he fulfilled his calling to glorify God, in love towards Him and his neighbour, remaining true to his creaturely being.

Subsequent to the Fall, man retained his freedom as formal category inseparable from his being; but, as he became totally depraved and consequently could no longer live in accordance with his being created in the image of God, he became a slave of sin, i.e., his freedom deteriorated to licentiousness. It is this licentiousness that is usually confused with freedom. Only in so far as man is regenerated and lives by faith in Christ can he once more live in conformity with his creaturely nature, in obedience to the Truth who sets him free.

Let us now focus on academic freedom. How does an educationist of the standing of John Dewey conceive of it? He sees it as "the freedom to teach in higher institutions of learning well-thought-out principles and demonstrated truth, or to direct the search for these without interference of political, bureaucratic or religious authority".[23]

It will be conducive to this exposition to state and scrutinise without delay the arguments in favour of such academic freedom. In his work *The teaching of controversial subjects,* Edward L. Thorndike asserts that such subjects should be dealt with "as stimuli to learning fundamentals".[24] There can be no objection to the view that all standpoints should be treated of at the university, provided that they be presented objectively in the sense already stated. Particularly no propaganda or indoctrination should be permitted. Hofstadter and Metzger point out that "university education is adolescent education, and that the young mind yields to the imprint of ideas as easily and uncritically as wax".[25] While Thorndike uses the term "fundamentals", may I remind you that we have already argued that the ultimate truth is not open to human reason or research.

H. K. Beale advances the argument "that, if left free, truth will overpower error in free discussion".[26]

Mindful of the fact that the Truth was crucified on this earth, one can hardly share his optimism.

Dewey rejects all interference of a "political, bureaucratic or religious" nature. As to bureaucracy, I may safely assume that there will be no dissentients.

The word "political" clearly refers to the state. In how far can the university be considered to be autonomous? I could accept the standpoint of Von Lübtow: "Unter der Autonomie ist die Selbständigkeit des Seins und Wirkens der Universität in der ihr eigentümlichen inneren Sphäre zu verstehen. Sie besteht darin dass die Universität ihre Angelegenheiten innerhalb der Schranken der Allgemeinen staatlichen Rechtsordnung selbständig ordnet und verwaltet".[27]

This view is in alignment with the XXIInd World Congress of *Pax Romana,* when it concludes: "Academic freedom represents the most important aspect of this autonomy. But, like all human freedom, it can never be absolute... The democratic State will be entitled to intervene whenever the constitutional principles on which it is based are endangered by a subversive attitude".[28] That means that the police may intervene under such circumstances, provided that they do not in any respect interfere with matters purely academical, and that no academician is intimidated, while legally performing his duty.

The remarks of Edward J. Bloustein in this connection are to the point, when he depicts the Neo-Marxist type of student as follows: "This is indeed a generation of rebels without a cause, a generation of nihilists, a generation despairing of the life we live and set on remaking it, without a vision of any alternative".[29]

Albert Sloman duly asks attention for the relative nature of the autonomy enjoyed by British universities, when he says that "it is a right which will be respected only as long as universities continue to meet their obligations. They must be governed in such a way that they remain sensitive to what society requires from them".[30]

It must be mentioned that while autonomy concerns the institution, academic freedom can, as all freedom, only refer to persons. The persons in this case, however, are those, who think, speak and act as *academicians*. What has been said, applies to the freedom of the academician *qua* academician to voice an opinion, to teach, to do research, to publish, *etc.*

A matter of primary importance in a multi-racial society is that of appointment at and admission to a university. When Roger Apery holds "that there is no such thing as ... French as opposed to German science"[31] it amounts to an over-simplification of the case. Reference has already been made to the diversity and multiformity within creation. Not only individuals, but also nations, reveal difference of endowment and aptitude: the French excel in diplomacy; the Germans distinguish themselves in theoretical insight; and they possess the genius of invention and music; the Romans are the creators of jurisprudence. And precisely by virtue of this multiformity the image of God, in which men individually and mankind as a whole are created, finds greater and more admirable expression.

In addition, it has been shown that a university has the closest relationship with the society from which it derives. It cannot be denied that in the Republic of South Africa, Universities that bear the stamp of the English, on the one hand, and that of the Afrikaans section of the community, on the other hand, have developed accordingly. If this applies to ethnic groups it will *a fortiori* have relevance to racial groups, where the differences are more pronounced. I could, however, not accept exclusion as a matter of principle, as all men are of the same status before God; but would regard it as a legitimate temporary rule of order, until all racial groups have advanced to that stage of spiritual maturity, which holds identity in high esteem and results in spontaneous separate development.[32]

Dewey is opposed also to religious interference. If he uses "religious authority" as synonymous with the institutional church, his position would be sound and worthy of support. The three spheres of life: the society, the church and the state, are sovereign within their own realm and responsible only to God. One or more of these may not encroach upon the domains of the others. The Calvinist cannot accept the right of existence of church-schools and universities. The name "Vrije Universiteit" indicates that this university is free from interference of the church as well as the state with regards to matters academical.

The so-called "conscience clause" in South African legislation must needs be broached here. According to this clause, religious convictions must in no way be a criterion with respect to appointments to the teaching staff of a university. The evident intention of the legislator was to ensure the neutrality of science. It has, however, been indicated that no science can be without presuppositions. Such legislation indeed demands the impossible, for, as Bavinck stresses, nobody can or may ever suppress his deepest beliefs. Neither the personality nor the truth admits of any compartmentalisation. Moreover, this legislation sets the conscience of both the parents and the student at naught: the parents, who are asked to break their baptismal vows, and the student, who is required to be strictly neutral.

The only solution is to be found in legislation allowing members of the community, who have a common philosophy of life, to establish their own university. The objection may be raised that this will lead to an undue multiplication of universities, but this is not the case. In this country the great majority of citizens are Christians. They can be classified in one of two categories: those who profess the *sola scripture, sola gratia, sola fide,* and those who do not. As to the rest of the population: the only section, which should not be allowed to found a university, are the atheists, for this would be incompatible with the written constitution of the Republic.

By way of recapitulation, academic freedom in Christian perspective amounts to the freedom of academicians in their pursuit of science and objective truth, in conformity with their creaturely nature in the image of God, in and through Christ, viz. as members of a university, having the revealed truth that God *is* as its cornerstone, and, as belonging to the societal sphere, free from church and state interference, and entitled to manage its own internal affairs in a constitutional manner, and which will investigate the truth, as revealed in created reality, in the light of the Word of God, most satisfactorily on the basis of God's providential ethnic multiformity.

The truth is at once the firmest foundation, the only liberating force, and the ultimate goal of all science. The *summum bonum* of the university must ever be to seek the truth, and to teach young men and women to deny themselves in love towards their neighbour and in the service of Him, who is the Truth.

1 H. Bavinck: *Gereformeerde Dogmatiek4*, Kok, Kampen, 1928, , p. 372.
2 Cf. Heb. 11 : 6.
3 Cf. John 14 : 6.
4 A. Kuyper: *Encyclopaedie der Heilige Godgeleerdheid2*, Kok, Kampen, 1909, III, p. 461. Cf. also W. Geesink: *Gereformeerde Ethiek*, Kok, Kampen, 1931, I, p. 156, and H. J. Störig: *Kleine Weltgeschicht der Philosophie3*, W. Kohlhammer Verlag, Stuttgart, 1953, p. 214.
5 Karl Jaspers: *Die Idee der Universität*, Springer-Verlag, Berlin, 1946, p. 12.
6 H. Bavinck: *op. cit.*, I, p. 28.
7 Immanuel Kant: *Kritik der reinen Vernunft*. Fünfte Auflage. Leipzig, 1881, p. 39.
8 Karl Jaspers: *op. cit.*, pp. 21—23.
9 Ludwig Raiser, Roger Apery and others: *Science and Freedom*, the proceedings of a conference convened by the Congress for Cultural Freedom, Hamburg, 1953, published by Martin Secker and Warburg, 1955, p. 101.
10 J. Calvin: *Institutes*, II, 2, 15—17.
11 *Institutes*, I, 6, 1—2.
12 M. V. C. Jeffreys: *Education Christian or Pagan*, London, 1952, p. 13.
13 A. v. d. S. Centlivres and others: *The Open University in South Africa*, Wynberg, Cape, 1957, p. 25.
14 Ernst Anrich: *Die idee der Deutschen Universität und die Reform der Deutschen Universitäten*, Darmstadt, 1960, p. 146.
15 K. Posthumus, Regeringscommissaris voor het wetenschappelijk onderwijs: *De Universiteit, doelstellingen, functies en structuren*, p. 12.
16 Gerhard Hess: *Die Deutsche Universität 1930—1970*, Darmstadt, p. 14.
17 Richard Hofstadter and Walter P. Metzger: *The Development of Academic Freedom in the United States*, New York, 1956, p. 262. Also cf.: *Vrijheid horizon der geschiedenis*. Een bundel opstellen onder redactie van dr. L. W. Nauta en prof. dr. J. Sperna Weiland, Nijkerk, 1966, p. 217.
18 J. S. Mill: *On Liberty*, the Harvard Classics, 25, pp. 214—5.
19 H. K. Beale: *Are American Teachers Free?* New York, 1936, p. 761.
20 Ulrich von Lübtow: *Autonomie oder Heteronomie der Universitäten*, Frankfurt am Main, 1966, p. 11.
21 Fred Clarke and others: *Church, Community and State in Relation to Education*, London, 1938, p. 26.
22 *Pädagogisches Lexikon, in voce Freiheit usw.*
23 *Cyclopedia of Education in voce Academic freedom*. Cf. also J. K. Beale: *op. cit.*, p. 774.

24 Edward L. Thorndike: *The Teaching of controversial Subjects,* Harvard University Press, 1937, p. 38. Cf. H. K. Beale, p. 751.
25 Richard Hofstadter and Walter P. Metzger: *op. cit.,* p. 411.
26 H. K. Heale: *op. cit.,* p. 752.
27 U. von Lübtow: *op. cit.,* p. 14.
28 *The Mission of the University,* being the Acts of the XXIInd World Congress of *Pax Romana,* Freiburg, 1952, pp. 198 and 199.
29 Walter P. Metzger, Edward J. Bloustein and others: *Dimensions of Academic Freedom,* paper on *The New Student and his role in American Colleges,* Chicago, 1969, p. 109.
30 Albert E. Sloman, Vice-Chancellor of the University of Essex. *A University in the Making,* London, 1964, p. 78.
31 Ludwig Raiser, Roger Apery and others: *op. cit.,* p. 246.
32 Prof. Heiko A. Oberman stated that he could not accept the "ideology" of separate development. In view of what I had said earlier, viz. that diversity and multiformity within God's creation come to pass under his all-wise providence and had to be accepted as such, I replied that spontaneous separate development was no ideology, but was founded on the principles revealed in Holy Scripture. Prof. Oberman answered that the Word of God does not contain axiomatic truths, relevant to science, but that its scopus was to reveal the living God.

It is clear that Prof. Oberman confuses philosophic postulates or mathematical axioms with *a priori* truths, revealed in Holy Scripture — truths which must and can only be believed by the regenerate heart. In this respect his argument is as fallacious as that of Karl Barth (Cf. *Kirchliche Dogmatik,* I, 2, pp. 583—4).

On requesting Prof. Oberman to inform Conference what substitute he would propose as the source of *a priori* truths instead of Holy Scripture, he furnished no answer.

Neither did he reply, when I asked him to explain to the gathering what ideology prompted Abraham Kuyper to write his brochure: *Eenvormigheid, de Vloek van het Moderne Leven,* a century ago.

No Calvinist will deny that Holy Scripture is *revelatio specialis,* proclaiming salvation in and through Christ. But redeemed man has the vocation to serve God in all spheres of life, as Paul wrote to Timothy: "So that the man of God may be well-fitted and adequately equipped for all good work" (2 Tim. 3 : 17).

May I also point out that there is no antithesis between the Bible, as revealing the living God, and as providing the ultimate *a priori* truths basic to science. On the contrary, precisely the faithful, who know and love God, will desire to glorify his Name in every realm of life, including science.

In order to eliminate all misapprehensions allow to explain that I do not hold the view (as a newspaper report alleged) that ethnic multiformity is a static condition. It certainly is dynamic, but it is a phenomenon, which has since Babel revealed itself *progressively.*

I also emphasised that *spontaneous* separate development is based on the fact that any spiritually mature person wants to be and remain himself. A great mind like Herman Bavinck subscribed to the dictum: *gratia non tollit naturam, sed perficit* (Grace does not annul nature, but perfects it). Cf.: *op. cit.,* III, p. 207 and *Handleiding bij het onderwijs in den Christelijke Godsdienst,* p. 116). In other words, the multiformity of creation must and will, as God's work, by his common grace, remain intact and always provide the structural pattern for saving grace.

Finally, it must be stressed that what I termed spontaneous separate development does in no way signify the subjugation of one ethnic group by another nor absolute segregation. It denotes the autonomous and coordinate co-existence of these groups in all brotherly love and mutual understanding, attended with the desire of each group to retain its own identity.

No individual may, however, be forbidden to marry any other on ethnic or racial grounds, for we are all created in the image of God. It stands to reason that the greater the ethnic and cultural differences, the more likely it is that tension will develop within such marriages, and that these consequently are imprudent and incompatible with the Christian ideal. What one does reject, is any preconceived attempt to promote integration by the propagation of intermarriage on the basis of the doctrine of egalitarianism — a doctrine which is unscriptural, in that it refuses to recognise the diversity of endowment and talent and the pluriformity in God's creation and providence.

SELECTED BIBLIOGRAPHY

H. Bavinck: *Gereformeerde Dogmatiek4*, I—IV, Kok, Kampen, 1928. Especially volume I is recommended for orientation as to Scriptural principles.

A. Kuyper: *Encyclopaedie der Heilige Godgeleerdheid2* I—III, Kok, Kampen, 1908—9. The concept of science from a Christian viewpoint is treated of in volume II.

Karl Jaspers: *Die Idee der Universität,* Springer Verlag, Berlin, 1946. A Philosophical treatise on the idea of a university.

A. v.d. S. Centlivres and others: *The Open University in South Africa,* Wynberg, Cape, 1957. This book presents the standpoint of the liberal empiristic university in South Africa.

G. Hess: *Die Deutsche Universität 1930—1970,* Darmstadt. The position of the University in Germany is described in this work.

R. Hofstadter and W. P. Metzger: *The Development of Academic Freedom in the United States,* New York, 1956. The title speaks for itself.

J. S. Mill: *On Liberty,* the Harvard Classics, 25, containing the well-known essay on freedom by the renowned philosopher.

The British Isles: Reflections on the Christian past, present and possible future with respect to the Christian reformation of higher education*

Mr Richard Russel

LET me divide my talk into three sections. First, a sketch of past and prevailing Christian attitudes to higher education in Britain. Secondly, a few words about our British universities. Thirdly a little about the past, present and possible future of the Christian Studies Unit.

In order to understand the dominant Christian attitudes to higher education one needs to look at the organization which has played a central role in forming the mind and worldview of evangelical leadership in every department of life. That organization is the Inter-Varsity Fellowship whose organization now also covers the Art Colleges, Polytechnics and Colleges of Education. Not only so, but the I.V.F. has played a decisive role in shaping the evangelical outlook through the whole English speaking world, and beyond that to the non-English speaking "mission fields". It is almost unknown to find an educated evangelical who was not a member of the I.V.F. while at university, which means too that one can be fairly sure that there are very few evangelical ministers who were not members. At present the membership in an I.V.F. group is about 5% of the university student population, and the Christian Unions constitute the largest student societies in most cases. (The year before last at Bristol University a few members of the C.U. became concerned about the state of Student Union politics and were easily

---

* An account of some of the main features of the British situation can be found in my 1973 dissertation *The Growing Crisis of the Evangelical Worldview and its Resolutions* (Department of Theology and Religious Studies, Bristol University, England).

elected to top union offices having the block vote of the C.U. behind them. Such participation would have been unknown until the last few years and is frowned upon by the senior I.V.F. people).

Before I rather critically characterize the I.V.F. let me mention three things to put my comments in perspective. First, I became a Christian, as did many people I know, through the I.V.F. Second, the entire C.S.U. committee were while at university members of the I.V.F. and we continue to enjoy cordial relationships with I.V.F. groups — a number of us are invited to speak with some regularity at I.V.F. meetings. Thirdly, and most importantly, the I.V.F. is the only significant witness to the Biblical Gospel on the British University campuses. The C.U. will contain, with rare exceptions, literally all the students who have a definite Christian commitment, and so it is the constituency which is and will be basic to any Christian reformation of higher education. Let me say that if the British I.V.F. gained a vision of what it could mean for Christian students to be *Christian* students then this would have an immense impact on the whole of English speaking Christianity and it could literally turn the British universities upside down. Let me now briefly recount some of the characteristics of the I.V.F. which seem to me to stand in the way of the Gospel disturbing and bringing peace to British academic life.

For our starting point we must turn back to the middle and later parts of the 19th century. In this period we see a retreat of Christianity before the challenges of Secular Humanism. The Tractarians (or Anglo Catholics) retreated into an idealized medieval past and into gothic and neo-gothic church buildings. The liberals continually adjusted the faith to "modern thought" and were engaged in an endless "strategic retreat". The evangelicals retreated into a concern with their own souls and onto the mission fields. It was this latter concern with personal piety and evangelism which was basic to the formation of the Student Christian Movement in the 1880's. In fact the visits of Moody and Sankey to Cambridge University played an important role. During the next few decades the S.C.M. was influenced by (a) doubts about the reliability of the Scriptures due to higher criticism and evolutionism (b) the recognition that the Christian faith had social, economic and political implications, and (c) the growing presence of high church Anglicanism having an incarnational rather than an atonement centred theology. Indeed it was over the doctrine of atonement that the I.V.F. broke away from the S.C.M. in order to reassert the earlier standpoint of the S.C.M., centred as it was on the cross, the individual and evangelism.

Over against this the S.C.M. asserted the incarnation, society and the amelioration of society by structural changes of a mildly socialist character. Both sides polarized and saw each other as departures from the Faith and literally defined themselves as the negation of the other. This polarization has left its mark on the I.V.F. ever since in term of the following general characteristics.

The I.V.F. has never produced any Christian critique of the liberal Humanistic university whereas the S.C.M. has produced a number e.g. A. S. Nash: *The University in the modern world* (1946) and Sir Walter Moberley: *The Crisis in the University* (1949). Indeed the major emphasis of the I.V.F. has been that one can be a "good student" in the Humanistic University *and* a "keen Christian", and that these roles are quite compatible. The only implication for being a Christian student is that (a) one evangelizes one's fellow students (b) one works honestly and industriously at one's studies. The consequence is that one can readily expect to find I.V.F. students holding whatever are the current philosophies and approaches in their field of study. The only time when there is some "Christian thought" about academic studies is when a subject like theology or philosophy or sociology or evolutionary biology gives rise to crises of faith and pastoral problems, and then the usual response is to discourage students from being involved in such subjects. The only concern therefore tends to be with spiritual survival and not with the Christian reformation of scholarship in terms of making every thought subject to the obedience of Jesus Christ.

Sadly there have been few *Christian* students, much rather there have been Christians who happened to be students or students who happened to be Christians. The essential link between faith and thought, or to use James' phrase, faith and academic works, has either not been recognised, or if dimly perceived not welcomed, or if welcomed then seldom able to come to any fruition as a lasting contribution to the Body of Christ. The life of the evangelical student is therefore divided between his Christian Union activities of prayer, Bible reading, fellowship, evangelistic meetings (and church) *and* his academic work. In the C.U. activities he is together with other Christians and experiences a measure of growth and blessing. In his academic work he is isolated as a Christian, for the only community which he can join there, and in which he must participate, is the secularized community of scholarship of his discipline with its one or many schools of thought. Even where one might expect students to wake up to the possibility of a Christian alternative where there are several conflicting secularist schools of thought (e.g. sociology) one usually finds that either they don't

322

get existentially involved in their discipline (and just want to pass the exams so they can 'help people' as social workers) or they become aligned with the neo-marxist or phenomenological or some other sociological school. Consequently if they do rarely meet together to discuss sociology it seems that they are usually more representatives of the secular schools of sociology than they are a part of the Body of Christ concerned to know the mind of Christ concerning sociological inquiry and social reality.

Whereas in the C.U. world the distinction between Christian and non-Christian, walking in the light and walking in darkness, is clearly and sharply made, in the realm of scholarship the student will not hear from his C.U. teaching that there is any such antithesis. In the latter realm it is assumed that he can work together with the unbelievers in the common scholarly enterprise. Even if he senses that there should be an alternative Christian scholarly tradition he will seldom if ever have heard of the work which has been done by Christian scholars in various parts of the world, and it is most unlikely that such work will be available in university libraries or bookshops. And even if such works are sometimes available, and especially if they are written abroad, a great deal of help is needed to make any sort of break with the secularized education he has had so far. Again he will receive little encouragement to follow up such lines of thought by his C.U. — indeed he may be regarded as having an unbalanced and unhealthy interest in his subject. Nor are his unbelieving tutors and lecturers likely to be very appreciative of his immature and blundering attempts to Christianly reform his subject. Even if he does manage to gain some small Christian insights then there is no way for them to provide the basis for further Christian work by subsequent students because there are no adequate channels of communication. It might be objected that there are Christian professors and lecturers in the British universities. For the most part their thought is difficult to distinguish from that of their non-Christian colleagues, nor is that surprising in view of their own educations and the complex and difficult matter of working towards a new framework for a discipline. Usually however there seems to be little concern to engage in such reformation and one suspects that in some cases the man's academic position was partly the result of exemplary conformity to the secular mind.

A further feature which follows from the C.U. ('grace') and studies ('nature') dualism is that those subjects are avoided which would most tend to put this dualism in question e.g. theology, religion, politics, sociology and philosophy. These are precisely the subjects where disturbing fundamental questions about the meaning of life and the ordering of society are raised. However while the evangelical student knows that eternal life is to know Jesus Christ, he seldom has much idea of what this means for human life now, except for the importance of evangelism. (In the C.U. context the 'ideal man' is always the minister or missionary). For the Christian student who lacks this 'high calling' to live in the 'realm of grace' the tendency is towards 'practical' or 'humanitarian' subjects (mathematics, natural science, engineering, law, economics and medicine) which have a clearly defined role in the *status quo*. (The qualifications of the academic vice-president of the I.V.F. clearly reflect such a distribution of subjects). This means that the Christian students are absent in precisely those disciplines which have been shaking the campuses, which provide the vocabulary for Humanist prophesy and where the religious direction of our country is being debated.

One final comment on the I.V.F. and S.C.M. is this. The S.C.M. has more or less disappeared from British universities. Many of its earlier social ideals seem to have been met by the development of the welfare state. Its Christian character has almost completely been eliminated by secularism. Its crisis is visible. The British I.V.F., as I have explained, is flourishing. However there is a hidden crisis which has been going on for years. When I.V.F. students leave university and their C.U. the 'simple gospel' teaching with which they are acquainted cannot begin to do justice to the many responsibilities of adult life. Consequently perhaps 50% to 70% or more of them drift away from the Christian faith because of the *irrelevance* of the 'Christianity' which they were taught. It could well be that the cost of sacrificing everything to evangelism is counter-productive even if one uses criteria which would be acceptable to the I.V.F. leadership. It is certainly counter-productive if a rich reformational vision of the Biblical faith is the criterion.

We now turn to make a few comments on the British universities. In a basic sense they are more 'training' rather than 'educational' institutions. One of the reasons for this is the degree of specialization which pervades them. Indeed it is usual to study only three subjects (e.g. pure and applied mathematics and physics or French, German and Latin) from the age of 16. At university a student may have one subject or occasionally two or three but usually no more than one by his last year. Such intense specialism means that one has little if any awareness of what the other disciplines are doing or how they relate to one's own. Lacking that knowledge also incapacitates one from any fundamental thought

324

about one's own discipline. The consequence is that almost everyone is turned into a minor academic technician. The history and philosophy of the various disciplines are neglected — indeed serious thought about one's discipline is usually regarded as the responsibility of another department, a responsibility seldom recognised by that other department! Some attempts have been made at academic integration and interdisciplinary studies. But for the most part they succeed in making evident the modern fragmentation of knowledge rather than providing any synthesis. (If any synthesis is present it is usually one provided by a Marxist framework of understanding). This situation puts immense difficulties in the way of attempting to develop reformational scholarship in Britain, for the students have great difficulties in grasping the general ideas which both transcend their own disciplines and yet which fundamentally direct them.

We come now to the work of the Christian Studies Unit. Let me say first that my foregoing account of the I.V.F. is a little dated and there are signs of improvement. Most of these one can trace to the influence of reformed ideas from outside of Britain. We are indeed indebted especially to Dr. Francis Schaeffer and Dr. Hans Rookmaaker for the way in which they have encouraged evangelical students to think about general cultural problems and to understand something of what they see around them. In its earliest beginnings the C.S.U. dates from 1967 when the first booklist was published and sent out. The publication and distribution of Christian literature on the various academic disciplines from a Christian perspective has been one of the major activities of the C.S.U. Over the last twelve months sales have exceeded £1000 and are likely to increase rapidly. We have also organised a number of conferences at Birmingham, Bristol, London and Rochester. The most significant developments however have occurred in the past few months. First, St. Werburgh's Church (an Anglican church) in Derby have provided a house, and some financial support for the secretary of the C.S.U. Secondly an 8 day summer school was held at St. Werburgh's in August attended by 60 students, lecturers and teachers and orientated to education and the social sciences. There was great enthusiasm for the idea of Christian scholarship and we all sensed that God's hand was upon the work we were doing. Plans are now maturing for further weekend and vacation conferences on the philosophy of science, aesthetics and art history, philosophy and theology. We hope to duplicate the papers from all these conferences and make them generally available. Whereas a few years ago we felt we were battling against the stream, we are now witnessing in Britain the emergence of increasing numbers of Christians concerned with knowing the ways of the Lord of the various aspects of human culture. There are now a number of Christian Arts Groups from which are coming new poems, music, plays and films.

At the last General Election a candidate stood for the newly formed Christian Party. In the economic sector we have seen the development of the Christian Industrial Enterprises Limited. There are several groups concerned with the establishment of Christian schools and in the church institution itself God's Spirit is moving in ways we have not experienced previously. It is in this exciting context that the C.S.U. can play a role in providing academic service to the whole Body of Christ. The Lord has given us an immense sense of expectation about the future — at precisely the time that we are witnessing so much disintegration in our national life. For us in Britain the idea of Christian higher education is a new thing and most of those involved with C.S.U. are under 30 years old, so we need all the help we can get from countries where Christian higher education enjoys wide support. May I urge in conclusion that priority is given to the translation into good English of much more reformational scholarly work with suitable editorial introductions and notes. May I urge that Christian scholars who are visiting Britain contact us so that we can arrange hospitality and put them into contact with those of similar interests. Secularised Western scholarship is now global and it is urgent that we think in global terms and for this to happen good communications are vital.

A few years ago an American philosopher Hazel E. Barnes wrote a book entitled *The University as the New Church* and maintained that the university now played the role occupied by the church in earlier times. Indeed the university is in many ways the spiritual centre of modern civilization in that it provides the major perspectives on life for those who occupy the most formative places in society. Our task is to penetrate this spiritual centre with the good news of the Kingdom of God for scholarship and science, because in Jesus Christ is hidden all the treasures of wisdom and knowledge. Those treasures should be manifest in our study groups, institutes, colleges and universities as lights upon a hill.

Co-ordination between reformed

Christian institutions in the Americas

Prof. John C. van der Stelt

Introduction

Due to limitations of space and time, this presentation of the problems and prospects in Christian higher education in the Americas will have to be brief. In keeping with the primary intent of our Conference, I will not belabour the obvious by discussing that which one can readily ascertain for himself from the catalogues of the various Reformed academic institutions. Instead, I will attempt to provide a succinct description of our past and present problems and of our future possibilities. It is to be understood that I cannot look at our American situation with eyes other than my own. It is my avowed aim to reflect upon our situation from the normed perspective of the transcending and yet ever-present Word and Spirit of God.

All the North American educational institutions represented at this Conference have as their goal the development of scholarship, instruction, and training in a biblically directed and historically relevant manner. None of our colleges, seminaries, and other higher educational agencies claims to be pure and have a monopoly on the truth. Although practical, at times even subtle principial differences do exist among these various institutions, the general approach of our reformed academies is characterized by the belief that life is religion, God's Word is normative for all things, Jesus Christ is the Redeemer of culture, and the Gospel liberates man and society from evil thought — and act — patterns.

Latin America

There is little I can say at this point about South and Central America.[1] What has been accomplished in the Latin American countries in the area of Reformed Christian higher education is (as yet) not too impressive. Worldcompromising papal religion and world-fleeing pentecostal Christianity have greatly contributed towards a fearful socio-economic and political vacuum in Latin America.

In the past, capitalism has filled this void with secular materialism; today, communism is pouring socialism and Marxism into this vacuum.[2]

Of the approximately fifteen million evangelical Christians spread throughout the seventeen Latin American countries, no less than sixty-three percent adhere to a pentecostalistic world-view. By the end of this decade the total number of evangelical Christians is expected to swell to nearly twenty-seven million. With some seventy-five thousand congregations at present, and an anticipated increase of another five thousand congregations per year, the training of clergy and other Christian leaders has become, to say the least, a mind-boggling one.[3]

Most of the present three hundred and sixty Protestant theological training centres are not much more than mere Bible Schools with highly inadequate library and instruction facilities. The contents of the theological curricula in these schools are often unrelated to the Latin American situation and are usually a perpetuation of peculiarly Western or North American views concerning such matters as Christ and culture, faith and learning, scholasticism and spiritualism, Bible and theology, *etc.*

Since evangelical and reformed missionary activity has been generally limited to the peasants and the poor, no significant inroads have been made as yet into the circles of higher education in Latin America. During the coming decade of debates and dangers in this vast part of America, what is going to be badly needed is the co-operation of such ministries as Reformed-Presbyterian missions,[4] the international radio and television work of the Back to God Hour,[5] the Inter-Varsity Christian Fellowship,[6] Liga para el Avance de Estudios Christianos (L.A.E.C.),[7] the Association for the Advancement of Christian Scholarship through its Institute for Christian Studies,[8] and the Latin American Theological Fraternity.

Problems in North America

Using the three main divisions of our conference theme in reverse order, I shall try to explain briefly our main educational problems under the headings *scholar, scholarship,* and *institutions.*

Scholar

The prevalence in North America of individualism has greatly hindered the development of communal Christian scholarship. Each person tends to be on his own. Inevitable results of such individualism have been a loss of office-awareness and a fostering of unhealthy

328

personalism and pietism.

What has really complicated the situation in evangelical Christianity at large, particularly during the last century, has been the phenomenal rise and impact of pre-millenarianism with its inbuilt inability to deal effectively with relevant issues in our present dispensation. One of the side-effects of this cultural docetism has been the rise of a remnant-syndrome, mixed with a vigorous eschatological expectation for Jesus to come back to deliver us from the burdens of this life.

A Christian with such a framework of mind and heart is much more interested in a personal witness to Christ, an apologetic defence of his beliefs, and a cultivation of certain peculiar morals than he is in genuine, integral Christian scholarship, in a careful study of the creational beams and girders of society and in a continuing unfolding and restoration of culture. If this type of Christianity does not ignore, then it at least minimizes the implications of the Cultural Mandate by suggesting that complex problems in life can be solved in a simplistic and biblicistic manner. It relativizes the question of redemption of scholarship, and it stresses the salvation of the scholar. The only way for a Christian scholar to make his personal life meaningful is to use his scholarship as a (lower) means for the (higher) end of the Great Commission's goal to save others for Christ. Instead of erecting signposts that witness to the powers of God's coming Kingdom, one must try to direct the lives of believing students with tracts, devotionals, and at times antiquated systems of thought to confessional hide-outs, where, it is believed, the Christian student and scholar can survive in the midst of a threatening and hostile world of learning, until the Kingdom comes with the return of Christ.

Scholarship

The result of such a personalistic religion and problematic eschatology is paralysis of integral Christian scholarship. Sin and salvation, it is believed, affect the personal life of the scholar rather than his supposed impersonal scholarship. The Word of God is directed to the abstracted "soul" of a thinker, and not to his thought-patterns and cultural activities.

This near-total blindness to the need for an *integral* Christian education, though less so now than before, still characterizes much of the ministries of such educational agencies as Inter-Varsity Christian Fellowship, Campus Crusade for Christ, Young Life Movement, University Christian Conference of Canada, and various denominational campus ministries.

When Christian scholars fail to see the need for a fundamental reformulation of basic systems of thought and a rudimentary re-structuring of society's order and priorities, scholarship is destined to remain an essentially non-Christian activity, in spite of the fact that it is performed by Christians for some ulterior purpose.

The sad, if not ironic, effect of such an approach with its implicit religious dichotomy has been the fostering, by default, of course, of the very thing that is to be avoided, viz. secularism on and off campus! It has opened the doorway to the existential threat of reducing the Christian's role in higher education to a mere endorsing of political, socio-economic, racist, and ecclesiastical practices which are highly questionable when viewed in the Light of the central Law of God's Kingdom.

With Kingdom-living truncated and restricted to a confessional sitting upon personal and ecclesiastical tree-stumps, Christian scholarship, though sincerely aimed at, is never really attained. Because Fundamentalists have refused and are unable to reformulate some of the most basic problems in the world of higher education, millions of well-intending North American Christians remain enslaved to, and hence continue, usually unconsciously, to propagate, such culturally paralyzing false dilemmas as individual or communal, personal or institutional, capitalistic or communistic, denominational or ecumenical, conservative or liberal, faith or reason, theology or philosophy, church or world, Bible or science, objective or sub-jective, particular or universal, principal or practical, ideal or em-pirical, private or public, feeling or thinking, Christ or culture, church or state, pessimistic or optimistic, love or law, *etc.*

This form of Christianity has not yet seen the possibility of genuine Christian scholarship. All it can do is devise different apolo-getic skills that enable Christian students to make maximal use of confessional airpockets which, in our modern world of science and research, are ever dwindling in number and size. In fact, it sets in motion the forces of a systematic retreat from real scho-larship.

Institutions

North American institutions of higher education have never been really free from some form of external control. In this respect, church and state have often deterred the process of historical indi-vidualization and differentiation. Most of the thirteen hundred and fifty non-church related colleges in the United States of America are in fact controlled by the state, and nearly all of these state-colleges have been established only during the last century. Most of

330

the five hundred and fifty-nine church-related and controlled colleges came into existence, however, more than one hundred years ago, and were staffed, of course, with faculty and presidents taken from the clergy of the various denominations.[9]

With the first amendment of the Federal Constitution of the USA, which ensured the legal separation of church and state, and with the famous Dartmouth College Case in 1819, which guaranteed denominational colleges freedom from state-interference, the road was opened for either the church or the state to determine the course of education.[10] At first, at least until the 1860's, the church took the lead, particularly the Presbyterian Church, in founding fairly numerous church-controlled colleges.[11] This unparalleled multiplication of church-related colleges diminished, however, with the waning of the American Western Frontier movement. From that time on, the state has taken over the lead in the area of college education.

On the post-college university level of higher education in the USA, approximately three hundred and twenty thousand students attend some kind of church-controlled university. Most of these Christian university students are Roman Catholic, *viz.* 186 000; the Methodists have some 55 500 students; the Baptists 33 500; the Mormons 23 250; Lutherans 10 500; Presbyterians 6 500; and other Christian groups a combined total of nearly 15 000 university students.[12]

The typical North American Christian higher educational institution is a cultural-historical expression and organizational embodiment of what has been stated above under *Scholar* and *Scholarship*. Given the church-state problem — understood in the sense of a dilemma between Christianity and world, religion and learning — Christian education *had* to become ecclesiasticized and function primarily as a scaffold for private, denominational religion, and only secondarily as a support for public life in the state and nation.

Whereas church and state used to be the cultural centres in our civilization, in our modern age this honour has fallen to the institutions of advanced education. Both church and state have now come under the "spiritual" guidance of the academies they control outwardly. However, with the loss of a clearly defined religious direction in our modern world of higher education, a somewhat frightening situation has developed in our North American culture: hedonistic materialism, Marcuseanism, mass media, mass recreation, and Eastern religions are now beginning to vie for control of the educational steering wheel.

Against this background and within this context one must see the relativity, at times even the ultimate meaninglessness and futility, of the work of so many Christians who are engaged in establishing, supporting, and expanding Bible Colleges, Liberal arts Colleges, Community Colleges, and various Campus Ministries. Either maintaining the *status quo* or trying to escape from it, often these well-intending, usually greatly sacrificing and genuinely struggling Christian fellow-believers fail to recognize the desperate need for an architectonic critique of our total situation and the need for a return to a reforming and reformed culture and education. It is precisely in this connection that we experience the greatest problem in co-ordinating our Christian higher educational endeavours especially within the specifically Reformed Christian communities.

Prospects in Christian Higher Education

Clarification

The present ideological and practical problems in the area of higher education are having a positive impact upon the Christian community. Christians are compelled by the contemporary crises to clarify more than ever before the specific nature and unique goal of true Christian scholarship. It is everything or nothing. Half-heartedness and vagueness no longer suffice. One can hear from secular and Christian educational corners the 'Macedonian' call to come over and help discover unity and meaning again for a broken and groping world. Increasingly the realization is dawning that, without a proper academic articulation of the basic principles proclaimed by churches, the message of the latter cannot be implemented in the rest of society. Educational malfunctioning cannot avoid having ill effects, sooner or later, upon all non-educational activities and institutions.

Contextual Renewal

God's Kingdom cannot be equated with any specific tradition, nation, race, culture, period, person, or institution. In this awareness, a small yet significant number of North American Christians are trying to rediscover its unique calling. Also in the area of education these Christians are beginning to draw the line of demarcation much more in a religious and confessional, rather than ethnic, racial, denominational, or national manner.

This rediscovery has resulted in an exciting, at times painful, realignment of various movements and forces that strive for renewal of life. What unites these different renewal groups is a communal awareness of the reality of God's Word, the scope of His Kingdom, the nature of Christian service, the meaning of history, and the

332

force of hope.

There has been no period in the history of both the United States of America and Canada that is comparable to the last twenty years as far as the number and nature of such basically reforming movements are concerned.[13] Since the middle of our century, the following numerically small, but principially strong, institutions of renewal have arisen in Canada: (1) Christian Labor Association of Canada; (2) Association for the Advancement of Christian Scholarship with its Institute of Christian Studies; (3) Committee for Justice and Liberty; (4) Christian Farmers' Organization; (5) Wedge Publishing Foundation; (6) Curriculum Development Centre; (7) Institute for Christian Art; (8) Alberta Christian College.[14] During this same time-span, the following institutional attempts at renewal have appeared on the USA scene: (1) Dordt College in Sioux Center, Iowa;[15] (2) Trinity Christian College in Palos Heights, Illinois;[16] (3) National Association for Christian Political Action; (4) The Kuyper Institute on the campus of Stanford University in California;[17] (5) The Reformed Theological Seminary in Jackson, Mississippi; (6) Christian Studies Center in Memphis, Tennissee.[18]

In both Canada and the USA, a number of psychiatric institutions and hundreds of Christian elementary and secondary schools, non-state controlled and non-state supported, have either continued from before World War II or have been started since that time. Calvin College, Calvin Theological Seminary, Westminster Theological Seminary, and Covenant Theological Seminary have experienced continued growth during the past two to three decades.[19]

It is not easy to break or bend established traditions. Ideas, especially when institutionalized, tend to be very rigid. Some severe birthpangs have accompanied some of these new beginnings. This has been true particularly within the sensitive area of higher education. Yet, here too, the spirit of sanctification and the sense of unity have resulted in a new consorting and have proved to be stronger than the disintegrating forces of competition, jealousy, and individualism.

Radical Christian Academy

Various Reformed Christian institutions of higher learning, aware of common problems and prospects, have begun to see the need for the establishment of a community of committed Christian scholars who refuse to be a country club of mere logicians. Logical acumen and apologetic astuteness are not believed to be viable alternatives to, for example, Marcuseanism and various other forms of materialism. The *raison d'être* of Christian higher education can no longer be the mere perpetuation of our given situation, especially not when the very nature of the latter is being questioned.[20]

More than ever before it is incumbent upon the Reformed community to be prophetic and to lead the way also in the area of education. The need of the hour is concentration on the interconnections and religious foundations of a rapidly disintegrating society. Mainly through its Institute for Christian Studies, the Association for the Advancement of Christian Scholarship has begun to zero in on this whole matter on a graduate level.[21] Also the Consortium of Reformed Colleges, established in 1974, has focussed its attention on this basic issue, at least in its first round of discussions.[22]

What seems to be a central theme in this renewed reflection on the fundamental identity of Christian scholarship is the biblical reaffirmation of the meaning of creation and creatureliness. The way to counteract humanistic secularization of the meaning of reality, to avoid spiritualistic docetizing of reality, and to abandon Roman-Catholic, Scholastic-Protestant, and Arminian-Evangelical compromising distorted understanding of creatureliness is to understand again the revelation of the *Christos* and the *Biblos* in connection with that of the *Logos*, by whom and through whom all things have been created.[23]

In the measure that colleges, seminaries, and other higher educational institutions recognize this, they have a unity of purpose, identity, and practice which enhances communal scholarship and fosters institutional co-operation. Failing to acknowledge this, they create conflicts among one another. Such conflicts necessitate the organizing of conferences between the disagreeing members of the Christian higher educational community for the purpose of rediscovering and retaining unity by trying to resolve the difficulties.

Having learned from the beginning and history of the Free University in Amsterdam and refusing to be satisfied with an oversimplified and patchwork type of Christian higher education, Calvin College, the Association for the Advancement of Christian Scholarship, Trinity Christian College, the National Union of Christian Schools, and Dordt College have all been involved, especially during this past decade, in serious attempts to formulate their respective educational philosophies. Confronted by ever increasing encroachments of the various -isms in our culture, these institutions felt the need for some kind of educational credal statement. It is telling, perhaps, that not so much our Reformed Seminaries as the various liberal arts colleges and the AACS have had to struggle with this complicated and urgent matter. The "Educational Creed" of the AACS, the "Christian Liberal Arts Education" of Calvin College, and "Scripturally-Oriented Higher Education" [24] of Dordt College are some of the most noteworthy educational statements thus far that reflect this concern to be reformational in the total curriculum and encyclopedia of knowledge.

In line with the vision of Abraham Kuyper especially, Reformed Christians in North America are aware of their formidable task to broaden and deepen the rather restricted vision of most forms of Anglo-American Puritanism and Presbyterianism. One of the things we in North America have learned from the Free University in Amsterdam is the Calvinistic understanding of a *radical* and *global* Christianity.

Contacts and co-operation

Various contacts exist between the North American Reformed Christian institutions of higher learning. One must think in this connection of students transferring from one college to another, students graduating from one of these colleges to enter one of the seminaries or the ICS, mutual consultation by the college administrators, instructors from one institution lecturing at a sister institution, sponsorship of joint conferences to discuss topics of mutual interest, and the establishment of graduate and post graduate seminars during the summer in certain academic disciplines for the purpose of creating a community of Christian scholarship that reaches across geographic and denominational boundaries.

As with any family that has many members, there are many problems we must constantly face and seek to overcome. Appealing for financial support — remember we have no tax equality in education in the USA and Canada — and seeking to recruit students and faculty from approximately the same community can at times become very complicated matters. Moreover, different denominational motivations and confessional leanings tend to becloud the real issue of Christian scholarship and education from time to time.

Conclusion

This First International Conference of Reformed Scholarship will greatly benefit us in the Americas. Looking at ourselves from a distance, we should be better equipped to relativize our often petty struggles and to radicalize our task of (re)formulating ideas for the purpose of reforming our own societies and cultures.

In our American hemisphere with its more than half a billion inhabitants, fewer than half of which live in Canada and the USA, the Reformed-Presbyterian community is *numerically* all but negligible. There are signs, however, that many evangelical Christians, particularly in the USA, are looking for a culturally more meaningful and cosmically more encompassing form of Christian discipleship.[25]

John Calvin once wrote to King Francis of France: "It is one of the characteristics of the divine word, that whenever it appears, Satan ceases to slumber and sleep", and "It is not we who disseminate errors and stir up tumults, but they who resist the mighty power of God".[26] The real test of Christian discipleship comes with the sustained commitment to our God as we seek to understand the complex issues of our day and age, train others for enlightened leadership, and support those who must implement in practical life the things we have been able and privileged to research and teach. Only in this way can we become and remain academic ambassadors of the *wisdom* of the world.

---

1 For general information about South and Central America see H. Blakemore: *Latin America* (Oxford: Oxford University Press, 1966) in *The Modern World* Series, C. H. C. Blount, general editor; Simon Collier: *From Cortés to Castro. An Introduction to the History of Latin America, 1492—1973* (New York: Macmillan Publishing Co., Inc., 1974); John Edwin Fagg: *Latin America. A General History* (New York: The Macmillan Co., 1969); William R. Read, Victor M. Monteroso and Harmon A. Johnson: *Latin American Church Growth* (Grand Rapids: William B. Eerdmans Publishing Co., 1969); John H. Sinclair: *Protestantism in Latin America: A Bibliographical Guide* (Austin: Hispanic American Institute, 1967).

2 From the time of the start of Western colonization of Latin America until the beginning of the eighteenth century the population of indigenous Latin Americans was reduced from thirty million to twelve million! With the increasing domination of the rich and middle class, trained mostly in North America, the mass of poor workers and peasants has become marginated and oppressed. In 1945 Pope Pius XII sent many priests to Latin America to oppose the threat of communism there. Within the last decade a number of Roman Catholic persons, such as Dom Helder Camara, Camilo Torres and Gustavo Gutierrez, have become very outspoken about this situation and are calling for some form of revolution theology. For further information, see the write-up of the Symposium on "Religious Education in Latin America" in: *Religious Education,* vol. LXVI (November-December, 1971), pp. 401—441; Dr. L. Schuurman: „Enkele Kerngedachten van de Latijns-Amerikaanse Theologie van de Bevrijding", *Gereformeerd Theologisch Tijdschrift,* 74th year (November, 1974), pp. 213—232; also the *Ecumenical Review* of the WCC concerning the work of the World Council of Christian Education (WCCE), which on January 1, 1972, became a subdepartment of the WCC.

3 William R. Read, *et al.: op. cit.,* pp. 40—70, 256, 310, 362, 372—377.

4 The Christian Reformed Church, for example, is supporting the work of some fifty missionaries in eight out of the seventeen Latin American countries.

5 Especially through the ministry of Rev. Juan Boonstra.

6 Cf. the work of Dave Howard and Samuel Escobar.

7 This organization, located in Grand Rapids, Michigan (Box 6151), USA, headed by John Roberts and H. der Nederlanden, seeks to translate and/or distribute relevant books. Its main objective is to reach out to Christian students and scholars with such publications as *El Hombre en el Mundo de Dios* and *El Estudiante Christiano en la Universidad Moderna* by Dr P. G. Schrotenboer; *Historia de la Salvacion y Santa Escritura* by Dr H. Ridderbos; *Incertidumbre Moderna y fe Christiana* by Dr. G. C. Berkouwer; *Enfoque Christiano de la Ciencia* by Dr H. van Riessen; *Religion Escritural y Tarea Politica* by Dr H. Evan Runner; *Una Critica Christiana del Arte y Literatura* by Dr C. Seerveld; *Evolution o Reformacion en la Biologia?* by Prof. Hebden Taylor and *El Evangelio y la Lucha de Clases* by Rev. Arnold Rumph.

8 On his way to this Conference Dr H. Hart last June addressed seminary and church audiences in San Juan (Puerto Rico), Lima (Peru), Santiago (Chile), and Buenos Airos (Argentina).

9 William Warren Sweet: *Religion in the Development of American Culture, 1765—1840: American College Movement* (New York: Charles Scribner's Sons, 1952).

10 W. W. Sweet: *op. cit.*, p. 163. The Dartmouth College Case gave trustees of privately endowed institutions the right to conduct colleges and universities, choose presidents and faculties, and determine the curriculum without fear of political interference.

11 *Ibid.*, pp. 165—174. The Baptists and Methodists were at first opposed to a trained clergy, unlike the Presbyterians, Congregationalists, Episcopalians, Lutherans and Reformed. Education played a dominant role in spreading Christian religion and culture across the land. Of all the colleges and seminaries that were started between 1830 and 1860 in the USA, approximately seventy percent disappeared again in a relatively short while, mainly due to financial hardships, denominational conflicts, fire, pestilence, and other debilitating factors. Cf. Henry D. Funk: "The Influence of the Presbyterian Church in Early American History". *Journal of Presbyterian History*, XI. (April, 1925), pp. 184—186.

12 Cf. *Yearbook of Higher Education* 1973/74 (Orange, N.J.: Academic Media, 1975). There are some one hundred and twenty theological seminaries in the USA. The total number of university students in Canada is a little more than three hundred thousand.

13 Many of these reformational stirrings in both Canada and the USA have been either triggered or else strongly supported by Dr H. Evan Runner's pioneering work for twenty years through the Guillaume Groen van Prinsterer Club at Calvin College, many members of which are now connected, directly or indirectly, with the Association for the Advancement of Christian Scholarship and its Institute for Christian Studies in Toronto, Ontario, Canada.

14 The Christian College Association of Alberta, Canada, hopes to start a Christian Junior College, right on the campus of the University of Alberta (19 000 students) in Edmonton, in September, 1976. Alberta is the only province in North America in which Protestant Christians receive partial tax support from the government for their own Christian educational institutions.

15 With a present enrollment of nearly one thousand students.

16 Its enrollment is around three hundred and fifty students.

17 The founder of the Kuyper Institute is Rev. Jon R. Kennedy, an independent Presbyterian minister and expert in the area of mass media — see his *The Reformation of Journalism. A Christian Approach to Mass Media* (Wedge Publishing Foundation, 1972). Since 1972 Kennedy has been teaching courses in mass media which are accredited by the University of Stanford. Presently, he is working on a publication called "Whole Earth Christianity" and is broadcasting every week a one hour news-talk show on cable television in the area of San Jose, California.

18 Through conferences, research, lectures, and publications this Center seeks to develop its own critique of vital issues and institutions. A somewhat related, though independent, agency is *Chalcedon* with Rousas J. Rushdoony as its sole research scholar. Both the Center and Chalcedon reject "big" government and tend to accept the basic tenets of free enterprise economics and politics.

19 Calvin College, with an enrollment of almost three and a half thousand students, differs from Dordt College and Trinity Christian College in that it is officially owned and controlled by the Christian Reformed Church. Nearly ten percent of the students at these three USA colleges come from the Reformed community in Canada.

20 The American Academy of Arts and Sciences has just published *American Higher Education: Toward an Uncertain Future*, vols. I—II (Boston, 1975). See also Sidney Hook, Paul Kurtz and Mire Todorovich (editors): *The Idea of a Modern University* and the *Philosophy of the Curriculum: The Need for General Education* (Buffalo, NY: Prometheus Books, 1975). There is an evident swing away from the Science-Ideal toward the Personality-Ideal in North American higher education — see "Second Thoughts About Man III: What the Schools Cannot Do", *Time* (April 16, 1973), pp. 78—85.

21 Since 1959 the AACS has sponsored some fifty-eight study conferences with a total of forty different lecturers and a combined number of at least ten thousand conferees, and it has presented six series of "Discovery" lectures in twenty-five communities throughout Canada and the USA. Since 1970 the ICS has conducted six basic, graduate-level summer seminars on such topics as hermeneutics, politics, economics, natural science, and philosophy. With its staff of seven, the ICS is doing basic research and teaches students from Canada, the USA, England, Lebanon, Australia, Holland, Japan and Latin America. In the near future the Institute hopes to obtain accreditation for its Ph.M. and Ph.D. programs. The aim of the ICS has best been set forth in *Place and Task of an Institute of Reformed Scientific Studies*.

22 Members of this Consortium are: Calvin College in Grand Rapids, Michigan; Hope College in Holland, Michigan; Trinity Christian College in Palos Heights, Illinois; Covenant College in Lookout Mountain, Tennessee; Dordt College in Sioux Center, Iowa; Northwestern College in Orange City, Iowa; and Central College in Pella, Iowa. The first lecturer to visit all these colleges and discuss a central issue with respect to Christian scholarship was Dr N. Wolterstorff.

23 The identity of these three and the relationships among them are presently being discussed in various Reformed and Presbyterian journals, books, and institutions. The issue is not first of all Christology, nor bibliology. In our age of despair, crises, and meaninglessness, what is at stake is the content of, for example, article I of the Apostles' Creed.

24 Copies of these documents can be obtained by writing to the respective

colleges. See also Arthur F. Holmes: *The Idea of a Christian College* (Grand Rapids: Eerdmans, 1975).

25 James Montgomery Boice "Is the Reformed Faith Being Rediscovered?" in *Christianity Today* (March 28, 1975), pp. 12—13. About the broader shift in USA Protestantism away from liberalism and toward rigorous conservatism, see *Time* (October 9, 1972), p. 84. Whether this shift is favourable to the cause of continued reformation remains to be seen, however. Theological orthodoxy does not necessarily result in cultural orthopraxis. Those evangelical Christians who are developing increasing appreciation for a dynamic and life-encompassing Christian life-style tend to become critical of the rigidity and limited scope of conservatistic Christianity.

26 *Institutes of The Christian Religion,* translation of Henry Beveridge (Grand Rapids: Wm. B. Eerdmans Publishing Co., 1953), pp. 17—18.

Developing reformed Christian study facilities: Indonesia, New Zealand, Australia and the South Pacific Islands

Rev. Stuart Fowler

1. *The background*

1.1. Christianity came to Australia and New Zealand with the coming of British settlement at the end of the eighteenth century. It was brought to most of the South Pacific Islands by missionaries of British background only in the nineteenth century.

1.2. The type of Christianity that came to the region in this way was, on the whole, not a type that is conducive to the development of Christian scholarship. It was generally a pietistic, individualistic type of Christianity which sees no place for a distinctively Christian contribution to social or political issues as such, and senses no need for the development of Christian scholarly endeavour, except in the area of theology.

1.3. As a result, social, political, and educational development has been frankly secular in character. Most people in the region would regard with considerable pride this secular tradition in social, political, and educational institutions. Attempts to break with this tradition in the interests of the kingdom of God are viewed with suspicion, and met with resistance, even from many Christians, because such moves are seen as introducing a dangerously divisive sectarian principle into the society.

1.4. In this tradition the Church, and other forms of organised Christian activity, have a respected and privileged, but strictly limited place. The conduct of public worship, the encouragement of private devotions, welfare programmes for the socially disadvantaged, pronouncements on moral issues, and evangelism aimed at adding converts to this particular restricted form of Christianity are the limits of the expected role of organised Christianity. There is, of course, no legal barrier to organised Christian activity far beyond these limits. There is the quite forbidding barrier of a strong cultural tradition which affects also the thinking of many in the Reformed ecclesiastical tradition.

1.5. While most people in Australia and New Zealand would claim some church affiliation, and nine out of ten profess to believe in God and have a Bible in their home, only 27% attend church regularly. Of this 27% attending church regularly, only 13% attend a Protestant church, and for many of these church attendance would be the limit of their involvement in Christian activity. In short, of the sixteen million people in Australia and New Zealand only a very small percentage would be active Christians, and fewer still would take seriously the authority of the Scriptures.[1]

1.6. In the South Pacific Island countries Christianity must compete with animism and non-Christian faiths. Here too the active Christian community, and still more so, the evangelical Christian community, is a minority in a society that, in general, is moving in a secular direction.

1.7. Christianity has a much older history in Indonesia than anywhere else in the region, going back some four hundred years. The oldest protestant church in Indonesia today, the Moluccan Protestant Church, was founded in 1534, though it only became autonomous in 1935. However, while there is this very early Christian presence in the Indonesian Islands, for a long time it was limited to a very small area, and only began to expand significantly throughout the Indonesian Archipelago extensively in the nineteenth century. The great majority of the Christian churches in Indonesia today were founded in the late nineteenth and early twentieth centuries.

1.8. The protestant Christian constituency of Indonesia, based on the membership figures of churches affiliated with the Indonesia Council of Churches, is around five million in a total population of one hundred and twenty million, or approximately 4% of the population. If Roman Catholics and protestant groups not associated with the Indonesia Council of Churches are included the figure could go up to around 8%. In the last ten years there has been an upsurge of interest in Christianity and the Indonesian churches today are steadily growing. However, there is also evidence of widespread erosion of confidence in the authority of Scripture which must militate against the development of a radically biblical scholarship.[2]

1.9. Among the various streams of Christianity that have developed in Indonesia in this century, there has been a significant stream, originating from the Netherlands, that has encouraged the development of Christian involvement in social and political life and in scholarship. On the other hand, there has been some strong criticism of this stream of thought from Indonesian Christians, contending that it has imposed on Indonesia a Western, and specifically a Netherlands, tradition that was not only unsuited to the Indonesian situation, but a hindrance to the proper development of Indonesian national identity, and a barrier to a truly biblical, Christian response by Indonesian Christians to their specific situation.[3]

1.10. In short, the general picture throughout the region is that, while it is impossible to give exact figures, the Christian community that has the respect for the authority of Scripture as the Word of God which is essential for reformed Christian scholarship, is a very tiny minority of the population. Among this tiny minority the prevalent type of Christian faith is one that does not foster enthusiasm for Christian studies except in the field of theology.

2. Significant changes

2.1. In recent years there have been significant changes within the Christian community, particularly in Australia and New Zealand, that have important, and encouraging, implications for the development of Christian scholarly endeavour.

2.2. In the first place, the wave of migration from the Netherlands has added a new and different tradition to the Australian and New Zealand Christian community. Although by no means all the Christians who have migrated from the Netherlands are enthusiastic supporters of Christian scholarly enterprise, among them there have been those who have brought with them what may be called the Kuyperian tradition which with its breadth of vision of the kingdom of God, provides an important stimulus to the development of Christian scholarship.

2.3. The most significant fruit of this vision in the education field, up to the present, has been the establishment of a vigorous and growing movement for parent-controlled Christian schools, particularly in Australia. Increased government sympathy and assistance for non-government schools in Australia in recent years has helped this movement to make more rapid progress in the establishment of Christian schools, six of which are now operating in key centres throughout Australia. In addition, there are three Christian schools associated with the congregations of the Free Reformed Churches of Australia.

2.4. However, valuable as this contribution from Christians in the Kuyperian tradition migrating from the Netherlands has been, it remains, at this stage, largely on the fringe of the Christian community in Australia and New Zealand, being regarded by most

342

Christians in the area as a Dutch peculiarity. Indeed, a fair assessment would have to agree that there has been some tendency by those within this tradition to see obedient Christian response in terms of transplanting to Australia and New Zealand the sort of Christian institutions developed in response to the significantly different cultural tradition of the Netherlands. There is often apparent a significant confusion between a particular cultural tradition and the Biblical insights that have been developed in that tradition. As a result, while the important Biblical insights inherited by Christians from the Netherlands in the Kuyperian tradition have had some impact on other Christians here and there, there has been no significant penetration of the mainstream of Christian thought in Australia and New Zealand. The very valuable heritage of Christian thought in the Netherlands can have a real impact in Australia and New Zealand, and the rest of the region, only as its important Biblical insights are thoroughly disentangled from the particular cultural tradition within which they have been developed.

2.5. More significant, therefore, at this present time, for the development of Christian scholarship in Australia and New Zealand is the growing awareness within the evangelical Christian community of the importance of Christian social and political involvement. Increasingly, it is being seen that it is not enough to have a private, personal faith, but that the Christian community should be grappling with the problems of man's life in all its aspects, including the social and political dimensions. This growing awareness of the breadth of concern of the gospel has little relation to the influence of migration from the Netherlands, but is part of a world-wide reaction within evangelicalism, reflected, for example, in the Congress on World Evangelisation held at Lausanne in July 1974.

2.6. This growing awareness of the life-encompassing breadth of the gospel is leading an increasing number in the evangelical community to look for some principial basis and direction for Christian action in society. Not content to remain with a mere Christian activism, or a moralistic protest, they are looking for more penetrating insights, the sort of insights that can be provided by a radically Biblical scholarship.

3. *Existing facilities*

3.1. In both Australia and Indonesia there are a number of theological colleges that are either explicitly reformed, or where teaching of a generally reformed character is offered. Among these mention may be made of the Theological College of Jakarta, the Theological College of Jogjakarta, the theological faculty of the

Satya Wacana University at Salatiga, the Reformed Theological College in Geelong, the Moore Theological College in Sydney, and the Queensland Bible Institute in Brisbane.

3.2. Outside the field of theology, study facilities are very limited. There is a "Christian leadership training" course in Indonesia designed to prepare church members for political and social leadership. There are annual study conferences for teachers in the principles of Christian education, sponsored by the National Union of Associations for Parent-controlled Christian schools in Australia, and this year, also in Australia, the Moore Theological College offered, for the first time, a short course of evening lectures on educational principles for teachers.

3.3. The only established institution in the region providing facilities for full-time Christian studies in areas other than theology, is the Satya Wacana Christian University in Salatiga, Central Java. Founded as an attempt to develop a serious Christian approach to scholarship within the context of the Indonesian situation, it has become a centre for higher education that attracts students, including many non-Christians, from many parts of Indonesia. Teaching staff come from a variety of Christian backgrounds and understanding, and also include some non-Christians.

3.4. There are three organisations in Australia and New Zealand that are committed to the establishment of Christian study facilities providing for full-time study in other fields as well as theology. One of these, the oldest, is the Association for a Christian University, which, since 1955 (then known as the Association for Higher Education on a Calvinistic Basis), has operated the Reformed Theological College in Geelong. The object of this Association is "to provide education at tertiary level (including a theological faculty) based on Biblical principles" but, until now, it has not been able to do more than provide theological training.

3.5. With the appointment of Dr. H. van der Laan as professor of Philosophy and Christian Education, the Association for a Christian University (ACU) expects to take the first step next year in expanding its study facilities beyond theological training. It is hoped that this will be the beginning of an Arts faculty in the projected Christian University.

3.6. The ACU, although an independent body, has close links, stipulated by its constitution, with reformed denominations, particularly the Reformed Churches of Australia and New Zealand. The small Reformed Presbyterian Church in Australia has also been closely associated with the development of the ACU since its inception, and more recently, a special relationship has been established between the ACU and the Presbyterian Church of Eastern Australia, another of the smaller Presbyterian denominations in Australia. These three denominations provide the support base for the ACU.

3.7. The other two organisations working for the development of Christian study facilities on a biblical basis are the Foundation for Christian Scholarship in Australia and the Foundation for Christian Studies in New Zealand. Founded in 1973 within a few months of each other, these two bodies have no special relationship with any denomination or group of churches, and have a membership and support base that is much wider than the reformed denominations.

3.8. While FCS (AUS) and FCS (NZ) are independent of each other, they are so very close in their vision, organisational structure, confessional commitment, and planning, working toward joint programmes for the two countries, that for the purpose of this report they may be treated together, (referred to simply as FCS).

3.9. While the FCS vision and planning is for the development of a community of Christian scholarship in Australia and New Zealand that will serve as a research and teaching centre for the whole region, there are no plans for the establishment of a University in the traditional sense. What is envisaged is a smaller, more flexible and open, community of scholars, whose work will be closely related to the situation of the Christian in the secular institutions of higher learning.

3.10. An expanding programme of lectures, seminars, study groups, conferences and literature publication is sponsored by FCS in a number of centres in Australia and New Zealand. All FCS work is at present conducted on an honorary basis, but it is becoming increasingly more difficult to meet the demand of an expanding programme on this basis.

4. *The challenge of the future*

4.1. In those parts of the region that have inherited the Western European tradition, there is a crisis of leadership in society. The old humanistic faith has fragmented and lost credibility. It has been exposed as impotent in the face of mounting problems, social, political, economic. In other parts of the region, only recently emerged, or still emerging, from colonialism, there is a search for a viable basis for national identity. As Christians in this situation we have a responsibility to provide positive, constructive leadership, speaking out with prophetic vision and insight in the name of Christ our Lord to a society adrift. The crisis of our age is also our opportunity.

4.2. There is a growing awareness of this responsibility among Christians who are committed to Scripture as the Word of God, but a great deal of confusion over how to go about the task. There is a stirring consciousness that, as Christians who take the authority of the Bible seriously, we should be speaking to the issues that confront our society today, but very little agreement about what we should be saying.

4.3. It is clear that the Christian community in this region faces an exciting challenge, and that there is a growing readiness among the people of God to rise to meet that challenge. What is lacking is both a depth of understanding and insight regarding the issues that confront us, and a clear sense of direction in developing Christian alternatives that are not just redecorated versions of the product of non-Christian thought.

4.4. In this situation, the development of radically biblical Christian scholarship over a broad range of disciplines must be regarded as a top priority task. Such a scholarship, by itself, will not, and cannot, provide the answer to the needs of the hour. What it can do, is serve the whole body of Christ in this crucial hour by providing the sort of critical insight into the prevailing forms of apostate thought, and the nature of the Christian alternative that is essential for the building of the clearly distinguished, and genuinely constructive contribution to the issue of today's world that alone will make today's Christian community an effective witness to the kingdom of God.

4.5. Christians in the Reformed tradition possess a rich heritage out of which they can make a unique and invaluable contribution to the whole Church in the area of Christian scholarship. But, if we are to do this we must develop the sort of openness to the Word of God that will allow us to respond in faith to the unique situation in which we are placed, not merely reproducing the institutions, methods, and strategies of other historical situations.

4.6. We must recognise that the base for Christian scholarship should be, and can be, wider than the constituency of reformed churches. Many who for one reason or another are not associated with a reformed church, share or can be led to share, the vision we have. As Prof. Sidney Rooy has said already in this conference: "We must work unitedly with all who share the biblical vision of a dynamic creation — salvation, kingdom — church, and election — covenant faith ... There are more biblically reformed people outside our historical pigeon holes than is often realized". In Australia and New Zealand we are currently proving the truth of these words in a significant way.

4.7. To achieve this wider base, however, we in the reformed tradition must learn to curb our fondness for Reformed banner waving, talking loudly and often of our Calvinistic science, our Calvinistic philosophy, our Calvinistic theology, our Reformed institutions. Such banner waving helps nothing and usually hinders communication with other Christians. If we are going to really share the biblical confession and vision we have inherited we must take down the unnecessary barriers to communication, and our banner waving is one of these. We need to stress our common ground with other Christians by speaking rather of a Christian scholarship, a Christian scientific endeavour, building Christian institutions for higher learning. To get people to listen to what we have to say is more important than to wave banners.

4.8. A second requirement in planning for the future is that we be flexible in our thinking about the type of study facilities to be developed, not limiting our thinking to the development of universities and colleges in the traditional sense. We must be open to a variety of ways of meeting the need.

4.9. In particular, in view of the significance of the secular institution for higher education in our society, we should give high priority to the development of Christian scholarship within the context of these secular institutions. One way of doing this would be through foundational studies presented in seminars, lecture series, and short term residential courses of study at both undergraduate and post-graduate level, so that Christian scholars will have the equipment and community necessary to enable them to develop a distinctively Christian contribution in their particular field of study within the framework of the secular institution. Some small beginnings toward this have been made already by FCS, but it needs considerable expansion.

4.10. A third requirement is the development of a full-bodied, radically biblical scholarship that will show clearly its Christian character in every branch of science and learning. We must work to correct the existing imbalance between theology and the other branches of learning in the Christian scholarly enterprise. Without minimising the importance of theology, we must recognise that all our talk about a distinctively Christian science and learning will never be credible until theology can be seen in a real, working partnership, not only with a Christian philosophy, but with special sciences that show a distinctively Christian character.

4.11. Fourthly, our planning for the future must ensure that Christian scholarly endeavour addresses itself to the issues of man's daily life where he is in today's world. It must keep in close contact with the world beyond its own institutions and immediate concerns. It must work closely with, and provide stimulus and support for,

Christian action groups that endeavour to develop authentic Christian alternatives in politics, in the arts, in social order, and in every other area of man's life in the world.

4.12. Finally, the Word of God alone must give authoritative direction to our endeavours. We must make constant, conscious effort to ensure that both the dogmas of contemporary society and the dogmas hallowed by tradition, yes, even Christian tradition, give way before that Word.

4.13. The prospects for Christian scholarship in the region are exciting and challenging. We must proceed in faith, confident that the Lord who has led us to this present situation will enable us to serve him faithfully in this situation, responding with an obedience to his Word that will establish, not merely a bulwark for the kingdom of God, but a commando force storming the citadels of secularism in the name of Christ our King.

---

1 Statistical information for this paragraph is taken from *Religion in Australia* by Hans Mol (Nelson 1971).

2 Statistical information for this paragraph is taken from *World Survey of Reformed Missions* (RES 1973); *Indonesia: Church and Society* by Frank L. Cooley (Friendship Press); *The Christian Faith in the Modern World* (RES 1970). 1967 census figures on church membership have been increased by 10 percent to allow for growth since then.

3 See Raden Soedarmo: *The Christian's Calling in the State* in the symposium *The Christian Faith in the Modern World* (RES 1970).

Japan in the Far East

Prof. Dr. Shintaro Tokunaga

1. *The status quo in the Far East*

Today's world is in an age of a huge structural change. The polarization of the world's nations which began after World War II shifted gradually to the multi-polarizing system centred around three or five great powers. After that, the number of emerging "new nations" belonging to "the third world" increased and they strengthened their voices in the international arena. We are now unable to find any effective solution to urgent problems such as population, material resources and food without taking account of the existence of "the third world".

The Far East is also rapidly changing. It has a vast area of land and a large number of inhabitants. The economic and political structures of the nations are quite different from each other. A number of races, languages, customs and religions co-exist there. It is almost impossible to grasp the Far East as a coherent and homogeneous unity. But there are some indications among the Far Eastern nations of displaying the following common characteristics to a greater or lesser extent:

◇ the existence of animism and syncretism,
◇ the exaltation of national consciousness,
◇ modernization in action,
◇ the succeeding withdrawal of the advanced nations,
◇ the growth of neutralism,
◇ the challenges of communism, especially of Red China.

As I have no time to deal with them in detail here, I would like to concentrate mainly on the status quo of Japan in relation to the other nations in the Far East.

2. *The status quo in Japan*

2.1. Population. The total population of Japan was 108 710 000 in 1973. It is the most industrialized and urbanized Western-like country in the Far East. There are a number of religions, such as various sects of Buddhism, Shintoism,[1] and syncretic "new religions" which appeared in succession especially after World War II. A certain author writes that more than 1500 religions probably exist in Japan. It is not too much to say that Japan is, in reality, a multi-religious country.

2.2. Christianity

Christians	Number	Ratio
Protestants	773 595	66,8
Catholics	383 934	33,2
Total	1 157 532	100,0

The ratio of Christians in the total population is only about 1%. Of the 20 main denominations listed in the Japan Christian Yearbook, 1975, the largest is the United Church of Christ in Japan (194 059), and the Reformed Christian Church in Japan is ranked as the sixteenth (5 798).[2]

2.3. The Japanese spiritual and socio-cultural conditions. In retrospect, the modern history of Japan shows that almost all of the big changes which came about in the past have been brought about by the influences and pressures from abroad rather than from internal reasons. The successive governmental authorities exerted one-sidedly from above their power and control on the people in order to catch up with and get ahead of the advanced countries in the West. Thus loyalty and patriotism became our imperative duty, and the outcome was the notorious "aggressive imperialism" of Japan.

The Emperor-Deification and Shinto-Shrine Worship were enforced through various methods and measures by the Ministry of Education, in spite of the existence of the Constitution of 1889 which guaranteed, though not in full, the freedom of religion. But it deserves to be noted that such a national policy modernized Japan on the one hand, while it extremely formalized national consciousness on the other. Japanese nationalism in its immaturity was easily turned into ultra-statism.[3] Soon after World War II, the ultra-statism was shattered with one stroke by the G.H.Q., and the old myth which had sustained the *ancien régime* lost its prestige and authority, while the anarchistic confusion of thought and belief began to appear. Such a mental and spiritual disorder is now more and more complicated because of the rapid growth of industrialization and urbanization and technological development.

Economic prosperity since the 1960's has entailed a great deal of complex problems in every sphere of life. The following tendencies in intellectual and spiritual life seem to be increasingly salient:

◇ fanatic actions, personal and collective, driven by self-interests,
◇ the spread of feelings of indifference, unrest, impatience, indignation, casual and temporal enjoyment of life, etc.,
◇ taking advantage of political and social ideologies for the purpose of justifying one's own selfish demands and self-assertion.

In accordance with the unprecedented prosperity, the secularization of religions has become conspicuous, that is, an inclination to discover the way for the salvation of humanity solely from the point of view of political and social changes and reforms. Thus the politicalization of religions is now more and more apparent.

On the other hand, State-Shintoism which seemed to have ceased, revived and vigorously resumed its activity in order to restore its authority and the prerogatives it had enjoyed in the past. Supported by various interest groups, the extreme right-wings and the bereaved family groups, State-Shintoism has been exerting its strong pressures on the National Government, the Upper and Lower Houses, leading bureaucrats and members of the House of Representatives. State-Shintoism is aiming directly at the nationalization of the Yasukuni Shrine for the time being, but it is clear that its real intention is to get governmental subsidies and to revive the lost position of the national religion. Thus the so-called "Yasukuni Problem" has become one of the urgent religious and political issues, because there is a possibility of violating the articles of the New Constitution of 1946 which guarantee the two principles of the freedom of religion and the separation of politics and religion.[4]

Faced with such internal and external signs of the time mentioned above, the responsibilities for evangelism have become all the more serious especially to the RCJ and her christians. But to undertake such responsibilities, it is absolutely necessary, above all, to establish and develop historical Reformed Christian theology. The responsibility for evangelism entrusted to the RCJ by Our Lord is, at the same time, to be that of our Institutions for Reformed Christian Higher Education in the country. These two can not be separated from each other.

3. *The Reformed Christian study institutions and facilities in Japan*

3.1. Some 70 Protestant seminaries seem to exist in Japan according to the Japan Christian Yearbook, 1975. Two of them should be mentioned here: The Reformed Christian Seminary in Kobe and The Japan Christian Seminary in Tokyo. Both of them are of a high academic standard and are wrestling with their tasks of theological investigation and education, standing on the basis of clear and firm Biblical theology. The former is related to the RCJ, while the latter is independent.

The RCS was established in 1974 under the General Assembly of the RCJ, but her predecessor was the Central Theological Seminary in Kobe, in pre-war time conducted by the Japan Mission of the PCUS. The number of graduates from our seminary amounted to more than 120. There are 32 students enlisted at present and there were also several students from Taiwan and Korea previously. There are two full-time professors and several regular instructors. In addition to these, our seminary invites guest professors from abroad on special occasions. The land and buildings of the seminary were given by the PCUS in 1960 and its budget is now met by designated donations from local congregations of the RCJ.

In June, 1975, Rev. Ryuzo Hashimoto was elected as the Principal of our seminary and the members of the Board of Trustees were re-elected for the purpose of finding solutions to various difficulties and promoting development.

3.2. The Japan Calvinist Association. The members of the JCA are 160 at present and most of them are Reformed Church ministers, laymen and college students. The JCA also holds full membership in the International Association for Reformed Faith and Action. It was organized in 1954. Its main purpose is to study Reformed and Calvinistic principles, present public lectures and publish Calvinistic literature. Three books have been issued by the JCA so far.

3.3. The friendly relations with other Reformed and Presbyterian churches within Japan. Some individual ministers and laymen of the RCJ participate in the activities of The Society of Evangelical Theology in Japan whose administrative office is at the Japan Theological Seminary in Tokyo. They are active in their work with friends from other denominations.

4. *Conclusion*

In short, the main spiritual and cultural characteristics of contemporary Japan might be summarized as follows:

◇ The prevalence of syncretism. This might be more or less common to other Asian nations.
◇ Progress of secularization in accordance with post-war modernization.
◇ Manifestations of traditional and mass-societal indifference to spiritual, cultural, social problems and aspects.

Facing up to and resisting the signs of the times in Japan, we can not but feel ourselves too weak to accomplish fully the great mission of evangelism. But we believe that the progress of the King-dom of God is due to the work of the Holy Spirit, not to the work of man. In order to carry out this mission in accordance with the will of God, in season and out of season, the unification of Reformed Christian theological studies and evangelism in earnest and incessant prayer is absolutely necessary.

Last but not least, I would like to make some concrete sugges-tions that Reformed Christian Educational Institutions in Japan seem to think desirable:

◇ an interchange of qualified teachers and students;
◇ an exchange of theological and educational intelligence, such as periodicals issued by educational institutions, contents of curri-cula, new devices and methods of teaching, specific problems and needs felt by the institutions, etc.;
◇ joint theological study projects especially on animistic and secu-larizing influences on today's churches and the theological world.

5. *Appendix*

The Shikoku Christian College was established by the PCUS in 1950. The original land and buildings, formerly part of Japanese Imperial Army installations, were purchased through the Presbyterian Pro-gram of Progress in 1949. The annual operating budget was at the beginning supplemented by regular subsidy from the Presbyterian Board of World Missions.

The S.C.C. had been a non-accredited four-year college, but afterwards acquired the recognition of the Educational Department of the Government as a co-educational college. The S.C.C. was registered officially as the Shikoku Gakuin University.

There are three academic facilities in the S.C.C.

1. Junior college: English.
2. Senior college: Four Departments.
   (1) English and American Literature.
   (2) Humanities (including Christian studies, Philosophy, History, Economics and Political Science).
   (3) Social Welfare.
   (4) Education.
3. Graduate School of Social Work.

The S.C.C. has 1 500 students and 100 faculty members. The number of graduates has amounted to 2 061 up to now. Some of them have gone on to seminary and the ministry (29), engage in Social

Welfare (120), Public Service and Teaching Profession (133), Business (676), Independent or Domestic Enterprise (81) and others (873).

The S.C.C. is located at Zentsuji City, Kagawa Prefecture on the Island of Shikoku with its population of 4 million.

All teachers are professed christians of some denomination, but the Reformed Christian teachers are six at present, although all teachers had belonged to the RCJ at its start.

---

1 *Shintoism.* The clear-cut features of Shintoism are very hard to grasp, for it contains ingredients which came from the folk-ways-Shinto, which had been shaped in the late medieval period. It is said that five fields mentioned below are included in the concept of Shintoism: 1. Shrine-Shinto; 2. Imperial-Household-Shinto; 3. Dogmatic-Shinto; 4. Sectarian-Shinto; 5. Folk-ways-Shinto. State-Shintoism, which played a tremendous role in Japanese aggressive militarism, had been shaped through combining Shrine-Shinto and Imperial-Household-Shinto during the period of the Meiji Restoration in 1868. Shigeyoshi Murakami: *The State Shintoism,* 1970, pp. 14—8. (Iwanami).

2 *The Reformed Christian Church in Japan.* The RCJ was born in Japan in 1946 in the midst of post-war confusion, and at its start adopted the Westminster Confession, the Westminster Larger and Shorter Catechisms as the confessional standards. The RCJ has 91 ministers, over 200 elders and 270 deacons and deaconesses. It has enjoyed co-operative relations with the foreign Missions, the Presbyterian Church, U.S., the Christian Reformed Church and the Orthodox Presbyterian Church. A resolution was passed at the General Assembly in 1966 as to the "priesthood of every believer" and now preparations are in progress for drafting a Declaration concerning the "relation of state and religion" in memory of the 30th Anniversary of the RCJ which will be held in April 1976.

3 It seems to me that the nationalism of the new nations in Asia and the statism of Japan are somewhat different from each other. The Asiatic nations have long been under the colonial domination of the advanced nations, and therefore, this nationalism started as a movement of anti-colonialism and self-determination; while Japan has never experienced such a situation, with the exception of the short period of occupation by the Allied Forces immediately after World War II. Japan had really devoted herself to catch up with and to get ahead of the civilized nations in the West. The outcome was that Japan jumped into statism, skipping the maturity of national consciousness.

4 If the nationalization of the Shinto-Shrine were effected, the politicalization of religion and the religionization of politics would possibly be brought about. Successive governmental authorities have had recourse to the dubious logic of the compatibility of the freedom of religion and the Shinto-Shrine Worship. Everyone was obliged to participate in the designated ceremony of the Shrine, since to do so was a national obligation and Shintoism was not to be regarded as a religion, but a national courtesy. But there was another implication in this logic. The National Government intended to keep in check the fanatic Shinto believers and the extreme rightists

354

who insisted strongly upon the governmental recognition of Shintoism as the sole national religion.

Reviewing the status quo in Europe

Prof. Dr. A. Troost

THE fact that I am not here to address you as an official delegate of the Free University of Amsterdam represents a tragic symptom of the "status quo of Reformed Study facilities" in Europe.

I do not intend to engage in a discussion of the reason why, regrettably, the Free University, of all places, is not officially represented here. I will not do so in this speech, nor will I do so during the discussion.

But I simply make mention of this fact as a symptom. It is a symptom of the weakness of christendom generally, Calvinism included. After all, all sincere christians desire to live according to God's Word. European Calvinism in particular was granted the blessing of vision allowing them to see, more clearly than christians elsewhere, that the gospel's relevance could not be confined to the church and to theology, but that, instead, God's Word is relevant for all of life's areas and for all the sciences.

This idea was elaborated for philosophy and the various sciences by Dr A. Kuyper and by his philosophical disciples in the movement for calvinistic philosophy. They were aware of their religious need to enthusiastically devote themselves to the inner reformation of theoretical thought itself. This was to be a biblical alternative to the pre-reformational idea of an external theological addition to, or critical commentator upon, non-christian science and theory supposed to be all right in the main.

It was such inspiration that led to the founding of the Free University, just as it also led to the founding of this university of Potchefstroom. This however, only constituted the beginnings of the calvinistic reformation in the realms of philosophy and the sciences. In terms of the theoretical enterprise we have never progressed beyond these beginnings. It is true, indeed, that a few small institutues in various parts of the world were inspired to their work in ways in which the Free University and Potchefstroom were also instrumental.

But it must be said that Calvinism generally has refused to accept this reformation of theoretical thought as its own. In the typically calvinistic countries of Europe, the Netherlands, Scotland and Hungary, the calvinistic reformation has affected little more than development in church and theology, but even within these areas we are faced by a hopeless state of fragmentation and division. In the Netherlands alone we already find ten reformed ecclesiastical denominations and at least four or five different theological institutes or faculties.

The present status quo is largely determined by the fact that the very soil in which the christian idea of science was conceived, the Free University, has experienced a change in character. It has testified to this change, first of all during the major congress of professors and lecturers of 1968 and subsequently in an official replacement of the foundational creed by a statement of purpose. The latter no longer represents the ideal of a calvinistic development of science, but the expressed wish to make the factual development of current science as such serviceable to political and social life.

Certainly, in a certain sense it may represent a truly biblical purpose, to the extent that the various tasks and talents within the kingdom of God ought to be carried out in the service of one's fellow man and of the world. But the change in question has been interpreted in drastically different ways. Most of those, employed by the Free University, experience this new statement of purpose as a liberation out of calvinistic isolation and as in principle a new way into communication with all major christian churches and trends of thought in a world-wide context. Others, by contrast, experience this new development as a renunciation of the calvinistic reformation in favour of a vague and inherently contradictory mixture of numerous non-calvinistic, and sometimes semi-christian or non-christian tendencies.

What lesson are we to draw from this — it seems to me tragic — history of Calvinism in Europe and in the Netherlands?

1. Calvinistic theology in its traditional systematics offers no guarantee for a christian life and it offers no points of contact for a christian development of scientific thought. In fact the remnants of Calvinism in Europe have, along the patterns of traditional Lutheran and Roman Catholic traditions, usually objected to the christian idea of theory and science. The price these remnants had to pay for this position, however, was either to be manoeuvred into a sterile, conservative position of isolation or to experience their own downfall as Calvinism, because of an inner powerlessness when faced with modern science in its development.

2. Calvinistic institutes and universities will do well to display some modesty and hesitancy when tempted to present themselves as the bulwarks of the Kingdom of God. Certainly this image may come to be used now and again in the midst of doing battle with the

powers of darkness in the western world, but it should be done only in humble acknowledgement of Ps. 127: "Except the Lord build the house, they labour in vain that build it: except the Lord keep the city, the watchman waketh but in vain".

God has kept his Kingdom fast for 19 centuries already without the aid of such "bulwarks".

3. Nevertheless the Scriptures call us to build ramparts and fortresses against the powers of unbelief and revolution. These spiritual powers are especially mighty in the areas of science in our times, and tempting too. For life in God's Kingdom, theoretic thought is not the most important. A biblical love, a biblical faith and a biblical view of life and society is more important than science. But nonetheless, in the 20th century the world and christianity need the service of theoretical thought for their life and their spiritual struggle.

4. More than ever before we will have to consider, that autonomous theoretical thought has been one of the most seriously worshipped idols of western culture for 26 centuries. Numerous calvinistic and orthodox theologians have burnt their incense at the altar of this god, in order to achieve human honour and acknowledgement in the world of science, and power and influence in the realm of the church.

5. A biblical sanctification of theoretical thought, as much as the proper exercise of an ecclesiastical office, requires fulfilment by the Holy Spirit and the power of Christ. Without infusion by the Holy Spirit the church becomes worldly, and that holds good as well for the theologian, the university or an institute for christian theory.

6. Definitely established in the divine order of creation is that the typical nature and structure of all the special scientific disciplines is bound to philosophical insights and frameworks of thought, while, in turn, philosophy finds its origin, direction and support in an ethos, an attitude of life. It is that ethos which must be renewed and reformed by the regenerating power of God's Word and Spirit.

7. If that be correct, it is a practical requirement of the utmost importance that theologians and philosophers from all areas of God's Kingdom speak together about the great difference and about the coherence between faith and theology. For it was precisely in Calvinism that the practical identification of faith and theology constituted the chief point of entry for the idolatrous worship of theoretical reason, a source of ecclesiastical schisms

and the fertile ground of relativism and apostasy.

8. What we need as calvinists in Europe is contact first of all with German-speaking christians in order to engage in a discussion about the possibilities of a christian theoretical enterprise. That would be an alternative to the traditional scholastic problem of the relation between two entities: faith and autonomous rational science that are inherently independent and estranged from each other.

I hope that the few German-speaking brethren in our midst will take up contact with the christian institutes for calvinistic science in the world with a view to such possibilities.

9. Finally I would suggest that it is highly necessary to co-ordinate the work done by the presently numerous small and financially weak periodicals, so that we may have just a few but effective means for mutual exchange of information and discussion, all for one and the same purpose: the advancement of Calvinism, with a special emphasis on the inner reformation of all scientific thought.

Creating facilities for Evangelical theological training in Africa

Dr. Byang H. Kato*

1. *Introduction*

The title suggested for this paper includes the words *Reformed Christians* and *Young African Countries*. I chose to omit these expressions to avoid any misunderstanding. *Reformed* in a technical sense would exclude by far the biggest percentage of Christianity in Africa including myself. But in a general sense, all Protestant Christians who have benefitted from the fruits of the Protestant Reformation may be called Reformed.

Young African Countries is a relative term. It is also viewed in some circles as a colonial-derogatory description. A term such as Black Africa is preferable.

I use the term evangelical to describe that section of the Christian Community in Black Africa that firmly believes in and lives according to the doctrinal faith hereby summarized:

1. The Bible: Revelation, inspiration, inerrancy and authenticity. Thus the Bible is the Word of God and the final authority in all that it affirms.

2. Jesus Christ: His virgin birth, sinless life on earth, historical death, resurrection and ascension. It also includes the purpose of His death — all summed up in 1 Cor. 15 : 3, 4.

3. Man: Created by God, perfect. Now fallen, totally depraved, deserving only God's condemnation. He can be rescued from this fundamental dilemma by faith in Christ alone (Eph. 2 : 8, 9). The saved Christian would normally seek to fulfil the demands of Christian ethics which includes his relation to other men within a political set-up. But the demands of Christian ethics must not be confused with the matter of salvation. Good works are the results and not the means of attaining salvation (Eph. 2 : 8—10).

4. Eschatology: The irreducible minimum of an evangelical

---

* It is with deep regret that we have learned of Dr Byang H. Kato's death by drowning on 19 December 1975.

belief concerning the life to come includes:

(a) Personal, physical return of Jesus Christ at a time not known by any created being, not even the Son during His earthly life (Mk. 13 : 32).
(b) Personal, physical resurrection of all people as individuals.
(c) The judgement of the living and the dead and retribution on the basis of the acceptance or rejection of Jesus Christ.
(d) Reality of Heaven and Hell. The righteous will enjoy heaven eternally, while the unrighteous will be tormented in hell forever.

Brethren of like precious faith as described above are warmly invited to the great fellowship of AEAM. Schools with this persuasion provide the facilities for evangelical theological training in Africa.

2. *Facilities for theological education*

2.1. Departments of theological education in universities. The following are some of the outstanding departments of religious education in Africa: Makerere University, Uganda; Nairobi University, Kenya; Ibadan, Nsukka, Lagos and Ife Universities in Nigeria; Faculty of Theology at Kinshasa, Zaire; Fourah Bay College, Sierra Leone; University of Ghana at Legon, Ghana.

This list is by no means exhaustive. It is only to illustrate the point. Although there are some evangelical professors in these departments, many of the courses are liberal in nature. The emphasis is rather on comparative religions, presenting religions as equal. For example, the department of religious study at Ibadan University symbolizes their presentation with the following design:

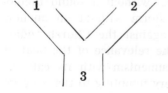

1. Islam.
2. Christianity.
3. African Traditional Religions.

The journal of this department is called *Orita,* which means a meeting point. This symbolism is open to various interpretations. But I can see the danger of universalism inherent in it.

The primary concern of these departments is academic achievement rather than the spiritual preparation of students for the ministry. While they have their contribution to make in the educational field, they are not the best for ministerial training.

2.2. Theological schools. There are at least 120 theological institutions in Africa. Very few of them are thoroughly liberal, although a number of them have teachers who are not evangelical as they cannot in good conscience sign the statement listed above.

These schools can be classified under four levels:

◇ *Level one:* requirement for entrance is merely the ability to read and write in the vernacular. Until recently, this level had the highest percentage of enrollment.

◇ *Level two:* Seven years of secular education before enrollment. The students then spend three to four years in the institution. Perhaps this level has the highest enrollment now. Many of the graduates are too young for the ministry. They usually start working in other fields of the ministry such as book sales, youth camps or other vocations.

◇ *Level three:* Nine years of secular education or its equivalent. Many students in this category are ambitious and usually aspire to go higher.

◇ *Level four:* Twelve years of secular education and above. About 12 schools of this level are presently available in Black Africa. Some of them have started issuing degrees, i.e. B.Th. But the big snag is that hardly anybody recognizes these degrees but the institutions themselves. Students with a first degree have nothing provided for them at the present. AEAM is exploring the possibility of meeting this need.

3. *Suggestions for meeting the need*

The Church in Africa can boast of about 100 000 000 "Christians" in its fold. It is irrelevant to spend time disputing these figures. But I must stress the point that a Church without a sound theological basis is like a drifting boat in a storm without an anchor. The wind of every doctrine is blowing against the Church today. The wind of contextualization is testing the relevance of the boat of Evangelical Theology. The ill-wind of ecumenism with its call for secularization of Christianity is proving very tempting to the average Christian. The wind of Black theology, with its legitimate quest for human dignity but without an adequate term of reference, appears convincing. The wind of African Theology with its rightful search for the African personality, yet failing to see the unique nature of Christian revelation, is very appealing. For the ship of evangelical faith to stand the test of the times, it must be grounded on the hope of our fathers. "We have this as a sure and steadfast anchor of the soul, a hope that enters into the inner shrine behind the curtain,

362

where Jesus has gone as a forerunner on our behalf, having become a high priest forever after the order of Melchizedek" (Heb. 6 : 19, 20).

Two things are necessary for the survival of the ship of our faith. On the one hand, there must be an uncompromising confidence in God's revealed Word. On the other hand, there must be the intelligent communication of this faith to the contemporary African mind. Along with this two-fold commitment, there must be another pair of oars: the head and the heart.

The woman preacher Kathryn Kuhlmann has humorously stated that some people have been educated beyond their intelligence. To have the head full of theological knowledge without a warm heart for personal soul winning and building men up in the faith could lead on to Kuhlmann's observation. To achieve these goals, I suggest that Evangelical Christians in Africa co-operate in leadership training in the following manner as the political situation allows:

1. It takes an African today to speak to an African on some of the current issues. Mission boards working in Black Africa should therefore put the matter of the training of Africans highest on their "priority list".

2. Where the Lord has blessed His church with material resources, the Christians in that part of Christ's body should consider it a privilege to share in the training of leadership for another part of Christ's body. Stewardship of personnel and material resources are both God's gifts to the Church. This assistance could be in the areas of awarding scholarships to students and building up the theological institutions.

3. Works published by an institution should be shared with other institutions. AEAM has a list of the names and addresses of over 100 institutions.

4. Where possible, institutions should be merged for the sake of efficiency and promoting unity among the brethren of like precious faith.

5. The possibility of the formation of a Theological Society should be explored. I have in my possession a long list of persons interested in such a move.

6. AEAM has launched the following ambitious programme to help towards meeting the urgent need of leadership training in Africa.

(a) BEST — Bangui Evangelical School of Theology — as reported in April 1975 *Afroscope.*

(b) Anglophone School of Theology. Plans for this school are still under way. A crucial meeting in November 1975 will consider this proposal.

(c) Accreditation. This is probably the most urgent need for theological institutions in Africa today. AEAM is therefore calling for a meeting of its Theological Commission in Nairobi 21—27 Nov. 1975. Principals of 19 theological institutions interested in accreditation have been invited. Support in prayer, counsel, finance and any other way will be deeply appreciated.

Evangelical Christianity in Africa is hereby admonished to walk the path of the early church. "And they devoted themselves to the APOSTLES' TEACHING and fellowship, to the breaking of bread and prayers" (Acts. 2 : 42).

May the Faithful Teacher of teachers, the Holy Spirit Himself, guide us all in these challenging days.

Co-ordination between Christian institutions in Southern Africa

Prof. Dr. J. H. Coetzee

1. *Introductory note*

A growing global approach to the world in a physical as well as in a spiritual sense, either in the form of utopian and humanistic dreams or in terms of a Christian and eschatological vision, accompanied by increasing personal contact and mobility or by means of various kinds of audio-visual forms of communication, have diminished limits of time and space. All of this constitutes perhaps one of the most striking features of our time. The ecumenical movement and awareness within the sphere of the institutionalized church, presents one aspect of this tendency. This conference bears witness to a reviving sense of ecumenicity or oneness amongst reformed Christian scientists in the field of higher education.

1.2. In introducing the topic assigned to me, it seems relevant and appropriate to state my belief that reformed educational institutions are also subject to the Christian ecumenical commitment. Without any doubt these institutions have a nature and vocation different from that of the church. The distinction as reflected in the different typological appellations of church and educational institution is indicative of their respective structures, nature and calling. The adjective "Christian" which applies to both, however, accentuates an essential similarity and relationship.

1.3. The educational institutions involved are concerned with one or more aspects of scientific work: exploring the unknown domains of natural and cultural phenomena by way of scientific research, transferring knowledge in their teaching assignments and/or implementing the acquired scientific materials either in professional or technological activities. Science in itself is essentially man's way of discovering cosmic realities in obedience to his cultural mandate and hence in conjunction with the revealed truth of the Word of God.

1.4. The general statement that science exists as a unity contains a greater truth than is perhaps usually understood. This thesis might appear to be challenged by the perceptible tendency to specialize up to the point of creating both the appearance and the reality of fragmented and hardly related bits and pieces of verified knowledge dispersed over an increasing range of disciplines, amongst millions of scientists and scholars associated with hundreds of thousands of educational institutions for research, training or applied science.

1.5. Essentially the existence of more than one Truth is irreconcilable, both logically and in principle. The same applies to science. In practice of course the reality of sin and its catastrophic effect on man, his intellect and his moral capacity, present a major barrier to the realization of this principle. The Apostle Paul, referring to the revealed truth, had to acknowledge: "For now we see through a glass darkly..." (1 Cor. 13 : 12). Nonetheless, Jesus Christ has overcome the world. Hence this oneness should be aspired to and be unfolded in the mutual acquaintance of and relations between those institutions and individuals committed to the quest for science "in thy light" (Ps. 36 : 9). It supposes a two-way action: co-operating according to their sphere of activities, their nature and vocation in the common struggle against the lie and for the sake of the Kingdom of God, to the honour of his Name, and at the same time in mutual encouragement, enlightenment and supervision of those participating.

2. *The Southern African scene*

2.1. In South and Southern Africa the ideal of harnessing institutions and academics to this idea of co-operation, co-ordination and perhaps integration, is up against numerous obstacles. The history of this sub-continent has left the present and emerging generations with a legacy of variety-in-conflict. Black and White divisions embedded in distrust, disassociation and social distance, are strengthened by a history of both political, physical and ideological clashes between Afrikaner and Englishman. Traditionally the Afrikaner people are the more general representatives of the reformed faith in the country.

2.2. A few broad lines might serve to indicate the situation at present. Christianity in Southern Africa today is a concept of kaleidoscopic hues and colours. It spans a wide field of faiths and denominations: Roman and Greek Catholics; Lutherans, different English, American, Dutch, orthodox and modernistic brands of Protestants, various shades of reformed or Calvinistic adherents, a variety of sectarian movements and for some at least also Judaism. Even within the camp of reformed Protestantism, a substantial part

366

of the fold is committed to traditionalism and could be counted as nominal adherents only.

2.3. These circumstances have, individually and collectively, a bearing on the task of co-ordination of reformed Christian institutions. The existing differences, both essential and peripheral, reflect on attitudes, approaches, readiness to co-operate and even on defining limits of contact and participation. Nevertheless, these obstacles ought to be regarded as challenges instead of being feared as dangers and viewed as reasons for adopting a passive stance.

3. *Co-ordination: Scope and possibilities*

3.1. Taken literally, the wording of the subject imposes certain limits on the scope of this paper. Confining myself to co-ordination between Christian institutions only, the answer would be relatively simple and easy. Co-ordination in this case could be promoted and implemented either by inaugurating some form of co-ordinating institution (which should however avoid the semblance or nature of a superstructure) or by having regular or ad hoc meetings of representatives on the levels of administration, teaching and research. A clear case can also be presented for something similar at the student level. Other possibilities present themselves either in the garb of independent contacts or coupled to or integrated with those mentioned above. These include regular or sporadic meetings of groups of teaching staff in conferences or symposia on related or interrelated fields of study and/or research. Exchange or co-operation of publications, seems to be self-evident. Additional possibilities to be considered would include a system for visiting teachers for shorter or longer periods and facilities for post-graduate students to do at least part of their work on the campus of another institution. Within the general pattern more precise *modi vivendi* should be developed for every case in question.

3.2. Unfortunately the situation is not that simple when viewed from the organizational angle. Christian institutions, officially recognized as such, are rather the exception. In reality only one *academic* institution can glory — in humility and gratitude — in the fact of being chartered as a Christian university.

3.3. On the other hand and as a reason for rejoicing, most of the other universities have associated with them a theological seminary *cum* theological faculty. This does not include theological training institutions independent from universities. A case in point is the regular contact between the theological faculties of the Afrikaans universities. In addition members of staff of these faculties and theological training schools meet in annual conferences for the sake of Old Testament, New Testament and other studies in the field of theology. These, however, are mostly limited to the Afrikaans universities. Those concerned with Christian missions are co-ordinated, in their personal capacities, in the South African Missiological Society.

3.4. The presence of a substantial number of Christian teachers on the staff of universities and other relevant institutions poses a credit point as well as a problem when approached from the angle of institutional co-ordination.

3.5. It should be regarded as self-evident that Christian institutions would profess via their representatives, where relevant and opportune, in whatever form of contact, their principles when confronted by colleagues from the "non-Christian" institutions. It is clear, however, that this is insufficient.

3.6. In the Republic members of the teaching staffs of the various universities involved in related academic disciplines meet more or less regularly either on a rather loose ad hoc footing or in structured associations. This is the case, for example with anthropologists and sociologists. These meetings offer opportunities, however limited, to profess, discuss and explain approaches and interpretations from the reformed Christian point of view. This, too, is not quite satisfactory.

3.7. In a number of cases teaching staff, subscribing to the principle of reformed Christian scientific work, are co-ordinated in either specific or more general academic associations. Explicit examples are COVSA (Christian Pedagogical Association of South Africa),[1] the SAVCW (South African Association for Christian Scholarship)[2] and VCHO (Association for Christian Higher Education).[3] These cases are mentioned as models which could be followed by all reformed teachers at the academic level in Southern Africa.[4]

3.8. In the absence of sufficient members of reformed Christian universities and parallel institutions for Christian education, the aim of co-ordination seems, for the present, to emphasize the co-ordination of individuals as well as institutions. In this regard, the question presents itself whether the SAVCW should not take the lead in initiating the establishment of groups of reformed Christian academics on the pattern of COVSA according to the need and nature of the different disciplines. I do not wish to convey the impression that SAVCW should elevate itself to a kind of super-organisation. Nonetheless, the idea forces itself on one's mind whether these groupings within the bounds of specific disciplines should not in one way or another be linked to the more inclusive SAVCW.

3.9. Whatever the form this is to take eventually, a thrust

in this direction would serve primarily to co-ordinate like-minded men and women within the precincts of their respective fields of study. In addition the SAVCW stands to gain by a move of this nature. As an auxiliary to or in default of official alliances between universities and related institutions, this might meet the need for, and could promote co-operation on, the institutional level.

3.10. Regular and/or ad hoc meetings, conferences, symposia, discussion groups with papers, addresses and discussions on both departmental and inter-departmental *niveau* seem the most natural activities of these co-ordinated units. Joint publications, journals, specialist papers, monographs recommend themselves as ways and means of mutual participation. So does exchange of publications independently sponsored by the different institutions. An indisputable need, however, exists for at least one journal of international standard published in an international language.

3.11. Initiating and promoting similar contact and co-ordination between reformed Christian students, appears to me to constitute an additional issue intimately related with the above mentioned cause.

4. *Reaching out*

4.1. Professor Stanford Reid touched on an aspect which appears to me relevant to this issue. It relates to the "feed-back" of Christian scientific work in a comprehendable, "simplified" form and way to those outside academic boundaries, strictly speaking. This presents itself to me as one form of relationship and bridge between university and society — to be more precise: between a Christian university and a Christian society.

4.2. May I briefly illustrate this point by introducing what, I believe, is a general problem. As a member of an editorial board of a reformed magazine with exactly the abovementioned goal, it is an extremely frustrating experience to exhaust oneself in a very often unsuccessful search for a reformed authority in a specific field to expound the reformed view both positively and in criticism of wayward tendencies of the day.

4.3. Ideally, panels of competent, enthusiastic and co-operative authors, primarily from the ranks of Christian scholars, should be available for this kind of work. But in many fields they are either totally lacking and/or harbour an attitude of non-involvement. This specially applies to technology, natural sciences, all aspects of the arts, politics, economics, the film, theatre, television etc.

4.4. A greater amount of co-operation as suggested in paragraph 3 might also promote new acquaintances and by interaction sharpen both insight and stimulate an increase of enthusiasm.

5. *In conclusion*

5.1. The charter of the Potchefstroom University for Christian Higher Education surely is not meant to be confined to a file in the strong room of the administration. Nor does it restrict the relevant implications to the confines of the university campus. It clamours for recognition and application inside and outside the physical boundaries of this institution. The university's task does not end with educating and training its own students and sending them out into the wider world of the nation's life so as to find a place somewhere in the complex spectrum of activities. It calls for reaching out to wider horizons. Its facilities should be available to those of similar convictions if they cannot be accommodated elsewhere. It must commit itself to the cause of Christian higher education inside and outside its own campus, inside and outside the borders of this country.

5.2. I am quite aware of the obstacles on the way to attaining the ideal posed in this paper. In addition to the hurdles I have tried to enumerate, lack of dedication and scarcity of funds are sure to form further obstacles on the road of those who dare to respond to the challenge. The victory, however, is to those who act in faith. "For by thee have I run through a troop; and by my God have I leapt over a wall" (Ps. 18 : 29).

---

1 This organisation publishes a journal *Fokus*. Address: P.O. Box 20027, Noordbrug 2522, South Africa.

2 The official publication of the S.A.V.C.W. is *Bulletin van die Suid-Afrikaanse Vereniging vir die Bevordering van Christelike Wetenskap*. Address: Prof. M. E. Botha, Dept. of Philosophy, P.U. for C.H.E., Potchefstroom 2520, South Africa. (Subscription R2,00 per year.)

3 The V.C.H.O. publishes a scientific journal called *Tydskrif vir Christelike Wetenskap* (subscription R2,50 per year) and a more popular periodical *Roeping en Riglyne*. Address: VCHO, P.O. Box 1824, Bloemfontein 9300, South Africa.

4 Apart from the above-mentioned organizations and their different publications I would like to mention the following:
The A.C.B. (Afrikaans Calvinistic Movement) which publishes a monthly paper *Woord en Daad* (Word and Deed). Address: P.O. Box 20011, Noordbrug 2522, Potchefstroom, South Africa. (Subscription R4,00 per year.)
Koers (Direction), a Calvinistic scientific journal of which six issues are published per year. Address: The Editor (at the moment Prof. E. J. Smit), "Koers", Potchefstroom University for C.H.E., Potchefstroom 2520, South Africa. (Subscription: R5,00 per year).
Perspektief (Perspective), a publication of the Department of Philosophy at the Potchefstroom University for C.H.E. (This journal can be received free of charge on request from the head of the Department of Philosophy.)

As Dr. D. Kempff will deal in a separate paper with the work of the I.A.C. (Institute for the Advancement of Calvinism) I merely mention it here to complete the list of names and addresses. More information can be obtained from The Director, I.A.C. (at the moment Dr. B. J. van der Walt), P.U. for C.H.E., Potchefstroom 2520, South Africa.

Calvin's critique of Calvinism

Prof. Dr. Heiko A. Oberman

THE theme of our conference as it was originally announced reads: "Reformed Higher Educational Institutions as a Bulwark for the Kingdom of God — Present and Future". And here I am, representing a professedly neutral institution, intended as a bulwark for progress, not for the Kingdom of God, a university soon to celebrate its 500th birthday, and an Institute which does not deal with the present or future, but with the Middle Ages and the Reformation.

I.

In approaching our theme it is important to realize in advance that we hail from different worlds, not merely from different continents. Our common bond, however, is that all of us regard this theme as rich — and perhaps even loaded. Let us tax and test this bond to the utmost in challenging each others' presuppositions with the same fearless openness for truth which characterized the Genevan Reformer. The shortest procedure for flushing out these presuppositions may well be a sketch of the history of Calvin research which can then be used as a compass to reveal where each of us stands. Such a sketch is of necessity tendentious; it must ignore the more subtle variations and nuances. Furthermore, this task is a baffling one because of the large number of publications to be taken into account. Dr Kempff's impressive *Bibliography of Calviniana: 1959—1974,* which has recently been published simultaneously in Potchefstroom and Leiden, gives eloquent testimony to the present state of affairs. Since Professor Nauta of the Free University prepared a more comprehensive discussion of recent Calvin research, for the last Calvin Research Congress in Amsterdam, I can limit myself here to what interests us most, the prevailing schools of Calvin interpretation. Enumerated as concisely as possible, I discern six basic types of schools.[1] In the second part of this paper I shall indicate six issues in recent scholarship which I regard as relevant to our theme of Calvin's challenge today.

1. *The classical interpretation.* Even today we can admire the excellent and comprehensive grasp of Calvin's dogmatic treatises and of the *Institutes* which was demonstrated by this school. Yet, not

unlike the German phenomenon in the field of theology when a reference to Scripture is replaced by a quotation from Martin Luther, the classical schoolinterprets Calvin with the pretence of presenting the Word of God itself. Valid theology is the reiteration of the positions described — and hence prescribed! — by Calvin.

2. *The confessional interpretation.* Calvin is here viewed through the eyes of the Westminister Confession and the Heidelberg Catechism: Scripture and predestination are seen to be the foci of his thought.

3. *The neo-orthodox school:* God's revelation is only grasped in Christ, *through* Scripture, *reflected* in predestination as the covenant of grace ("Gnadenwahl").

4. *The Dutch school* (Abraham Kuyper and Herman Bavinck) stresses the sovereignty of God over all cultural manifestations of life; hence it includes a theology of society, of the state, of politics, yet not in the strict sense of the word 'theocratic'. In his assessment of "Kuypers idee eener christelijke cultuur" Arnold A. van Ruler — a true theocrat, the first to design a theology of hope — concludes that "de gemeene gratie uitsluitend de functie van een leer van het aanknopingspunt in het groot heeft".[2] For Kuyper common grace has the sole purpose of keeping the machine of creation running and of preparing for the conversion and rebirth of individuals, and not, as Van Ruler sees it, of sanctifying creation as the one and single eschatological (= now) purpose of God. We shall return to this point in our discussion of decisive points in contemporary Calvin research.

5. *The anti-orthodox interpretation.* Not characteristic of any particular group, this view builds upon some mythical and some historical elements. Calvin is described as the enemy of culture and of research; as the murderer of Servetus, and the manager of police-controlled Geneva.

6. *The historical school.* Originally in reaction against all forms of 'theological' interpretation, this school has made giant strides by trying to abstain from taking sides in the debate around the right 'use' of Calvin. It thus has little patience with any form of confessional interpretation, be it orthodox or neo-orthodox; yet, *de facto* it has done the most to answer the theses implied in the anti-orthodox view. The humanist Calvin, the editor of Seneca's *De Clementia,* is shown not to be a passing stage but to determine: 1. his interests in education; 2. his concern with affairs of state — and both with a wide ecumenical horizon.

Although all six 'types' or 'schools' are represented in this country, I expect that most will recognize themselves as belonging to the position I have described as II, III or IV. Yet the most substantial and lasting contribution in the last type described has been made by a South African, André Malan Hugo († 1975) who not only provided us with a fine study entitled *Calvijn en Seneca*[3] (Groningen, Djakarta, 1957), but also — together with the English translator of the *Institutes,* Ford Lewis Battles — an exemplary critical edition of *De Clementia* (Leiden 1969).

We mention André Hugo at the end of our presentation of the six types partly so that we may honour a scholar who died too young, leaving a sizable gap which will not be readily filled in the ranks of international scholarship; and partly because his work shows in a nutshell the extent to which the historical method can help us to demythologize long-venerated Calvin images and allow us ultimately to bridge the divide between the dogmatic and the anti-dogmatic types, orthodox veneration and anti-orthodox iconoclasm.

II.

In the second part of this presentation I intend to touch upon some six key issues which deserve our renewed attention in view of new developments in the field.

Their common scope can perhaps best be designated as "Calvin's critique of Calvinism". As a minority group in a divided world Calvinism is understandably inclined to assume an apologetic attitude, to defend the status quo and to point proudly to the achievements of Calvinistic principles and institutions. An assessment of these from the perspective of Calvin may well provide us with a platform for reorientation, renewal and reform. At the same time, recent research may show us the limits of Calvin himself, the respects in which he was a product of circumstances that do not apply to us to the same extent.

1. *Calvin the Humanist.* Calvin as the twenty-three year old commentator on Seneca is not yet the reformer; as a matter of fact he does not yet see how reform can be possible without detriment to the Church Catholic. Indeed, as Hugo has pointed out, the writing of this commentary may well have "served him as a temporary means of escape from the inner conflict occasioned by that problem".[4] But in 1532, in this year before his conversion — and that means before his discovery that the Church Catholic is a community of believers obedient to the Word of God rather than to the Church of Rome — Calvin placed himself within the ranks of those who were

called the *humanistae theologizantes*. In a decree of 22 August 1523 the Sorbonne had decided "that all new translations of the Bible made from Hebrew or Greek into Latin were of no value to the Church, but were pernicious", a decree confirmed by the Council of Trent in 1546. In 1532 Calvin opted for the 'resourcement', the renewal, of the human spirit through a return to the classical sources; in 1533 he found that 'resourcement' in the Scriptures as providing access to the life of the Spirit. For us it is important to realize that it would be a mistake to play off Calvin the Christian against Calvin the humanist scholar. From the very beginning stages of Calvinism these two, the campaign against obscurantism and the struggle for reform of the Church, belong together. Where they are separated an orthodoxy is bound to emerge which is blind to the needs of the mind and the body alike, and which isolates the Church from society.

2. *Renewal and the unity of the Church.* Calvin could very well have become a 'Nicodemian' or an Erasmian Christian, avoiding confrontation *(tumultus!)* and trusting that the new culture of the mind would suffice for the reform of the Church. But Calvin, the student of law — even in that last year of 1532—1533 in Orleans — carried his legal interests over into his study of theology and continued to be concerned with structures, organizations, and politics as the *Ordonnances Ecclésiastiques*, as well as Book IV of the *Institutes*, document.

In a very bold and — to use an epithet seldom applied in a scholarly presentation — a wise chapter in the volume honouring Paul Oskar Kristeller on his 70th birthday, William Bouwsma discusses the tension between two thrusts in humanism, between two spirits in one breast, the 'Stoic' and the 'Augustinian' elements: on the one hand, Stoic consolation and on the other, the Augustinian call for social engagement and political action.[5] Writing on "The Two faces of Humanism", he observes: "Humanists of more Stoic tendencies, like Erasmus, seem to have been less likely to become Protestants than those of the more Augustinian kind. But the more Augustinian humanist might end up in either the Protestant or Catholic camp".[6]

Why then did the 'Augustinian' Calvin end up becoming a Protestant? As the letter to Cardinal Sadoleto (1539) indicates, it was the doctrine of the Church which proved to be the decisive locus in Calvin's conversion. Augustinianism, Biblical studies and the freedom-hungry protest against tyranny as voiced in his commentary on Seneca were all factors in this event. Yet most importantly in this combination the possibility of opting out of reality and sublimating the longing for the renewal of the Church through the escape hatch of the invisible Church was excluded. For the whole Reformed tradition it was to be of lasting importance that for Calvin it is impossible to participate in the Church Catholic of the Creed without also participating in the local, visible church. At times in Calvinism this had led to an overemphasis on the completeness of the *ecclesia loci*. But Calvin's vision blocks that kind of cheap ecumenism which transcends and escapes the hardships of urgent Chuch reform by reference to the invisible Church universal. Within this context, Calvinism has striven from its very beginning for Church unity in faith and order. But it should be added that at the same time Calvinism has suffered most from splinter groups which absolutized their own local traditions. Here I discern the greatest threat resulting from the presently disrupted relations between the churches in this country and the World Council of Churches. Withdrawal can be the necessary attitude over against a political organization, but in the Church of Christ the truly Calvinist course of action is to hang on, to seek communion and to provide for communication — till the partner-churches proceed with *de facto* excommunication... much to their own detriment.

3. *Conversion and the Eucharist*. A point of seemingly less immediate interest concerns the two short Latin words "subita conversio". Calvin himself uses these words in his Psalms Commentary of 1559 to describe his conversion.[7] Taken literally, the phrase means "sudden conversion" and it has been understood in this sense by those inside and outside of the Reformed family who have seen in Calvin the divinely ordained prototype of conversion. True conversion has to be sudden, datable; yes, indeed, 'clockable', and those who could not pass this test could not be part of the fold.

Much research has been directed toward understanding this reference to conversion. As a matter of fact, the right understanding of the even smaller word 'subita' could have helped decisively in this effort. Throughout the Middle Ages "subita" marks the work of God in contrast to the time-consuming achievements of man. "Subita" does not refer to a time-unit but to the divine agent, to the vertical in contrast to the horizontal dimension.

Conversion is, as Calvin likes to emphasize, penance, which in turn is the work of the Holy Spirit and which lasts as long as life itself. Conversion cannot be made into an emotional proof of one's belonging to the elect.

The gravest danger, however, proved ultimately not to lurk in a Calvinistic pietism — which I am prepared to defend as the precious core of the Reformed tradition — but in an elitist doctrine of the Eucharist. The "Half-Way Covenant" of the New England Pu-ritans documents[8] how this central sacrament and focal point of Calvin's theology is debased into a sign of progress by the Saints, instead of being regarded as the necessary food for faith — essential for survival on the trek towards the Kingdom.

4. *Scripture and Science.* In 1973 when the 500th anniversary of the birth of Nicolaus Copernicus was celebrated, numerous articles utilized the occasion in order to associate Calvin — as well as the other reformers — with obscurantism. The words of Thomas S. Kuhn were readily quoted: "Protestant leaders like Luther, Calvin and Melanchton led in citing Scripture against Copernicus and in urging the repression of Copernicans".[9]

R. Hooykaas has eloquently opposed the myth that Calvin mentioned and rejected Copernicus in his works: "There is no lie so good as the precise and well-detailed one and this one has been repeated again and again, quotation marks included, by writers on the history of science, who evidently did not make the effort to verify the statement. For fifteen years, I have pointed out in several periodicals concerned with the history of science that the 'quotation' from Calvin is imaginary and that Calvin never men-tioned Copernicus; but the legend dies hard".[10]

The reason why the voices of historians were not heeded is no mystery: it was not Calvin, but some of his followers who con-strued a division between faith and science which tragically forced many a Christian to choose between the two. Hence Calvinists themselves gave credence to this distortion of Calvin.

As far as Calvin himself is concerned, in his commentary on Genesis he points out that the story of creation does not compete with "the great art of astronomy", but that it accommodates and speaks in terms of the unlettered *idiota,* the man in the street.[11]

In the name of Calvin much damage has been done in later times and stores of faith and piety have been sacrificed on the altar of rigid inspiration theories. Calvin's exegetical methods were far ahead of his own time; it is our task not to fall behind him today.

5. *Piety between Theology and Moralism.* My fifth point concerns that elusive entity best called the spirituality of Calvin. It has often been argued that the influence of the *Devotio moderna* (Collège de Montaiguy and its principal since 1483, John Standonck!) extends through Calvin far into the Reformation period. And indeed, it is remarkable that a strong Calvinism flourished most easily in those areas which had been centers of the *Devotio moderna:* the Low Countries and the Rhine valley.

However, the more we are able to grasp what it is that characterizes this late medieval reform movement, the better we are able
to see some of the unique characteristics in Calvin's spirituality.
While *devotio* stood for the fundamental disposition toward God
as well as for an attitude of contempt toward the world, *pietas,*
Calvin's key word, represents the life of sanctification through intensive involvement in this world. It is another sign of ecumenical
openness in Reformation studies[12] that it was a Jesuit, Father Lucien
Richard, who made a major advance at this point.[13] He argued that
Calvin's *pietas* stands for a new spirituality which is grounded
in his understanding of the knowledge of God. Piety is derived
simultaneously from the Word of God and the internal testimony
of the Spirit. "Simultaneously" is to be underlined since the Spirit
provides that inwardness and personalism which are also to be
found in the *Devotio moderna.* But at the same time this form of
spiritual communication is set in the objective context of theological knowledge of the Word of God. Thus, Calvin's spirituality
differs radically from that of the *Devotio moderna* on three essential points. First, it is a spirituality of service to the world; second,
it is based on a new Word-directed religious epistemology; and
third, it stresses the inner unity of Christian life and theology.[14]
In those instances where Calvin's spirituality has given way to
Calvinist morality, it has relapsed into the ethics of the *Devotio
moderna.* We have a clear task of reform ahead of us here.

6. *Calvinism and the democratic ideal.* Our last point concerns the
most highly sensitive issue of the relation of Calvin to democracy.[15]
I begin here with some quotations which document the radically
opposing interpretations which have been applied to Calvin: "Calvin
was as much in favor of the democratic form as he was opposed
to the monarchical one".

"Calvin was a great propagator of democracy, but he energe-
tically tried to ward off its abuses and excesses". — Émile Doumergue.

"From considering only his political ideas, one would certainly
be entitled to conclude that Calvin was not a precursor of modern
democracy". — Charles Mercier.

"If Calvin mixes democratic elements with aristocratic constitutions, he nevertheless remains completely foreign to the dogmas
of modern democracy ... he does not believe either in popular
sovereignty or in individual rights". — Marc-Edouard Chenevière.

" 'Democracy' is not a term in favor with Calvin. He does not
advocate democracy in and of itself: he fears its deterioration into
anarchy. Nevertheless, his notion of 'aristocracy tempered by democracy' approaches our conception of representative democracy. It

becomes unmistakably clear in his later writings that the ideal basis of government is election by the citizens". — John T. McNeill.

The key to this apparent mystery of these many interpretations is held once again by the historian who is prepared to place Calvin in the context of his time. In this respect I find most validity in the conclusion of Hans Baron: "Calvinist political thought helped more than any other tendency of the time to prevent a full victory of absolutism, and to prepare the way for constitutional and even republican ideas".[16] Michael Walzer has demonstrated the transition from the sixteenth to the seventeenth and following centuries: "What Calvinists said of the saint, other men would later say of the citizen: the same sense of civic virtue, of discipline and duty lies behind the two names".[17]

Yet, in working through the sources I have come to the conclusion that Calvin's own ideal of state government is best described in terms of a form of aristocracy. This is marginally tempered by group interests to which we may validly assign the name 'democratic expressions'. To put it crudely, either reiterating Calvin or using his political views as a blueprint for contemporary society would spell sheer tyranny,[18] the very state of affairs he had challenged as a young humanist. As was the case in each of the previous five aspects I have discussed, this shows us once again that to reiterate is the surest path to distortion.

Allow me to conclude with a quotation from Calvin himself, a statement which bears reiteration because it reveals the living centre of his piety and faith. In his sermon on II Sam. v. 4 — 'David reigned forty years' — Calvin notes that this was by no means an unchallenged or uninterrupted reign: 'ce n'a pas esté du premier coup en perfection'. Then he proceeds ('c'es pour nous, que cecy est ecrit') to apply this text to the contemporary rule of God, giving here his religious testament, which is characteristically at the same time a political eschatology:[19]

" ... though we know that God rules, yet insofar as our Lord Jesus Christ is hidden in him and his very reign is hidden in this world, it has no splendour but it is little esteemed, indeed rejected by the majority. Therefore, we should find it not at all strange that our Lord Jesus Christ, though he has been established as King by God his Father, does not at all have the authority among men which He is entitled to. Furthermore, today there is no certain time limit ('terme' = kairos) indicated to us. When we see the rule of our Lord Jesus Christ is limited, since there is only a handful of people who have accepted him, and since for every one city which has received the Gospel there are large countries where idolatry rules, —

when we thus see that the rule of Jesus Christ is so small and despised according to the world, let us cast our eyes upon this figure which is given us here (in the rule of David), and let us await the end (terme), which God knows, for it is hidden to us. I say, let us await in patience, till his Kingdom is established in perfection and God gathers those who are dispersed, restores what is dissipated and sets in order what is confused."

"...let us not desist, as far as it is in us, from praying to God that he advances and enlarges (his Kingdom) and that each man apply to this with all his power; and let us allow ourselves to be governed by him in such a way that he is always glorified in us, both in life and in death."

This text stems from Calvin's last sermons which were not published till recently and hence virtually 'lost'. Yet with this testament of faith and piety in hand, we are in a position to answer the question raised in the theme of this conference quoted at the beginning of this paper.

In this faith I find the bulwark for the Kingdom of God — present and future.

---

1 For a more elaborate discussion of the first three schools I refer to Henry Van der Goot: "A typology of 'Schools' of Calvin interpretation in 19th and 20th century theology", prepared for the University of Toronto.
2 Nijkerk, s.a. (1943), p. 147.
3 *Calvijn en Seneca. Een inleidende studie van Calvijn's Commentaar op Seneca, De Clementia, anno 1532* (Groningen-Djakarta, 1957).
4 *Ed. cit.*, p. 16*
5 *Itinerarium Italicum. The Profile of the Italian Renaissance in the Mirror of its European Transformations. Dedicated to Paul Oskar Kristeller*, H. A. Oberman with Th. A. Brady, Jr., eds. (Leiden, 1975), pp. 3—60; 56.
6 *Ibid.*, p. 57.
7 "...subita conversione ad docilitatem subiget". *Opera Calvini* 31, 22 f. Cf. most recently A. Ganoczy: *Le jeune Calvin. Genése et Evolution de sa vocation réformatrice* (Wiesbaden, 1966), pp. 272—304; 298.
8 Cf. E. Brooks Holifield: *The Covenant sealed: The Development of Puritan Sacramental Theology in Old and New England, 1570—1720* (New Haven, 1974).
9 *The Copernican Revolution* (Cambridge, Mass., 1957), p. 196.
10 *Religion and the Rise of Modern Science* (Edinburgh-London, 1972), p. 121.
11 *Calvini Opera* 23, 20—22.
12 Cf. R. Bäumer: "Das katholische Calvinbild" in H. Jedin, R. Bäumer: *Die Erforschung der kirchlichen Reformationsgeschichte seit 1876 und 1931* (Darmstadt, 1975), pp. 99—102. This survey omits the significant contribution by L. G. M. Alting van Geusau: *Die Lehre von der Kindertaufe bei Calvin* (Bilthoven-Mainz, 1962).
13 *The Spirituality of John Calvin* (Atlanta, 1974).
14 Cf. the appreciative review by Joseph N. Tylenda, S. J. in *Theological*

Studies 36 (1975), pp. 356—358.

15 For literature see the excellent workbook by Robert M. Kingdon and Robert D. Linder: *Calvin and Calvinism. Sources of Democracy?* (Lexington, 1970). The following quotations here on p. XIII f.

16 "Calvinist republicanism and its historical roots", *Church History* 8 (1939), pp. 30—41; 41.

17 *The Revolution of the Saints* (Cambridge, Mass., 1965), p. 2.

18 Basil Hall's words of caution — à propos W. Fred Graham: *The Constructive Revolutionary: John Calvin and his Socio-Economic Impact* (Richmond, Va., 1971) — are to the point: "...he (Calvin) was a party to reducing the small amount of democratic procedure allowed". "A sixteenth-century miscellany", *The Journal of Ecclesiastical History* 26 (1975), pp. 309—321; 318.

19 *Supplementa Calvinia* I, 105, 34—36. Cf. my "The 'Extra' Dimension in the Theology of Calvin", *The Journal of Ecclesiastical History* 21 (1970), pp. 43—64; 46.

The conflict between the Lutheran and Calvinistic churches about the relevance of faith for public life and the consequences of this conflict for Calvinistic research

Dr. R. Mokrosch

1. *General and historical summary of the conflict*

The age-old dispute between Lutheran and Calvinistic churches about the relevance of the reformatory faith for public life had begun even before Calvinism was born. I refer to the dispute of the *First Generation of the Reformation* about the issue, whether "justification solely through faith without the works of the law", was retarding or promoting the shaping of public Christian life. Is the principle of justification a reformatory principle of the entire organization of public life or has it nothing to do with it? Does it reform all spheres of public life, such as culture, economy, politics, education and science, or does it only reform the inner-being of man? The left wing of the reformers, e.g. Thomas Münter,[1] the farmers,[2] the Anabaptists[3] etc., put this question to the Lutherans long before Calvin. They demanded a "consequent reformation". They were not content with a reform of the faith, which would at best bring about the reform of the church and the sacraments. They insisted on a reform of the entire feudal system and the entire monarchical authority. The reform of the inner being should be accompanied by the reform of external, public life.

Precisely this demand was also the focal point of the *Second Generation of the Reformation,* the reformation of Calvin in Geneva. To be sure, Calvin had, as far as contents were concerned, nothing in common with the left front of the reformation, but in a formal respect he had exactly the same aim: the reform of the entire public life by virtue of the reform of faith. His interest was transferred from the doctrine of justification to ecclesiology and ethics.[4] Church discipline, church order, education and deaconal duties within the context of the Geneva Refugee-and-poverty-relief-program, were at the center of his activity.[5] He was not content to reform simply one section of human life, but was concerned with the reformation of all of public life.

This public relevance of Calvinistic theology became, for the *Third, Fourth and subsequent generations* a common heritage, which held the most disparate reformed trends together under the vague common concept of "Calvinism".

No matter how different the doctrines, liturgies, ethical concepts and the traditions of the Huguenots, Congregationalists, Puritans, Presbyterians or the Waldensians were — they all felt themselves committed to this heritage of Calvin: not only a reform of doctrine, but also of life; not only a reform of the church but also of the community. This claim exposed them, as the permanently suppressed minority, to cruel persecution,[6] — while the Lutheran churches had long since compromised with the authorities on the basis of "sovereign church government":[7] they had agreed to a fine distinction between an internal church government by the ministers on the one hand which concerned only the spiritual life, and an external church authority by the provincial governor on the other hand, which concerned external public life. They had thus surrendered all means of direct influence on the organization of public life. Very rarely the Calvinists attacked them for this attitude, but they in return attacked the Calvinists all the more vehemently. To the orthodox Lutheranism of the 17th and 18th centuries, it was inconceivable why the Calvinists allowed themselves to be persecuted more frequently on account of political and social reasons than dogmatic principles.

In *recent times*, this conflict between Lutherans and members of the reformed church about the relevance of Calvinism for public life, has once again revived.[8] In the first years after the outbreak of 1945, the question was passionately discussed — at least in Germany — whether after the failure of christianity and the churches, christian policy, christian social work and christian education were even permissible. The Lutheran churches saw themselves corroborated, they never wished direct influence, but only indirect influence over politics, social work and education. They had always warned against a christianizing and christian penetration of public life. The Reformed churches, on the other hand, never relinquished their claim to a christian formation of public life; they wished to make good again that which they had been guilty of during the Nazi regime. Four examples should sufficiently explain the contrast between the Lutheran and Calvinistic churches during the *1950's and 1960's*.

(1) During the debate on rearmament and the development of atomic power at the beginning of the 1950's, the Calvinists radically declined any form of conventional or atomic rearmament (on account of their consequential christian policy[9]), while the Lutherans, owing to their policies of political insight without christian penetration, agreed to rearmament.

(2) It was exactly the opposite in the case of the vehement dispute over confessional schools and confessional social institutions at the end of the 1950's. While the Calvinists on account of their consistent social and educational policies, defended the old confessional schools and institutions, the Lutherans on the other hand, abandoned them on the grounds of social and pedagogic principles.[10]

(3) In the 1960's both confessions, in spite of their ecumenical alliance, united on the question of the anti-racial programme, the violence- and resistance thesis, the development and educational assistance programmes of the ecumenical council of churches: the German Calvinists, on account of their christian attitude on politics, welcomed the actions of the ecumenical council; the Lutheran Churches, on the other hand, owing to their policy of non-interference concerning christian penetration, reacted with reserve and scepticism.[11]

(4) Also in the wider area of "the democratization of church and community", polarization was unavoidable: while the Calvinists, in accordance with their principle of "the kingdom of all believers", generally supported this process, the Lutherans reverted to their principle of "priesthood of all believers" and let kings remain kings and subjects remain subjects.

The dispute between Lutherans and Calvinists on the relevance of faith for public life, also has theoretical origins and different practical results: the Lutheran Churches wish to help the inner law of political, social and pedagogical processes free of christian penetration. They therefore tend to *keep* church and state, christianity and public life *apart*. The practical results are, as history has proved, a most conservative political attitude but an openmindedness in social and pedagogic matters. The Calvinistic churches, on the other hand, go for consistently christian politics, social work and education in order to organize public life on a christian basis. They thus tend toward a close *relationship* between church and state, and between christianity and public life. The practical results of this attitude are — as the history of at least the German Calvinists has proved — a highly receptive, progressive policy, but a differentiated conservative attitude in the social and pedagogic spheres.

384

These various opinions of the Lutheran and Calvinistic churches in public life, naturally have consequences for their research institutes and their public financing. Before I discuss these consequences, however, I should like to mention a few key words related to the special and actual problems of the conflict, with reference to the general and historic summary of this struggle. By means of the examples of (a) Calvinistic-Christian policy, (b) Calvinistic-Christian social work and (c) Calvinistic-Christian education, I should like to illustrate the Calvinist's criticism of the world and the Lutheran criticism of this Calvinistic criticism.

2. *Special and actual problems of the conflict*

2.1. Calvinistic-Christian policy[12] is based upon three pillars: on the claim of the Lordship of Christ over church *and* state, on the concept of the kingship of all believers, and on the covenant of the Old Testament. All three pillars lay down certain norms for Christian policy.

The future Lordship of Christ, according to the opinion of the Calvinists, will not only apply to the church but also to the state. State and church are only different educational instruments of God, preparatory to the kingship of Christ. In the sense of a "Zweireichelehre" (two-realm doctrine) they are, admittedly, personally and jurisdictionally different, but they have to watch, like two eyes, over the same subject matter: namely over the *christianity of the state* and over the *orthodoxy of the church.* The church must orientate itself in accordance with this norm of Christian policy. It may not leave the state to its own devices.

The second pillar is the *Kingdom of all believers,* which expects from every christian the political responsibility of a king. Not only one person, but all people are an image and an instrument of God. This conception gave birth to the Geneva aristocracy and later became the cradle of modern democracy. It demands from every believer the practice of Christian policy in accordance with *democratic* norms.

The third pillar is the *covenant* of the Old Testament. Exactly as God sealed a covenant with man, so too mankind should amongst themselves and with God seal a covenant in the form of a constitution. Constitutions have religious importance for Calvinists. Should they be violated, then resistance, as prescribed by the Scottish Confession of 1560, Article 14, should be offered and if necessary by means of violence. *Loyalty to the constitution,* or should the occasion arise, *resistance* is expected of each Calvinist.

Christian-Calvinistic policy is based upon these three pillars with their three norms: Christian state on the basis of the sovereignty of Christ, democracy on the basis of the kingdom of all believers and loyalty to the constitution or resistance on the basis of the covenant.

The opposition of the Lutherans is apparent: they reject a Christian state, do not consider the democratic form of state as eternally valid and forbid violent resistance. Should the Christian policy become a christianized, i.e. Christian ideological policy, their criticism is legitimate. But it is illegitimate should it cripple the struggle of the Calvinists against governments which violate their own constitution and democracy and mock the sovereignty of Christ.

2.2. Calvinistic-Christian social work[13] is not based upon the need of visible signs for the assurance of election. Max Weber's famous thesis of the relationship between puritanical faith in election and capitalistic commercial zeal has often been proved false in theory and practice. That, however, does not imply that Calvinistic social work has nothing to do with election: the chosen one desires to pass on the mercy bestowed upon him by God. The knowledge of his election which has not made him arrogant but humble, automatically leads him to social service. This social service is of a Christian nature because the chosen one carries out God's divine will ("Heilsplan") in accordance with Calvin's *providentia Dei* doctrine (the doctrine of the providence of God). The assurance of election is the first root of Christian social work in Calvinism.

A second root is *biblical ethics*. Calvinism has accepted neither the law of nature nor a natural morality, but solely the Bible as a source for its social work. It has never been interpreted biblically but always spiritually. The Calvinists have interpreted the words of Christ: "Give without receiving" concerning the dispute on tax-taking, in such a way that only from the rich and not from the poor, may tax be taken. Biblical ethics were adapted to the prevailing social and economic situation, without sacrificing its spirit.

A third and final root of Calvinistic social work is the Calvinistic *vocational understanding*. Every occupation and not only priesthood, as was the case during the Middle Ages, is service to God. Each occupation should serve God and fellow-man and is thus Christian social service.

The consciousness of election, biblical ethics and social vocational understanding are the roots which have produced the widely ramified tree of a Calvinistic social order (cf. the "Elberfelder-system"). They carry a confessional and Christian stamp, but they are not ideological.

The scepticism of Lutheran social ethics once more directs itself against the *Christian credentials* of social work: Should social work adjust itself according to purely Christian norms, it could possibly violate social needs. In the third world for instance, purely Christian social work would totally overwhelm native culture. Furthermore, purely Christian social work could always be exposed to the danger of eventually attributing the assurance of election and justification to their social success.

The claim of these objections is to be borne in mind: Calvinistic-Christian social work was only too often misused to promote a colonial import of Christianity; and social successes were often regarded as visual proof of election. This, however, does not exclude the claim to specific Christian social work in accordance with social orders. Christians must remain the salt of the earth, even when they often resemble sugar.

2.3. Calvinistic-Christian education[14] is the crux of Calvinistic public work. Because the chosen and the justified should always progress in sanctification, they must be educated throughout their lives, i.e. not merely as youths but also as adults. Church and State in conformity with Calvinist tradition are co-operatively responsible for this education in school, in adult catechism and in church order and discipline. Calvinistic churches in western democracies reluctantly and with heavy hearts agreed to the separation into a state-and-church-responsibility in the field of *general* education. Up to this day, however, they vehemently oppose the separation of state and church in religious education, because they are unable to distinguish between preaching and religious teaching. Religious education is, as far as they are concerned, proclamation, and general education is educating towards becoming children of God. Therefore, every form of education should be Christian, even though it be the responsibility of the State.

The Lutheran pedagogues and the theological pedagogues, in agreement with practically all educational planners, are allergic to this pedagogical conception — at least in the Federal Republic of Germany. The general trend of Western European educational systems tends towards deconfessionalizing schools and universities, in order to establish public "schools for all". Even religious education in schools should be separated from the influence of churches and confessions.

The Lutheran churches obviously opposed the latter tendency but they wholeheartedly support the first tendency. This is brought about by their Lutheran heritage: behind every form of Christian education they suspect the attempt at a salvation-pedagogical selfjustification. It was specifically this "Education to become children of God" which Luther opposed so passionately in the Catholic educational concept (in the *via antiqua* and in the *devotio moderna)* and in the humanistic educational ideal. To him becoming a child of God could only be a gift and could never be attained by education.

Because of this uneasy heritage the Lutheran churches have admittedly at an early stage, sacrificed strategically important commanding positions, but by means of this, they have also done the educational policy a great service; educational planning in Europe has, on account of the emancipation from the church, received its impetus and the education policy in the third world was and is, constantly warned by the Lutheran educational planners against the import of European-Christian patterns of life and thought.

But this warning against every form of the Christianizing of education naturally has its limits where it hinders the Christian élan of more recent emancipatory educational institutions. If Christian education is executed — inter-confessionally and ecumenically: both these conditions should indeed be complied with — then it should not be unnecessarily retarded, but exclusively demanded.

3. *Consequences of the dispute in Calvinism-research*

In a concluding resumé, I should like to distinguish between the *status quo* of Calvinism-research in Germany and the *status* as it should be in future.

The *status quo* is portrayed by the sober statement that we in Germany admittedly have various Calvinistic theologians, but only two institutions which concern themselves with Calvinism-research: Firstly there is our Institute for the Late Middle Ages and Reformation in Tübingen, where under the leadership of Prof. Oberman theological and profane-historical interweaving of Calvinistic theology, — especially Calvinistic ecclesiology, church-order and church discipline — and Calvinistic legal thought in the late middle ages, are investigated. Secondly, the institute in Würzburg which, under the leadership of Alexandre Ganoczy, investigates the hermeneutic of Calvin in his exegetical writings and the legal thought in his church orders and political writings. There is no other institute in Germany! To complete the meagre extent of this yield, it must be mentioned that Prof. Oberman is Dutch and A. Ganoczy is a Hungarian Catholic. Whatever institutionalized Calvin research exists, is moreover imported.

It probably borders on speculation, should one consider this meagre sphere of research as a result of the public relevance of Calvinism — because there is decidedly more institutionalized Luther-research —, but I cannot stifle this speculation: a theological conception which is *not* publically so relevant as that of Calvinism, is certainly sooner and more willingly supported by the secularized public. Indeed, it must be added, that only 17 percent of the German Protestants are Calvinists, but that too I consider a result of the German tendency not to allow the Church too much influence in public life. To me, it seems no coincidence that it should have been the Catholics who have taken a protective interest in Calvinism-research.

Finally, allow me, in view of this meagre *status quo,* to enumerate *seven requirements,* which could be important for the *extension of Calvinistic research in future.*

1. Calvin and Calvinism-research must be more vigorously pursued there where the relevance of Protestant belief for the construction of public life is negated or affirmed, doubted or only half-heartedly supported.

2. This research receives its legitimacy from this actual social problem which should not induce the manufacturing of instant results, but exactly the opposite, namely a long-term, historically correct assignment.

3. Calvin and Calvinism-research should always go hand in hand, because no reformer such as Calvin can be researched as solely reflected in his historical influence.

4. Calvin and Calvinistic theology may never be researched as pure history of ideas, but should always be researched as the history of the church, in profane history, i.e., social history, economical history, cultural history etc. This claim results from their personal demand to shape public life.

5. Calvin- and Calvinistic thought must — as is the case with the Tübingen Institute — be researched in its late middle age interweaving and must, if necessary, be separated from it. Specifically owing to the fact that this reformatory thought is so intimately amalgamated with public life, it has adapted numerous relics from late medieval legal thought and city life.

6. Calvin and Calvinism-research should, as in Tübingen, be executed inter-confessionally and not confessionally — specifically because Calvin is justly considered the "Man of the evangelical union".

7. Institutionalized, Calvin and Calvinism-research should, if possible, be co-ordinated with theological education and/or Christian public work. Only thus can the results of this research be tested and revised in public.

---

1 Thomas Müntzer repeatedly accuses Luther and the Wittenberg Reformers of having an "untried faith" and believing in a "sweet Jesus". In place of this he demands a "faith proven through suffering" and a belief in a

"bitter Christ" (cf., for example, "Vom getichten Glauben", 1524, §§2.11.14, G. Franz: *Gesamtausgabe* and "Protestation odder Empietung", 1524, §5, Franz). I consider this contrast to be a precursor of the subsequent one between "inwardness" and "outwardness". This is supported by Müntzer's charge that the Lutherans have a "beschissene Demut". The assumption that Müntzer in the last months of his life (beginning first in August, 1524, not before!) aspired to a reform of the entire magistracy stems from his so-called "Sermon to the Princes" in 1524 (cf. especially the demand for a transference of power from the princes to the people: "Das Schwert ist notwendig, um die Gottlosen zu vertilgen, Rom. 13 : 4. Damit das recht geschehe, sollen das unsere Väter, die treuen Fürsten, tun, die Christus mit uns bekennen. Wenn sie das aber nicht tun, so wird ihnen das Schwert genommen werden," Franz) and his participation beginning in March, 1525 in the Peasants' Revolt in Thuringia.

2   The various articles of the peasants from the year 1525 (for example, the Twelve Memmingen Articles, the Letter of Articles by the Black Forest Peasants, the Articles of the Stühlinger Peasants, the Mühlhausen Articles, the Allgau Articles, the Erfurt Articles, the Frankish Articles) along with the carrying through of the "new law" often demand the reinstating of the old (feudal) law". Thus, one can in no way designate the Peasants' Revolt as purely an "anti-feudal movement". However, common to all the peasants is the demand for a fundamental reform of the magistracy and the law.

3   The Anabaptist movement — at least in the form in which we encounter it in the 1527 Manifesto and in Michael Sattler's "Schleitheim Articles" (cf., especially Article 6, "Vom Schwert") — advanced no claim for a public and revolutionary enactment of its reform demands for church and state. It is much more the case that the Anabaptists consistently preached non-violence (cf. C. Baumann: *Gewaltlosigkeit im Täufertum*, Leiden, 1969). This in no way means that their reform demands are to be taken less seriously than those of Müntzer and the peasants.

4   This 'shifting of importance' does not appear in the first version of the *Institutes* in 1536, but it does occur in the famous tract of 1539 against Cardinal Sadoleto (cf. *Calvini opera selecta,* ed. Petrus Barth, vol. 1, pp. 457—489, esp. pp. 464—471).

5   Cf. the appropriate paragraphs in the "Ordonnances ecclesiastiques" of 1541 and in the Geneva Church Ordinances of 1561.

6   A few historical examples: The anti-episcopal struggle of the Scottish and English Presbyterians before and during the English Revolution was a fight for freedom against secular as well as ecclesiastical absolutism. The Calvinist ecclesiology of John Knox (cf. for a comparison of Knox's ecclesiology with that of Calvin, V. E. d'Assonville: *John Knox and the Institutes of Calvin* (Durban-Pretoria, 1968), chap. 8) and that of Thomas Cartwright had political implications which emerged fully only in the Puritans' struggle for the freedom of Parliament and of religion. The best insight into the social and political reform tendencies of the seventeenth-century Huguenots comes from the history of the Huguenots' tribulations written by their best theologian, Jean Claude, in 1686, or shortly after the revocation (1685) of the Edict of Nantes (1598): "Plaintes des protestants cruellements opprimés dans le royaume de France". The numerous Huguenot educational institutions established since the mid-seventeenth century — such as their Berlin school and at the court of

Friedrich William I — display the integral reform-mindedness of the Huguenots. — The social-political reform tendencies of the Waldensians in Switzerland and the Piedmont, though not so pronounced, can be traced in particular characteristics. Cf. Franz Lau: „Die Geschichte der Waldenser", *Evangelische Diaspora*, 26 (1955), 218—234; Valdo Vinay: "Der Anschluss der romanischen Waldenser und die Reformation und seine theologische Bedeutung", *Theologische Literaturzeitung*, 87 (1962), 89—100. W. Wattenbach: *Über die Inquisition gegen die Waldenser in Pommern und Brandenburg*, Berlin, 1887; and W. Erk: *Waldenser, Geschichte und Gegenwart*, Frankfurt 1971.

7 On the history of the territorial church government from the Confession of Augsburg (1530) to the Prussian General Code of 1794, see the ever useful treatment by K. Rieker: *Die rechtliche Stellung der evangelischen Kirche Deutschlands* (1893).

8 The following draws on the churches' official statements in the forms of opinions, synodal acts and declarations, and position papers by the churches' governing bodies concerning current social and political problems since the end of World War II. Because most of these were never printed, I can cite them only indirectly.

9 The co-signers of the famous "Atom-Memorandum" by Professor Hahn, the nuclear physicist, were mostly Reformed Christians.

10 See the debates which took place in the Rhenish Evangelical Church under the presidency of Beckmann.

11 See the declaration of the VELKD (= Vereinigte Evangelisch-Lutherischen Kirchen Deutschlands) to the "Anti-racism Program" in 1968/69.

12 On the following see the mass of secondary literature, esp. J. Moltmann: „Die Ethik des Calvismus", in his *Das Experiment Hoffnung* (Munich, 1974), pp. 131—144; and his *Calvin-Studien* (Neukirchen-Vluyn, 1959), pp. 310—333. Also, K. H. Esser: "Demokratie und Kirche am Beispiel Calvins", *ZRP*, 26 (1971).

13 Relevant here are André Biéler's writings for and lectures to various committees of the World Council of Churches, and esp. his "Gottes Gebot und der Hunger der Welt". *Calvins Sozialethik*, Polis, vol. 24 (Zurich, 1966).

14 See R. Hedtke: *Erziehung durch die Kirche bei Calvin*, Pädagogische Forschungen des Comenius-Instituts, Heidelberg, 1969.

On Calviniana literature

The study done by the Institute for the Advancement of Calvinism

Dr. D. Kempff

1. *Introduction*

At the Potchefstroom University for Christian Higher Education there are various institutes. The aim of such an institute is that it specialises in a special area or in a special direction. In accord with the essential character of this university, there is also an institution called the Institute for the Advancement of Calvinism. True to the thought-climate of John Calvin himself, this Institute in its advancement of Calvinism does not want to glorify some human being. Calvinism simply means a special Christian world and life view and could just as well be called reformed christianity. This will immediately become clear when we enter into the activities of this Institute.

2. *The Institute for the Advancement of Calvinism*

2.1. Character, aim and working procedure. The I.A.C. was established in 1966 and succeeded the work of the Calvinistic Foundation which was established in 1962. It started with a part-time director. In July 1974 a full-time director was appointed and the Institute received a centre of its own. It is an interfaculty institution, having representatives of all faculties in its council as well as representatives of the departments of Philosophy and Interdepartmental Philosophy, as well as from the Afrikaans Association for Calvinism.

A large part of the work of this Institute consists of stimulating studies and publishing results. By giving assignments to people, these people are stimulated in a specific direction or they are stimulated to think about a special research area. The results of this are made known in a wider circle.

The financing of the I.A.C. is done by the Potchefstroom University for Christian Higher Education.

2.2. Publications. The following publication activities can be mentioned:

2.2.1. Pamphlet series on important issues. Articles on topical matters, seen from a Calvinistic or Reformed Christian point in view by authorities in their respective fields, are circulated monthly. Up to September 1975, 95 issues have been published in Afrikaans and each month about 5 000 are sent to recipients free of charge. The addresses are mainly in South Africa. It is intended to issue some of these pamphlets in English too, for circulation here and abroad.

The title of No. 93, by prof. J. A. L. Taljaard, elucidates the series and its object. It reads (translated) *Christian-Calvinistic scientific endeavour: what it is not and what it desires to be.*

2.2.2. Brochures: The scope of these studies is bigger; the intention, however, is identical. They are in Afrikaans and are sold. Examples: *The Authority of Scripture* (S. C. W. Duvenage); *The Calvinist and Art* (P. D. van der Walt); *Human Rights* (J. D. van der Vyver). In preparation i.a. *The philosophy of the Idea of Creation* (H. G. Stoker), collected articles on *Pollution*, on the *Energy Crisis in South Africa*, on *Futurology*, etc.

2.2.3. Larger works. The I.A.C. aspires to publish more comprehensive works at least every five years. Two have been issued. In 1969: *Die atoomeeu — In U Lig* (The atomic age in the light of the Word of God). It has the character of a *Festschrift* on the occasion of the centenary of the P.U. for C.H.E. In 1974: *Reformasie en Revolusie* (Reformation and Revolution).

Both contain a minimum of 20 articles written by Calvinists here and from abroad, dealing with various subjects from a reformational point of view.

Plans for more extensive works are being considered, i.a. the papers read at this conference. Also a series on Christian scientific endeavour in the different scientific disciplines. This could include a bibliography on Christianity and the sciences. (More on this later in this paper. Cf. 5. Research: Christianity and the Sciences).

3. *Calviniana-research*

There was a suspicion that in South Africa people talk a lot about Calvin and Calvinism, but that study about him and his influence is necessary. That is why a large research project was planned in this connection, with the financial support of the Human Sciences Research Council.

About this research we can mention the following particulars:

3.1. A thorough listing was made of all relevant books in the library of the Potchefstroom University for Christian Higher Education. This includes articles in collections. Further, we have checked what other books in this field can be found in other South African libraries, in order thus to acquire the total picture of the available sources in our country. An almost complete catalogue was made of the available works. It is an alphabetical catalogue, mentioning authors, title, subjects, etc. This catalogue is available in the library of the Potchefstroom University for Christian Higher Education, at the I.A.C. and at the Human Sciences Research Council in Pretoria, so that any researcher can easily determine what book is available and where in our country.

At the same time, with the help of the Potchefstroom University Library, we paid attention to the acquisition of books that were not available and considered to be important.

3.2. A bibliographical study of Calvin and Calvinism was started. This was in continuation of a similar project that had been started earlier already. We mention in particular Alfred Erichson: *Bibliographia Calviniana* (1900, reprinted in 1960). It contains a bibliography of works by and about Calvin from the sixteenth century up to 1900. We can mention that this work is not complete, but its completion is receiving attention elsewhere. Then there is Wilhelm Niesel: *Calvin-Bibliographie, 1901—1959* (1961). This work contains about 1 600 entries of books and articles. The intention that we had was to do bibliographical research from 1959/1960 up to 1971. In the course of our research various things became clear, however:

3.2.1. Items from South Africa are seldom mentioned. For that reason we went into this area a lot deeper and the result was another I.A.C. publication in a series of Calvin-causeries: Kempff, D.: *Bibliography of South African Calviniana* (1973, 150 p's). Important items dated before 1959 have been placed in the international bibliography of which mention will be made later. (Cf. 4. A Calviniana-Bibliography.)

3.2.2. Research and checking indicated that Niesel's work has important shortcomings, for example, concerning theses which appeared in the U.S.A. and elsewhere before 1959 and also concerning various kinds of articles. That is why our research went back to 1900 and we in fact found many items that we included in our bibliography.

3.2.3. There did not exist systematised bibliographical information with respect to opponents of Calvin and fellow workers of his. Neither about his various influences on certain people and countries. For that reason we also paid attention to those people (for example the Huguenots, Butzer, Knox, Servet, Cranmer, Arminius) and countries up to about 1650. We have also collected information about the views on the direct influence of Calvin and his friends throughout the ages or concerning a direct discussion about Calvinism as such. But the application of Calvinistic principles in specific areas (for example, Calvinistic Philosophy) has been left out, in order to give attention to that in another research project.

394

3.2.4. Because the date of publication was postponed, the actual research has been continued, so that information of a very recent date could also be placed.

3.3. The result of this research was a publication by the I.A.C. and Brill in Leiden of Kempff, D.: *A bibliography of Calviniana 1959—1974.*

It appeared in 1975 and comprises 294 pages. The date *a quo* (1959) is in the light of what was mentioned above, not quite correct, even though the main emphasis is on that date and on the information that is *post Niesel*. Concerning the *ad quem* (1974), we can say that a few items of 1975 have been added. In any case there is a need for a succeeding volume or for a continuation of this kind of research and publication of its findings. Later we will have to say more about this. (Cf. 4. A Calviniana-Bibliography.)

3.4. As an aim of the Calviniana research of the I.A.C., we also pay attention to the following:

3.4.1. A series of Calvin causeries. The intention is to present annotated bibliographies about specific subjects and about material that is available in Potchefstroom and South Africa. As the collection grows, these publications will also grow in size and significance. The intention is to make knowledge of existing studies available in broader circles and also to offer an evaluation and in that way to stimulate study and research.

There have already appeared, in Afrikaans, causeries about Calvin's view of Scripture, Calvin on the State and law, and on Calvin and the ecumenical calling of the church.

It is our future intention to publish causeries about, for instance, Calvin and ethics, music, church and state, education, church government and discipline, culture, God, anthropology, etc.

4.3.2. Yet another large project which the I.A.C. will initiate is called: *The impact of Calvinism on South African society.*

This includes also the Reformational heritage of the 16th century and its roots in the pre-Reformation period and further back. As a scheme for this research the following main points can be mentioned:

◇ Reflection on fundamental principles of Calvinism (as a basis for the rest of the programme).

◇ Historical approach on the backgrounds of our Calvinistic heritage in Europe.

◇ The links between European and South African Calvinism during different phases of contact.

◇ The impact of Calvinism on different spheres of life in South Africa.

The results of this research will, as they become available, be published in a series called *Studies about the influence of Calvinism in South Africa*. At the end of this project (probably 1984) a synopsis of the results of research will appear in one or more volumes.

4. A Calviniana-Bibliography

It seems proper to present a few more particulars about *A Bibliography of Calviniana 1959—1974*.

4.1. Research about this started in South Africa and made use of all possible publications and sources. This includes larger bibliographical studies (for example L. R. de Koster: *Living themes in the thought of John Calvin)* and checking of literature lists in books and theses. It also included going through journals and journal indexes, for example: *Internationale Bibliographische Zeitschriften-verzeignis*.

4.2. With the aid of a bursary made available by the Human Sciences Research Council, this research was continued overseas. This called for visits to at least 45 libraries from the Vatican to the Library of Congress. In addition, material has been acquired from other libraries, bringing the total to 60. Direct aid has been received from several academics in various countries, of whom some are present here today.

4.3. Smaller and larger articles, of greater or lesser importance, have been included. In some countries this may be valuable, even if the scientific depth of the items is not very great. If we have erred, it is probably *per excessum* and not *per defectum*. It was our intention to be as complete as possible and in the final analyses, we collected more than 3 000 items.

4.4. An analysis and overview of the items and data in the bibliography will give you an idea of the importance of the contents and of the present condition of Calvin study in the world (all numbers are minima in die various categories):

◇ Theses before 1959: 45 for Ph.D. degrees and 53 for other degrees.
◇ From 1959: 100 theses for doctor's degrees and 30 for other degrees.
◇ 58 of these degrees were in Theology.
◇ Countries in which this kind of study was done are the following:

U.S.A. 125
France 29
Switzerland ..,... 18

Germany (Western) 15
Italy 8
Netherlands 7
South Africa 7
Scotland 6
England 5
Canada 5
Ireland 4
Austria 2
Wales 1
Sweden 1

◇ Articles before 1959 are 350 and after 1959, 1 000.

◇ There are 35 books before 1959 and from that date 100, excluding theses, while of 30 books reprints have appeared, excluding the actual works of Calvin himself.

This information is relevant only for the first part of the bibliography (works about Calvin).

4.5. The second part of this work deals with Calvinism.

◇ There are 120 items about Calvin's influence, 140 about the Reformation, 160 about Calvinism in general and other subjects such as Calvinism and the church, culture, authority.

◇ Various reformers who worked in close relationship to Calvin are entered with items on the number of pages mentioned: Beza (3), Brez (1), Bullinger (2), Butzer (11), Farel (1), Knox (4), Laski (1), Viret (1).

◇ Countries in which the influence of Calvin was noticeable and studies dedicated to that topic are U.S.A., Eastern Europe (3 pages), England (with various sub-headings), France (subdivided), Germany and Austria, Italy and Spain, The Netherlands (including Belgium), Scotland and Switzerland. The second part takes 110 pages or provides about 1 200 items.

5. Research: Christianity and the sciences

In the above-mentioned research about Calviniana we often came across material about the relationship between Christianity and the sciences or the influences of reformed christianity on the sciences. Because there is much need for bibliographical information about this, we have started a second research project.

In broad outline there are certain points of agreement with the project we have already mentioned:

◇ This time it is under supervision of the Department of Inter-departmental Philosophy, it is financed by the Human Sciences Research Council and the researcher, Dr. D. Kempff, works in a part time capacity.

◇ A catalogue of books at Potchefstroom has already been made and is available. Checking of the other libraries in the country is almost finished.

◇ Research has been done to find relevant journal articles. We mainly went back to 1900. Already more than 2 000 items have been found.

◇ Available books and theses have been checked for lists of literature. Relevant works, as mentioned for example in *Dissertation Abstracts,* have been ordered by the Potchefstroom University Library and as they are received they are checked immediately and thoroughly.

◇ The research will surely be continued and completed overseas.

◇ It is our intention also to publish this bibliographical information in systematised form in a book. Again we will separate the items into certain subjects and scientific branches.

6. *Organization and future*

Our research, specifically about Calviniana, Christianity and the Sciences, had a specific organization. Scientific work is never done in isolation. One has to take account of the past and of other people that move and publish in the same area. Especially in the area of the Human Sciences the following points are important:

◇ Man is limited in his abilities and has to co-operate with others and has to check their findings.

◇ Already published results or conclusions do not become out-dated so quickly and will always have to be taken into account.

◇ We can certainly accept insights that are valuable, while finding out about errors can help us in preventing from making those errors ourselves.

For this reason there are libraries that collect the necessary information and make this available to the researcher. A bibliography and/or a catalogue are a part of our organization to make information available. The advantage of a bibliography is that this will be available everywhere and it directs our attention to studies that have already been done and to results that have already been recorded.

The forces of Reformed Christianity, also in scientific areas, are small in comparison with the rest of the world. For that reason we are so much the more called to co-operate and to use our forces jointly for specific tasks. In any case we have to try not to compete, but much rather to complement one another.

Finally, the following thoughts:

◇ In the noting down and making available of material we have to try in future to engage in teamwork.

◇ In passing on information we can be eyes for one another to see and feet for one another to progress on the path of our calling.

◇ In buying books we can complement one another, so that not everyone tries to make his own stock (or kingdom) as exhaustive as possible, especially because it is probably not all going to be used very economically. Making things available in exchange to one another can certainly be accomplished.

How all of this will have to happen, we do not now specify, but we leave it for discussion at this conference.

Resolutions

Votes of thanks

1. The Conference gives thanks and praise to our Heavenly Father for His steadfast love and goodness both in bringing us together in the fellowship of His Son, Jesus Christ our Lord, and in bestowing upon us the gifts of His Holy Spirit for the advancement of christian higher education.

2. The Conference expresses its gratitude and deep appreciation to the Potchefstroom University for Christian Higher Education and its Institute for the Advancement of Calvinism for the idea of the conference and for its meticulous planning and organization. All testify to the fact that delegates, observers and friends have benefited from the labour of love performed by the university staff. We marvel at their unceasing work in providing an incomparable hospitality displayed in a truly christian spirit of generosity.

3. The Conference moreover thanks the board of the "Vereniging voor wetenschappelijk onderwijs op gereformeerde grondslag" (Association for scientific education on a reformed basis, the association in the Netherlands which supports the Free University of Amsterdam), for its moral and generous financial support of the Conference.

Other resolutions

4. Affirmations
   The Conference of Reformed Institutions for Christian Higher Education confesses anew the sovereignty of our Triune God over all spheres of life.
   On this basis the Conference affirms that:

4.1. the reformed christian institutions and associations for higher education can and should serve as instruments for the acknowledgement and extension of the Kingdom of God on earth, especially in preparing and motivating their students for this service;

4.2. these institutions can accomplish their mission in this world properly only if they exist, are and act wholly in Christ and regard their members (faculty, administrative staff and students) as image-bearers of God;

4.3. the institutions for christian higher education, in common with all individuals and all other institutions, are under the authority of the Word of God according to the Scriptures of the Old and New Testaments and as summarized in the commandment to love God and to love one's neighbour as oneself;

4.4. it is the calling of institutions for christian higher education to make their own contribution in the search for the solution of basic and practical problems which confront the world, and to do so on the basis of the Word of God;

4.5. institutions for christian higher education share and participate in each other's burdens, problems and achievements;

4.6. institutions for christian higher education should try to co-ordinate their research programmes as well as sharing their scholarly achievements with each other and making them available to the world at large;

4.7. institutions for christian higher education have the critical task of testing all scholarly results as well as all cultural, political and social institutions and their achievements in their own scholarly way according to God's will for this world;

4.8. institutions for christian higher education, to fulfil this purpose, must develop among their students a critical mind shaped by the Word and Spirit of Jesus Christ, for them to be better equipped, spiritually and intellectually, to take up their responsibilities in society.

Planning for the future

5. Second Conference and Steering Committee

This First Conference resolves that:

5.1. a second international conference of reformed institutions for higher education be held in 1978;

5.2. a steering committee be appointed, comprising representatives from various continents, whose task it will be:

5.2.1. to establish mutual contact between reformed institutions for christian higher education as well as christian scholars and professional people in other institutions;

5.2.2. to consider the future formal organization of our reformed scholarly intercourse and the collaboration of our institutions for higher education and, in order to avoid fragmentation of our wider aims, to consider how this responsibility ought to be related to the work of the only world-wide and non-ecclesiastical association of reformed people, namely, the International Association for Reformed Faith and Action;

5.2.3. to plan (give shape to and determine content of) the programme for the second conference.

5.3. The following persons be appointed to the steering committee:

I. Achineku (Central and Northern Africa).

M. D. Barnes (North America).

H. J. J. Bingle (Advisory capacity).

J. C. Coetzee (Southern Africa).

J. D. Dengerink (Europe).

E. D. Fackerell (Australia and New Zealand).

R. Hashimoto (Asia).

S. H. Rooy (South America).

P. G. Schrotenboer (As secretary of the RES).

B. J. van der Walt (Advisory capacity).

N. Wolterstorff (As representative of Calvin College) and

5.4. Calvin College in the U.S.A. (along with such other members of the Consortium of Reformed and Presbyterian Colleges who wish to co-operate) be requested to act as host and to co-operate with the steering committee in whatever other way necessary, and that Potchefstroom University for Christian Higher Education be requested to act as host should Calvin College not be able to do so.

6. Theme of Second Conference

6.1. The Conference having discussed:

6.1.1. the order and structure of the institutions of christian education;

6.1.2. the character and service motive of and problems relating to christian educational institutions;

6.1.3. the role of lecturers and students and their respective authority;

6.1.4. the facilities of and relationship between various reformed christian institutions, resolves that the second conference discuss the *task* of christian higher education.

6.2. The Conference suggests as the theme of the second conference:

The responsibility of christian higher education in relation to the problems of modern society.

Motivation:

The Conference desires a serious study of the exact meaning of the responsibility of christian higher education regarding the many problems demanding attention in modern society.

6.3. The Conference suggests that this study of christian responsibility be discussed in relation to some of the following:

6.3.1. the international economic order particularly with regard to the world-wide problem of affluent and poor countries;

6.3.2. international relations and national self-interests and the promotion of justice in relation to these;

6.3.3. the ecological crisis and the biblically-enjoined cultural mandate;

6.3.4. the biblical concept of work and culture in relationship to technological development, particularly mass production;

6.3.5. the role of the family in modern society;

6.3.6. the development and use of nuclear power;

6.3.7. critical investigation of the concept "democracy".

6.4. The Conference declares its desire that the roster of speakers for, and delegates to the successive conferences should represent a wide range of academic disciplines and related fields of activity.

7. Clearing House

The Conference requests Potchefstroom University for Christian Higher Education to act, until the next conference and in co-operation with other reformed institutions for christian higher education, as a clearing house for the collection and dissemination of information concerning

7.1. the availability of courses with a biblical approach to the various scientific disciplines;

7.2. bibliographies of printed material, including books, doctoral theses, articles and papers which deal scripturally with the various scientific disciplines;

7.3. the availability of curricula for christian primary and secondary education;

7.4. the translation, either projected or in progress, of works with biblical insight into the various scientific disciplines;

7.5. scholarships available at reformed institutions for higher learning, with the aim of enabling reformed christians from countries where reformed study facilities are not available, to enrol at institutions for christian higher education so that they may be encouraged and guided to work towards the establishment of such institutions in their own countries;

7.6. ways whereby younger reformed institutions could be helped especially in being supplied with library books.

8. Translation

8.1. The steering committee should consider appointing a sub-committee whose mandate shall be to select for translation in English key works with biblical insight into the various scientific disciplines.

8.2. This translation sub-committee if appointed should delegate the actual translation of such works to appropriate committees, institutions or organisations, taking into account current translation projects.

8.3. The above-mentioned translation sub-committee should attempt to ensure the highest quality of the translations to be done.

9. Subjects for study

The Conference suggests that the following subjects are in urgent need of study by individuals, study groups and institutions and that the results of these studies be published. This list of subjects has been compiled from suggestions and motions submitted to the committee on motions and does not reflect their order of importance.

9.1. The crisis in modern education: its spiritual background and historical roots.

9.2. The history of christian institutions for higher education: reasons why a number of them have lost their christian character and others might be in danger of losing this character (spiritual decay; lack of living contact with the Word of God and of active prayer; lack of understanding of the universal meaning of creation; fall and redemption; adaptation to non-christian thought; massification; the desire "to be like the surrounding non-christian universities"; etc.).

9.3. The desirability or necessity for an educational creed formulated specially for the tertiary institutions.

9.4. The meaning of christian scholarship with regard to the scholar, the field(s) of research, the methods to be applied and the results to be achieved.

9.5. The meaning of academic freedom in the light of the creed of the christian institution.

9.6. The nature and origin of the variety and the unity of the sciences. The relation between philosophy, theology and the other sciences.

9.7. The effect which the relation between philosophy, theology and the other sciences must have on the content, organisation and adaptation of research and curricula in the christian institution for higher education.

9.8. The relation between research, scientific teaching and professional training within the christian academic institution.

9.9. The non-christian student in the christian academic institution.

9.10. The ministry of the academic institution to the non-academic world (basis, nature, the way in which this is to be carried out, etc.).

9.11. The meaning of "critical scholarship, critical university and critical education".

9.12. Educational technology and its impact upon christian education.

9.13. University didactics developed from christian perspective.

9.14. The christian responsibility towards adult education.

9.15. The rise of humanistic futurology and the necessity for a christian approach, particularly to education.

9.16. The character of the academic teaching situation and of the interdisciplinary approach in the institution for christian higher education.

9.17. The impact of our christian principles on the structure of the university, especially with regard to the following:

9.17.1. The role of the state in the government of the university.

9.17.2. The role of the state in formulating scientific and research policy.

9.17.3. The meaning of scholarship as a profession.

9.17.4. The historic influence of humanism in the structure of the 'faculties' e.g. of arts and of science.

9.18. A scripturally based christian philosophy of education founded upon a christian anthropology.

9.19. The practical implications of the central facts in God's redemptive work, namely Christ's death and resurrection, for the character and task of all institutions for christian higher education and also, specifically, for all the academic disciplines.

9.20. Structural stability and change in the sphere of christian higher education.

9.21. The question of authority in institutions for christian higher education.

10. Relation P.U.—F.U.

The International Conference of Reformed Institutions for Higher Education held at Potchefstroom, South Africa, in 1975 regrets the absence of a delegation from the Free University of Amsterdam.

While refraining from passing judgement on the differences of opinion between Potchefstroom University and the Free University which caused the absence of a delegation from the Free University, the Conference does not wish to detach itself from this conflict and hence urgently appeals to both universities to establish renewed and permanent contact. The Conference welcomes the news that the initiative for such contact has already been taken.

In this connection the Conference stresses the following considerations:

10.1. During various discussions in the course of the Conference, such as in the reports of delegates from various countries it was apparent that a meaningful discussion of science can only take place, as we have joyfully experienced, with due reference to the fullness of life (political reality included) and even more so when scientific practice is intended to be of service in the Kingdom of God in its universal meaning.

10.2. It is essential to continue discussion on the normative perspective of the Kingdom of God within society as part of the contact between christian institutions for higher education (from a scientific point of view) since this will benefit the institutions in sharing each other's problems and recognising and respecting each other's responsibilities in the situation in which they have been placed.

10.3. The estrangement of two of the largest institutions of reformed conviction would be detrimental to the common objective as supported by the Conference during all discussions. Therefore, it has to be vigorously countered.

11. Christian Commitment

This Conference urges christian scholars/teachers to respond to every opportunity offered by the Lord to carry their scholarship into institutions of higher education, whether christian or secular, so that, by manifesting their christian commitment through their scholarly activities they may bring the critical and constructive powers of the Christian gospel to bear upon the whole intellectual sphere in order that all men may fulfil their God-given calling.

First International Conference for

Christian higher education

Review and preview

Dr. B. J. van der Walt

International conferences are certainly nothing new in our times. An international conference of reformed people in the area of Christian higher education is, because it is the first time in history that a thing like this has taken place.

In the thirties of this century there were several international conferences of Calvinists. After the second world war, IARFA (the International Association for Reformed Faith and Action) picked up the threads and built up world wide activity on a small scale. But never was an international conference with the specific purpose of dealing with Christian Higher Education held.

The international gathering about which this article reports, was therefore a special occasion. Because this was a beginning, a first attempt of this kind, we must not overrate the value of this event. Just as is the case with all new things, there was the problem of lack of experience; no previous examples could be used to build on. So there were problems, and I will not leave those problems unmentioned. By showing what the problems were, we can improve in the future. However, the purpose of this short report is to accentuate the positive. Did the conference succeed in its purpose? Which concrete results were attained?

Christians, even more than others, ought to know that all human attempts and trials show their failures. But possibly during this meeting there were still some signs of the coming of the Kingdom of God.

By means of posing questions we will try within a short space to give an overview of the various events.

1. *When?*

After a year's period of preparation, including a world tour by the secretary (Prof. J. C. Coetzee), the meeting became a reality between 9 and 13 September 1975. Actually there were plans and consultations several years before the event.

The whole thing now seems to be old news! The fact that this report about the conference appears almost a year after it happened, does have a few advantages, too. In the first place a number of reports from East and West and from North and South have appeared, as a result of which it is possible in a more objective manner to determine how the participants did think about the conference afterwards. Secondly, as a result of the conference certain other events have already taken place. For example a Clearing House has been established at the Potchefstroom University for Christian Higher Education and a delegation of the Free University of Amsterdam has started a dialogue with the P.U. So this report is in some ways quite up to date.

2. Where?

How could South Africa, with its so called racial discrimination, be the host of an international, multi-racial conference?

It must be credited to both the organisers of the conference and also the guests from all over the world, that even though the conference took place *in* South Africa, it did not continually deal *with* South Africa's internal political problems.

The Potchefstroom University did not make any attempt at justifying or propagating the political convictions of its country. And the guests did not force the host to continually talk about these problems.

In his article "Calvinists in Potchefstroom" *(The Reformed Journal,* Nov. 1975, p. 8) Prof. N. Wolterstorff correctly says: "It would be a mistake to suggest that wandering debates about apartheid constituted the main significance of the conference". Exactly for that reason it is regrettable that Wolterstorff's article does give the impression that the apartheid problem did constitute the main diet of conference. He himself says very little about the conference, as if this were less important. If he had wanted to write about the politics of South Africa, he could better have used another, more fitting title. Then he would not have created the impression that the political course of S.A. overshadowed the entire conference.

The initiative was taken by the Institute for the Advancement of Calvinism at P.U. for C.H.E. When it appeared that the Free University of Amsterdam would not be able to organize such a meeting as was originally intended, the P.U. took it upon itself. As one of the few full universities of a Christian character in the world, the P.U. was able to undertake this financially. Large financial offers needed to be made, for very many of the delegates had to be subsidized with free travel costs to far off South Africa. However, for the P.U. it was a great privilege to be able to provide this service. In exchange, it gave the P.U. much more than it could ever have given: it brought expansion of perspective, stimulated self-critique, brought about a new idea of its responsibilities (in international relations also) and provided inspiration for the future.

3. Who?

The following statistics give an idea of the extent of the conference. On the average between 250 and 400 people attended the sessions. There were 130 delegates (72 from South Africa, 58 delegates and 7 observers from abroad). There were representatives from 76 different institutions (52 from abroad and 24 from inside South Africa). All continents were represented and delegates came from 19 countries. From the African continent they came from South Africa, Rhodesia, Malawi, Zambia, Kenya and Nigeria. Europe was present in France, Germany, Holland, England, Scotland. From North America, Canada and the U.S.A. were there. South America was represented by Argentina. Asia had people from Japan, Korea and Indonesia. Finally, Australia and New Zealand came from the Australian Continent.

Since these statistics show the truly ecumenical character of the gathering, it is very much to be regretted that the Free University of Amsterdam could not be represented. But the conference did adopt a motion in which it officially expressed its sorrow about this fact. In that motion the P.U. and F.U. were advised to repair the broken contact, with the next international conference and with future international action in mind too. As remarked in the beginning, this conversation has already taken place in Potchefstroom. It is to be hoped that as the results become available,*

---

* Seeing that the report of the consultations which were held at Potchefstroom from 2nd to 5th March only reached the I.A.C. office in September, after this report had already gone to press, the results of the meeting cannot be discussed here. Apart from the printed report of the Free University, titled *Verslag van een samenspreking tussen delegaties van de Vrije Universiteit en de Potchefstroomse Universiteit vir Christelike Hoër Onderwys* (July, 1976), there is also a written commentary made by the P.U. for C.H.E. on this report, and a reply from the F.U. delegation (dated 16 August 1976) to this P.U. comment.

the various journals that have reported about the conference, will also report about the results of this dialogue.

4. Why?

It was the considered opinion of the P.U. for C.H.E. that for a long time now we have been ready to bring together representatives of Christian Higher Education on a world wide basis and also to gather reformed Christians from whatever institution they might be. We would like to gather these people in order to:

◇ get to know one another better;
◇ discuss together the idea of Christian scholarship, the task, calling, problematics and opportunities of, and for, Reformed Christian Institutions for Higher Education for the remainder of this century.
◇ Work on a practical plan, based on responsible principles, for the advancement and promotion of the work of the various Reformed Christians in Scholarship and of such institutions in various parts of the world; in order that we may get to know the dangers which threaten to undermine the Christian character of these institutions and to weaken the methods that we are trying to develop; so that we may find ways to counteract these dangers.
◇ Promote closer co-operation and co-ordination between related institutions and to strengthen the work of all the small minority groups of Reformed Christians in various parts of the world.

Insofar as a first gathering of this kind can be called successful we may conclude with joy that this first conference succeeded beyond expectations. The Lord did not withhold his blessing hand from us. Many reports from various parts of the world, give good testimony of the gathering with much praise.

5. What about?

The theme of the conference was: "Reformed Higher Educational Institutions as bulwark for the Kingdom of God — present and future". This theme invited quite a bit of criticism. Doesn't it indicate the old idea of a closed university that does not allow social problems within its walls, exactly at a time when it is so important that the university need to be open to social problems? Can one really say that the service of Christian Higher Education has the character of a bulwark within the Kingdom of God? Isn't this too negative a view? Is it also not true that such a theme is just a bit arrogant: Can human institutions indeed be called a bulwark within God's Kingdom? Must we not be a bit more humble? According to many the bulwark idea reminds one too much of Abraham Kuyper's cultural optimism and of the Afrikaner's so-called laager mentality. Thus it would be a theme of bygone days.

Fortunately this initial impression of isolationism was rejected by the conference itself. As reported by P. G. Schrotenboer's *R.E.S. News Exchange:* "Contrary to the possible impression that the theme may give that the conference was an exercise in isolation, the speakers from all parts of the world expressed an openness to modern society and faced head-on the relation of the college and university to society today. ... The service motive was strong throughout the conference..." Our looks were not only directed within, but indeed also toward the outside. Actually it is fortunate that this first conference was focused more on the Christian institution, the Christian teacher and Christian academic endeavour itself. The second conference, which is planned for 1978 in Grand Rapids, Michigan, U.S.A., can now spend more time on directing our attention towards outside problems and to the relationship between science and society. If one were not to have one's own house in order, particularly the house of Christian Higher Education, it would not help much to try to provide services of value for the outside world!

I do not believe, as many do today, that the university only earns its laurels in its service to society, and especially to the Third World. When we look at the relationship of university and society in such a way that the university merely becomes a social tool, we do injustice both to university and society.

The central theme was divided into various sub-themes, with a number of papers for each. On the first day the conference dealt mostly with different aspects of "The Christian Institution". On the second day the main theme was: "Christian learning/scholarship/science". The third day called our attention to "The Christian Scholar". The last day dealt with the very important matter of "Co-ordination between Christian Institutions". The fact that there were no less than 35 papers, shows what a lot of hard work was done. That all this had to be done within four days, will also show, however, that there was not much occasion for in-depth discussion. Fortunately all papers were handed out to the delegates beforehand, so that afterwards they still had lots of material for reflection as well.

The intensity of the program did have a specific reason: the response to the invitation of the organisers for papers was far beyond expectation. As a result, persons who had offered to read papers almost had to be asked to withdraw their kind offer again — something the organizers did not want to do. At the next conference we shall either have to spend more time on each paper or we shall have to have fewer papers in order to allow deeper discussions and reflection.

Of course, one cannot possibly satisfy all people. This conference also, did not succeed in that respect. Delegates from Africa and the East found some of the subjects too theoretical and somewhat irrelevant for their situations, while precisely these papers were an academic banquet for many of the Westerns! An advantage of the great variety of papers was, that everybody probably did get at least a little bit that was significant.

6. *How did things go?*

In the different reports we continually meet evaluative terms such as the following: important, interesting, mind-expanding, fascinating, insightful, stimulating, well organised, etc. Another theme accented by most reports is that of the wonderful spirit of solidarity, spiritual unity which was experienced during the conference. This was especially revealed in the communality of all that was done:

◇ We *listened together* to one another. We acquired insight into views and viewpoints of others, into problems and possibilities of Christian education under varying circumstances all over the world.

◇ We *thought together* about deep theoretical problems and difficult practical stumbling blocks.

◇ We *talked together.* Of course we did not only talk during official sessions. Sometimes we talked till very late in the night. Not all had equally much to say. Fortunately for the talkative ones there were the more silent ones, who liked to listen! Fortunately for those who liked to listen there were those who liked to talk !

◇ We *sang together.* Who can describe the great experience when so many people from so many nations from all over the world sing praise to God in one world language?

◇ We also *prayed together.* It was moving to hear everyone who led in devotions, call upon the name of God in his own language, even though one could understand nothing of it.

◇ One must not think that we did not also *differ together.* The differences were necessary, for otherwise it would have been a terribly dead and dull gathering.

◇ We also *relaxed together* and enjoyed ourselves. Apart from the fact that all delegates stayed within the same residence, they were also able to eat all meals together. A fantastic dinner, at which the State President of South Africa gave a speech, was offered to the delegates. During the one day off, the conferees inspected a gold mine and travelled to a farm and after the conference there was a four-day tour with all sorts of memorable things to see, among other things the famous Kruger Game Reserve and one of the Black Universities (The University of the North).

◇ May it be true that in the future, locally as well as internationally, we will be able to *struggle together* for the coming of Christ's Kingdom. The conference clearly showed how much work is to be done yet and how little has been achieved.

The beautiful, unforgettable spring days of September 1975 were days of a real meeting of minds and persons, such as we had not had before. May this be a prelude to a new spring in the area of Christian Higher Education.

Without a doubt the secret behind the notable unity between people of different colours and different cultures was no doubt their common faith. In the thirties of this century, ecclesiastical fights and divisions every time caused the shipwreck of international Calvinistic action. (One could read W. G. de Vries' thesis *Calvinisten op de tweesprong. De Internationale Federatie van Calvinisten en haar invloed op de onderlinge verhoudingen in de Gereformeerde Kerken in Nederland in de dertiger jare van de twintigste eeuw.* Groningen, De Vuurbaak, 1974). It is an immense step forward that ecclesiastical division at this conference did not play any role. Even differences in political conviction were not able to torpedo the gathering.

Personal contacts of great value have been built up across borders. When we met informally, we got acquainted, we exchanged information and we even made close friendships.

7. *What about the future?*

This is the last but possibly also the most critical question. It would not be very hopeful if we would have to be satisfied with the conclusion: We had a nice conference. Fortunately this was not the case. It is true that we did not decide to establish a formal organisation or even more closely formalised ties. But this was wise. Something like that needs time to ripen and should not hastily be forced. However, the motions that were accepted during the last day of the conference, do open the curtains of the future considerably. Some of the decisions are already being worked out. We mention some of them.

7.1. The *Steering Committee* has already had two meetings (the first in Potchefstroom and a second in Grand Rapids) in order to pay attention to a number of matters, but especially to begin organising for the next conference at Calvin College, in August 1978. Provisional plans for the Grand Rapids Conference look something like this:

The theme of the conference will be "Christian education and its world mission: The responsibility of Christian instiutions of higher education to justice in the international economic order".

The conference is to be divided into two parts, the whole to cover five days. The major part of the conference will be devoted to the subject of justice in the international economic order and the responsibility of the Christian community. This subject will be introduced by a consideration of the role in society of institutions for Christian higher education. All this will be preceded by a worship service including an orientation address.

The role in society of institutions for Christian higher education

Kingdom, church, world

To open the discussions of the conference, there should be a perspective-setting lecture. In this, the idea would be developed that the Church is God's people in the world called to be witness, agent and evidence of the coming of His Kingdom. Institutions for Christian higher education are institutions sponsored by the Christian community in order to accomplish a certain phase of that comprehensive task.

School in Society

This lecture would first develop in more detail the relation of the institution for Christian higher education to its sponsoring Christian community. From there, the lecture would go on to discuss the relation of the institution for Christian higher education to the institution of the church, and to such institutions of general society as the state and business organizations. The lecture would not merely discuss how these entities are related ideally, but would touch on the concrete problems actually experienced. One of these is:

414

How can the educational institutions with integrity face the issues of the day while remaining in solidarity with, and giving leadership to, the institution of the church and the Christian community?

Theory and Praxis

An analysis of the relation between theoretical and non-theoretical praxis as diverse responses to the Word of God and his creation. How do scholarly results get "translated" into non-scholarly categories? How do and should scholars treat issues presented to them by society? Can only that scholarly research be justified which has an immediate relevance for society? To what extent should scholarship be guided by a social reformist impulse? What is the nature and place of "basic" research? (Though the relation of theory and praxis has been a vital issue from the very beginning of Western thought, a special confrontation with the Marxist and neo-Marxist views on this matter will be necessary).

Justice in the international economic order

God's Call for Justice

Again, we open with a perspective-setting lecture. The biblical concept of, and call for, economic justice would be developed.

Within this context, there would be some consideration of the biblical vision of man as called to be a steward of the riches of the earth in the service of his fellows. There would have to be some consideration of the relation of love and justice; and the anti-totalitarian vision of a well-structured society as one composed of various institutions each with its proper limited domain of authority under God, would have to be touched on.

The Facts of Justice and Injustice

What are the actual relations between the so-called dominant and dependent countries with respect to economic justice (income distribution, distribution of natural resources, access to and utilization of those resources, etc.)? What are some of the factors that shape these relations (e.g. technological skills, social stratifications, primary and secondary resources)?

The Economic Systems

What are the major economic systems, and what bearing does their diversity have on justice in the economic order?

Economic Justice and the Future

Here there would be an attempt to uncover the fundamental trends, the fundamental dynamics, at work in the international economic order which affect just and unjust distribution. On the basis of these trends, what does the future hold with respect to justice in the international economic order — relations between the so-called dominant and dependent countries, relations among dominant countries with different economic systems, etc.?

Norms for the International Economic Order

What are some of the basic norms concerning justice in the international economic order? What would a just order look like? What should we be working towards? What, for example, determines rights to resources? to products produced by human labour? to income? Does the US have a right to resources in Bolivia, for example? Do future generations have a right to resources? Instead of thinking in terms of rights, should nations think in terms of stewardship? (This topic is obviously related to that above. This, however, is more detailed and specific. That one deals with the basic biblical vision. This one deals with "middle axioms".)

Strategies for Change/Preservation

On the basis of the foregoing, what should be the witness of the Christian to the states, the businesses, etc. of the world? That is to say, what are some of the basic strategies for change that those institutions ought to be working toward? What are some of the wholesome institutions and arrangements that they should be preserving?

The Role of Our Institutions

What practical steps can the Reformed institutions of higher education take to promote the cause of justice in the international economic order? That is to say, what can we do to promote the adoption of the above-suggested strategies of change and of preservation? What research and teaching programmes should be undertaken? What is the possibility of co-operation among various institutions? Can there be a division of labour? Can there be a regular exchange of results?

7.2. The Steering Committee has also considered establishing an international organisation as from the next conference. The proposed name is *International Alliance of Reformed Institutions for*

7.3. The P.U. has acceded to the request of the conference to establish a *Clearing House* for the next 3 years (1976—1978), aimed at furthering consolidation and the opening of perspectives for the future.

We may report with great joy that Potchefstroom University has found this project so important that it has made available an amount of R45 000. The director of the IAC, with the help of a secretary, hopes to devote his full-time attention to this matter, starting in July 1976. In order to prevent stagnation or even the cessation of all action, it is necessary to build on what has been achieved already.

The following tasks are regarded by the Clearing House as of prime importance for the next few years:

1. General *documentation* work.
2. Encouraging the *exchange of publications* between various institutions.
3. The collection and publication of *bibliographies and (if possible) annotated bibliographies* about Christian Higher Education, Christian academic work in general, and the results of Christian scientific endeavour in the various disciplines.
   Something like *The (International) Reformed World of Learning* would be a publication with valuable source material.
4. The collection and making available of *relevant information*, for example, concerning the history of various institutions, teachers' and students' numbers, courses that are offered, students' activities, etc. This information may be useful in determining the possibilities at various institutions and may help to advise about exchange of students and teachers.
5. *Translation* of existing key books in various disciplines and of courses with a reformed perspective from other languages into English.
6. *Publication* of essays, articles, brochures, books and collections in English. These may be manuscripts which had never been published before, or have been distributed only in a limited way. They can also be entirely new publications that have been produced at the request of specialists with a Christian conviction.
7. *Scholarships* and other sources of financial help can be surveyed in order to encourage students to study at various institutions for Christian Higher Education. This would be of value for students and teachers at larger institutions who, for the sake of

further enrichment, would like to study elsewhere, but especially for students and teachers at smaller or younger institutions which do not yet themselves have the necessary funds or study facilities. It even holds for students at so-called neutral institutions who desire to do their work in the light of Scripture.

8. *Exchange of lectures.* This may be very fruitful and teachers at various institutions could engage in a mutual exchange for a few months, teaching as guests at other institutions and thereby also making themselves aware of what is going on in the various countries.

9. *Help for younger and/or smaller institutions.* In this area much can be done even if it is only to help them expand their libraries.

10. *Encouragement and advice for the establishment of study groups,* organizations or institutions for Christian Higher Education in areas or countries where nothing of this kind exists at all.

11. *Regular newsletter,* containing brief news items and mutual exchange of opinion, the announcement of important publications, reviews, etc.

12. *Research about primary and secondary education* — among others the establishment of curricula from a Christian point of view. Even though the Clearing House operates more in the area of higher education, we should not, if time permits, neglect this important area.

For the moment these are mere plans. To realise this twelve point, three year plan the Clearing House will need everyone's help. Only if we join hands, can something be achieved; and — fortunately — for the time being we don't even have to stick our hands into our pockets !

Activity and money, however, cannot guarantee any success. We shall be planning and labouring in vain if God will not bless our weak efforts and use them to his honour. Please do not forget therefore to pray the Lord for his blessing on this wonderful, new and challenging international action.